CLARENDON LIBRARY OF LOGIC AND PHILOSOPHY

General Editor: L. Jonathan Cohen

THE PROBABLE
AND
THE PROVABLE

THE PROBABLE
AND
THE PROVABLE

=

L. JONATHAN COHEN

CLARENDON PRESS · OXFORD

1977

Oxford University Press, Walton Street, Oxford OX2 6DP

OXFORD LONDON GLASGOW NEW YORK
TORONTO MELBOURNE WELLINGTON CAPE TOWN
IBADAN NAIROBI DAR ES SALAAM LUSAKA ADDIS ABABA
KUALA LUMPUR SINGAPORE JAKARTA HONG KONG TOKYO
DELHI BOMBAY CALCUTTA MADRAS KARACHI

© *Oxford University Press 1977*

British Library Cataloguing in Publication Data

Cohen, Laurence Jonathan
 The probable and the provable. - (Clarendon library of logic and philosophy).
 1. Evidence (Law) 2. Probabilities 3. Law - Philosophy
 I. Title II. Series
 347.06   K   77-30148

 ISBN 0-19-824412-6

Printed in Great Britain by
Billing & Sons Limited, Guildford, London and Worcester

To my
Mother

Preface

SOME of the work on this book was done during tenure of a two-year Radcliffe Fellowship and I wish to thank the Radcliffe Trustees for this award. I also wish to thank my College for several periods of sabbatical leave that were devoted to the book, and to thank Yale University for a visiting professorship in the fall semester of 1972/3 which enabled me to test out some of my ideas on a wide spectrum of North American audiences.

The book was planned and written as a single, sustained argument. But earlier versions of a few parts of it have appeared separately. An earlier version of §§1–11 appeared as *Probability: The One and the Many* (British Academy Annual Philosophical Lecture), 1975. An earlier version of §§32–5 appeared as 'How Can One Testimony Corroborate Another?' in *Essays in Memory of Imre Lakatos*, ed. R. S. Cohen, P. K. Feyerabend, and M. W. Wartofsky, 1976, pp. 65–78. A few paragraphs of §42 had earlier versions in 'A Note on Inductive Logic', *Journal of Philosophy*, 70 (1973), 27 ff. A Spanish translation of parts of chapters 4, 5, and 7 is due to appear in *Teorema*, during 1977. I am very happy to make the usual acknowledgements in connection with all these earlier publications.

For work that straddles several disciplines it is important to have the right kind of friends and acquaintances. I count myself as having been particularly fortunate to receive a good deal of initial guidance and encouragement from Professor Sir Rupert Cross and from Professor A. M. Honoré in regard to the legal issues involved in my argument. Later details I discussed again and again with Dr. A. Zuckerman, and I owe very much to the patience and generosity with which he let me use his time for this purpose.

On the mathematical side I am grateful to my colleague Dr. P. Neumann for some valuable help with the algebra of §35, and to Professor S. Kripke for some sage advice about multiple quantification in modal contexts.

Professor Sir A. J. Ayer kindly read the whole book in type-script and the final version profits at a number of places from his perceptive and judicious comments. Mr. C. A. B. Peacocke also read the whole book in typescript and I am particularly grateful to him for discussing with me each stage of the proof advanced in §§56 and 57. At various times I have also been greatly helped by discussions or correspondence with Professors I. Levi and W. Salmon, despite the considerable differences in our several points of view. Further valued help on points of detail has come from Dr. J. Leiber, Mr. Lloyd Humberstone, and the Oxford University Press's referee.

I have also learned much from contributors to discussions on the numerous occasions on which I have lectured or read papers on topics connected with the book during the years 1972–6. I have always found such public discussions very stimulating, and since I have unfortunately kept no record of the individual names of those taking part I can only express my gratitude collectively to the audiences of my lectures at Oxford and to the institutions that invited me elsewhere. These latter were the statistics departments at Connecticut and Yale Universities, U.S.A.; the mathematical institute at the University of Athens, Greece; the philosophical departments, societies or colloquia at British Columbia, Calgary, and Simon Fraser Universities, Canada; at Florence University, Italy; at Valencia University, Spain; at Bristol (the Fry Lectures), Dundee, East Anglia, Glasgow, Keele, Stirling and Warwick Universities, and the London School of Economics and Political Science, U.K.; and at Boston, Brown, City of New York, Columbia, Indiana, Johns Hopkins, Pennsylvania, Pittsburgh, Rhode Island and Rochester Universities, and Vassar College, U.S.A.

I have discussed almost every point in the book at some time with Dr. Jonathan Adler. These conversations have been immensely useful in helping me to clarify issues and guard against objections, and I am very greatly indebted to him. Without his penetrating, lively, and sympathetic interest in the subject my own thinking would undoubtedly have lacked an especially powerful stimulus. But both in his case and in those of the others whose names I have mentioned I should add that I take full responsibility for the final state of the text and for any errors, inadequacies, or incoherences it may still contain whether these be legal, mathematical, or philosophical.

Finally I must pay tribute to the astonishing accuracy with which Miss Patricia Lloyd has read my various manuscript formulations and to the skill and patience with which she has typed draft after draft.

30 July, 1976   L. J. C.

Contents

Introduction

MOST people, when they have grown out of the school-room, never encounter any proofs of mathematical theorems. But there is another kind of proof, in instances of which almost every adult takes an occasional interest. Indeed for some people proofs of this other kind turn out to be more important than anything else in their lives. I refer to proofs, or purported proofs, of particular facts in courts of law—the proofs without which justice would indeed be blind. Does the evidence prove that the fashionable physician murdered his elderly patients in order to expedite his receipt of their legacies? Has the well-known financier been libelled when described as a man who misleads investors? Can you yourself prove the negligence of the contractors whose bad craftsmanship on your roof seems responsible for the rain's getting through to damage your furniture? Within the framework of such proofs a rich variety of issues arise about the probability with which this or that point has been established. We can all imagine ourselves as jurors charged with the task of judging how far one witness's testimony has corroborated another's or whether the circumstantial evidence offered is an adequate substitute for what appropriate eyewitnesses might have said. But what is the nature of these gradations or evaluations of proof? How are they most correctly determined? What is the structure of the probabilities with which they deal? What rational principles bind them, setting up implications or inconsistencies between one such probability-judgement and another?

Without an adequate answer to these questions our intellectual culture is defective in at least two respects. First, we cannot, in theoretical jurisprudence, complete a comprehensive account of what the administration of justice entails. Secondly, we cannot be sure that our philosophy of probability is powerful enough to embrace every part of its domain.

Not surprisingly, therefore, early modern theories of probability were much occupied with problems about legal proof. Within the framework of the mathematical calculus of chance, for which Pascal and Fermat had laid the foundations, Leibniz and Bernoulli sought to develop a theory of probability that would have among its principal goals the provision of an adequate analysis for gradations of legal proof. They, and others like them, were convinced that the mathematics of the Pascalian calculus revealed the underlying structure of forensic probabilities. Indeed, many contemporary writers still believe this. They believe, for instance, in a complementational principle for negation, viz. $p(B,A) = 1 - p(\text{not-}B,A)$, where '$p(B,A)$' is to be read 'the probability of B's truth on the evidence of A's'. They believe in a multiplicative law for conjunction, viz. $p(B \& C,A) = p(B,A) \times p(C,A \& B)$. These and the other familiar Pascalian principles are supposed to govern the gradations of legal proof, just as the Pascalian calculus is commonly called by mathematicians *the* theory of probability.

But, if one takes a careful enough look at some of the problems involved, quite large cracks begin to be discernible in the alleged closeness of fit between Pascalian calculus and forensic probability. Attempts can be made to paper over these cracks, but no such attempt could be fully successful. Paradox after paradox emerges from any sufficiently thoroughgoing attempt to represent the logic of legal proof in terms of the calculus of chance. The object of the present book is both to establish the existence of these paradoxes, and also to describe a non-Pascalian concept of probability in terms of which one can analyse the structure of forensic proof without giving rise to such typical signs of theoretical misfit. Neither the complementational principle for negation nor the multiplicative principle for conjunction applies to the central core of any forensic proof in the Anglo-American legal system.

There are thus four main tasks to be accomplished in the following pages.

First, the book aims to show that, if forensic proof in Anglo-American courts is analysed in terms of the mathematical calculus of chance, the anomalies and paradoxes which are generated are too numerous and too serious for intellectual comfort.

Secondly, a differently structured concept of probability

will be described in a degree of detail that enables its merits and demerits to be appropriately evaluated. Moreover, to guard against the suspicion of an *ad hoc* solution the book will explore the interconnections of this non-Pascalian concept of probability with certain other familiar patterns of human reasoning. The general aim here will be to establish the rationality of the concept and the depth of its entrenchment in human culture.

Thirdly, I shall try to show that this particular non-Pascalian concept of probability can indeed perform the forensic tasks for which any Pascalian concept seems illsuited. And I shall also try to show that the non-Pascalian concept has some important uses even outside the somewhat stylized institutional framework of legal proceedings. For to show the former without the latter would not sufficiently explain why people are normally content to have such serious issues determined as they are in the courts.

Fourthly, to avoid accusations of word-play, I need to show too that the title of this non-Pascalian concept to be called a concept of *probability* is quite a strong one. The concept is not a mere homonym of its philosophically better-known fellow— I shall argue—but is generated necessarily by any defensible theory of probability that is powerful enough to bring all the familiar species of Pascalian probability within the reach of its analysis. In order to understand properly how Pascalian probability can have the variety of different uses it genuinely does have—in gambling, quality control, insurance, statistical inference, signal-transmission theory, and so on—one has to suppose an over-arching semantics of probability that forces one to admit the possibility of a certain non-Pascalian concept. Specifically one has to think of probability as degree of provability and then to envisage the gradation of provability even in certain kinds of system that, as it turns out, exclude Pascalian principles.

But different readers may well have different levels, or orders, of interest in these several issues. The philosopher who is primarily interested in the general theory of probability will perhaps need to be convinced at the outset, on fundamental grounds, that a non-Pascalian concept of probability could have an important use and need not be merely a mathematical freak. He will need to be shown too that it could be a probability properly so called. Only then will he be prepared to follow arguments which are designed to show, first that some non-Pascalian concept is needed for the analysis of forensic proof, and secondly that this concept has such-or-such a particular nature. On the other hand, a reader whose primary interest is in jurisprudence may not be so heavily committed already to Pascalianism. Indeed, he may well be readier initially to learn about the relatively concrete paradoxes to which a Pascalian analysis of forensic proof gives rise, than to follow the somewhat more abstract arguments which are necessary to establish the terminological credentials of non-Pascalian probability. He will be content to turn finally to the latter arguments as a matter of theoretical completeness, rather than to demand them initially as a precondition of giving any serious attention to the issue.

Accordingly the book's four constituent Parts have been written in such a way that they may be read in different orders by different kinds of reader. If a reader's primary interest is in jurisprudence or if he is as yet scarcely acquainted with philosophical writings about the general problem of probability he would do best to start with Part II (the paradoxes inherent in a Pascalian analysis of legal proof), and, after reading on through Parts III and IV (the non-Pascalian concept and its uses), he could come last to Part I (the theoretical credentials of non-Pascalian probability). But if the reader's primary and informed interest is in the general problem of probability he should go straight through the book, from Part I to Part IV, in the order in which these Parts are printed.

PART I

CAN THERE BE A NON-PASCALIAN CONCEPT OF PROBABILITY?

I

The Problem for a Polycriterial Theory of Probability

Summary

§1. Recent philosophical theories about probability have tended to be polycriterial rather than monocriterial. §2. Identity of mathematical structure does not suffice to explain why such-and-such criteria are all criteria of probability. §3. Nor can a family-resemblance theory explain this (or any other) conceptual unity.

§1. *One criterion, or many?*

A philosophical theory of probability, like many other kinds of theory, is concerned to increase understanding by revealing the underlying unity that generates superficial diversity. We are familiar with many apparently different types of probability: the probability of drawing an ace from a well-shuffled pack of cards, the probability that a British lorry-driver (any one you choose) will survive till the age of seventy, the probability that a radium atom will disintegrate within twenty-four hours, the probability that Excalibur will win the 1979 Derby, the probability (on the evidence before today's court) that the defendant uttered the slander of which the plaintiff complains, the probability (on available experimental evidence) that all cervical cancer is caused by a virus, and so on. A philosophical theory of probability seeks to interpret all these probabilities as relative frequencies, perhaps, or as degrees of belief, or as natural propensities, or as logical relations between propositions, or as truth-values in a multi-valued logic, or as some other uni.ary type of structure.

The unity sought has thus characteristically been a unity for criterion of gradation, in the sense to be described in the next paragraph, rather than for method of assessment, and the difference between these two types of unity is sufficiently important to deserve a brief initial digression.

A criterion of gradation is a relatively well-accepted pattern of intrinsic differentiation in degree or quantity, while a method of assessment is a strategy for discovering such degrees or quantities within appropriate limits of accuracy. The centigrade scale is a criterion of gradation for temperature, which (at sea level) regards 0° as the heat of melting ice and 100° as the heat of water beginning to boil; while the application of an appropriately marked off mercury thermometer is a familiar method of assessment for temperature so conceived. Correspondingly we may need to distinguish between the truth-conditions and the justification-conditions, respectively, for a proposition stating the temperature of, say, a person's blood. Some methods of assessment may be applicable to more than one criterion of gradation, like the use of a measuring-tape marked off in centimetres as well as in inches when these different criteria of length are defined in terms of a standard metre-bar and a standard yard-bar, respectively. Also a particular criterion of gradation may admit several methods of assessment, some perhaps more accurate than others. The hours and minutes of the passing day admit of being measured by more than one kind of clock. And the logical structure of a criterion of gradation may not always be entirely the same as that of its methods of assessment. For example, if car A is travelling at more miles per hour than car B, and car B than car C, then A is travelling at more miles per hour than C; but the actual measurements cannot be relied on to exhibit this transitivity in every case since the readings on any actual speedometer are subject to some margin of error.

Realists and anti-realists may dispute the nature of the relation between what I have called a criterion of gradation and a corresponding method of assessment. Perhaps anti-realists will prefer to see the relation in every case as a relation between two different methods of assessment—an impracticable and a practicable one, respectively. But the distinction has at least to be proposed in order for this dispute to arise, and failure to draw some such distinction produces no less confusion in regard to probability than it does in regard to other topics. In particular a mono*criterial* account of probability is quite compatible with accepting a plurality of methods for *assessing* probabilities. Samples of different sizes or structures may be used for estimating the probability that a lorry-driver will survive till the age of seventy, even if the criterion of relative frequency is in fact always in mind.

Nevertheless, even when all this has been said, a monocriterial theory of probability is notoriously difficult to sustain. A relative frequency account, like von Mises's, seems to fit the actuarial probability of a lorry-driver's survival till age seventy much better than it fits the prediction that Excalibur will win the Derby in 1979, since it seems to imply that a probability should be predicated collectively rather than distributively— i.e. predicated of sets rather than of their members. A personalist account, like Savage's seems to fit tipsters' predictions better than it fits scientific generalizations over unbounded domains, since bets on the truth of a single prediction can be decisively settled in a way that bets on the truth of an open-ended generalization cannot and betting quotients are therefore a more realistic criterion of belief-intensity in the former case than in the latter. And similar objections—some of which will be mentioned later—can be made to each of the familiar monocriterial accounts.

Accordingly in recent decades there has been a substantial trend of opinion towards some kind of polycriterial account of probability. Rival monocriterial theories claim to refute one another. But a polycriterial account supposes this or that monocriterial analysis, if internally consistent, to be not wholly refuted by the diversity of the facts—merely restricted in its domain of application. Popper[1] made an important contribu-

---

[1] K. R. Popper, 'A Set of Independent Axioms for Probability', *Mind* XLVII (1938), 275 ff., reprinted with further developments in K. R. Popper, *The Logic of Scientific Discovery* (1959), pp. 318 ff.

tion to this trend by showing, in 1938, that it is possible to
construct the mathematical calculus of probability as a purely
formal system, in which nothing whatever is assumed about
the nature of the probability-function except that its logical
syntax conforms to the axioms of the system. For example, its
arguments do not have to be sets, as Kolmogorov's treatment
implies them to be.[2] This establishes that the syntax of mathematical, i.e. Pascalian, probability can be given a representation
which is entirely neutral between all the rival monocriterial
theories. But it does not suffice to show that more than one
semantical interpretation of the calculus can function as a
viable theory of probability that is properly so called. Here the
work of Reichenbach and Carnap has been a turning-point.
Reichenbach[3] sought to demonstrate in 1934 that the possibility
of conceiving probabilities as the truth-values of a multi-valued
logic was not incompatible with the possibility of achieving a
semantic analysis of probability in terms of relative frequency.
And Carnap[4] showed later that the possibility of an analysis in
terms of relative frequency was also not incompatible with the
possibility of conceiving probability as a logical relation.

But the trouble with a polycriterial account of probability is
that, when faced with this apparent plurality of criteria, it
seems content to pursue the ideal of step-by-step descriptive

[2] A. Kolmogorov, 'Grundbegriffe der Wahrscheinlichkeitsrechnung', *Ergebnisse
der Mathematik* 2. 3 (1933), translated by N. Morrison as *Foundations of the Theory
of Probability* (1950). On the limitations of Kolmogorov's axiomatization cf. Tom
Settle, 'Induction and Probability Unfused', in *The Philosophy of Karl Popper*, ed.
P. A. Schilpp (1974), p. 733. But Kolmogorov's treatment is an abstract one in so
far as it does not restrict what can be elements of the (finite) sets with which it
deals.

[3] H. Reichenbach, *Wahrscheinlichkeitslehre* (1935), translated by E. H. Hetton
and M. Reichenbach as *The Theory of Probability* (1949). Cf. also George Boole,
An Investigation of the Laws of Thought (1954), pp. 247 ff. There were difficulties in
Reichenbach's proposal: cf. E. Nagel, *Principles of the Theory of Probability* (1939),
for a general critique of the different interpretations that have been proposed for
the calculus. Certain mathematically significant variations in the axiomatization
of the calculus of probability do not substantially effect the issues under discussion
in the present book and will therefore be ignored. On these variations cf. J. J.
Mehlberg, 'Is a Unitary Approach to Foundations of Probability Possible?' in
Current Issues in the Philosophy of Science, ed. H. Feigl and G. Maxwell (1961), pp.
287 ff., and T. L. Fine, *Theories of Probability: An Examination of Foundations* (1973).

[4] R. Carnap, *Logical Foundations of Probability* (1950). On Laplace's contribution
here cf. C. Howson, 'The Development of Logical Probability', in *Essays in Memory
of Imre Lakatos*, ed. R. S. Cohen, P. K. Feyerabend, and M. W. Wartofsky (1976),
p. 289.

adequacy rather than that of explanatory simplicity. When confronted with the inherent difficulties of the problem, it acknowledges the anomalies that face this or that monocriterial theory, and seems content to be driven by them to postulate a fundamental duality or multiplicity rather than a fundamental unity. It has apparently to surrender the prime goal of theory— unification—and then risks degenerating, as difficulties multiply, into mere natural history.

§2. *The mathematicist theory*

Is there any way in which polycriterial tolerance can be incorporated into a single explanatory theory? Can any unifying principle be found to underlie the plurality of probability-criteria that the diversity of the facts drives us to accept? Or is the word 'probability' a merely accidental homonym as we move from one criterion's domain of application to another? That is the main problem with which this part of the book is concerned. But before proposing my own solution I shall first briefly consider two other possible proposals.

One tempting way to deal with the problem is to argue that the required unification is to be found in the identity of the underlying calculus. A probability-function, it may be said, can now be defined quite formally by the axioms of the Pascalian calculus, and it can also be shown, in the case of each worthwhile criterion, why any function that conforms to the criterion must be a probability-function. For example, Ramsey showed this in regard to the belief-intensity criterion and Braithwaite in regard to the relative frequency criterion.[5] What more, it may be asked, is needed? What more can a theory of probability do?

But this proposal serves to highlight the nature of the problem rather than to solve it. It sheds no light on *why* there should be such a diversity of semantical criteria, each satisfying the axioms of the calculus in its own way and each having some substantial utility or interest of its own. There may well be other purposes for which it is useful to define probability functions in terms of their formal or mathematical structure. But such a definition will not serve our present purposes. The

[5] F. P. Ramsey, *Foundations of Mathematics* (1931), pp. 181 f.; and R. B. Braithwaite, *Scientific Explanation* (1953), pp. 115 ff.

mathematical calculus is not a theory of probability in the required sense of 'theory'.

After all, a monocriterial account—a relative frequency theory, say, or a personalist theory—does at least purport to go beyond familiar data. It claims to show, at least in principle, how a value is generated by the probability-function in relation to any pair of arguments of the appropriate type. We are thus put into the position of being able to check the plausibility of the theory in relation to other data than those on which it was founded. But a purely formalist account does not do this. It describes the common structure that, as it happens, certain familiar concepts have. But it makes no contribution towards explaining why they *all* have it. It does not indicate in general terms either a sufficient or a necessary semantical condition for being a concept of the type that will, on investigation, always be found to have that structure. As a symptom of this fault, the formal, mathematicist account does not enable us to discern any new examples of the structure it describes. It lacks any consequence analogous to that which Bacon[6] and Leibniz[7] long ago saw to be essential for any genuinely explanatory theory in natural science—the prediction of some hitherto unnoticed truth.

Moreover a formalist account is not only insufficiently explanatory for the above reasons. It also explains too much, so far as it explains anything at all. A formal axiomatization of probability is in principle open to non-standard interpretations. A formalist account is thus implicitly willing to apply the term 'probability' far beyond the limits imposed by its normal semantics.[8]

§3. *The family-resemblance theory*

Deficiency of explanatory power also vitiates a very different scheme—semantical rather than syntactical—for presenting a unitary but polycriterial account of probability. J. L. Mackie has recently argued that the term 'probability' has at least five basic senses, that are not mere homonyms. These five

---

[6] Francis Bacon, *Novum Organum* I. ciii and cxvii.

[7] In his letter to Couring of 19 Mar. 1678, published in *Die philosophischen Schriften von G. W. Leibniz*, ed. C. J. Gerhardt (1965), vol. i, pp. 196.

[8] Cf. p. 35, n. 4 below.

senses have grown out from and been nourished by a central root of meaning, he says—'which hovers between the extremes of guarded assertion and good but not conclusive reasons for believing'[9]—and they can all be explained as the result of a series of natural shifts and extensions. 'Probability', on Mackie's view, 'illustrates the thesis of J. S. Mill (recently taken over by Wittgenstein and his followers in their talk about family resemblances) that "names creep on from subject to subject, until all traces of a common meaning sometimes disappear" '.[10]

Now, if this were intended as a genuinely historical account of the matter, in the spirit of Mill's remarks, it would need to be accompanied by evidence that Mackie's supposed sequence of semantic shifts and extensions actually took place in the required temporal order. Mackie offers no historical evidence of this kind and, in the light of Hacking's recent researches,[11] it is highly doubtful whether it could be offered. Most of the current ways of talking about probabilities seem to have grown up together.

If, however, the aim of Mackie's account is somehow to make sense of the current situation, irrespective of historical etymology, it suffers from a defect inherent in the family-resemblance approach to conceptual problems. For example, men ride petrol-tankers, horses, and tractors, but not oxen; oxen, horses, and tractors, but not petrol-tankers, are used on farms for pulling things; petrol-tankers, tractors, and oxen stay on the ground while horses sometimes jump; and all petrol-tankers, oxen, and horses have their front and rear means of locomotion approximately the same height, while most tractors do not. But no one supposes it appropriate to mark *this* particular nexus of family resemblance by carrying over the name of one of the four sorts of objects to describe the other three sorts. The fact is that some groups of four or more sorts have common names, and some do not, even when the sorts exhibit family resemblance to one another. So unless the exponent of a family-resemblance approach to probability tells us why *his*

---

[9] J. L. Mackie, *Truth, Probability and Paradox* (1973), p. 188f.

[10] Ibid., p. 155, quoting J. S. Mill, *System of Logic* Bk. I, ch. i, §5.

[11] I. Hacking, 'Jacques Bernoulli's *Art of Conjecturing*', *British Journal for the Philosophy of Science* 22 (1971), 209 ff., and 'Equipossibility Theories of Probability', *Brit.Jour.Phil.Sci.* 22 (1971), 339 ff. Cf. also I. Hacking, *The Emergence of Probability* (1975).

supposed nexus of family resemblance generates a common name, in contrast with others that do not, he has not explained anything. But if he does do this, and does it adequately, he has to go beyond a merely family-resemblance account. It will certainly not be adequate to say that a common name is generated when the resemblances are sufficiently close, if the only test of sufficient closeness is the use of a common name. And again a symptom of failure to achieve a genuine explanation is the failure of the theory to imply any further checkable consequences. The family-resemblance account imposes an all-too-familiar kind of gloss on the data we already have, but cannot be relied on to lead us to anything new.

2

Probability as Gradation of Provability

Summary

§4. Instead, probability is to be viewed as a generalization on the
notion of provability; and different criteria of probability may be
seen to be appropriate in accordance with whether the proof-rules
that we have in mind as a basis of analogy are general or singular,
necessary or contingent, extensional or non-extensional. §5. Proof-
criteria that are general, necessary, and extensional generate probabilities that are appropriate to games of chance. §6. Proof-criteria
that are general, contingent, and extensional generate probabilities
that are appropriate to empirical statistics. §7. Proof-criteria that
are general, contingent, and non-extensional generate probabilities
that are appropriate to the measurement of causal propensities.
§8. Proof-criteria that are singular and necessary generate probabilities like those of Carnapian confirmation-theory, and proof-criteria
that are singular and contingent generate probabilities appropriate
to subjectivist, or personalist, theory. §9. Probability-statements are
evaluations of inferential soundness, and cannot be elucidated as
acts of guarded assertion.

§4. *The degree-of-provability theory*

The problem then is to present a polycriterial account of probability that avoids being purely syntactical, as the family-
resemblance account does, but is also genuinely explanatory,
which that account is not. We want to know how such very
different criteria of probability are applicable in different
contexts, when they are still felt to be, in some important sense,
criteria of the same thing. And the clue to a solution of the
problem is to be found by bearing in mind that in the Latin
ancestry of the European concept of probability there is to be
found not only the notion of approvability, on which leading
philosophers[1] have tended to concentrate for their etymologies

---

1 e.g. William Kneale, *Probability and Induction* (1949), p. 20.

in recent years, but also that of provability. So let us see what follows if we regard probability as a generalization on the notion of provability, and thus as a mode of evaluation for inferences rather than for statements.

This idea is by no means wholly new to philosophy. Even Locke contrasted demonstration with probability as different forms of proof. He wrote[2]

As demonstration is the showing the agreement or disagreement of two ideas, by the intervention of one or more proofs, which have a constant, immutable and visible connexion one with another, so probability is nothing but the appearance of such an agreement or disagreement, by the intervention of proofs, whose connexion is constant and immutable, or at least is not perceived to be so, but is, or appears, for the most part to be so, and is enough to induce the mind to judge the proposition to be true or false, rather than the contrary.

But, to simplify the situation, it is better to regard demonstrability as a limiting-case of probability rather than as an opposite of it. This too is a familiar idea from the work of de Morgan, Keynes, Waismann, and others.[3] What seems hitherto unexplored, however, is the possibility of founding a polycriterial, rather than a monocriterial, account of probability on this basis.

In any artificial language-system one formula B is said to be provable from another A if and only if there is a primitive or derivable syntactic rule that licenses the immediate derivation of B from A. But the kind of provability that concerns us in the present inquiry is not purely syntactic. So, to avoid confusion, let us speak of a (primitive or derivable) syntactic proof-rule as being inferentially sound, in an interpreted system S, if and only if the conclusion of any derivation which it licenses is true whenever the premiss or premisses are. Then the hypothesis to be considered is that probability is degree of inferential soundness. To grade the probability of B on A is to talk qualitatively, comparatively, ordinally or quantitatively about the

---

[2] John Locke, *An Essay Concerning Human Understanding*, Bk. IV, ch. xv, §1.

[3] A. de Morgan, *Formal Logic, or the Calculus of Inference, Necessary and Probable* (1847); J. M. Keynes, *A Treatise on Probability* (1921), pp. 133 ff.; and F. Waismann, 'Logische Analyse des Wahrscheinlichkeitsbegriffs', *Erkenntnis* 1 (1930), 228 ff. Cf. K. R. Popper, *The Logic of Scientific Discovery* (1959), p. 356: 'In its logical interpretation, the probability calculus is a genuine generalisation of the logic of derivation.'

degree of inferential soundness of a primitive or derivable rule that would entitle one to infer B immediately from A. And, just as demonstrative provability, when philosophically reconstructed, is always relative to the primitive derivation-rules of some particular deductive system, so too degree of probability is always relative to some particular criterion.

What makes this account inherently polycriterial is that, just as there are several different ways in which deductive systems, regarded as interpreted logistic systems, may be distinguished from one another in accordance with the type of provability regulated by their respective derivation-rules, so too different criteria generate correspondingly different types of gradation for inferential soundness. Indeed it turns out that all the main differences between commonly discussed criteria of probability are revealed in this way, provided that attention is not confined to the rather limited variety of derivation-rules that is normally at issue in metamathematical proof-theory.

To categorize the type of provability regulated by the primitive derivation-rules of a deductive system, where these rules are inferentially sound, at least three important questions need to be asked. All three are questions that are also familiar in many other contexts of philosophical analysis. Briefly stated, the questions are: Is a typical statement about such provability general or singular? Is its truth necessary or contingent? Is it extensional or non-extensional?

A typical statement about provability in a deductive system S is general if, as commonly in mathematical logic, the primitive derivation-rules of S set up proof-schemas, legitimating the inference from any formula or formulas of a certain kind to a corresponding formula of another kind. Proofs may then be conducted wholesale in these terms, with individual formulas never specified. On the other hand a typical statement about provability in S is singular if each primitive derivation-rule legitimates an inference only from one specific sentence to another, as from 'There will never be a nuclear war' to 'London will never be destroyed by hydrogen bombs'.[4]

---

[4] I shall say nothing here in regard to deductive systems that have both singular and general rules, or in regard to systems that have rules which are singular in regard to their premisses and general in regard to their conclusions or vice versa. The probability-functions that correspond to such mixed systems seem to be as little

Familiar examples of necessarily true statements about probability are those for which the corresponding conditionals are truths of classical logic, say, or arithmetic. For example, 'If A and if A then B, then B' is the necessarily true conditional that corresponds to the statement that 'B' is provable from 'A and if A then B'. The derivation-rules are then deductive in the logician's or philosopher's rather specialized sense of 'deduction'. But a statement about provability is contingent if it relates to derivation-rules which are read off from some physical theory, like the rules of classical mechanics or special relativity which are needed to prove—or to 'deduce', in the everyday sense of that word—from astronomical data that the next eclipse of the sun visible in England will be on 11 August, 1999.

Finally, a statement about provability is extensional if it remains true whenever co-extensive terms are substituted for one another in the formulas about which it speaks. But such a statement is non-extensional if it does not always remain true under these circumstances, as is often held to be the case in the logic of indirect discourse.

Accordingly, on the proposed hypothesis (that probability is a generalization of provability), three analogous questions may be asked as a step towards disambiguating the comparative sentence-schema of natural language '. . . is more probable than –.–.–. on the assumption –––', or towards determining the variety of meanings available for a functor[5] 'p[..., –––]' that maps probabilities on to numbers.

Should the blanks of the comparative sentence-schema be filled by expressions signifying membership of this or that class, as when formulas that may constitute the premisses (or the conclusions) of a particular proof-rule are classed together if and only if they supply different subjects to the same specified predicable?[6] Or should these blanks be filled by expressions

---

used as they are studied. But I regard it as a virtue, rather than a vice, of the analogy between probability and provability that it generates several types of probability-concept which are, as it turns out, not exemplified or approximated in philosophically familiar patterns of human reasoning. A theory ought to be substantially richer than the data it explains: the extra content is a means of testing the theory and thereby a stimulus to further research; cf. §§10–13 below.

[5] I use the term 'functor' for an expression denoting a function.

[6] In using the term 'predicable' here, rather than 'predicate', I follow the example of P. T. Geach, *Reference and Generality* (1962), pp. 23 f., in another con-

designating this or that fully determinate proposition, as when the premisses and conclusion of a proof are fully specified? Secondly, should the completed sentences, if true, be taken to formulate necessary truths of logic or arithmetic, or should they be taken instead to formulate contingent truths about the world? And, thirdly, should the completed sentences be regarded as preserving their truth-values whenever terms that have identical extensions replace one another therein, or not?

Analogously, are the fillers for the argument-places in a rationally reconstructed probability-functor to be conceived of as monadic predicables, or as sentences? Is an accepted equation of the form $p[\ldots, ---] = n$ to be regarded as necessarily, or contingently, true? And is the left-hand side of such an equation as extensional as the right-hand side?

Thus whether we regard ourselves as being concerned with *discovering* the meanings of natural-language sentences about probability, or with *inventing* meanings for the formulas of a formal system, at least three of the most important questions that can be asked about demonstrative provability can also be asked about probabilities. Moreover these three binary dimensions of categorization provide a matrix within which all the familiarly advocated criteria of probability can be accommodated in distinct pigeon-holes.

Some briefly sketched examples will clarify these claims, and help to substantiate them. But it would be both disproportionate and distracting in the present book to attempt a full presentation and discussion of the various familiarly advocated criteria of Pascalian probability.

§5. *Proof-criteria that are general, necessary and extensional*

Suppose first that statements about probability are to correspond to expressions that signify *general* rules of demonstrative inference, concerned with any formulas of a certain kind. The probability-functor will therefore be assigned predicables as fillers for its

---

text. I assume here, for simplicity's sake, that we are dealing only with monadic predicables. There are well-known difficulties about the introduction of polyadic predicables into the argument-places of mathematical probability functors (cf. R. Carnap, *Logical Foundations of Probability* (1950), pp. 123 f.), though the theory of inductive probability-functions developed in §§40–66 below is not exposed to these difficulties.

argument-places. Suppose too that the resultant equations are *extensional* and, if true, *necessarily* true. Here, where we are dealing with predicables and construing them extensionally, we shall be able to grade the inferential soundness of the derivation-rule at issue in terms of its success rate. For example, the probability of a number's being prime, if greater than 10 and less than 20 may be said—informally—to be ·5, because out of eight such numbers just four are primes. But this is tantamount to stating a rule that entitles us to infer a sentence with 'is a prime' as predicate, from a sentence with 'is greater than 10 and less than 20' as predicate, whenever both sentences have the same subject, and claiming that the rule has a 50-per-cent reliability for contexts to which it is applicable. And it is applicable wherever no other available premiss is relevant to inferring that conclusion: i.e. the numeral that is the subject of both premiss and conclusion in each case is supposed to be picked at random. Similarly the probability of any one outcome in a six-outcome game of chance is one-sixth, because a rule which says

From an outcome's being either A, B, C, D, E, or F infer its being A

has a one-sixth reliability wherever it applies. And again such a rule applies wherever the other circumstances are not unfavourable to its application: e.g. it applies to random throws of a well-balanced cubic die on to a flat surface. This kind of rule correlates two sets of equally specific and mutually exclusive outcome-types, one of which is the set described in the premiss and the other of which is the intersection between this set and the set described in the conclusion. The soundness of the rule is assessed *a priori* by calculating the ratio that the size (i.e. cardinality) of the latter intersection bears to the size of the set with which it is correlated.

This kind of probability-statement has often been taken to presuppose a principle of indifference between alternative outcomes. But that principle creates notorious difficulties, not least about why it is needed for some kinds of probabilities and not for others. And if one recognizes what kind of gradation of inferential soundness is being made by these probability-statements, one can see the problem in its proper perspective.

We do not need a special principle of indifference here but only a proviso about other circumstances' being not unfavourable; and that proviso is no different from the one which needs to be made whenever a necessarily sound rule of inference is applied to contingent issues. There is a familiar rule that 2 and 2 make 4, but the rule applies to counting the apples in a bucket only if there is no hole in the bottom.

Thus the limitations of this kind of criterion of probability are quite apparent. The conception of probability as an *a priori* calculable ratio between one set of mutually exclusive outcomes and another applies well to set-ups of assumed randomness, like games of chance. Absence of empirical evidence that one outcome (out of the game's set of equally specific, mutually exclusive, and jointly exhaustive outcomes) is more probable than another is just what characterizes a game as a game of pure chance. But in science, as has been justifiably remarked, one does not obtain knowledge out of ignorance. So this classical criterion of probability has no application to findings in the natural or social sciences. Moreover, because this criterion is concerned with the extensions of predicables, what it makes probability-functions map on to numbers are ordered pairs of *sets*. So the criterion assigns probability-values collectively, not distributively, and it cannot guarantee application of the collective value to individual outcomes. There is a ·5 probability that any number you choose which is greater than 10 and less than 20 will be a prime, but there is certainly not a ·5 probability that the number 15 is a prime. There is a ·5 probability of landing heads for any coin-toss. But there is certainly not a ·5 probability that yesterday's toss of tails was actually heads.

§6. *Proof-criteria that are general, contingent, and extensional*

Suppose next that we consider the probabilistic analogue for rules of demonstrative inference that are general, extensional and *contingent*. Here again the most obvious crtierion of gradation for demonstrative soundness is by the ration of one set-membership size to another.[7] The reliability of the rule

[7] An objector might be inclined to argue that wherever probabilities are defined over sets the resultant equations are necessarily true, because, whatever two sets are named, those two sets have the same size-ratio in each possible world.

From a man's being a lorry-driver, infer his survival till
age seventy

may be assessed empirically by estimating, from samples
appropriate to some chosen confidence-level, the ratio of
the number of lorry-drivers surviving till seventy to the total
number of lorry-drivers. But we might also, instead of talking
about ratios, seek to grade the reliability of this rule, as
Reichenbach's work suggests,[8] by the truth-value in a multi-
valued logic of a certain combination of propositional sequences,
like the proof of a multiple conclusion from a multiplicity of
premisses. We should then have a mode of gradation for inferential soundness that was not only contingent and extensional
but also concerned with singular, rather than general, inference-
rules, in that it applied to (sequences of) specific sentences
rather than to predicables.

The conception of probability as an empirically estimatable
relative frequency, or as the limit of this frequency in a long
run of randomly chosen samples, has the advantage of indicating a precise and interpersonally objective source of quantitative determination in very many types of statistical problem.
But again probability-values are being assigned collectively,
not distributively. So this conception, if strictly construed, has
the disadvantage of not indicating any simple, direct and
trouble-free method for assessing the probabilities of mere
individual events. If in these terms we speak of the probability
that John Smith, *qua* lorry driver, will survive till seventy, we
are not so much speaking about John Smith *tout court* as about
any randomly picked lorry-driver, and we are still not speaking
specifically about John Smith *tout court* if we get nearer to

---

However the argument seems too powerful to be valid, for it applies to numbers as
well as to sets and thus generates necessary truth for, say, the statement that the
ratio of the number of men's colleges to the number of women's colleges in Oxford
is 18 to 5. My remarks in the text must be construed as being intended in a sense
of 'necessary truth' in which this statement is not necessarily true while it is necessarily true that the ratio of the number of primes to the total number of integers
between 10 and 20 is 1 to 2. My sense is therefore one in which the necessity of a
statement's truth depends not only on the sets, numbers or other things it refers to
but also on its mode of reference to them, so that, for example, some true statements
of identity may be contingent. It would be out of place to say more about this
currently much discussed topic in the present context.

[8] Op. cit. (1949 edn.), pp. 387 ff.

identifying the intersection of relevant sets to which he belongs and speak of him *qua* fifty-year-old, British, diabetic, father of four children, living next to an asbestos factory, son of a suicide, and so on.[9] We are grading a probability for a certain type of person, not for the individual, John Smith. Also since this conception of probability applies to predicables, not to complete sentences, it does not indicate any obviously plausible way to assess the strength of scientific hypotheses in relation to experimental evidence. Anyone who seeks in it a foundation for inductive logic is handicapped from the start. Nor does the conception of a probability as a truth-value solve any epistemological problem that cannot be solved by conception of it as a ratio, since the precise truth-value to be assigned has still to be assessed by consideration of the relevant ratio, whether this be a relative frequency in a statistical sample or a proportion of favourable alternatives in a game of chance. It is possible that the conception of probability as a truth-value in an appropriate multi-valued logic has the intellectual advantage of linking probability theory with logic. But it does not help to indicate how any such probabilities may be ascertained, except in the limiting cases of 0 and 1.

§7. *Proof-criteria that are general, contingent, and non-extensional*

Let us now examine the probabilistic analogue for rules of demonstrative inference that are general, contingent, and non-extensional, like statements of causal laws.

There are, no doubt, some statements about causes—especially anecdotal statements—in which identically referring terms are inter-substitutable. Compare, e.g. 'Cicero's speech caused Catiline to leave Rome' and 'Tully's speech caused Catiline to leave Rome'. But such statements do not concern us here. What we do need to bear in mind is that one physical property may be co-extensive with another and yet need to be

---

[9] So in Reichenbach's interpretation a statement about the probability of a single case has no meaning of its own. It represents 'an elliptic mode of speech' and, 'in order to acquire meaning, the statement must be translated into a statement about a frequency in a sequence of repeated occurrences' (ibid., pp. 376–7).

The relative-frequency analysis of probability is further restricted in application by the fact that the introduction of a limiting value presupposes an ordering for the set of samples which determine relative frequency in the long run. There ought to be some pre-analytical rationale for this ordering.

distinguished from it in order to constitute the causal explanation of it. For example the property of elasticity can be defined
(for macroscopic objects) in non-chemical terms. But to
explain why a particular kind of thing has such elasticity might
conceivably involve reference to the fact that that kind of
thing has a certain molecular structure which is coextensive
with the property of elasticity. So the explanation would be
essentially non-extensional.[10] What happens, then, when
analogously the probability-functor has predicables to fill its
argument-places but the resultant equations are contingent
and non-extensional? Since coextensive predicables may not
now be substituted for one another, we have to suppose that
such a probability-function maps ordered pairs of properties,
attributes, or characteristics, not ordered pairs of sets, on to
numbers. So the soundness or reliability of a rule of inference
is then graded by the strength of the contingent, physical
connection between two characteristics, as perhaps with the
rule that would entitle us to infer from a thing's being a radium
atom to its disintegrating within twenty-four hours. Indeed, to
treat a radium atom's probability of disintegration within
twenty-four hours as a so-called 'propensity' of the atom is in
effect to grade the soundness of such a rule of inference by the
strength of this physical connection. Or rather, *if* a worthwhile distinction is to be drawn between interpreting the
mathematical calculus of chance as a theory of relative frequencies and interpreting it as a theory of propensities, *then*
an essential, though curiously seldom noticed, feature of
difference between the two interpretations is that the former
makes probability-equations extensional and the latter makes
them non-extensional. But in both cases the same method of
assessment is available. The probability may be estimated from
relative frequencies in appropriate samples.

   This conception of a probability as a measurable physical
connection between two characteristics—a 'propensity', as it is
sometimes called—has the advantage of allowing probabilities
to be predicated distributively of individual objects in well-
understood environments, like radium atoms in experimental

   [10] This is a relatively mild type of non-extensionality. There are various degrees
of tougher resistance to substitutivity: cf. L. Jonathan Cohen, *The Diversity of
Meaning*, 2nd edn. (1966), pp. 194 ff.

situations. If a particular object has the one characteristic, it may be said to be subject to the weakish connection linking that characteristic with the other.[11] But, if this conception is ever justifiably applicable, it can be so only so far as the strength of the connection is immune to interference by other causal factors—or only when some actual or possible scientific theory is supposed, as perhaps ideally in atomic physics,[12] to predict or explain the precise strength of the particular connection involved, quite apart from sample-based estimates of that strength. Since the connection is then regarded as not being purely accidental, the terms signifying what are taken to be connected may with good reason be understood non-extensionally, like the terms of a statement asserting a causal law. The connection lies between one property, attribute, natural kind,[13] or other characteristic, and another, not between two sets.[14] But where other factors might interfere and no theoretical explanation of the precise strength and nature of an empirically estimated probability is supposed obtainable, as in the case of the probability that a fifty-year-old lorry-driver—anyone you please—will die within the next twenty years, there is no reason not to conceive the probability extensionally as the ratio of one

[11] Certain kinds of subjunctive conditional statements about probability also require a propensity analysis rather than a relative-frequency one: cf. §85, p. 306ff, below.

[12] For a criticism of Popper's analysis of quantum-theoretical probabilities as propensities cf. P. Suppes, 'Popper's analysis of probability in quantum mechanics', in *The Philosophy of Karl Popper*, ed. P. A. Schilpp (1974), pp. 760 ff.

[13] Admittedly W. V. Quine, *Ontological Relativity and Other Essays* (1969), pp. 131 ff., has attempted to reduce the concept of a natural kind to the wholly extensional concept of a set of objects that match each other in respect of their parts, like the molecules of a particular chemical element. But this makes the logical analysis of a concept depend on the infinite divisibility of matter. If matter is not infinitely divisible, there must be some level in the study of natural kinds (perhaps sub-atomic physics) at which objects cannot be classified together in terms of their matching parts. Cf. §90 below.

[14] Philosophers have disputed whether such a propensity-type probability 'belongs to' an individual atom, say, or to an experimental set-up. On the proposed analysis it belongs to both, though in different ways. On the one hand it connects a certain type of experimental set-up with a certain type of event. On the other hand each instance of such a set-up is thereby subjected to the connection. From this point of view to dispute whether a propensity belongs primarily to a set-up or to its instances is as philosophically pointless as disputing whether we should say that being penetrated by a bullet causes a heart to stop beating, or rather that the bullet in the individual victim's heart causes it to stop beating. But cf. D. H. Mellor, *The Matter of Chance* (1971), pp. 70 ff.

set's members to another's. Similarly, where set-ups of assumed randomness are concerned, as in games of chance, it is appropriate to conceive a proability as an *a priori* calculable ratio between one set of equally specific and mutually exclusive possibilities and another rather than as the empirically measurable strength of a physical connection. If we do start to measure the physical connection between a coin's being tossed and its landing heads, we are in effect checking how far the assumption that we are dealing with a game of chance is appropriate.

§8. *Proof-criteria that are singular and either necessary or contingent*

I am trying to show how the hypothesis that probability is degree of inferential soundness is bound to generate a poly-criterial account of probability in accordance with the different criteria of gradation that are appropriate to grading the soundness of familiarly different kinds of inference-rule. And I have so far confined myself almost entirely to general inference-rules, whether these be necessary or contingent, extensional or non-extensional. I shall turn now to singular inference-rules and to the analogous probability-functions, which take fully formed sentences as fillers of their argument-places.

If such an inference-rule is necessary, rather than contingent, the analogous gradation of inferential soundness will have entailment as the upper limit of the relation between premiss and conclusion and contradiction as the lower limit, and whatever intermediate relations obtain will also obtain necessarily. For example, Carnap's programme for inductive logic supposed that these conditions were satisfied by the confirmation-relation between a statement of experimental evidence, e, and a scientific hypothesis, h. According to Carnap the probability of h on e is to vary with the extent to which the range of e is contained within the range of h, where the range of a sentence s in a language-system L is the class of those state-descriptions in L—i.e. descriptions of possible worlds—in which s holds true. Different range-measures then provide different methods of assessment for probabilities formulated in the appropriate artificial language-system. But there is a strong constraint on the application of such necessarily true statements of probability, similar to that already noticed in the case of other necessarily true evaluations of demonstrative soundness. The price to be paid for deriving practical benefit from a necessary truth is that conditions must be just right for its application, whether it be applied in evaluating the probability of a tossed coin's landing heads or in summing the apples in a barrel. Carnap's logic would be usefully applied to the evaluation of scientific predictions only if the differing measurements assigned by the chosen range-measure to different sentences could be made to fit the actual structure of Nature. The range-measurement of a sentence stating the situation S to exist would have to reflect somehow the strength of Nature's potential for bringing S about.

The conception of a probability as a logical relation between propositions, corresponding to a singular rule of demonstrative inference, has the advantage of not precluding the association of probabilities with individual events. It achieves this by allowing the assignment of probabilities to the propositions reporting these events. But even if such a conception can be adapted, as is notoriously difficult, to languages of richer structure than monadic first-order predicate calculus, it seems inevitably to confront its users with the need to make some evidentially unsupported decision, like the choice of a preferred Carnapian range-measure out of an infinity of available ones. Such a decision might sometimes be a matter of considered policy as regards the degree to which prior probabilities should be allowed to influence our calculations. But there seems no way in which the decision can be appraised for truth or falsity in the light of empirically discoverable facts. So, as a philo-sophical reconstruction of how people actually reason with one another, the logical theory of probability is applicable only where some such *a priori* decision may legitimately be imputed.

It is natural to wonder therefore, so far as the probability-functor is to take fully formed sentences as fillers of its argument-places, whether we should not do better to conceive statements about probability as being capable only of contingent, not necessary truth. In such a conception probability is not a logical operation on propositions, but perhaps a psychological or epistemological one. Statements about probability are analog-ous to singular rules of inference that are empirically validated, and the task for a criterion of probability is to provide a gradation for the inferential soundness of such rules. And one familiar way of doing this is to grade how strongly a rational man does, or should, believe in the truth of the conclusion when the truth of the premiss is given him. The inferential soundness of a rule deriving B from A might thus be calibrated in terms of the lowest odds at which a man who distributes all his wagers coherently might bet on B if given A, where at least a necessary condition[15] for coherence is that the bettor should not distribute his bets in such a way as to ensure an over-all loss of money.

Conception of probability as degree of belief escapes diffi-culties like the arbitrariness of choosing a particular range-measure in Carnapian inductive logic. By grading probabilities in terms of acceptable betting odds within a coherent betting policy, the so-called subjectivist or personalist approach can plausibly claim that all sufficiently informed and identically motivated rational men would agree about such probabilities.[16]

---

[15] On various possible conceptions of coherence here cf. H. E. Kyburg, Jr., and H. E. Smokler (eds.), *Studies in Subjective Probability* (1964), editorial introduction p. 11. There are problems about the impact of a rational man's interests on the betting odds he will accept. Some of these problems are resolved by C. A. B. Smith, 'Consistency in Statistical Inference and Decision', *Journal of the Royal Statistical Society* (Series B) 23 (1961), 1–37. But a non-coherent betting policy might be quite rational for a non-acquisitive man: cf. the remarks of G. A. Barnard, in the discussion of C. A. B. Smith's paper, ibid. pp. 25–6.

It would also be possible to grade belief in the truth of the conditional proposi-tion 'If A is true, then B is true' by a quotient for betting on its truth. But not all subjectivists, or critics of subjectivism, distinguish as carefully as they should between $p[B,A] = n$, $p[A \rightarrow B] = n$ and $A \rightarrow p[B] = n$: cf. n. 21, p. 30, below.

[16] Of course, a proof that invokes a contingent rule of inference can always be transformed into one that invokes a necessary rule, if the contingent rule is trans-formed into the major premiss of the new proof. Analogously a contingently true probability-statement can, in principle, always be reconstructed as a necessarily true one in which the facts warranting the contingent truth are included in the evidence for the new probability: i.e. the contingent probability $p[B,A]$ warranted by C, becomes the logical probability $p[B,A \& C]$. But, if the ways in which the content of A and the content of C affect the value of $p[B,A \& C]$ are highly dis-parate, this mode of construction serves no useful purpose. There may also be a problem about substitutivity. On both the logical and the personalist accounts probability-statements are non-extensional, in the sense that contingently co-extensive predicables are not always inter-substitutable *salva veritate* in such statements. But, whereas logically equivalent expressions would normally be inter-substitutable therein on a logical account, they would not be inter-substitutable on a personalist account unless the rationality of a rational bettor is taken to include logical omniscience.

It is unimportant here whether we take probability-expressions to be relational predicates, as in

The proposition that it will rain this afternoon *is highly probable on the evidence of* the proposition that the barometer is falling this morning,

But, presumably because it is not easy to become so rational, well-informed and conventionally motivated and because, with wins being undiscoverable, betting on open-ended generalizations is hardly an appropriate activity for rational men, few researchers in the natural or social sciences have in fact adopted this personalist approach.

§9. *Probability-statements as evaluation of inferential soundness*

I have only sketched the situation very summarily and incompletely, because no more is necessary here and to say more about these topics would divert attention from the main topic of the book. But what I have said so far should suffice to show that each of the familiarly advocated criteria of probability fits neatly into place within the matrix generated by three primary questions about deductive systems and their proof-rules. If we view probability-statements as evaluations of inferential soundness, we are led naturally to recognize their inherent capacity for heterogeneity; and since different kinds of deductive system are appropriate to different tasks we can understand why such widely differing criteria of probability have actually been put forward. A monocriterial account of probability is as viciously Procrustean as a monocriterial account of goodness that would identify the criteria of a good pen, say, with those of a good gardener.

A polycriterial account of probability is thus to be seen as no more requiring a family-resemblance analysis than does a polycriterial account of goodness. The criteria of a good pen can be distinguished quite uncontroversially from the criteria of a good gardener. But not only is the term 'good' not a mere accidental homonym in these contexts, as Aristotle long ago remarked:[17] we do not have to give a family-resemblance, successive-shift-of-meaning account of it either. There is an underlying nuclear meaning of the word which enables us to

---

or sentence-forming operators on sentence-pairs, as in

It is highly probable, on the evidence that the barometer is falling this morning, *that* it will rain this afternoon.

So in the informal discussion I shall use either idiom as stylistically convenient. For the purpose of formalization, however, it is necessary to opt for one idiom or the other: cf. §66 below.

[17] *Nicomachean Ethics*, 1096[b], 26–7.

use it in judging the value of indefinitely many different types of thing. In this meaning it is no more a homonym, or a polyseme, than is 'value' itself. So, too, like many other terms of appraisal or evaluation—like 'good', 'valid', 'legitimate', 'beautiful', etc.—the term 'probable' turns out to have, quite compatibly with its single nuclear meaning, a wide variety of criteria of gradation, which may be regarded as determining the existence of a correspondingly wide variety of different concepts of probability.

But whatever the nuclear meaning of such an evaluative term is (and sometimes a philosophical characterisation of it is rather difficult) this nuclear meaning would certainly be useless without some appropriate criterion to complement it in any particular context of use. And therein lies a substantial difference between the nuclear meaning of such an evaluative term and any original root of meaning for a descriptive term, like 'game', say, from which various other meanings may have developed by a process of family resemblance. The latter is self-sufficient in a way that the former is not.

It seems reasonable to accept, then, that the vocabulary of probability is, at bottom, the proper terminology for grading and evaluating the soundness of proof-rules. And, if one accepts this, one can see not only why, because there are different kinds of proof-rule, there must also be correspondingly different criteria of probability, but also why there was an opportunity for some philosophers[18] to be excessively impressed by the use of the vocabulary of probability in the utterance of guarded assertions. Evaluative terms like 'good' and 'probable' lend themselves very readily, as predicates in simple categorical sentences, to the performance of rather characteristic types of speech-act, such as commendation and guarded assertion, respectively. The reason why one cannot say

On my evidence Excalibur will probably win the race, but in fact it will lose

is just because this would be both to assert, albeit guardedly, and to deny the same thing. But that such evaluative terms have to

---

[18] e.g. S. E. Toulmin, 'Probability', *Proceedings of the Aristotelian Society*, supp. vol. xxiv (1950), 27 ff.; J. R. Lucas, *The Concept of Probability* (1970), pp. 1 ff.; and J. L. Mackie, op. cit., pp. 158f.

be assigned meanings independently of these performances becomes clear when we consider their use in the antecedents of conditional sentences, and in other more complex contexts, that are incapable of performing speech-acts of commendation, assertion, etc.[19] And where the term 'probable' is not used assertorically it does not exclude the negation of what is said to be probable, as in

If on my evidence Excalibur will probably win, but in fact it will lose, my evidence is not as complete as I should like it to be.

Nor does the guarded-assertion theory help us much to see how, at its heart, probability is a relation. By appealing to such familiar types of utterance in ordinary speech as 'It is probable that Peter will come to the party', where reference to the evidence has been omitted because it is unnecessary, the guarded-assertion theory invokes an ellipse as a paradigm, and directs attention to the rhetorical, rather than to the logical, structure of discourse. Here as elsewhere[20] the surface forms of ordinary

---

[19] M. Dummett, *Frege: Philosophy of Language* (1973), pp. 327 ff., has recently defended the applicability of sentential operators to sentences already containing force-indicators in certain special cases. But his arguments do not have the generality that would be required to sustain a 'guarded assertion' theory of probability. For example, where '⊢' functions as a sign of assertive force, he remarks (p. 351) that we could have a use for the complex form 'If (⊢A), then (⊢B)' construed as meaning 'If I were to assert (agree) that A, then I should assert (agree) that B.' Now suppose that 'Λ' were a sign of guarded assertion. Then presumably there would be a corresponding use for the form 'If (ΛA), then (⊢B)' as meaning 'If I were to assert (agree) guardedly that A, then I should assert (agree) that B.' But this would not be a use paraphrasable by 'If it is probable that A, then B.' For though it happens to be true that if I were to assert (agree) guardedly that it will be cloudy this afternoon I should also assert (agree) that I am excessively cautious in my weather predictions, it is not true that if clouds are probable this afternoon I am excessively cautious. Nor is there any obvious use for a sentence of the form 'If (ΛA), then I should prefer not to assert (agree) guardedly that A', though there is an obvious use for 'If it is probable that A, then I should prefer not to assert (agree) guardedly that A.'

[20] For instance the normal German word for probability, *Wahrscheinlichkeit*, has more etymological connection with the notion of approvability than with that of provability. Though *probabel* and *Probabilität* are occasionally used today, *wahrscheinlich* goes back into the seventeenth century. But the long-standing tendency to treat *wahrscheinlich* and *scheinbar* as opposites does indicate that in its semantics *wahrscheinlich*, like *probable*, has an underlying concern with interpretation of evidence. It is noteworthy also that even in constructing the mathematical calculus of probability as a purely formal system it is less restrictive to take the dyadic functor as primitive and define the monadic functor in terms of it, than to adopt the

language are a particularly unrevealing guide to the philosophical student of probability. More specifically, what I have in mind is that any analysis for the term 'probable', that is to allow interpretation of the mathematical calculus of chance as a logic of probability, must at least elucidate a certain well-known fact. This is that the following three expressions do not necessarily have the same truth-value for particular A, B and n, viz.: $p[B,A] = n$, $p[A \to B] = n$, and $A \to p[B] = n$.[21] And the guarded-assertion theory is inherently incapable, on its own, of elucidating this fact, because all three expressions can function equally well as forms of guarded assertion where the truth of A is the only known or assumed evidence.

But the proposed analysis of probability as degree of inferential soundness achieves the required elucidation quite simply. For

---

reverse procedure: cf. K. R. Popper, 'Replies to My Critics', in *The Philosophy of Karl Popper*, ed. P. A. Schilpp (1974), p. 1132, and Tom Settle, 'Induction and Probability Unfused', ibid., p. 733.

[21] Three equivalences are at issue here, all of which are demonstrably false for mathematical probability:

(i) $(A)(B)(n)(p[B,A] = n \leftrightarrow p[A \to B] = n)$.

Whereas elementary logic gives us $p[A \to B] = p[-B \to -A]$, it is demonstrable that $p[B,A]$ is not in every case equal to $p[-A, -B]$: cf. L. Jonathan Cohen, *The Implications of Induction* (1970), p. 113.

(ii) $(A)(B)(n)(p[B,A] = n \leftrightarrow (A \to p[B] = n))$.

Consider any case in which $p[B,A] > p[B]$ and A is contingently true.

(iii) $(A)(B)(n)(p[A \to B] = n \leftrightarrow (A \to p[B] = n))$.

Consider any case in which A logically implies B, A is contingently true, and $p[B]$ < 1, or in which A is necessarily false and $n < 1$.

Because of these non-equivalences the term 'conditional probability' is an unfortunate name for $p[B,A]$: 'dyadic probability' is less misleading.

I have assumed here that the conditional $A \to B$ is truth-functional. Even without that assumption it can still be shown that $p[B,A]$ is not necessarily equal to $p[A \to B]$: cf. D. Lewis, 'Probabilities of Conditionals and Conditional Probabilities', *Philosophical Review* lxxxv (1976), 297 ff. However, Lewis's interpretation (ibid., pp. 306–8) of dyadic probabilities is scarcely tenable. He conceives of $p[B,A]$ as measuring the assertability of the truth-functional $A \to B$, even though this cannot account adequately for the fact that, while the assertability of the truth-functional $A \to B$ reduces with high $p[B]$ as well as with high $p[-A] \times \dfrac{p[-B \ \& \ A]}{p[A]}$, $p[B,A]$ reduces with the latter and not with $p[B]$. In contrast with Lewis's interpretation, the conception of $p[B,A]$ as measuring the provability of B from A does account for the latter point quite unproblematically, and it implies accordingly that $p[B,A]$ does not measure the assertability of the truth-functional $A \to B$.

according to that analysis an expression of the form of p[B,A] = n grades the soundness of inferring B from A, and this must be different, in principle, from grading the soundness of inferring A→B since, notoriously, there are deductive systems in which one particular formula may be demonstrable from another even though the truth-functional conditional linking the two is not demonstrable. Similarly, since according to the analysis what are commonly called 'prior' probabilities—and would better be called 'monadic' ones—correspond to inferences from the null class of assumptions, an expression of the form A→p[B] = n tells us what level of soundness to assign, if what A says is true, to the derivation of B from no assumptions at all. But the expression does not imply that B must be derivable from A with just this level of soundness—which is quite another issue and dealt with instead by p[B,A] = n. Nor does it tell us, unconditionally, that the truth-functional conditional linking A and B must be derivable with this level of soundness from no assumptions—which is again an obviously different issue and dealt with by p[A→B] = n.

Perhaps someone will object that provability normally has certain properties that do not carry over into probability. For example, it is normally the case that, if C is provable from A (without the help of the principle that contradictions imply anything whatever), then C is provable from A and B (without the help of principle that contradictions imply anything whatever). But it would be quite fallacious to claim that for any n, if p[C,A] = n and p[A,B] > 0, then p[C,A & B] = n.

The answer to this objection is a simple one. It is that when one treats a given mode of gradation G as a generalization of a particular quality Q, or Q as a limiting-case of G, one does not imply that every feature of Q is generalized in G. Thus one does not count it as an objection to treating the concept of temperature as a generalization on the concepts of hot and cold that, for any person's hand at a particular time, there is some intermediate degree of temperature—the same as that of the hand—which does not have a distinctive feel. Rather, part of the fall-out from any successful philosophical proposal to treat G (e.g. probability) as a generalization of Q (e.g. provability) is a clarification of which features belong to Q in virtue of its being merely a particular quality, as it were, or a limiting-case, and which features belong to Q independently of this status. For example, the mathematical calculus of probability includes the principle that, if $p[C,A] = 1$ and $p[A,B] > 0$, then $p[C,A \& B] = 1$, but not the principle that for any n, if $p[C,A] = n$ and $p[A,B] > 0$, then $p[C,A \& B] = n$.

3

The Completeness Issue

Summary

§10. Completeness, as a property of certain deductive systems, may be viewed as a limiting-case of probabilistic complementationality. §11. It follows that proof criteria for incomplete systems generate probabilities that do not conform to the mathematical calculus of chance. Such probabilities measure what Keynes called 'weight' and have a non-complementational negation principle. §12. One such probability is that which the consequent of any generalized conditional has on the truth of its antecedent, if this probability is equated with the level of inductive support that exists for the generalization. §13. This concept will be shown to play an important part in the way in which lay juries are expected to assess proofs of fact in Anglo-American lawcourts.

§10. *The connection between deductive completeness and mathematical probability*

I remarked earlier that a good explanatory theory, in philosophy as in natural science, should always predict some hitherto unnoticed type of truth, and I used this point as one argument against both formalist and family-resemblance theories of probability. Such theories merely put a gloss on what we know already about the polycriterial nature of probability and do not lead directly to the discovery of some hitherto unacknowledged criterion. It is clearly incumbent on me, therefore, to show that my own analysis of probability in terms of inferential soundness does lead to such a discovery; and the remainder of the present book could be regarded as being devoted to this end.

The familiar criteria of probability were pigeon-holed within a matrix that was generated by three binary dimensions of categorization. The three questions 'General or singular?', 'Necessary or contingent?' and 'Extensional or non-extensional? —questions that arise naturally in any categorization of inference-rules—were applied to gradations of inferential soundness and were found to generate enough distinctions to accommodate all the philosophically familiar types of criteria in separate pigeon-holes. It follows that, if further questions of this sort can usefully be asked, some or all of the pigeon-holes may be subdivided and we may have not only a fuller character-ization of the familiar criteria, but also an indication of some philosophically unfamiliar ones. If both of the latter results are obtainable, we shall have substantial confirmation of the present analysis.

Well, there is certainly another important question that arises about any deductive system in relation to its inference-rules: is it complete or not? We are here concerned with probability in any interpreted system in which negation is expressable. So let us adopt the definition that such a system is complete just so long as any formula B is provable from the axioms if and only if not-B is not provable. Now, if probability is to be conceived as degree of inferential soundness, the demonstrative provability of B from A is a limiting-case of probability, where $p[B,A] = 1$. Hence, if we conceive this limiting-case as an instance of provability in a complete system, we may take $p[\text{not-}B,A] = 0$ to state that not-B is not provable from A; and, in general, the probability of B on A should be expected to vary inversely with the probability of not-B on A. For we cannot, in such a complete system, assert anything about the non-probability or non-provability of B except in terms that imply asserting something about the probability or provability of not-B. What emerges is the familiar complementational principle for negation: $p[B,A] = 1 - p[\text{not-}B,A]$. Complete-ness, as a property of certain deductive systems, may thus be viewed as a limiting-case of probabilistic complementationality.

In an incomplete deductive system, on the other hand, there must be at least one well-formed formula such that neither it nor its negation is provable. That is to say, when provability is described in terms of probability, there must be an A and a B such that both $p[B,A] = 0$ and also $p[\text{not-}B,A] = 0$. It follows that where criteria of probability are invoked which are analogous to the primitive derivation-rules for an incomplete deductive system the familiar complementational principle for negation cannot apply. If we ever wish to reason in terms of such probabilities, our statements must have some other logical structure than that articulated by the familiar mathematical calculus of chance.

I do not wish to suggest, however, that the only fruitful way of classifying probability-criteria is by reference to questions that arise about deductive systems in relation to their inference-rules. In particular it is important also to consider possible differentiations in the type of gradation of inferential soundness.[1] More specifically, is this gradation to be viewed as one that *measures* inferential soundness by a countably additive function which maps its argument-pairs on to real numbers, or is the gradation of inferential soundness rather to be viewed as *ranking* the soundness of inferences by a function that is not even finitely additive and maps its argument-pairs on to integers, or is this gradation instead to be viewed as being merely *comparative*? In the measure-theoretical case there are well-known arguments that, with the help of relatively uncontroversial assumptions (such as that probability-functions take as their arguments the elements of a Boolean algebra), establish[2] a multiplicative principle for the probability of conjunctions—$p[B \ \& \ C, A] = p[B, A] \times p[C, A \ \& \ B]$—though in the case of ordinal grading a multiplicative principle is obviously unworkable. Now a complementational principle for negation and a multiplicative one for conjunction are in substance all that is required[3] to guarantee conformity to the Pascalian calculus of probability. So an appropriately comprehensive explanation why several widely different kinds of probability-function conform to this calculus is that they all measure inferential soundness by criteria analogous to rules of inference in a complete deductive system (for the elements of a Boolean algebra),[4] while the differences between these different kinds

[1] Yet another relevant question, which is unimportant in the present context, would concern whether the proof (probability) is interpersonal or valid only for a particular person.

[2] Cf. R. T. Cox, *The Algebra of Probable Inference* (1961) pp. 4 ff.; and J.R. Lucas, *The Concept of Probability* (1970), pp. 33 ff.

[3] Ibid. Cf. R. T. Cox, loc. cit., and J. R. Lucas, loc. cit.

[4] But, while this does seem a sufficient condition for conformity to the Pascalian calculus, it is hardly a necessary one. Non-standard (i.e. non-probabilistic) interpretations of the calculus are certainly possible. For example, the dyadic functor 'p[..., ---]' might have a reading that was appropriate to taking the numerals 'o' and 'ı', instead of sentences or predicables, as fillers for its argument-places.

of probability-function are analogous to corresponding logical differences between kinds of inference-rule.

§11. *The grading of probabilities by evidential weight*

A probability that is analogous to demonstrability in an incomplete system has much in common with what Keynes long ago referred to as the 'weight' of evidence.[5] Though the absence of a required axiom precludes us perhaps from having a demonstrative proof of B, it may nevertheless be conceived to be compatible with admitting some degree of provability for B since so many of the axioms we need for proving B are there. 'B is *almost* demonstrable', we might say. Similarly Keynes said that

> One argument has more *weight* than another if it is based on a greater amount of relevant evidence. . . . It has a greater amount of *probability* than another if the balance in its favour, of what evidence there is, is greater than the balance in favour of the argument with which we compare it.

Weight, Keynes was convinced, cannot be analysed in terms of mathematical probability. An equation of the form $p[B,A] = n$ is not more likely to be right, he said, if of higher weight, since such an equation states the relation between A and B with equal accuracy in either case.

Nor is an argument of high weight one in which the probable error is small; for a small probable error only means that magnitudes in the neighbourhood of the most probable magnitude have a relatively high probability and an increase of evidence does not necessarily involve an increase in these probabilities.

Keynes did not feel sure, so he said, that the theory of what he called evidential weight had much practical significance. But perhaps that was because he seems to have envisaged it wrongly, like Peirce before him[6], as a mere auxiliary to the theory of mathematical probability, and not as an independent criterion of probability in its own right. Correspondingly the measures

---

[5] J. M. Keynes, *A Treatise on Probability* (1957), pp. 71 ff.

[6] C. S. Peirce, *Collected Papers*, ed. C. Hartshorne and P. Weiss, vol. ii (1932), p. 421.

developed by statisticians for grappling, in effect, with what Keynes took to be the problem of evidential weight—measures like Fisher's significance levels or Neyman's confidence intervals—are designed to operate on, or make statements about, estimates of statistical magnitudes like mathematical probabilities. They do not constitute criteria for the inferability of B from A that judge by nothing but the relevant 'weight' of A.

What happens if we do judge inferability in this way? We obtain a positive gradation of inferability for B only if the evidence is, on balance, in favour of B, and the level of this gradation then depends just on the amount of the evidence. Only if the evidence were, on balance, in favour of not-B, would we instead, by grading the amount of relevant evidence we have, obtain a positive gradation of inferability for not-B. So, when we obtain a positive gradation of inferability for a proposition from possible evidence, we obtain none for its negation. In other words, where the truth of A is not itself disprovable, if $p[B,A] > o$, then $p[\text{not-}B,A] = o$. But the converse does not hold—the negation principle is non-complementational—since A might be indecisive or wholly irrelevant in regard to B. The evidence might neither favour B on balance nor not-B. We should then have both $p[B,A] = o$ and $p[\text{not-}B,A] = o$. And this is like saying that in an incomplete deductive system it does not hold that, if not-B is not provable from A, then B is so provable, since it might be the case that neither B nor not-B is provable.

Perhaps someone will object that, if $p[B,A] = 1$ is to be taken as stating the demonstrative provability of B from A, $p[B,A] = o$ *must* be taken to state B's demonstrative disprovability. Hence—the objection continues—the non-provability of both B and not-B is not really represented by $p[B,A] = o$ and $p[\text{not-}B,A] = o$, but rather by $p[B,A] = \cdot5 = p[\text{not-}B, A]$.

But, if provability is to be put on a scale and made a matter of degree, there are at least two prima-facie candidates for its lower limit. One is disprovability, the other non-provability. Whereas the former kind of scale can embrace the lower limit of the latter as $p[B,A] = \cdot5 = p[\text{not-}B,A]$, the latter kind of scale can also embrace the lower limit of the former, since the disprovability of B can always be represented by the provability of not-B. So provability is generalizable just as plausibly by being opposed to non-provability in incomplete systems as by being opposed to disprovability in complete ones.

Again, some philosophers may wish to defend Keynes's failure to accept evidential weight as a criterion of probability, just on the ground that incomplete deductive systems cannot accord with the complementational principle for negation. Such a philosopher would hold it safe to conceive probability as degree of inferential soundness only so far as complete systems are concerned. Since an extension of the analogy to incomplete systems breaks the guarantee of conformity to familiar principles of the mathematical calculus of chance, he prefers to restrict the inferential-soundness analysis in a way that will maintain a guarantee of that conformity. But this philosophical position, which I shall call 'mathematicism', has three substantial demerits.

First, it has an inelegant lopsidedness. Why should there not be gradations of inferential soundness for incomplete systems as well as for complete ones, and if so, what better term can there be for these gradations than 'probabilities'? Certainly none of the other three binary dimensions of categorization for provability did anything to restrict the scope of the semantical connection between probability and inferential soundness. So what is there about the completeness–incompleteness distinction that justifies its doing this? One can hardly say that incomplete deductive systems are very rare or always unimportant.

Secondly, if probabilistic analogues for incomplete systems are rejected just because their structures do not conform to the mathematical calculus of chance, the life-blood of probability is being identified with a purely formal structure rather than with a semantical feature. Yet, as we have already seen, a mathematicist account of probability cannot provide an explanatory theory of the required sort—a theory that will *explain* the diversity of identically named criteria which are actually in use. Just as a syntactic homogeneity that was semantically unelucidated did not suffice to explain the semantic fact that different criteria are all equally named criteria of probability, so too a merely syntactic heterogeneity does not suffice to invalidate a semantical argument for identity of nomenclature. Indeed, the old example of non-Euclidean geometry, and the more recent one of non-Zermelian set-theory, should warn anyone against being too quick to deny the possibility of what we might term—from partial analogy with those examples—a non-Pascalian calculus of probability. The point here, however, is not that one member of some set of axioms for the Pascalian calculus has been shown mathematically to be independent of the others. Nothing of philosophical interest emerges here until is is shown that for semantic reasons some non-Pascalian calculus is equally entitled to be described as a calculus of probability.[7]

Thirdly, in everyday life we very often have to form beliefs about individual matters of fact in a context of incomplete information. We need something better then than a concept of probability which is conclusively applicable to our inferences only on the assumption that we already have all the relevant premisses. What may well serve our purposes instead is a concept that not only tells us which conclusion is favoured by the evidence we do have, but also grades how extensive a coverage of the relevant issues is achieved by this evidence.

But is such a concept more than just a philosophical possibility? Does it play any role in actual human reasonings? If so, what are its criteria of evaluation and its syntactic principles? And is an account of these criteria and principles to be constructed *ad hoc*, as an analysis of human reasoning about probabilities in certain specialized contexts, or does it connect with some much more general and pervasive structure of reasoning? These are the questions with which later parts of the present book will be concerned. When they have been answered satisfactorily we shall have substantial confirmation for the degree-of-provability theory of probability. It will have led us to new knowledge.

§12. *Mathematical and inductive probability*

It is widely assumed that there are in any case two ways to state probabilities—an expert, exact, numerical way and a popular, loose, qualitative way. We can state either that the

---

[7] But I do not wish to suggest that the non-Pascalian calculus developed in §66 below is the only one of any philosophical interest. Another obvious candidate for consideration is the proposal to take the propositions of a non-classical (non-Boolean) logic as arguments of the probability-function. Cf. also p. 47, n. 14, below.

probability of one inch of rain on a June day in Oxford is ·14, say, or that heavy rain is rather improbable in Oxford in June. The numerical style of statement is supposed at home in the natural and social sciences, the qualitative in everyday life. But the two styles of statement are assumed to differ solely in precision and expertise. The relation of the one to the other is allegedly like that between a statement that there were, say, fifty-three people at last night's party and the statement that there were a lot of people there. Both concepts of probability are assumed to conform in structure to the principles of the mathematical calculus of chance—the multiplication principle for conjunction, the complementational principle for negation, and so on. It is just that in the one case conformity is sharp, rigorous and computable, while in the other it is rough, indeterminate and a matter for judgement. For example, when given any two real numbers in the closed interval $\{0,1\}$, we can compute their product. So we can always compute $p_M[B \,\&\, C, A]$ if we know $p_M[B, A]$ and $p_M[C, A \,\&\, B]$, where $p_M[\ \ ]$ signifies a specifically mathematical (Pascalian) probability. But we cannot be expected to be able to compute whether 'moderate' is the product of 'fairly high' and 'high', As one mathematician has put it[8]

Probable inference of every kind, the casual and commonplace no less than the formalised and technical, is governed by the same rules and . . . these rules are all derived from two principles, both of them agreeable to common sense and simple enough to be accepted axioms.

But the numerical-qualitative dichotomy is not at all the point for which I shall be contending. My point will be that alongside the various concepts of mathematical probability— i.e. the concepts which conform to the familiar principles of the mathematical calculus—there is at least one other kind of concept which has a rather different structure. This other kind of concept, which I shall call 'inductive probability', is not just a loose and popular form of mathematical probability. It differs from mathematical probability as a square differs from a circle rather than as a chalk-on-blackboard circle differs from a geometrically perfect circle. For example, it has quite

[8] R. T. Cox, *The Algebra of Probable Inference* (1961), p. 29.

different principles for negation and conjunction. Moreover, it involves a comparative or ordinal gradation of probability rather than a quantitative and measurable one. So it lends itself particularly well to use in areas of reasoning where it is not possible to count or measure the evidence. No doubt in everyday life we do also have loose and qualitative ways of stating mathematical probabilities. But these are not to be confused with loose and qualitative statements about inductive probability, which are hardly less common. In fact, whereas both loose and exact modes of statement are now familiar in relation to mathematical probability, my claim is that only the looser form of statement has hitherto been common in relation to inductive probability. Just as the numerical, exact way of stating mathematical probabilities has gradually emerged in the last three centuries as the result of much painstaking effort by philosophers and mathematicians, so too the numerical, exact way of stating inductive probabilities, which I shall propose in Part III of the book, is the outcome of an attempt to reconstruct in more precise form the loose and inexact way of stating them which is widely prevalent.

The mathematicist theory has also sometimes been attacked on the ground that it compounds together the kind of probability that may be assessed by a scientific hypothesis and the grade of inductive support that belongs to such a hypothesis itself. On the one hand, we are told, there is the probability of a one inch rainfall on any June day in Oxford, say, while on the other there is the probability that a hypothesis stating this probability is true.

But that is not my point either. Inductive probability is not just a special form of inductive support. On the contrary it is crucial to distinguish inductive support—the support characteristically desired for hypotheses in experimental science—from inductive probability. Roughly, the inductive probability of a first-order, singular proposition S on the evidence of another, R, will turn out to vary directly with the inductive support that exists for the first-order generalization of which the conditional making S consequent upon R is a substitution-instance. For example, $p_I[Sa,Ra]$ will vary with $s[(x)(Rx \rightarrow Sx)]$, where $p_I[\ ]$ signifies a specifically inductive probability and $s[\ ]$ signifies grade of inductive support. Thus whereas inductive support belongs most intimately and directly to universally quantified conditionals, in relation to the results of testing them, inductive probability belongs rather to the consequents of substitution-instances of such conditionals relatively to their antecedents. As a result the logical syntax of statements about inductive probability will turn out to differ in several important respects from that of statements about inductive support.

So perhaps Hume came close to the nub of what I am arguing, when he claimed[9] that 'probability or reasoning from conjecture may be divided into two kinds, *viz.* that which is founded on *chance*, and that which arises from *causes*.' But this strand in Hume's epistemology has had little influence on subsequent philosophers, presumably because it was not fortified by satisfactory accounts of the two main kinds of reasoning about probability. On the one hand Hume seems to have thought that all reasoning about mathematical probabilities was based on the principle of indifference; whereas that principle has at best a rather confused relevance to just one of the several different concepts of mathematical probability (cf. §5 above). On the other hand Hume's account of reasoning about causal probability was vitiated by his obsession with enumerative induction, as I have argued in another book.[10]

In that book I set out a detailed case for a certain account of the logical syntax of propositions about inductive support. My account was designed to fit, not enumerative induction, but a systematically developed version of that form of inductive reasoning (championed by Bacon, Herschell, and Mill) which proceeds from the results of testing hypotheses, with appropriate controls, under relevantly varied experimental conditions. I shall not repeat here any of the text of the previous book. But

---

[9] D. Hume, *A Treatise of Human Nature*, Bk. I, Pt. III, §XI: Selby-Bigge edn. (1888), pp. 124 f.

[10] *The Implications of Induction* (1970), pp. 125 ff. I shall refer to this book hereafter as *TIOI*. In *TIOI*, however, the word 'probability' always denotes what I here call Pascalian or mathematical probability, because when I wrote *TIOI* I had not yet realized either the importance of the concept of inductive probability or the strength of its title to be so called. Hume came closer still to the non-mathematical concept of probability that I have in mind when he added, with characteristic inconsistency, that there is a third species of probability 'arising from Analogy' and remarked that 'without some degree of resemblance . . . 'tis impossible there can be any reasoning: but as this resemblance admits of many different degrees, the reasoning becomes proportionately more or less firm and certain' (op. cit., Bk. I, Pt. III, §XII, p. 142).

I shall put forward some new and independent arguments which lead to the same conclusions as before about the logical syntax of Baconian support. In addition I shall reformulate the two arguments that this kind of inductive support is not expressable in terms of mathematical probability, in order to show that the essential thrust of those arguments is not affected by any of the criticisms that have been advanced against either of them. When the autonomy of inductive (Baconian) *support* has been thus vindicated, the theory of inductive (Baconian) *probability* can be developed therefrom.

§13. *The example of judicial proof*

Even if it were possible to describe, self-consistently, a concept of inductive probability, that concept might nevertheless be unused or unusable in practice. So it is necessary to show at least one important job that a concept of inductive probability can do and any concept of mathematical probability cannot. But there is a very serious difficulty to be got round here. The difficulty is that where many people feel most inclined to doubt the applicability of the mathematical calculus, viz. in regard to the probabilities about individual facts on which they found very many of their everyday decisions, the framework of discussion seems too loose and indeterminate to provide any secure footing for argument. The multiplicational principle for conjunction, and the complementational principle for negation, for example, are deeply entrenched features of the mathematical calculus. But when a farmer reckons the probability that he will both have a good crop of apples this year and also have someone to help him pick them, who can say whether his reckoning about this conjunction of events conforms— even very roughly—to a multiplicational principle? When he balances the probability that his barley will be ready for harvesting next week against the probability that it will not, who can say whether the one probability is—even very roughly —the complement of the other?

However there is one field of discussion where an everyday concept of probability is undeniably used within a fairly determinate framework—in British, Australasian, and North American courts of law. Wherever jurymen are instructed to use the same notions of probability and certainty as they use in their more important decisions about their own affairs, we can investigate the working of an everyday concept of probability within a juridical framework that provides some relatively secure footings for argument. All the familiar features of court-room proof—testimonial corroboration, circumstantial evi-dence, presumption of innocence, balancing of probabilities, etc.—operate there as constraints on the adequacy of our analysis. Just as geometry, number theory, etc. have long supplied philosophers with paradigms of that kind of proof which rests on principles of deductive reasoning, so for proofs of individual facts at varying levels of probability we can find rigorously structured paradigms in the lawcourts.

The older writers on probability—Bernoulli, Boole, etc.—did in fact often take their examples from the courts. Since then very many uses have been developed for the mathematical concept of probability in the natural and social sciences and more recent writers on the subject have tended to be pre-occupied with these. Indeed one leading modern writer[11] has even gone so far as to claim that 'it is characteristic of legal analysis, as well as of classical physics, not to be satisfied with open-ended, probabilistic results.' But this claim is quite erroneous and, as we shall see, runs directly counter to the normal standard of proof in civil cases. In the philosophy of probability there is much of value still to be learned from the courts.

Accordingly in Part II of the book I shall begin my argument against the Pascalian, mathematicist theory by arguing against its applicability to the standards for proof of fact in British, Australasian, and North American courts of law. Mathematical probabilities are admittedly sometimes cited in the courts. But when they are so cited (for example, in relation to life expectancy) they constitute part of the evidence from which a conclusion is to be drawn. They are not the probabilities with which certain conclusions are to be drawn from the evidence. Hence, if the mathematicist theory does not fit the mode of reasoning that is proper for lay juries, and jurymen are supposed to carry the principles of their everyday reasonings into the jury-room, the mathematicist theory must be wrong for much of everyday discourse also.

[11] P. Suppes, *A Probabilistic Theory of Causality* (1970), p. 8.

In Part III I shall go on to construct a fairly thorough account of the semantics and syntax of inductive probability. And at the outset of Part IV I shall argue that this inductive form of probability fits judicial discourse perfectly. It obviates all those difficulties that the mathematicist theory encounters there. Nevertheless certain objections may be raised against the inductivist account.

Some critics are sure to declare that they find the principles of inductive probability counter-intuitive. But, even if this is true, it would not constitute an objection. Intuition has no more important a function in philosophy than it has in science. In both it may suggest hypotheses to investigate, but in neither is it an oracle of theoretical truth. An expression of the view that such-or-such a principle is intuitively evident, or counter-intuitive, as the case may be, sometimes belongs in a thinker's autobiography, but never deserves a place in the publication of his arguments for or against that principle. If several people found the concept of inductive probability counter-intuitive, this might have force against a claim that everyone without exception operates with that concept. But it would have no force at all against the more modest claim, which I advance, that the concept is actually used by some people (especially in the lawcourts) and is at least available for anyone to use.

Other critics may be inclined to suggest that, even if the concept of inductive probability can be shown to be used by judges, advocates and lay juries in British, Australasian, and North American lawcourts, it may still have no important fields of employment outside these courts. However, such a criticism would display a serious misunderstanding of the nature of judicial proof. Admittedly many proofs of fact that would be widely accepted as such outside the courts would not be accepted inside them, because of some special legal requirements about admissibility of evidence, corroboration, etc.[12] But the converse does not hold. Any proof that conforms to the appropriate legal constraints would normally be accepted as a

---

[12] Perhaps the best-known set of restrictions on admissibility concerns hearsay evidence. But there are very many others. One important instance of a requirement for corroboration is to be found in the English law for rape trials. On the general nature and origin of such constraints cf. J. B. Thayer, *A Preliminary Treatise on Evidence at the Common Law* (1898), pp. 267 ff.

proof outside the courts.[13] If this were not so, we should hardly be so willing to entrust our liberty, property or reputation to the arbitrament of juries within the framework of established legal procedures. Moreover, quite apart from proofs of individual facts, there are a number of other fields of employment for a concept of inductive probability that have nothing whatever to do with the law. I shall show in Part IV that a theory of inductive probability can shed a good deal of new light on some much-discussed problems about the nature of historical and statistical explanation, the criteria for rational acceptance or belief, the analysis of dispositional statements, and the possibility of scientific knowledge. Once these further contexts are taken into account as well, the importance of inductive probability can hardly be open to question.

In any case, even if a non-Pascalian concept of probability were used only in the courts, and not outside them, it would still be of quite considerable interest. We are not entitled to suppose that questions affecting life, liberty, property, and reputation are debated with any less appropriate degree of care and thoroughness in the courts, than are questions of scientific interest in the laboratory. So judicial discourse about probability is hardly less worthy of logical and philosophical attention than are the various forms of scientific discourse that are indisputably concerned with mathematical probabilities.

In short, the central thesis of the book will be that the notion of inductive probability exists alongside that of mathematical probability as a standing instrument of human reason. Neither is reducible to the other by any possible process of logical analysis. Nor can either permanently take the place of the other in our actual reasoning, since they perform such different kinds of task. And, if this thesis is established, substantial confirmation will have been found for the degree-of-provability theory of probability that was outlined in §§1–11

---

[13] The law does occasionally require or permit a certain proposition to be treated as if it had been proved when that proposition is not in fact proven in the normal way, e.g. in regard to the death of a man who is shown to have disappeared for at least seven years. But such a proposition is a presumption. What is proved, by the normal standards of proof that laymen can apply, is not the presumption itself but grounds for making it, despite the fact that lawyers sometimes speak of this as proving the presumption (e.g. R. Cross, *Evidence*, 3rd edn., (1967), p. 129).

above. That theory will not merely have accounted for the variety of philosophically familiar forms of probability, and have explained their common conformity to the principles of the mathematical calculus. It will also have led to the discovery of a hitherto unanalysed notion of probability, and have helped to explain its conformity to quite different syntactic principles. Specifically, the theory led us to see the possibility of a concept of probability that allows p[not-B,A] = o alongside p[B,A] = o and normally has p[not-B,A] = o when p[B,A] >o; and we shall find not only that such a concept is generated by the Baconian style of inductive reasoning but also that it is actually employed in lawcourts and elsewhere.[14]

[14] Inductive probability will turn out to meet neither of the two main conditions for Pascalian probability: it is neither additive nor complementational. A concept of probability that is complementational but not additive is familiar from recent work on comparative probability: cf. T. L. Fine, *Theories of Probability: An Examination of Foundations* (1973), pp. 15 ff. It would be interesting to know whether there are any important uses for a concept of probability that is additive but not complementational.

PART II

SIX DIFFICULTIES FOR A PASCALIAN ACCOUNT OF JUDICIAL PROBABILITY

4

What are the Standards of Proof in Courts of Law?

Summary

§14. There are two main standards for proof of fact in English and American courts. The plaintiff in a civil case must prove on the balance of probablities, and the prosecutor in a criminal case must prove his conclusion at a level of probability that puts it beyond reasonable doubt. §15. Does the concept of probability involved here conform to the principles of the mathematical calculus of chance? Some philosophers have claimed that it does, some that if such a probability were measurable it would do so, and some that it is not even in principle a mathematical probability. §16. The third of these views is the most defensible, but it has never been properly argued or substantiated hitherto. So the following six chapters will be devoted to bringing out some of the anomalies or paradoxes that result from any attempt to interpret Anglo-American standards of juridical proof in terms of mathematical probability.

§14. *The difference between the criminal and civil standards*

The ordinary British or American citizen who serves on a jury is customarily assumed, or urged, to use the same standards of probability and certainty in the deliberations of the jury-room as he uses in his everyday life. Thus in 1849 Baron Pollock charged his jury with the words[1]

> If the conclusion to which you are conducted be that there is that degree of certainty in the case which you would act upon in your own grave and important concerns, that is the degree of certainty which the law requires and which will justify you in returning a verdict of guilty.

Philosophers of law have therefore tended to seek an elucidation of juridical standards of proof in terms of some overall theory of probability. Like jurymen they have modelled their conception of probability within a lawcourt upon their conception of probability outside it.

But for philosophy in general the opposite direction of modelling is more illuminating. It is so difficult to find arguments for saying just how probability is conceived in everyday life that it is worth while trying to see what light can be shed on this conception by an investigation of judicial probability. That is, it is worth while studying what kind of structure a concept of probability must have if it is to serve the relatively specialized and determinate purposes of advocates, jurymen, and judges. For there is good reason to believe that just such a concept must also be in use outside the courts for a vast variety of everyday purposes. Otherwise the whole system of lay justice would be founded on an illusion.

Now in English and American law there are at least two standards of proof. In a civil suit the plaintiff is often or normally required to prove the facts of his case on 'the preponderance of evidence', or 'the balance of probability', if he is to win. In a criminal case the prosecution establishes the guilt of the accused only if it proves its case up to a level of probability which is near enough to certainty for the conclusion to be put 'beyond reasonable doubt'. Though the exact terminology that should be used in describing these two standards of proof is sometimes disputed, and a third standard is sometimes invoked

---

[1] In *R.* v. *Manning*, 1849, 30 C.C.C. Sess. Pap. 654, quoted by R. Cross, *Evidence*, 3rd edn., (1967), p. 89 n. 1. Cf. J. B. Thayer, op. cit., p. 275: 'As regards the main methods in hand, they are still those untechnical ways of all sound reasoning of the logical process in its normal and ordinary manifestations; and the rules that govern it here are the general rules that govern it everywhere, the ordinary rules of human experience, to be sought in the ordinary sources, and not in law books.'

in American courts, the hard core of the doctrine is not in dispute at all.[2] It is certainly the law now that in order to determine issues of fact some high and absolute level of probability is required from the prosecution in criminal cases, while the level of evidence required to be successful in a civil suit is often or normally relative to the level of evidence offered by the unsuccessful party.

§15. *Theories about judicial probability*

But what is the nature of this juridical concept of probability, so often and so confidently employed? In particular, is it a mathematical probability? i.e. does it conform to the mathematical calculus of probabilities that Pascal originated? If it does, it has a quite determinate and well-studied structure.[3] For example, the mathematical probability of anything—whether or not we can actually measure it—is normally conceived as a real number greater than or equal to 0 and less than or equal to 1. Again, the mathematical probability of an event obeys a complementational negation principle whereby the probability of the event's occurrence and the probability of its non-occurrence always sum to 1. Also, mathematical probability obeys a multiplicative conjunction principle, whereby the probability that two independent events both occur is equal to the mathe-

[2] Cf. R. Cross, *Evidence*, 3rd edn., (1967), pp. 87 ff., and E. W. Cleary (ed.), *McCormick's Handbook of the Law of Evidence*, 2nd edn., (1972), pp. 793 ff. It is not easy to determine exactly when, and how, Anglo-American law came to accept the double standard. But that is not an issue with which I am concerned here. Some kind of differentiation of standard has certainly been long in existence: cf. E. W. Cleary, op. cit., p. 799.

The expression 'proof on the preponderance of evidence' is often used for the main standard of proof in civil cases. But it is clear that the preponderance thus referred to must be preponderance of probative force, rather than preponderance of mere volume. E. W. Cleary, op. cit., pp. 793 ff. gives reasons for agreeing with J. P. McBaine, 'Burden of Proof: Degrees of Belief', 32 *Californian Law Review* 246f. (1944), that the three commonly occurring formulations 'proof on the preponderance of evidence', 'proof by clear, cogent and convincing evidence', and 'proof beyond reasonable doubt', should be interpreted as requiring proof that a proposition is probably true (i.e. more probably true than false), that it is highly probably true, and that it is almost certainly true, respectively.

If the argument of the present book is valid, then the non-existence hitherto of a sufficiently developed theory of inductive (Baconian) probability will suffice to explain why judges and lawyers have sometimes found it difficult to interpret these standards in terms that substantially improved upon the ordinary understanding of their meanings.

[3] Cf. nn. 1, 2, and 3 of Ch. 1, pp. 7f., above.

matical product of their individual probabilities. Or, more generally (so as to cover the case of non-independent outcomes), the
principle is that

$$p_M[B \ \& \ C, A] = p_M[B, A] \times p_M[C, A \ \& \ B],$$

where '$p_M[\ldots, ——]$' means 'the mathematical probability of
the conclusion that ... on the premiss that ——' or 'the mathematical probability of a thing's being ... when it is ——'. So
something quite definite and quite important is at issue if we
ask whether or not the concept of probability that is invoked in
stating standards of proof is a mathematical probability.

Three different ways of answering this question are to be
found in the literature.

Some writers have held without qualification that the probabilities involved are, or ought to be taken as, mathematical
ones. The nineteenth-century Irish mathematician George
Boole, for example, had no hesitation in applying the mathematical theory to the probability that a person accused in a
criminal court is guilty.[4] He apparently did not see anything
at all chimerical in the asumption that such a probability was
a measurable quantity. Nor has this type of view been confined
to mathematicians or to the past. It is also be found occasionally in contemporary American law journals, where the probability is sometimes conceived objectively as the measure of a
frequency, and sometimes subjectively as the measure of a
juror's strength of belief.[5] Similar views have been expounded
in Continental Europe in relation to Continental legal systems.[6]

In somewhat greater numbers commentators have held that
such a probability is in principle mathematical but not in
practice calculable—because of the complexity of human
affairs, the paucity of relevant statistical data, or the difficulty

---

[4] George Boole, *An Investigation of the Laws of Thought* (1854), ch. xxi.

[5] e.g. V. C. Ball, 'The Moment of Truth: Probability Theory and Standards of
Proof', 14 *Vanderbilt Law Review*, 1961, 807–30; and M. O. Finkelstein and W. B.
Fairley, 'A Bayesian Approach to Identification Evidence', 83 *Harvard Law Review*
489–517, (1970). Cf. also R. J. Simon and L. Mahan, 'Quantifying Burdens of
Proof: A View from the Bench, the Jury and the Classroom', 5 *Law and Society
Review* 319–30, (1971), and G. R. Iversen, 'Operationalising the Concept of
Probability in Legal-Social Science Research', ibid., 331–3.

[6] e.g. P. S. de Laplace, *Essai philosophique sur les probabilités* (1819), ch. xiii, and
Rupert Schreiber, *Theorie des Beweiswertes für Beweismittel in Zivilprozess* (1968). On
Bernoulli's debt to Leibniz here cf. I. Hacking, *The Emergence of Probability* (1975),
pp. 85–91, and L. Couturat, *La Logique de Leibniz* (1901), pp. 240 ff.

of measuring intensity of belief. The probability at issue in a particular case is some percentage or other, they say, but no one can ever determine exactly which. Their thesis is, as it were, a subjunctive or counterfactual one. If we *could* measure such a probability, they are saying, it *would* conform to mathematicist principles, but in practice we cannot measure it. Often these writers take for granted, or leave implicit, the general thesis that such a probability is a mathematical one, and content themselves with drawing attention to particular consequences of that fact or with emphasizing the practical impossibility of making exact numerical determinations. For example, T. Starkie insisted that

in thus referring to the doctrine of numerical probabilities it is the principle alone which is intended to be applied in order that some estimates may be formed of the force of independent and concurring probabilities. The notions of those who have supposed that mere moral probabilities or relations could ever be represented by numbers or space, and thus subjected to arithmetical analysis, cannot but be regarded as visionary and chimerical.

More recently L. H. Tribe has argued eloquently for the view that, except perhaps in very special cases, the quantification of judicial probabilities is undesirable. Its appearance of precision is inevitably misleading, he thinks, and tends to undermine important human values. But he nowhere disputes the view that all the probabilities involved obey the principles of the mathematical calculus. His objection is just to the actual quantification of these probabilities, not to their conformity with the structural principles of the mathematical calculus.[7] Similarly J. Michael and M. J. Adler hold that in a trial of fact the probability of a proposition is not determinable exactly, though they assume that it obeys the mathematical theory's complementational principle for negation and they state that it is high if and only if over ·5 and very high if and only if over ·75.[8] Or again, Z. Cowen and P. B. Carter tell us that though such probabilities are not measurable the criminal

[7] T. Starkie, *A Practical Treatise of tne Law of Evidence* (1842), vol. i, pp. 568 ff.; and L. H. Tribe, 'Trial by Mathematics; Precision and Ritual in the Legal Process', 84 *Harvard Law Review* 1329–93, (1971).

[8] J. Michael and M. J. Adler, 'The Trial of an Issue of Fact', 34 *Columbia Law Review* 1285 ff. (1934).

standard is 'considerably higher than the merest fraction over 50%', and that on any given issue the criminal standard is always higher, 'and always the same percentage higher,' than the civil standard on the same issue.[9]

Others have held instead that the probabilities involved are not even in principle mathematical ones. But it is not easy to make out what alternative structure these writers assign to such a probability or how they justify what they do say about it. With characteristic forthrightness Bentham declared that the doctrine of chances (i.e. the mathematical calculus of probability) is inapplicable to the measurement of probative force[10] and proposed his own scale of measurement. For example, where the probative force of evidence was increased by the number of witnesses, the increase would always, according to Bentham's scheme, be determinable with mathematical exactness by summing the number of concordant witnesses and subtracting the number of discordant ones.[11] But Bentham gave no reason for preferring addition here to, say, multiplication, and subtraction to division, or for supposing that the evidence of each concordant witness was, *ceteris paribus*, to be treated alike rather than subjected to some such law as that of diminishing marginal utility.[12] Also, Bentham held that the odds a witness will accept for a wager on the truth of a proposition are a measure of the probability he assigns to the proposition.[13] But since it can be shown that fair betting odds within a suitably coherent system of wagers constitute a measure that conforms to the axioms of mathematical probability,[14] there is at least a prima-facie inconsistency in

---

[9] Z. Cowen and P. B. Carter, *Essays on the Law of Evidence* (1956), p. 254. Cf. also the Hon. Mr. Justice Eggleston, 'Probabilities and Proof', 4 *Melbourne University Law Review* 180–211, (1963–4).

[10] J. Bentham, *Works*, ed. J. Bowring (1843), vol. vi, p. 224; and *A Treatise on Judicial Evidence* (1825), p. 41.

[11] Cf. *Works*, vol. vi. p. 233; and *A Treatise on Judicial Evidence*, p. 41. J. S. Mill was more commonsensical about this: cf. his *A System of Logic*, Bk. III, ch. xviii, §3 (1896 edn.), pp. 353 f.

[12] Other difficulties in Bentham's proposal are mentioned by Dumont in his edition of Bentham's writings on the subject: *A Treatise on Judicial Evidence* (1825), pp. 45 f.

[13] *Works* (1843), vol. vi, 233

[14] Cf. R. Carnap, *Logical Foundations of Probability* (1951), pp. 165 ff. The original discovery of this fact seems to have been made independently by F. P. Ramsey, B. de Finetti, and L. Savage.

Bentham's position. Again, in Wills's *Principles of Circumstantial Evidence* we find it stated[15] that

> the terms CERTAINTY and PROBABILITY are essentially different in meaning as applied to moral evidence from what they import in a mathematical sense; inasmuch as the elements of moral certainty and moral probability . . . appear to be incapable of numerical expression.

Yet the same authority informs us that,[16] where several independent circumstances concur and point to the same conclusion, the probability force of the evidence 'increases according to a geometrical rather than an arithmetical progression', although 'neither the combined effect of the evidence, nor any of its constituent elements, admits of numerical computation'. It is not clear how two probabilities that are incapable of numerical expression or computation may nevertheless be multiplied together: how is multiplication distinguished from addition in this curious non-quantitative domain? But at least the learned writer was consistent in thinking that his probabilities cannot be mathematical ones. For he tells us that the product of multiplying them together is a probability that is greater than either multiplicand on its own; and mathematical probabilities do not behave in that way. The only real number multiplicands that have such a product are positive numbers greater than 1 or negative numbers of any size, whereas all mathematical probabilities are less than or equal to 1 and greater than or equal to 0. Other writers too[17] have approved the thesis that

> where a number of *independent* circumstances point to the same conclusion the probability of the justness of that conclusion is not merely the *sum* of the simple probabilities of these circumstances but the multiplied or compound ratio of them.

But unfortunately none of the authorities who approve this

[15] 7th edn. (1936), p. 9.
[16] Ibid., p. 434f.
[17] J. R. Gulson, *The Philosophy of Proof (in its relation to the English law of judicial evidence)* (1905), p. 139 (quoting W. M. Best). Cf. also T. Starkie, *A Practical Treatise of the Law of Evidence,* 3rd edn. (1842), vol. i, p. 568 ff., who combines this thesis with the view that mathematical probabilities *are* involved.

thesis tell us how they would justify it,[18] nor do they provide us with any systematic account of the concept of probability that they take to be involved.

§16. *The nature of the argument against a mathematicist theory*

The third of these three views is in principle by far the strongest, though in practice it has been by far the least well stated. Its intuitive or dogmatic assertions about the incorrectness of mathematicism need to be replaced by a sufficiently cogent set of genuine arguments. And its vague and incoherent references to a non-mathematical concept of probability need to be replaced by a detailed account of the structure of such a concept, an explanation of its title to be called a concept of probability, and a demonstration of its ability to perform smoothly and easily those tasks that the concept of mathematical probability can only perform with great difficulty or paradox.

The remainder of Part II will therefore be devoted to pointing out some serious difficulties in the mathematicist approach to judicial probability, whether this approach be exact and quantitative in form or loose and qualitative. It will be left to Parts III and IV to show just what kind of non-Pascalian account is appropriate. Undoubtedly mathematical probabilities do sometimes have a role to play in judicial trials of fact. But where they do so, I shall argue, they constitute part of the grounds for the trier of fact's conclusion, not graduations of the extent to which these grounds support his conclusion.

Nor does it make any difference if we regard lawcourt reasonings about matters of fact as would-be justification for a certain act that the jury, or other trier of fact, is to perform rather than as would-be proof of one or more propositions that the trier of fact is to believe. The merit of the reasoning has to be assessed in both cases, and what are at stake are the principles controlling such assessments.

For the most part there will be no need to cite actual cases or other sources of law. The relevant legal doctrine is scarcely obscure or in dispute. Purely legal controversies about burden of proof, admissibility of evidence, causal responsibility, etc., need not concern us. Instead, what are relevant, and have

---

[18] One prima facie plausible way of trying to justify it is criticized below in §37 (pp. 114 ff.).

mostly passed unnoticed, are various paradoxical consequences of construing the standards of juridical proof in terms of mathematical probability. Imaginary cases will illustrate these consequences as well as, or better than, real ones, because the points at issue can be made to stand out more clearly. Merely to describe such paradoxical consequences is to provide reasons for rejecting the mathematicist account, because the overriding aim of juridical proof in the Anglo-American system is to keep broadly in touch with lay conceptions of justice and sound reasoning. Admittedly, these arguments against the mathematicist account will not be conclusive ones, since those who are prepared to accept all its paradoxical consequences are entitled to continue holding the assumptions that generate them. This is often what happens in philosophy. But at least it will have been shown how unnecessarily extravagant a price has to be paid for maintaining the mathematicist account. The choice will be between insisting that there is only one normal type of logical syntax for probability, which is given by the mathematical calculus, and admitting that there are at least two, only one of which is given by the mathematical calculus. The former approach economizes in types of probability, but achieves this economy at the expense of a considerable variety of paradoxes. The latter approach can avoid all such paradoxes, but is committed to the existence of more than one normal type of syntax for probability.

5

The Difficulty about Conjunction

Summary

§17. In most civil cases the plaintiff's contention consists of several component elements. So the multiplication law for the mathematical probability of a conjunction entails that, if the contention as a whole is to be established on the balance of mathematical probability, there must either be very few separate components in the case or most of them must be established at a very high level of probability. Since this constraint on the complexity of civil cases is unknown to the law, the mathematicist analysis is in grave difficulties here. §18. To point out that such component elements in a complex case are rarely independent of one another is no help. §19. A mathematicist might therefore claim that the balance of probability is not to be understood as the balance between the probability of the plaintiff's contention and that of its negation, but as the balance between the probability of the plaintiff's contention and that of some contrary contention by the defendant. However, this would misplace the burden of proof. §20. To regard the balance of probability as the difference between prior and posterior probabilities is open to other objections. §21. To claim that the plaintiff's contention as a whole is not to have its probability evaluated at all is like closing one's eyes to facts one does not like.

§17. *The constraint on complexity in civil cases*

The rule for civil suits requires a plaintiff to prove each element of his case on the balance of probability. If this probability be construed as a *mathematical* probability, the conjunction principle for such probabilities would impose some curious constraints on the structure of the proof.

The most natural way to construe the requirement of a balance of mathematical probability is as a requirement that the probability of the plaintiff's case, on the facts before the court, be greater than the probability of the defendant's. Then, in accordance with the complementational negation principle for mathematical probability, the probability of each of the plaintiff's factual contentions would have to be greater than ·5 in order to exceed the defendant's relevant probability. But what shall we say then about the probability of the plaintiff's case as a whole—about the probability of the conjunction of his various contentions? It too, presumably, should not fall below ·5, or there would be a balance or probability in favour of at least one of the plaintiff's contentions being false. Justice would hardly be done if a plaintiff were to win on a case that, when considered as a whole, was more probably false than true. Hence on the mathematicist interpretation the court would need to keep a close eye on the separate probabilities of those various contentions, in case they were not high enough to produce a greater than ·5 probability for the conjunction, when this is calculated in accordance with the standard multiplicational principle.

For example, if the case has two independent elements, at least one of the two component contentions must have a substantially higher probability than ·501. Perhaps a car driver is suing his insurance company because it refuses to compensate him after an accident. Suppose the two component issues that are disputed are first, what were the circumstances of the crash, and secondly, what were the terms of the driver's insurance contract. Then, if each of these two issues is determined with a probability of ·71, their joint outcome can be determined with a sufficiently high probability, since ·71^2 is greater than ·501. But if one of the component issues is determined with only a ·501 probability, then the other component issue must be determined with a probability of very nearly 1. Otherwise the product of the two probabilities would not be high enough to satisfy the requirements of justice. Or, in other words, if one of the component issues is determined on the balance of probability (whether this balance be understood to lie at ·501, ·51, ·6 or even a higher figure), the other must, in effect, be determined beyond reasonable doubt. But though this constraint seems a necessary consequence of construing the standard in civil cases to require proof on a balance of mathematical probability, it seems to be a rule that is unknown to judges and unrespected by triers of fact.

Another unfortunate consequence of applying the conjunction

principle for mathematical probabilities in such a way is a severe constraint on the number of independent component issues in a single case. For example, if a series of independent points are all conjoined in a single allegation, and to establish each point a separate witness (or group of witnesses) is needed, then the higher the number of witnesses (or groups of witnesses) that is needed, the more reliable each witness (or group of witnesses) has to be. So if no witness (or group of witnesses) were ever to have a more than ·9 probability of speaking the truth, no case could ever deserve to win which conjoined more than six component points that were mutually independent and each required a separate witness (or group of witnesses)— since ·9^7 is less than ·5. An even lower limit could be imposed on the practicable number of such component issues if the balance of probability was thought to involve a mathematical probability substantially higher than ·501. For example, not more than three such issues would be practicable if the plaintiff had to achieve a level of ·7 in order to win. And a ·7 probability seems scarcely too high a level for the determination of civil issues affecting a man's fortune or reputation, or the conduct of great commerical enterprises. But, if the conception of juridical probabilities as mathematical ones were to force the court to refuse justice in cases involving highly complex issues of fact, that conception would be seriously inexpedient.

No doubt the defendant will often accept several of the plaintiff's component points. If he concentrates his effort on refuting just one or two of the elements in the plaintiff's case, he may well calculate that in practice he will have a better chance of persuading the jury to give judgement against the plaintiff than if he refuses to admit anything and tries laboriously to demolish each of the plaintiff's points in turn. Hence in many complex cases the difficulty about compounding mathematical probabilities would not in fact emerge. The points accepted by the defendant there could each be assigned a mathematical probability of 1, and all that is necessary is that the disputed point or points should compound to a figure higher than ·501, or ·7, or wherever the threshold of balance is conceived to lie. This policy will also minimize the costs that the defendant might have to pay if he loses. Nevertheless it is in principle always open to the defendant to contest each of the component points in the plaintiff's case, and sometimes it may in practice be in his interest to do so, especially when the trier of fact is a judge sitting without a jury. An insurance company, for example, may wish to fight the plaintiff's interpretation of his contract of insurance, for fear of similar liabilities in other cases. But it may also wish to fight the plaintiff's version of the circumstances of his accident, since the chance of success may be greater; and perhaps, for a plausibly different account of the accident to be shown possible, it may be necessary to disprove several of the plaintiff's allegations. So the difficulties latent in the mathematicist analysis would then become operative.

§18. *The independence issue*

Four possible ways of trying to circumvent these difficulties will be considered in §§18–21.

One way is to argue that the mathematical probabilities of component points in a civil case are rarely independent. For example, what was actually done by the parties to a contract may well be relevant to determining the terms of the contract. Hence the principle that normally operates here is not the one that is valid only for independent probabilities, viz.

$$p_M[B \,\&\, C, A] = p_M[B, A] \times p_M[C, A].$$

Instead it is the more general principle that is valid also for dependent probabilities, viz.

$$p_M[B \,\&\, C, A] = p_M[B, A] \times p_M[C, A \,\&\, B].$$

Consequently, it may be argued, the mathematical probability of the conjoint outcome need not be much lower than that of each component outcome, since we may suppose $p_M[S, Q \,\&\, R]$ to be substantially greater than $p_M[S, Q]$ where R and S are two component points in the plaintiff's case, and Q the total evidence.

But the trouble with this argument is that quite often the margin of inequality between $p_M[S, Q]$ and $p_M[S, Q \,\&\, R]$ in such a case is very slight, or $p_M[S, Q \,\&\, R]$ is even less, not greater, than $p_M[S, Q]$. For example, suppose the component issues of a suit for non-performance of contract are the terms of the contract and the actual performance of the defendant. If the actual performance of the defendant constitutes a premiss that is relevant to inferring the terms of the contract then the plaintiff's allegation of a discrepancy between terms and performance will be harder to prove than if the defendant's actual performance were irrelevant to inferring the terms. More specifically, suppose that the plaintiff in his proof of the terms of contract has to prove both the place where the defendant was to build the plaintiff a house and also the date by which the building was to be completed, and that he also has to prove that no house had been completed at that place by that date. Suppose none of the three probabilities is to be regarded as independent of the others, and the plaintiff proves the component issues of his case so effectively that the probabilities to be multiplied together are ·8, ·8, and ·75. The mathematicist account seems to lead inevitably to the paradoxical conclusion that he should lose his case, since ·8 × ·8 × ·75 is less than ·5.

§19. *Does the balance of probability lie between the plaintiff's and the defendant's contentions?*

A second way of trying to rescue the mathematicist theory here is to argue that the above-mentioned difficulties arise because the phrase 'the balance of probability' is wrongly construed as denoting the balance between the probability of a certain proposition (or event) and the probability of its negation (or non-occurrence). This construction ensures (since the mathematical probability of not-S is always $1 - s$ when the mathematical probability of S is s) that nothing can be established on the balance of probability if its own probability is less than or equal to ·5. And that in turn severely restricts the extent to which the probabilities of component conclusions can be compounded by multiplication. Therefore, it might be argued, we should not construe the phrase 'the balance of probability' as denoting the balance between the probability of S and the probability of not-S, on Q, where one party to the case asserts S and his opponent asserts not-S, and Q states the facts before the court, but rather as denoting the balance between the probability of S and the probability of, say R, where one party asserts S, the other asserts R, and S and R, though mutually inconsistent, do not exhaust the domain of possibilities. For example, the plaintiff might claim that the defendant was the driver of a car that collided with his own car at 2 a.m. on 20 October 1971, and the defendant might claim that he

was at home in bed at that time on that day (when he might
have claimed instead that he was at a party, or that he was
working late, or that he was abroad, and so on). It would
follow that S might be established 'on the balance of probability' if S was shown to have a probability of, say, ·2 on Q,
and R a probability of ·1. A plaintiff could then establish each
of any number of independent component points on the
balance of probability, in this sense, and the conjunction
principle for mathematical probability would still allow him
to have established the conjunction of his component claims
on the balance of probability, in the same sense. For, where
each s_i and r_i are real numbers, if $s_1 > r_1$, $s_2 > r_2$, . . . , $s_n > r_n$,
then $(s_1 \times s_2 \times \ . \ . \ . \ \times s_n) > (r_1 \times r_2 \times \ . \ . \ . \ \times r_n)$.

This way out of the difficulties might fit some kinds of case,
such as those that involve more than two parties or where the
court is asked for some kind of declaration. But it scarcely fits
the standard type of two-party civil case, where the defendant
wins if he disproves the plaintiff's allegation. To suppose it
fits these cases would be to suppose that the defendant is always
required there not merely to counter the plaintiff's allegation,
however he may do this, but also to establish some positive
claim of his own. Such a supposition introduces a general
category of *onus probandi* that does not at present exist, and
belongs to a system of law based on inquisitorial objectives
rather than to one based on the adversary procedure. Even in
the previous paragraph's example the actual issue before the
court would be whether or not the defendant was the driver of
the car involved in the collision, not whether the defendant was
the driver of the car or in bed at the time. Also, if there is
direct evidence of a fact alleged by the plaintiff, the case may
stand or fall with the reliability of the plaintiff's witness. The
issue is then a straightforwardly dichotomous one, between
reliability and non-reliability. Or an allegation by the plaintiff
may itself be negative in form, e.g. that the defendant never
paid him his wages, and then the issue between plaintiff and
defendant must again be assigned a straightforward dichotomy
of outcomes: were the wages paid or were they not? Similarly,
in a suit for libel, one issue may be the truth or falsity of the
proposition alleged to be libellous. But all the plaintiff has to
do in that connection is to establish the falsehood of this

proposition. If he sets out to establish the truth of some other proposition inconsistent with the alleged libel, it is as a means of establishing the falsehood of the libel, not as an end in itself.

§20. *Does the balance of probability consist in the difference between prior and posterior probabilities?*

Thirdly, yet another interpretation for the phrase 'proof on the balance of probability' might be suggested. Perhaps this means not that the probability of the desired conclusion should be greater than that of its negation, nor yet that the probability of the winning party's contention should be greater than that of some contrary contention, but that the facts should be favourably relevant to the desired conclusion. That is, the probability of the desired conclusion on the facts before the court should be greater than the prior probability of that conclusion (rather than equal to, or less than, this). In short, perhaps the requirement is that $p_M[S,Q] > p_M[S]$. The apparent advantage of this interpretation is that we avoid the previous difficulty about burden of proof, and yet, however many independent component points $S_1, S_2, \ldots, S_n$ we have, the probability of the conjunction $S_1 \& S_2 \& \ldots \& S_n$ on the facts before the court is always greater than the prior probability of this conjunction if the probability-on-the-facts of each of the component points is greater than its prior probability.

Such an interpretation may in practice even work as well for non-independent outcomes as for independent ones. Nevertheless the interpretation is scarcely tenable. The trouble is that in certain circumstances it allows a plaintiff to prove his over-all case on the balance of probability even if he fails to establish one or more of his component points on its own. For example, suppose the plaintiff has to establish four independent points S_1, S_2, S_3, and S_4. Suppose the prior probabilities of each of these is ·5, and each of S_1, S_2, and S_3 has a ·9 probability on the facts, while S_4 has a ·4 probability on the facts. In these circumstances $p_M[S_1 \& S_2 \& S_3 \& S_4, Q] > p_M[S_1 \& S_2 \& S_3 \& S_4]$, even though $p_M[S_4,Q] < p_M[S_4]$. But the courts would not normally allow a plaintiff to win unless he had established each of his component points on the balance of probability. The latter is a necessary condition for victory as well as a sufficient one. When the necessity of this condition is borne in mind, the proposed interpretation can easily make the plaintiff's case appear juster than the courts will allow,[1] rather as, when we bear in mind the sufficiency of the condition, the standard mathematicist interpretation—in the way that we have already seen—makes victory often seem less just than they allow.

Perhaps this particular difficulty in the proposed interpretation could be obviated by supposing some appropriate legal requirement. 'It's a matter of law, not common sense', we may be told, 'that each component point should be established on the balance of probability, quite apart from any need there may be to establish the over-all case.' But such a rule of law requires a rationale, and it is difficult to see where this is to come from if not from an impossibility of ever proving the over-all case on the balance of probability without so proving each component element.

Moreover there is a further difficulty that cannot be obviated in such a way. The proposed interpretation assumes that some positive prior probability is uncontroversially assignable to any contention that comes before the court. But why should this be so? If the level of a probability affects the issue of litigation, justice requires that both parties should have the opportunity to lead evidence relevant to its determination. The very idea of a distinction between prior probabilities that cannot be argued in court, and posterior ones that can, seems to reek of procedural injustice.[2]

§21. *Does the plaintiff's contention need evaluation as a whole?*

There is also a fourth way of trying to avoid the difficulties generated by the multiplicative nature of the conjunction principle for mathematical probability. If the rule about balance of probability cannot be reinterpreted so as to escape the

---

[1] The same difficulty arises for the previous interpretation of 'proof on the balance of probabilities'. If a series of positive contentions by the defendant are to counter the series of contentions by the plaintiff, the plaintiff's over-all case might have a higher probability than the defendant's even if at least one of the plaintiff's component contentions had a lower probability than the defendant's corresponding counter-contention. This kind of difficulty is also rather crippling for any proposal to take favourable relevance as a criterion of confirmation in natural science, as in M. Hesse, *The Structure of Scientific Inference* (1974), p. 134. Some evidence is allowed to confirm the conjunction of two theories even though it disconfirms one or both: cf. R. Carnap, *Logical Foundations of Probability* (1950), pp. 391 ff.

[2] Cf. also §36 (pp. 107 ff.) below, where this issue is discussed at greater length.

difficulties that confront it, perhaps we should seek to achieve the same end by restricting the rule's range of application. It might be argued that these difficulties arise only if we suppose that in a civil suit the case *as a whole* must win on the balance of mathematical probability. The difficulties all stem, it might be said, from the attempt to compound together into a single over-all figure the various different probabilities relating to disputed component issues. So there is an obvious way to avoid the difficulties while still supposing that the probabilities established by juridical proof are mathematical ones. Where more than one issue of fact is disputed in a case, we seem to be out of trouble if we apply the rule about balance of probability only to each component issue and not to the case as a whole. The plaintiff wins, we might say, if and only if he establishes each component point on the balance of mathematical probability. Hence there is no point in compounding the separate probabilities together, and then the multiplicativeness of the conjunction principle for mathematical probability does not generate any constraints on the practicable number of component issues or on the levels of probability at which these may be resolved.

However, for a mathematicist to evade the difficulty by claiming that the outcome of a complex civil case should not be evaluated as a whole, is rather like closing one's eyes in order to pretend that what one does not see does not exist. For, if nevertheless such an outcome were to be evaluated as a whole in accordance with the principles of mathematical probability, the result that would emerge in very many cases would be the opposite of what the courts themselves would declare. Even though the probabilities of three independent components in a plaintiff's case were, say, ·8, ·8, and ·75, a mathematicist evaluation would give the case as a whole to the defendant, not to the plaintiff. What kind of justice would it be to disregard this fact, if mathematical probability was really what was at stake?[3]

The same point emerges particularly starkly in regard to

---

[3] Much the same question can be raised in reply to those philosophers of science who, like I. Levi, use an analogous argument in defence of a rule permitting acceptance, or belief in the truth, of any proposition exceeding a certain threshold of mathematical probability on the evidence: cf. §88 (pp. 316 ff.) below.

criminal cases. Presumably on the mathematicist interpretation proof beyond reasonable doubt is proof at a level of probability that is not more than some very small interval short of certainty. But even if each element of the alleged crime is proved at this level—e.g. if it is proved that the accused's finger pressed the trigger, that the victim died as a result of the shot, and that the accused intended such a result—the conjunction of the elements may still not be proved thereby at the appropriate level. What kind of justice would it be to execute a man, or send him to a long term of imprisonment, if the crime as a whole had not been proved to be his responsibility?

6

The Difficulty about Inference
upon Inference

Summary

§22. Where a proof in a civil case involves several tiers of inference, the courts normally insist that each tier prior to the final one should rest on proof beyond reasonable doubt. A mathematicist analysis, however, would permit many multi-tier inferences to go through even though each tier was proved merely on the balance of probabilities. §23. So this kind of analysis has to suppose that the courts' requirement here springs from a special legal rule. But the rationale of such a rule is obscure if the mathematical analysis is correct. On the other hand the courts' requirement here does jibe with common-sense ideas about chains of inference.

§22. *Permissiveness in regard to two- or many-stage proofs*

The multiplicativeness of the conjunction principle creates a further difficulty if we come to consider certain other kinds of proof. So far we have been considering situations where two or more component and co-ordinate points have to be proved in order to constitute, in conjunction with one another, the plaintiff's over-all allegations in a civil suit. A typical example was when A alleges both that B contracted with him to build a house in a certain place by a certain date and also that B did not perform his part of the contract. The only tolerable way of envisaging all these situations in terms of mathematical probability, we have seen, is to expect proof on the balance of probabilities for each component point and not for the over-all allegation. This escape-route has to be paid for by accepting a consequential risk of injustice. But there are other situations in which the conjunction principle for mathematical probability creates difficulties from which even this escape-route will not rescue us.

Consider now those proofs which proceed by what is known

in some lawcourts as 'inference upon inference'. Such a proof essentially contains two or more stages of probabilistic reasoning rather than a multiple one-stage structure. It contains, say, a proof of R from Q and then a proof of S from R, rather than proofs of R and S directly from Q. For example, the testimony of witnesses might establish a certain probability that A's finger infection was caused by accident, and perhaps this causation might in turn establish a certain probability that A's death was caused by accident. A question then arises about how high the probability must be at each stage of the proof—from Q to R and from R to S, respectively—if the conclusion S is to be established on the balance of probabilities.

If the probabilities involved are mathematical, the answer to this question is again determined by multiplication. By the familiar principle we have

$$p_M[R \& S,Q] = p_M[S,Q] \times p_M[R,Q \& S]$$

and therefore, where $p_M[R,Q \& S] > 0$,

$$p_M[S,Q] = \frac{p_M[R \& S,Q]}{p_M[R,Q \& S]}$$

So, where $p_M[R,Q \& S] > 0$, we must have

$$p_M[S,Q] \geqslant p_M[R \& S,Q]$$

and, since by the same familiar principle

$$p_M[R \& S,Q] = p_M[R,Q] \times p_M[S,Q \& R],$$

we must also have, where $p_M[R,Q \& S] > 0$,

$$p_M[S,Q] \geqslant p_M[R,Q] \times p_M[S,Q \& R].$$

For example, we should achieve an over-all probability of not less than ·501 if both $p_M[R,Q]$ and $p_M[S,Q \& R]$ achieved a level of ·71. In other words, the mathematicist allows proof on the balance of probability to be transitive—e.g. to proceed from Q to S if it proceeds at the first stage from Q to Q & R and at the second from Q & R to S—just so long as the arithmetical product of the several stages' own probabilities is high enough.

But the trouble is that even on this condition the courts and textbooks do not normally accept the transitivity of proof on the balance of probability. Wigmore, for example, quotes with approval the rather strict principle that is stated in a judgement of Lockwood, J.:[1]

[1] J. H. Wigmore, *A Treatise on the Anglo-American system of Evidence in Trials at Common Law*, 3rd edn. (1940), vol. i, §41, p. 439, quoting Lockwood, J., in New

When an inference of the probability of the ultimate fact must be drawn from facts whose existence is itself based only on an inference or chain of inferences, it will be found that the Courts have, with few exceptions, held in substance, though not usually in terms, that all prior links in the chain of inferences must be shown with the same certainty as is required in criminal cases, in order to support a final inference of the probability of the ultimate fact in issue.

This is not a restriction on the admissibility of evidence of a certain kind, like the hearsay rule, nor a requirement that a conclusion of a certain kind be evidenced in some specified way, like the English rule requiring corroboration of an alleged victim's testimony in cases of rape. It is a quite general constraint that is imposed on probabilistic proof, whatever the type of evidence and whatever the type of conclusion. So it seems to be a restriction that stems from the courts' understanding of what is meant by 'proof on the balance of probability'. But if that is so the probabilities in question cannot be mathematical ones, since the only restriction imposed by the mathematicist theory on the transitivity of probabilistic proof is the requirement that the product of the several stages' own probabilities should itself reach an appropriate level. This restriction is so liberal that it allows proof on the balance of probabilities to be transitive even if there are as many as six successive stages of less than certain proof (each with a probability of ·9, say), so long as an overall level of ·501 suffices— whereas Wigmore's principle disallows this transitivity even when there are only two such stages.

Apparently the multiplicative nature of the conjunction principle for mathematical probability is again creating difficulties. In Chapter 5 that principle turned out to be excessively severe on proofs involving a number of co-ordinate components. Here the same principle appears to be excessively liberal in regard to proofs that have one stage dependent on another.

Perhaps someone will be tempted to object that I have engineered this appearance of excessive liberality by taking a

---

York Life Insurance Co. v. McNeely, Ariz. 79 Pac. 2d. 948. Lockwood himself held that 'this rule is not based on an application of the exact rules of logic, but upon the pragmatic principle that a certain quantum of proof is arbitrarily required when the courts are asked to take away life, liberty or property'. Cf., however, the opinion of Maxey, J., cited ibid., p. 437.

typical case of inference upon inference to proceed first from Q to Q & R and then from Q & R to S. 'True transitivity', it may be objected, 'involves proceeding from Q to R, not to Q & R, and then from R alone to S. The relevant probabilities are therefore $p_M[R,Q]$ and $p_M[S,R]$ and from these we have to determine $p_M[S,Q]$.'

But the trouble now is that the mathematicist approach is too restrictive to fit. It does not allow proof by inference upon inference even under the constraint which the courts impose— the certainty of all inferences prior to the last. Even where, in a two-stage proof, $p_M[R,Q] = 1$ and $p_M[S,R]$ is fairly high, $p_M[S,Q]$ may be zero. For example, the probability of a man's being an inhabitant of England on the evidence that he's an inhabitant of Oxfordshire is 1, and the probability of a man's living outside Oxfordshire on the evidence that he's an inhabitant of England is fairly high. But the probability of a man's living outside Oxfordshire on the evidence that he's an inhabitant of Oxfordshire is zero.

If the probabilities with which judicial proof operates here were mathematical ones, the courts would apparently be ready to accept arguments that are obviously and blatantly invalid. In fact a mathematicist analysis for inference upon inference guarantees transitivity only where every stage subsequent to the first has maximum probability. It is thus directly opposed to the principle of work in the courts, which requires instead that every stage prior to the last should have maximum probability. Consequently the courts cannot be using a standard of proof that hinges on mathematical probabilities.

§23. *Is the constraint on inference upon inference a purely legal matter?*

There seems to be only one way in which supporters of the mathematicist theory can accommodate the difficulty. They have to claim that the non-transitivity of proof on the balance of probability is a purely legal matter—an additional restriction that is logically supererogatory but imposed by the courts out of some abundance of legal caution. But such a treatment of the difficulty is unsatisfactory because it creates a mystery which it does not resolve, viz. what precisely is the explanation of the restriction? Why should the courts be so reluctant to take advantage of inferential liberties offered here by the conjunction principle for mathematical probability, especially when they are apparently so willing to ignore inferential restrictions imposed by that principle elsewhere (cf. Chapter 5 above)?

The situation is particularly puzzling because of the nature of the additional constraint. In a two-stage inference, for example, what is required, according to Wigmore, is that the first stage should prove beyond reasonable doubt, though the second stage may prove only on the balance of probability. At first sight it is tempting to explain this as being a way of ensuring that the probability of the over-all conclusion should not be lower than that of any stage on its own. But the explanation will not work. For on a mathematicist interpretation a two-stage inference could achieve such a result equally well if (contrary to Wigmore's principle) the second stage proved beyond reasonable doubt when the first stage proved only on the balance of probability. After all, multiplication is a commutative operation. So there is a mystery not only about why juridical proof on the balance of probability should be non-transitive even when the probabilities involved are fairly high, but also about why the requirements for inference upon inference should be precisely what they are.

Again, it will not help to suppose that what is required, in inference upon inference, is to view each stage of the inference as being based on favourable relevance. Admittedly, favourable relevance is not transitive. Consider, for example, the situation where $p_M[Q,R]$ is the probability of a man's living either in England or in Scotland on the evidence that he lives in Oxfordshire, and $p_M[S,R]$ is the probability that he lives in Scotland on the evidence that he lives either in England or in Scotland. So, if proof on the balance of mathematical probability is construed as proof by favourable relevance, it is quite clear why the former is not transitive. But neither do we have $p_M[S,Q] > p_M[S]$ as a necessary consequence of $p_M[R,Q] = 1 > p_M[R]$ and $p_M[S,R] > p_M[S]$. (Consider Q as 'x is a university graduate but temperamentally lazy', R as 'x is literate', and S as 'x has above average earnings'.) So the favourable relevance interpretation cuts out too much. It does not even allow inference upon inference in the cases where the courts allow it.

In general, if the foundation of an argument is only of

moderate strength, it seems prudent to believe that a strong superstructure cannot give us substantially more reliable results in the end than a weak one: any over-all conclusion is bound to be rather unreliable. But if the foundation is really strong then even a moderately strong superstructure will give us substantially more reliable results than a weak one. To indulge in a long chain of inference is rather like lowering yourself out of an upstairs window by a real chain. You have less distance to fall if the links at the lower end of the chain are weak than if those at the upper end are. Or again, we commonly suppose a factual conclusion to be proved—whatever the strength of the proof—only if the premises of the proof are not themselves controversial. Proof is something that may depend on what is probably inferable from known facts, but not on what is certainly inferable from probable ones.

This tends to suggest that in their customary attitude towards inference upon inference the courts are not imposing some peculiarly legal constraint but merely giving explicit expression to commonsense ideas about proof and probability. Correspondingly it will be shown later (in §72) that the rationale of Wigmore's principle can be fully elucidated if we construe the standards for judicial proof in terms of inductive probability.

7

The Difficulty about Negation

Summary

§24. Because of the principle that $p_M[S] = 1 - p_M[\text{not-}S]$, the mathematicist analysis implies that in civil cases the Anglo-American system is officially prepared to tolerate a quite substantial mathematical probability that a losing defendant deserved to succeed. §25. There is a limit to the extent that this difficulty can be avoided by supposing a higher threshold for the balance of probability. Nor are the proper amounts of damages held to be proportional to the strength of a winning plaintiff's proof. §26. If there were a legal rule excluding statistical evidence in relation to voluntary acts much of the paradox here would disappear. But it would be unnecessary to suppose such a rule if the outcome of civil litigation could be construed as a victory for case-strength rather than as the division of a determinate quantity of case-merit.

§24. *The paradox of the gatecrasher*

The negation principle for mathematical probability generates another kind of difficulty. The mathematicist account has to accept that if the judicial probability of an accused's guilt is x, the probability of his innocence is $1 - x$. Hence, if x were high enough for an accused's guilt to be beyond reasonable doubt and his condemnation therefore legally just, the probability here that a man who should, according to law, be condemned is innocent would be $1 - x$. Similarly, on the mathematicist account, the probability in a civil case that the unsuccessful litigant deserved to succeed would be $1 - x$ when the probability that the successful litigant deserved to succeed was x.

Now this kind of thing might be just tolerable in relation to criminal cases. If the level of mathematical probability at which further doubt is held to be unreasonable is fixed sufficiently high, then perhaps the extent to which the legal system officially admits the probability that a condemned man is innocent becomes sufficiently small. But what about those civil cases where British and United States law requires only a preponderance of probability? A substantially lower level of probability must constitute the threshold of proof in any such case. Correspondingly, if mathematical probabilities are at issue and a complementational negation principle applies, the probability that the unsuccessful litigant deserved to succeed may be by no means negligible. Suppose the threshold of proof in civil cases were judicially interpreted as being at the level of a mathematical probability of ·501. Would not judges thereby imply acceptance of a system in which the mathematical probability that the unsuccessful litigant deserved to succeed might sometimes be as high as ·499? This hardly seems the right spirit in which to administer justice.

Consider, for example, a case in which it is common ground that 499 people paid for admission to a rodeo, and that 1,000 are counted on the seats, of whom A is one. Suppose no tickets were issued and there can be no testimony as to whether A paid for admission or climbed over the fence. So by any plausible criterion of mathematical probability there is a ·501 probability, on the admitted facts, that he did not pay. The mathematicist theory would apparently imply that in such circumstances the rodeo organizers are entitled to judgement against A for the admission-money, since the balance of probability (and also the difference between prior and posterior probabilities) would lie in their favour. But it seems manifestly unjust that A should lose his case when there is an agreed mathematical probability of as high as ·499 that he in fact paid for admission.

Indeed, if the organizers were really entitled to judgement against A, they would presumably be equally entitled to judgement against each person in the same situation as A. So they might conceivably be entitled to recover 1,000 admission-moneys, when it was admitted that 499 had actually been paid. The absurd injustice of this suffices to show that there is something wrong somewhere. But where?

No doubt we must all in practice accept that *de facto* injustice will sometimes be done to a litigant even in the best of legal systems. His lawyers may present his case badly, his key witnesses may disappear, his opponent's witnesses may be prepared to perjure themselves, the judge may sum up one-sidedly, the jury may bring in a perverse verdict, and so on.

From long experience of the working of human institutions we cannot avoid accepting a substantial probability that a deserving litigant will in fact be unsuccessful. But the probability now under discussion is a different one. It is characteristically assessed not by external critics of courts and other human institutions, but by triers of fact within the courts. It is not the sociologically discoverable probability, in a particular jurisdiction, that a deserving litigant will be unsuccessful, but the legally admissible probability on a particular occasion, even when all key witnesses are present and say what they believe, that the unsuccessful litigant deserved to win.

§25. *What is the threshold of proof in civil cases?*

Perhaps you are tempted to object here that this shows only that the threshold of proof in civil cases must be assumed to lie at a much higher level of mathematical probability than ·501. But note three things.

First, to require a much higher threshold would very much worsen the difficulties about conjunction that were discussed in Chapter 2. Even if the threshold were set no higher than a mathematical probability of ·7, and there were no more than two independent component outcomes, the probabilities of each of the latter would have to reach ·85, in order to achieve a sufficiently high probability for the outcome as a whole. In effect the conjunctive principle for mathematical probability would now be so restrictive in civil cases that no one could ever envisage assigning a probability to the outcome as a whole if there were more than three such component outcomes.

Secondly, the higher the threshold level is put, the less plausible it is to suppose that this is what is meant by the phrase 'the balance of probabilities'. If a threshold of ·8 or ·9 is required, the mathematical probability of the loser's deserving to win should not be higher than ·2 or ·1, respectively. But the difference between ·8 and ·2, or between ·9 and ·1, is an overwhelming one, not a mere 'preponderance'. With such a standard of proof in civil cases, the difference from the criminal standard would almost disappear.

Thirdly, even if the threshold is put as high as a mathematical probability of ·8, this still seems to represent a scandalously high level of admissible doubt for a legal system to endorse *de jure.* To endorse a ·8 threshold is as if to allow, for any particular civil suit, that if in no more than four-fifths of the situations relevantly similar to the facts before the court the actual outcome is similar to what a plaintiff claims, he ought to win his case. Even if you think of the ·8 threshold subjectively, as a degree of belief, you presumably still have to adjust your degree of belief to the objective frequencies. So with a ·8 threshold the legal standard of proof entitles the jury in effect to assume for any such suit, in default of countervailing evidence, that the case before the court belongs to the category of situation that prevails in four-fifths of relevant examples, not to the category that prevails in one-fifth. Such a thesis seems just about as paradoxical as supposing that, if a bookmaker thinks a horse has a four-to-one chance of losing a particular race, he is wise to accept any number of wagers on the horse's win at those odds. Instead he must either limit the amount of money he has at stake or progressively shorten the odds. Correspondingly, if the award of damages in a civil suit were normally adjusted in size to the mathematical probability that the plaintiff deserved to win, one would feel it somewhat juster for the threshold of proof to be thought of as a mathematical probability of say, ·8. A relatively small award where the critical level was only just reached, and a relatively high one where it was greatly exceeded, would seem a fair arrangement. But no such arrangement is known to the law. It has sometimes been held that a specially high level of probability is required in civil suits where serious culpability is at issue, as perhaps where fraud or adultery is alleged.[1] But there is no rule requiring that the award of damages in a successful civil suit be adjusted in size to the mathematical probability that the defendant deserved to win,[2] and in any case no such rule could cover actions for

---

[1] Cf. R. Cross, *Evidence*, 3rd edn. (1967), pp. 92–9.

[2] Note that it is awards of damages that are primarily relevant here, not awards of costs. Similarly there is no rule in criminal cases requiring that the force or cogency of a piece of evidence should be adjusted to the enormity of the crime or the weightiness of the consequences attaching to conviction. Cf. William Wills, *Principles of Circumstantial Evidence*, 7th edn. (1936), ed. V. R. N. Gattie and M. Krishnamachariar, p. 333. Macaulay put the point very clearly in his *Essays* (1852 edn.), p. 143, quoted by Wills, op. cit., p. 335: 'The rules of evidence no more depend on the magnitude of the interests at stake than the rules of arithmetic.' Notoriously juries have failed to convict where they thought the penalty ensuing would be heavier than the crime merited. But what was happening then was just

specific performance or actions for a declaration, decree, injunction, order, grant, etc. On the mathematicist account a man might apparently lose his whole fortune if those of his circumstances that were in evidence tended to place him on the majority side of some critical division even though he actually belonged with the minority.

§26. *When are statistical probabilities admissible evidence?*

What can the mathematicist reply here? One line of defence for the mathematicist account might be to argue that the appearance of injustice in such examples as that of the rodeo is due to a faulty judgement of relevance. Perhaps the man sued for his admission-money had once been a boy-scout, and the defence could have led evidence to the effect that 90 per cent of ex-boy-scouts are uniformly honest in matters of money. That is, if the court were told all the circumstances that were relevant to the statistical probability of the man's having bilked the rodeo organizers, the reference class for calculating this probability would be rather different. Instead of its being just the class of people at the rodeo, it might be, say, the class of ex-boy-scouts at the rodeo, and the statistical probability that a member of that class has failed to pay for his admission at a rodeo might be known to be much nearer ·2 than ·501.

But the trouble with this line of argument is that even without the evidence about the boy-scouts no court would convict the man. Moreover, though an honest man at the rodeo might be absolved from suspicion by character evidence, there may be other cases in which the paradox is sustained. Even when all relevant circumstances have been taken into account, the mathematical probability in the plaintiff's favour might be, say, ·501, ·7, or ·8. An apparent injustice would then be officially countenanced by the legal system on the mathematicist account, whenever a man's relevant circumstances tended to place him on the majority side of some critical statistical division even though he actually belonged with the minority.

---

that their verdicts were determined by their moral consciences rather than by their factual beliefs. The cases discussed by J. M. Keynes, *A Treatise on Probability* (1921), pp. 24–7 are different again. They are not concerned with the degree to which a plaintiff has proved his case but, on the assumption that it is proven, with the question whether the size of the damages may be related to the probable extent of the plaintiff's loss.

So the mathematicist approach to juridical probability needs to be defended in some other way. Perhaps it might be argued instead that paradoxes of the kind under discussion arise only because the possiblity of statistical evidence is being entertained in relation to issues where statistical evidence is inappropriate. 'Statistical evidence', it might be said, 'is inadmissible whenever the thing to be proved is a fact about an individul that involves a significant element of decision or voluntariness.[3] Paradoxes of the kind alleged do not in fact arise, because they are precluded by the legal rules for admissibility of evidence.'

But even if the courts would not normally allow statistical evidence to establish a probability about a defendant's voluntary act at issue, their reluctance to do so requires an explanation. It cannot be because this evidence would be regarded by any clear-thinking and reflective person outside the courts as irrelevant to such an issue. What the keen salesman says to you, for example, is based on the latest statistics of reactions by different kinds of customers to different kinds of selling ploys. Instead the mathematicist's explanation has got to be that, if it does not specifically exclude statistical proof for voluntary acts, a legal system that accepts proof on the balance of probability would thereby condone a substantial probability of injustice. But why then do authoritative textbooks on the law of evidence never mention such a rule of exclusion? No need for the rule seems to be felt in normal practice. And this in turn suggests that the concept of probability normally invoked in stating standards of proof is not one which in fact entails such a possibility of injustice. The paradox is more plausibly avoided by rejecting the mathematicist philosophy of proof than by supposing statistics irrelevant to questions about voluntary acts.

An important part of the trouble seems to be that, if standards of proof are interpreted in accordance with a theory of probability that has a complementational principle for negation, the litigants are construed as seeking to divide a determinate quantity of case-merit, as it were, between them. Such an interpretation treats it as an officially accepted necessity that the merit of the loser's case in a civil suit varies inversely with that of the winner's, and this generates paradox where proof

[3] Cf. W. B. Stoebuck, 'Relevancy and the Theory of Probability', 51 *Iowa Law Review* 858, (1966).

is allowed on the mere balance of the two probabilities. Nor can we say then—as lawyers sometimes do say in practice—that the defendant's case is equally good on the facts in both of two similar lawsuits, while the plaintiff's case is better in one than the other. But we can say this quite consistently, and avoid the paradox, if we abandon any complementational principle for negation. We may then suppose litigants to be taking part in a contest of case-strength or case-weight, rather than dividing a determinate quantity of case-merit. The only possibility of injustice that is then officially countenanced is the possibility that one side may not have put forward as strong a case as it could. But where that happens it is the fault of the litigant or of his lawyers or witnesses, not of the legal system. We shall see later (§73, pp. 270 ff.) that if standards of juridical proof are interpreted in terms of inductive, rather than mathematical, probabilities this is precisely what follows.

The point under discussion has not gone unnoticed in the courts. A Massachusetts judge once remarked

It has been held not enough that mathematically the chances somewhat favour a proposition to be proved; for example, the fact that coloured automobiles made in the current year outnumber black ones would not warrant a finding that an undescribed automobile of the current year is coloured and not black . . . After the evidence has been weighed, that proposition is proved by a preponderance of evidence if it is made to appear more likely or probable in the sense that actual belief in its truth, derived from the evidence, exists in the mind or minds of the tribunal notwithstanding any doubts that may still linger there.[4]

---

[4] Lummus, J., in 'Sargent v. Massachusetts Accident Co.' 307, Mass. 246, 29 N.E. 2d 825, 827 (1940) quoted by V. C. Ball, 'The moment of truth: probability theory and the standards of proof', in *Essays on Procedure and Evidence* ed. T. G. Rondy Jr. and R. N. Covington (1961), p. 95.

Another interesting judgement in this connection was given by Brandon, J., in 'The Brimnes' (1973) 1 All E.R. 769ff. The relevant issue at stake was whether a telex message received at a time known to be between 17.37 and 18.37 was received after a telex that was received at a time known to be between 17.30 and 18.00. The judge thought that the court could 'only do its best' by taking a mean time of 18.07 for the former message; that, if this was wrong, the court could say that the former message was 'more likely' to have been later than the latter one; and that, 'if neither of these two approaches is justified, the position is that, whichever side needs, for the purpose of its case, to establish affirmatively that one of the two events preceded the other, has failed to discharge the burden of proof resting on it.' Of these three alternatives the third is the one most in keeping with the

In other words the standard of proof in civil cases is to be interpreted in terms leading one to expect that, after all the evidence has been heard, a balance of probability in favour of a certain conclusion will produce belief in the truth of that conclusion among reasonable men. So we need a concept of probability that admits a threshold for rational acceptance, or moderate belief, which is quite distinct from the threshold for belief beyond reasonable doubt. Inductive probability, it will turn out, has just the required property, but mathematical probability cannot have it (§89, pp. 318 ff).

---

arguments of the present book, the second apparently adopts the mathematicist account of proof on the balance of probability which this book rejects, and the first breathes a spirit of pragmatism and compromise which is sometimes as valuable in practice as it is difficult for any theory to embrace.

8

The Difficulty about Proof beyond Reasonable Doubt

Summary

§27. We are more inclined to hold that a particular conclusion falls short of certainty because there is a particular, specifiable reason for doubting it, than to hold that it is reasonable to doubt the conclusion because it falls short of certainty. Hence a scale of mathematical probability is otiose for assessing proof beyond reasonable doubt. What we need instead is a list of all the points that have to be established in relation to each element in the crime. §28. Not that a high statistical probability is necessarily useless; but it must enter into a proof as a fact from which to argue rather than as a measure of the extent to which a conclusion has been established, and its relevance must also be separately established.

§27. *Reasons for doubting guilt*

I have argued so far that the mathematicist account of judicial probability runs into grave difficulties in regard to conjunction, transitivity, and negation. These kinds of difficulties arise in any attempt to give a mathematicist interpretation to the legal standard of proof in civil cases. But the difficulties that arise for a mathematicist account of judicial proof are not confined to civil cases. In the present chapter and in Chapter 10 I shall discuss two such difficulties that arise in regard to proof of fact in the criminal courts.

According to the mathematicist theory, presumably, it is unreasonable to doubt the guilt of an accused if this is established by the evidence with some very high level of mathematical probability. But just how high a level must this be? It is not difficulty to see why a juror would baulk at answering such questions. We are more inclined to hold that a particular conclusion falls short of certainty because there is a particular, specifiable reason for doubting it, than to hold that it is reasonable to doubt the conclusion because it falls short of certainty. Even if a scale of mathematical probability were to be used for assessing how close a particular conclusion was to certainty, the crucial reason for doubting the conclusion would very often not be the fact that the probability was no higher than, say, ·95, but rather the specific item in, or feature of, the evidence that prevented this probability from rising any higher. What makes it reasonable to doubt the guilt of the accused, perhaps, is the shifty demeanour of one of the key witnesses against him or the absence of any evidence of motive. Correspondingly, even if a scale of mathematical probability could be used for assessing how close a particular conclusion was to certainty, its assessments would very often be quite superfluous as reasons for doubting guilt. The proof's degree of validity could be judged without regard to the scale of mathematical probability. The scale would be otiose. This is another price that has to be paid by those who insist on conceiving all judicial probabilities as mathematical ones.

What seems to be needed in practice for assessment of proof in a criminal trial is a list of the various points that all have to be established, and of the various let-outs that all have to be barred, in relation to each element in the crime, if guilt is to be proved beyond reasonable doubt. Wherever we have or assume such a list a scale of mathematical probability seems altogether otiose. The strength of the proof depends just on the extent to which the list has been covered.

§28. *The role of statistical probabilities in judicial proof*

Not that very high mathematical probabilities are always useless in judicial proofs of fact. Far from it. But where they are important they enter into the proof as part of the grounds for its conclusion, not as gradations of the extent to which its grounds establish the conclusion. They are given in evidence by expert witnesses, not estimated by jurors in the process of deciding on their verdict. This is easily seen if we consider a typical case in which a mathematical probability may be important, such as a case that involves an issue of identification.

Suppose that A is accused of murdering B and that part of the evidence against A is a threatening letter found in B's house which, though unsigned, has been typewritten on a machine that has the same peculiarities (broken or twisted type) as A's typewriter. More specifically, suppose that there is expert evidence asserting the presence of just three mutually independent peculiarities in the machine on which the letter was typed, and of just the same three in A's machine. Suppose the expert evidence is that each of these peculiarities is normally found, on average, in only one out of ten machines. Then, if this evidence is correct, the mathematical probability of a typewriter's having all three peculiarities will be ·001 ; and the mathematical probability that any randomly selected pair of typewriters have, independently of one another, all three peculiarities will be one in a million. It is tempting thence to infer a ·999,999 mathematical probability that the letter's having been typed on a machine with those peculiarities is dependent on the fact that A has such a machine, and therefore apparently a ·999,999 mathematical probability that A typed the letter.

Now obviously, even if there were such a high mathematical probability of this, it would not establish that A was the killer. Even if A had a motive for killing B he might not have had an opportunity and even if he had had an opportunity he might not have taken advantage of it. There are obviously problems about how the convergence of circumstantial evidence can prove a conclusion beyond reasonable doubt. But I shall discuss these problems in Chapter 10. What I want to emphasize here is that even if, in the situation described, it can be shown to be highly probable that A typed the letter, this high probability is not to be identified with the ·999,999 mathematical probability described by the expert witness.

The expert evidence was that the mathematical probability of two typewriters' having all three peculiarities independently is one in a million. Two stages of inference are then needed in order to reach the conclusion that A typed the letter. The first stage of inference is to assume a ·999,999 mathematical probability that the letter's having been typed on a machine with those peculiarities is dependent on the fact that A has such a machine. The second stage concludes therefrom that A typed it. Let us consider each stage separately.

The first stage moves from a proposition about typewriters

in general to a proposition about the machine on which the letter was typed and the machine owned by A. But for such a move to be justified it would need to be shown that there were no relevant circumstances differentiating these machines (or this machine) from the sample on which the expert witness based his estimate. For example, perhaps these peculiarities are found especially often in the typewriter's of B's acquaintances because of certain mutually independent factors causing the type to become broken or twisted in this way, such as the frequency with which certain letters or combinations of letters occur in the language, vocabulary, or names of B's acquaintances. To exclude reasonable doubt about a connection between A's machine and the typing of the letter, some appropriate testimony would be needed about the relevant circumstances of the machine and the letter. What counts at this stage in the proof is not just the evidence that there is a high mathematical probability of such a connection in general, but also the evidence that that probability is relevant to the particular case. The strength of the proof—the gradation of its validity—depends on the extent to which both propositions are established. To assess this extent in terms of a mathematical probability would be otiose for the same reasons as those mentioned at the beginning of the present section.

The point is strengthened when we come to consider the second stage of the proof that A typed the letter. The premiss of this stage is that A's machine is somehow connected with the typing of the letter. But what is the connection? Was the machine itself used to type the letter? Or was another machine rigged to resemble A's machine so as to frame him? If A's machine was used, did A himself use it? And if he used it did he do so voluntarily? If in the circumstances of the case doubt about any of these issues would not be merely fanciful, the prosecution must lead evidence to exclude it. So again the extent of the proof's validity is not identifiable with a mathematical probability of ·999,999. It is identifiable instead with the extent to which any reason has been excluded for doubting the significance of this mathematical probability for the issue in hand—viz. the question whether A himself typed the letter.

There are indefinitely many other ways in which a statistical probability may enter into a juridical proof, whether in criminal or in civil cases. There are other kinds of identity issues, and issues about affiliation, occupational disease, actuarial risk, quality control, jury selection, and so on.[1] But in every normal case the role of a statistical probability may be conceived analogously to the example just discussed. The statistical probability enters the case in the form of expert evidence, and its level of significance for the outcome has to be assessed in the light of other evidence by a mode of assessment which, at least on the face of things, need not itself have anything to do with mathematical probability. We shall see later (§§58–62) that this mode of assessment—this calibration of relevance or of the exclusion of reasons for doubt—is precisely the mode of assessment that determines inductive probability.

---

[1] Cf., e.g., Paul Sigal, 'Judicial Use, Misuse and Abuse of Statistical Evidence', 47 *Journal of Urban Law* 165 ff. (1969); Michael O. Finkelstein, 'The Application of Statistical Decision Theory to the Jury Discrimination Cases', 80 *Harvard L.R.* 338 ff. (1966); Thomas H. Liddle III, 'Mathematical and Statistical Probability as a Test of Circumstantial Evidence', 19 *Case Western L.R.* 254ff. (1968); and R. F. Coleman and H. J. Walls, 'The Evaluation of Scientific Evidence', *Criminal Law Review* (1974) 276 ff.

9

The Difficulty about a Criterion

Summary

§29. No familiar criterion of mathematical probability is applicable to the evaluation of juridical proofs. Statistical criteria have already been shown to be inapplicable. Carnapian criteria require a unanimity about range-measure, which cannot be assumed. §30. To suppose that jurors should evaluate proofs in terms of a coherent betting policy is to ignore the fact that rational men do not bet on issues where the outcome is not discoverable otherwise than from the data on which the odds themselves have to be based. §31. So the onus is on the mathematicist to propose some other criterion, which is not excluded by any of the special circumstances of judicial proof.

§29. *The inapplicability of Carnapian criteria*

Jurors and judges must be supposed to have some criterion, or system of criteria, for the probabilities of proofs, however tacit, imprecise, and intuitive this criterion or system may be. There must be some rationale behind their assignments and comparisons of probability—some rationale that justifies public confidence, ensures a reasonable degree of agreement, and underwrites the rejection of perverse verdicts. But it is very difficult to say what their criterion can be if the probabilities involved are mathematical ones. Nor is this difficulty just a difficulty about what can be managed in practice. Each of the more familiar modes of assigning values to mathematical probability-functions seems in principle inappropriate.

We have already seen, in §28, how statistical probabilities enter into judicial proofs. They constitute premises which can uphold the conclusion of a proof only in accordance with their degree of relevance. Not surprisingly, therefore, in the words of the Massachusetts judge already quoted,

the fact that coloured automobiles made in the current year out-numbered black ones would not warrant a finding that an undescribed automobile of the current year is coloured and not black, nor would the fact that only a minority of men die of cancer warrant a finding that a particular man did not die of cancer.

Even if the statistical probability of a current automobile's being coloured is a fact before the court, the trier of fact has still to determine the probability with which it may be inferred from this fact that a particular automobile is coloured.[1] Even if the former probability is a high one, the latter may not be.

But, if the probability of a proof—i.e. the probability of a conclusion on the facts—can thus never be identified with a statistical probability or relative frequency, what other criterion of mathematical probability can be appropriate? Are we to suppose, perhaps, that triers of fact tacitly operate a Carnapian system? Such a system evaluates probabilification in terms of a ratio of ranges. The probability of h on e is measured by the ratio of the range of the conjunction h & e to the range of e, where the range of a particular sentence in the system is the class of those state-descriptions (available within the system) in which that sentence holds true. But whether or not this system has any other application it suffers from a very serious disadvantage so far as application to judicial probabilities is concerned. Notoriously it generates not just one confirmation-function, but, varying with the range-measure, an infinite number of different confirmation-functions, for assessing probabilities.[2] So that the level of probability with which a given piece of evidence establishes a certain conclusion varies according to the confirmation-function selected. How then is there to be the uniformity that justice requires in the administration of the law? How can juries be expected to agree whether something has or has not been established on the balance of probability? Certainly no rule of law stipulates which confirmation-function is to be used in the jury-room. So a range-theoretical account of judicial probability would only be plausible if we could suppose that in practice there is just one confirmation-function that jurors use. But then, since

---

[1] Cf. what was said above p. 21, and f.n., about the application of the relative-frequency analysis to the probability of a single case.

[2] The classical text is R. Carnap, *Logical Foundations of Probability* (1951). Cf. also R. Carnap, *The Continuum of Inductive Methods* (1952); and R. Carnap and R. C. Jeffrey (eds.), *Studies in Inductive Logic and Probability* vol. i (1971).

people are supposed to assess probabilities inside the jury-room in just the same way as they assess them outside, there would have to be just one confirmation-function that everybody uses also in ordinary life. And the Carnapian theory, with its essentially pluralistic outlook, provides no rationale for the existence of such a surprising unanimity in the choice of confirmation-function. Indeed, if even Carnap recognized no compelling argument for the choice of just one range-measure,[3] how could a jury of laymen be expected to do so? And, if no such argument exists, then at the heart of the jury system, on a range-theoretical account, there is implicit an arbitrary and rationally indefensible act of choice. We must in fact now construe Carnap's work as having shown that, even when a jury comes to a correct conclusion by its own standards, another conclusion might have been equally reasonable. This is the price a mathematicist must be prepared to pay for adopting a range-theoretical analysis of judicial probability. But it is a high price to pay when the matter at stake might be a man's life, liberty, property or reputation.

§30. *The inapplicability of betting odds*

Another commonly invoked criterion for the assignment of a mathematical probability is the acceptance or acceptability of appropriate betting odds within a coherent betting policy. So perhaps well-behaved jurors, who are fully self-conscious in their reasoning, should be supposed to measure the strength of their belief in the correctness of a particular verdict by reference to the odds they would accept if wagering on its correctness? This measure, the betting quotient, would be the ratio of the favourable figure to the sum of the two figures, and would have the structure of a mathematical probability. Odds of 4 to 1 on the plaintiff's case, say, would give a betting quotient or mathematical probability of ·8. It would then apparently be possible for judges or legislators to stipulate a degree of mathematical probability that could be taken as putting the guilt of an accused person beyond reasonable doubt and a lower degree of mathematical probability that would suffice for the decision of civil cases.

[3] R. Carnap, 'Inductive Logic and Inductive Intuition': Reply to J. Hintikka, in *The Problem of Inductive Logic*, ed. I. Lakatos, (1968), p. 314.

But in fact such a procedure would be grossly fallacious. A reasonable man's betting practice is subject to two additional constraints, besides his knowledge of relevant data.

One constraint is that he only wagers on discoverable outcomes. Bets must be settlable. In each case the outcome must be knowable otherwise than from the data on which the odds themselves are based. When the horse-race is finally run, the winner is photographed as he passes the winning-post. When the football match is finally played, each goal is seen as it is kicked. Consequently wagers on past events or on the truth of scientific generalizations over an unbounded domain, or on any issue where the whole truth cannot be directly observed, are only intelligible in a context of total or partial ignorance about the relevant data. Knowing nothing, or only a little, about the local archaeological evidence I can wager you, on the basis of experience elsewhere, that there was no Roman settlement at Banbury; and to settle the bet we can excavate and see. But, if all the appropriate excavations have already been done, and we know their results, there is nothing to wager about. Similarly, to request a juryman to envisage a wager on a past event, when, *ex hypothesi*, he normally already knows all the relevant evidence that is likely to be readily obtainable, is to employ the concept of a wager in a context to which it is hardly appropriate. There is no time machine to take us back into the past. So there is no sure way of discovering whether the accused is guilty, or the plaintiff's statement of claim is true, except by looking at the relevant evidence. If one asks a juryman to envisage a wager in such a context, one is hardly entitled to expect a rational response.

Perhaps it will be objected that since people do sometimes wager sensibly about past events, as on the existence of a Roman settlement at Banbury, they can reasonably be assumed to have a general technique for assigning betting-quotient probabilities to past events on given evidence Why then cannot a jury employ such a technique for the solution of its own special problems about probabilities? The answer to this objection is that it still does not succeed in attaching significance to the conception of judicial probabilities as betting quotients. The argument against a betting-quotient analysis of judicial probability is not that there is no sufficiently general technique for devising betting-quotients: the argument is rather that in certain situations the operational acceptance of a betting quotient is irrational. So talk about assigning probabilities, when probabilities are understood in the proposed way, involves the absurdity of talk about accepting reasonable bets on unsettlable issues.

Moreover, another constraint on rational betting practice has to be mentioned here. No one bothers about odds unless the amounts at stake are of some consequence. Only the very poor bet seriously in pennies. But when the amounts at stake begin to rise a prudent man tends to be more and more cautious about the odds he will accept for a given size of stake. Bookmakers shorten the odds on a horse not only when they hear of its latest wins elsewhere but also when they begin to be concerned about how much they would lose if it won the current race. So there is little sense in asking a man what odds he would accept on a certain outcome unless the value of the units wagered is also specified. Every juryman would have to be instructed separately by the judge, in accordance with the judge's estimate of what would be an appropriate sum of money for that juryman to envisage wagering. Consequently every accused would be at risk not only in relation to the evidence, but also in relation to the judge's estimates of how much importance each juryman attaches to the gain or loss of this or that sum of money. Such a system certainly does not yet exist anywhere, and its institution seems scarcely likely to promote the ends of justice.[4]

§31. *The hiatus to be filled*

My point here is not that there is anything intrinsically and universally wrong with evaluating mathematical probabilities in terms of statistical frequencies, range-overlap or betting

---

[4] Nevertheless some writers have supposed that the probability of a defendant's guilt should be gauged in this way: e.g. G. R. Iversen, 'Operationalising the Concept of Probability in Legal–Social Science Research', 5 *Law and Society Review* 331–3 (1971).

F. P. Ramsey, *Foundations of Mathematics* (1931), p. 176ff., suggested a way of surmounting the difficulty about bettors' varying attitudes to gain and loss: the bet that provides a measure for a probability is to be conceived of as being made in terms of the difference between certain values of the bettor's preference-function. But it encourages irresponsibility if the ordinary juror is required to gauge probabilities in this way, since the bet would be unsettlable and so no actual gain or loss could ensue. Cf. also p. 26, n. 15.

odds. Far from it. Some or all of these criteria no doubt have very many useful fields of application. But for one reason or another, it seems, none of them is applicable to the task of evaluating the strength of a proof in a British or American lawcourt. Nor is there any well-understood game of chance to which the selection of a certain proposition, as the conclusion of a judicial proof, may be assimilated. Nor is there any well-established theory that encompasses mathematical probabilities for such propositions, like the probabilities of sub-atomic physics. Nor am I arguing just that it is rather difficult in practice to obtain exact measurements of proof-strength in the court so as to accord with one or other of these criteria. My point is that none of these criteria are applicable, so no assessment that accords with any of them is possible even in principle.

It is therefore incumbent on the mathematicist, if he wishes to defend his position in relation to judicial proof, to propose some other mode of evaluation. This must be a set of truth-criteria for statements of the form $p_M[S,R] = n$ that satisfies two conditions. First, it must not be excluded from application to judicial proof by any of the characteristic constraints on the latter. Secondly, it must invoke some definite measure that is comparable with the appeal to statistical frequencies, range-ratios, coherent betting odds, games of chance, or the properties of physical particles. Until such a set of truth-criteria has been produced the mathematicist theory is in a rather weak and paradoxical position. It assumes the existence of a mode of evaluation that satisfies certain rather restrictive conditions. But it cannot describe how this mode of evaluation operates, let alone how actual assessments are to be made in accordance with it.

10

The Difficulty about Corroboration
and Convergence

Summary

§32. Testimonial corroboration, and the convergence of circumstantial evidence, exhibit a common logical structure. §33. The
traditional Bernoullian analysis of this structure is unsatisfactory
because it gives the wrong result wherever the corroborating or
converging probabilities are themselves less than .5. §34. No account
in terms of mathematical probability can do better unless the prior
probability of the conclusion is taken into account: compare the
failure of Ekelöf's principle. §35. But, though an apparently satisfactory mathematicist account can be given when the requisite
independence conditions are properly formulated, it entails the
assignment of a positive prior probability to any conclusion that
has to be proved. §36. This conflicts with the normal rule that a
jury should decide a case solely on the facts before the court. §37.
The difficulty can be avoided if the juridical probability of S on R_1
& R_2 is conceived as the mathematical improbability of R_1 & R_2
on not-S. But this abandons the theory that the juridical probability of S on R_1 & R_2 is identical with the mathematical probability
of S on R_1 & R_2, and leaves obscure the justification for moving
from the original probability to its contrapositive.

§32. *The common structure of testimonial corroboration and circum-*
stantial convergence

Two familiar patterns of argument in British and American
judicial proof share a common logical structure that is very
difficult to elucidate in terms of mathematical probability. One
such pattern is to point to the mutual corroboration of different
witnesses. The other is to point to the convergence of different
items of circumstantial evidence. Let us first see what logical
structure is shared by these two patterns of argument, and then
explore the difficulties to be met with in any attempt to give a

mathematicist account of it. The structure is to be found in both civil and criminal cases, but some aspects of the mathematicist's problem emerge most sharply in regard to the latter. So I shall concentrate on examples of that type.

At its simplest testimonial corroboration occurs when two witnesses both testify, independently of one another, to the truth of the same proposition. On its own the admitted fact that A testifies that p would do something to raise the probability that p, and so would the fact that B testifies that p. But both facts together raise this probability substantially more than either would alone, provided that one important condition holds good. This condition is that neither fact may be causally connected with the other (other than through the truth of what is testified). If one witness has been told what to say by the other, or is influenced by what he hears him testify, or is involved in any other kind of collusion, there may be no genuine corroboration. But if there was no special reason to suppose that the two testimonies would be identical, they must give each other some degree of corroboration.

Two items of circumstantial evidence converge when both facts, independently of one another, probability the same conclusion. Suppose it has been established beyond reasonable doubt that A was due to inherit under B's will, so that A had a motive for murdering B. Then this fact on its own would do something to raise the probability that A was B's killer. Similarly, if it were established that A was a guest of B's at the time, so that he had an opportunity to commit the murder, this too, on its own, would do something to raise the probability that A was the killer. But both facts together raise this probability substantially more than either would alone, provided that a certain important condition holds. This condition is, roughly, that neither fact is dependent on the other except through the guilt of the accused. If all and only those who had a motive for the crime are known to have been deliberately invited by B to his house at the same time (as would appear to happen in some detective stories!), there is no genuine convergence. But if there was no special reason to infer A's presence in the house from his having had a motive, or vice versa, the two facts do converge to increase the probability of his having been the killer.

It is easy to describe in general terms the logical structure that is common to corroboration and convergence. If a conclusion, S, has its probability raised by each of two premises, R_1 and R_2, when these are considered separately, and R_2 is unconnected with R_1, unless through the truth of S, then the conjunction of R_1 and R_2 makes S more probable than does R_1 alone. But how is it possible to elucidate this familiar principle in terms of mathematical probability?

§33. *The traditional, Bernoullian analysis*

The elucidation that has been most commonly proposed is at least as old as James Bernoulli's *Ars Conjectandi*.[1] I shall discuss it in the admirably perspicuous form in which it was expounded by George Boole.[2]

Let p be the general probability that A speaks truth, q the general probability that B speaks truth; it is required to find the probability, that if they agree in a statement they both speak truth. Now, agreement in the same statement implies that they either both speak truth, the probability of which beforehand is pq, or that they both speak falsehood, the probability of which beforehand is $(1-p)(1-q)$. Hence the probability beforehand that they will agree is $pq + (1-p)(1-q)$ and the probability that if they agree they will agree in speaking the truth is accordingly expressed by the formula

$$w = \frac{pq}{pq + (1-p)(1-q)}.$$

This formula can obviously be applied also to the convergence of circumstantial evidence, with as much plausibility as to testimonial corroboration. Let p be the probability that fact A incriminates a person correctly, and q the probability that fact B does so. It would then be required to find the probability that, if they independently agree in whom they incriminate, they both incriminate correctly. Now, if they agree indepen-

[1] Part IV, ch. iii.

[2] Cf. 'On the Application of the Theory of Probabilities to the Question of the Combination of Testimonies or Judgments' (originally published in *Transactions of the Royal Society of Edinburgh*, xxi, 1857) in George Boole, *Studies in Logic and Probability* (1952), pp. 364 f. Boole acknowledged a debt here to Cournot and de Morgan, though he unfortunately omitted to postulate the independence of p and q. This old analysis has undergone a good deal of adverse criticism, not always for the same reasons: cf. J. M. Keynes, *A Treatise on Probability* (1921), pp. 180 ff. But it is still occasionally adopted as if it were unexceptionable, e.g. by Rupert Schreiber, *Theorie des Beweiswertes für Beweismittel im Zivil Prozess* (1968), p. 41.

dently in whom they incriminate, this convergence implies that they either both incriminate correctly with a probability of pq, or both incriminate incorrectly with a probability of $(1-p)$ $(1-q)$. So it looks as though just the same formula should express the probability that, if facts A and B do converge, the person whom they incriminate is guilty.

The formula is obviously plausible enough when p and q are independent of one another and both greater than ·5, and nothing is at issue but the truth or falsehood of testimony, or the correctness or incorrectness of an incrimination. The formula then always assigns w a greater value than either p or q , and so it looks as though corroboration, or convergence, as the case may be, has taken place. But unfortunately the formula also tells us that if the mathematical probability of A's telling the truth (or of A's being correctly incriminatory) is less than ·5, and ditto for B, then the mathematical probability that they are both telling the truth (or incriminating correctly) is even less. So one common type of testimonial corroboration, or convergence of circumstantial evidence, is not elucidatable in this way. One witness, for example, may seem rather unreliable because of his shifty demeanour, and another may seem rather unreliable because of his bad eyesight. Yet perhaps, quite independently, they both testify to precisely the same set of propositions even though each could have told any number of other stories. In such a case Boole's formula produces a lower probability for their joint veracity, whereas normal juries would assign a higher one. Boole's formula makes the two testimonies undermine one another, whereas our problem is to elucidate why in fact they corroborate one another. Similarly, the fact that the accused had a motive for murdering the victim may be only mildly incriminatory, since perhaps four other people also are known to have had motives, and the fact that he had an opportunity to commit the murder may also be only mildly incriminatory, since perhaps four other people are also known to have had opportunities. But the combination of motive and opportunity in one person out of the nine is more seriously incriminatory, and Boole's formula cannot represent this. If the mathematical probability of the accused's guilt on the evidence of motive were ·2, and that of his guilt on the evidence of opportunity were also ·2, Boole's formula gives a mathematical probability of approximately ·06 for the accused's guilt on the combined and converging evidence.

It might accordingly be tempting to propose the following correction of Boole's analysis: 'One testimony about an issue cannot be independent of another if they are both true, since what makes them both true is the same underlying fact. But one testimony may be independent of another when they are both false, since so many different things can be said instead of the truth. Hence, if p is the mathematical probability that A's testimony is false and q is the mathematical probability that B's testimony is false, then pq is the probability that both testimonies are false, $1 - pq$ is the probability that either the testimonies differ in truth-value or they are both true, and $1 - p$ is the probability that A's testimony is true. Therefore the probability that, if A's and B's testimonies both have the same truth-value, they are both true must always be greater than the probability that A's testimony is true.'

However, the independence that is properly required here is a relation between probabilities, not between events. Now what precisely are the probabilities at stake? If we take them as the probability that A's particular testimony is false and the probability that B's particular testimony is false, they are certainly not independent, since, in view of A's and B's agreement, the falsehood of the one testimony certifies the falsehood of the other. If instead we follow Boole, then the probabilities at stake are the probability that any randomly selected testimony of A's is false and the probability that any randomly selected testimony of B's is false. These probabilities may well be mutually independent if A and B are unconnected with one another. But so too then may be the probabilities that any two randomly selected testimonies of A and B, respectively, are true. Hence the probability that any two randomly selected testimonies of A and B are both true will be less than the probability that any randomly selected testimony of A alone is true.

§34. *The need to take prior probabilities into account*

The immediate trouble with Boole's formula is not that it treats truth and falsehood symmetrically, but that it envisages a situation in which the domain of possibilities is a binary one. For Boole the choice has to be between a witness's speaking the truth and his speaking falsehood. Yet, if the evidence of one unreliable witness is understood to corroborate that of another in terms of mathematical probability, this corroboration seems to occur just because there are so many other stories that each could have told. The domain of possibilities is a multiple one. Similarly when two pieces of circumstantial evidence converge to incriminate the same man, the mathematical probability of his guilt seems to be increased just because there are so many other men that either piece of evidence might have incriminated.

But what this means is that any adequate representation of corroboration in terms of mathematical probability must take into account the prior probability that a certain story—which is one out of so many competing possibilities—is true, as well as the probability of its truth on the evidence or this or that witness's testimony. Where agreement is relatively improbable (because so many different things might be said), what is agreed is more probably true. Similarly any adequate representation of convergence in terms of mathematical probability must take into account the prior probability that, say, the accused—who is one out of so many possible criminals—committed the crime, as well as the probability of this on the facts before the court. Where the guilt of any arbitrarily selected man is relatively improbable, a particular man's possession of both motive and opportunity is more probably significant. Boole's formula could hardly be expected to give us what we want here because it fails to take account of a vital element in the situation. The underlying trouble with the formula is that it takes no account of the relevant prior probabilities.

Indeed these prior probabilities *must* be taken into account if each of two corroborating or converging premisses may itself give a less than ·5 probability to the desired conclusion. In such a case it cannot be the absolute level of the conclusion's probability on the premiss that makes the premiss eligible to corroborate, or converge towards, the conclusion, since by the usual complementational principle for negation the denial of the conclusion then has a greater absolute probability. So instead what is vital is that the premiss should raise the probability of the conclusion. However low $p_M[S,R]$ may be, if it is

greater than $p_M[S]$, $p_M[\text{not-S,R}]$ will be less than $p_M[\text{not-S}]$.
More recently another principle of convergence or corroboration has been suggested by Ekelöf. At first sight this new principle seems to avoid the difficulties that the Bernoulli–Boole principle encounters. It is at least concerned with the (dyadic, conditional) probability of a hypothesis on the conjunction of two evidential statements, rather than with the (monadic, unconditional) probability of the conjunction of two hypotheses.

Let us suppose that in an action concerning a highway accident there are two facts tending to prove that one of the cars concerned had a speed exceeding 60 m.p.h.; length of the braking marks, and a witness who observed the collision. We further make the unrealistic assumption that by examining a great number of similar situations it has been possible to ascertain that each of these evidentiary facts implies in 3 cases out of 4 a faithful description of reality, whereas in the fourth case it has no value whatever as evidence of the speed of the car. At least if the value of each evidentiary fact is independent of that of the other, the value [sc. of the combined evidence] must be greater than 3/4. But how much greater? The length of the braking marks proves that the speed exceeded 60 m.p.h. in 12 out of 16 similar cases; at the same time this is proved by the witness-statement in 3 out of 4 remaining cases. The convincing force of the combined evidentiary facts would thus be 15/16.[3]

According to Edman[4] the principle that Ekelöf has in mind is

$$w = p + q - (pq)$$

where p and q are the separate forces of two converging but independent evidential facts and w is their combined force. This principle has the advantage that, unlike the Bernoulli–Boole principle, it seems to work just as well where p or q, or both, are less than ·5. oS long as both p and q are less than 1 and greater than 0, the combined force w is greater than either p or q alone.

---

[3] Per Olof Ekelöf, 'Free Evaluation of Evidence', in *Scandinavian Studies in Law 1964*, ed. Folke Schmidt (1964), p. 58.
[4] Cf. Martin Edman, 'Adding Independent Pieces of Evidence', in J. Hintikka *et al.*, *Modality, Morality and Other Problems of Sense and Nonsense: Essays dedicated to Sören Halldén* (1973), pp. 180—8. Edman claims to report a proof by Halldén of Ekelöf's principle. But the significance of his symbols is neither defined clearly nor illustrated by any example, so that it is not possible to say exactly where the proof goes wrong.

But this is only a superficial merit. Ekelöf's principle does not escape the underlying difficulty about prior probabilities that wrecked the Bernoulli – Boole solution of the convergence problem. Consider a case where p is ·25 and is the mathematical probability that the criminal was a male on the evidence that he had long hair, and q is ·25 and is the probability that the criminal was a male on the evidence of testimony to that effect by a supporter of the women's liberation movement. By Ekelöf's principle these two evidential facts converge to give an increased value to the combined evidence of ·44. Yet if the mathematical probability that the criminal was a male, on each separate piece of evidence, is ·25, the probability that the criminal was a female is ·75, and so the combined evidence has a force of ·94 in favour of the conclusion that the criminal was a female. We thus have the paradox that, according to Ekelöf's principle, the two pieces of evidence converge in opposite directions at the same time. Or—to put the point in other words—the evidence of the witness, on Ekelöf's view, corroborates whichever conclusion you prefer to draw from the fact that the criminal had long hair; and evidence that purports to corroborate opposite conclusions does not in fact corroborate either. Moreover, if the force of the combined evidence is to be conceived of as a mathematical probability, we have a straightforward contradiction between the calculation that the probability of the criminal's being a male is ·44 and the calculation that the probability of the criminal's being a female is ·94, since presumably the probability of being a female is in fact the complement of the probability of being a male.

What has gone wrong here? Obviously the trouble is that some of the posterior probabilities involved—viz. those of ·25— are lower than the corresponding prior ones, if the prior probability of the criminal's being a male is, say, ·5. In fact therefore the evidence decreases the mathematical probability that the criminal is a male and increases the mathematical probability that the criminal is a female. We should normally infer in such a situation that the evidence converges in the direction in which it increases the probability. But to represent such an inference we need some other principle than Ekelöf's. We need a principle that takes some appropriate account of prior probabilities.

§35. *A demonstrably adequate analysis of corroboration and convergence in terms of mathematical probability*

If we do take account of the relevant prior probabilities, the axioms of the mathematical calculus guarantee that corroboration or convergence takes place under appropriate conditions. But in order to make this clear it is necessary to spell out the nature of those conditions rather more precisely than hitherto. We shall then be in a position to determine also whether or not a mathematicist analysis of corroboration and convergence is applicable to the occurrence of these patterns of reasoning in British and American lawcourts.[5]

Typically we have a situation in which, if S is the proposition to be established and R_1 and R_2 are the two premises, then both R_1 and R_2 raise the probability of S. That is to say, $p_M[S,R_1] > p_M[S]$ and $p_M[S,R_2] > p_M[S]$. Hence, if the prior probabilities were evenly distributed over a binary domain, like the truth or falsity of S, they would each be equal to $\cdot5$, and we should have each of the two posterior probabilities, $p_M[S,R_1]$ and $p_M[S,R_2]$, greater than $\cdot5$, as the proper working of Boole's formula requires. But with a larger domain for evenly distributed prior probabilities, each of the prior probabilities would be less than $\cdot5$, and the posterior probabilities could then be less than $\cdot5$.

There is also another important requirement. The premises, in a case of corroboration or convergence, are supposed to be unconnected with each other unless through the truth of the conclusion. This involves two independence conditions.

First, if one witness is to corroborate another—i.e. if what the two witnesses agree about is more probably true—one witness must not be more inclined to give false testimony when the other does. For example, there must be no conspiracy to deceive. But it will not matter if one witness is less inclined to give false testimony when the other does. The first independence condition is therefore that $p[R_2,R_1 \ \& \ \text{not-}S]$ must not be greater than $p[R_2, \text{not-}S]$, where we can take R_1 to be the fact

[5] For purposes of expository simplicity I confine my examples of convergence in the text to proof of agency in criminal cases. But the same pattern of reasoning is obviously applicable to other issues and to civil cases: e.g. a man's having a house built for himself in London, and joining an amateur dramatic society there, may converge to indicate an intention to reside there.

that the first witness testifies to S, and R_2 to be the fact that the second witness testifies to S. Similarly, if one piece of evidence is to converge with another, the former must not be particularly prone to indicate an incorrect conclusion when the latter does. For example, the fact that a man is scared of the police and the fact that he has recently committed a similar crime do not converge to raise the probability of his having committed the present crime, since even if he is innocent of the present crime his other misdeed is likely to make him scared of the police. But it will not matter if on the assumption of the man's innocence one fact lowers the probability of the other. For example, the two converging facts may be that the accused walks with the same limp as the murderer and that he was seen to jump over the victim's garden wall. In short, R_1 must not be favourably (though it may be unfavourably) relevant to R_2 on the assumption that S is false.

Secondly, if one witness is to corroborate another, the former's inclination to give true testimony must not be reduced, but may be increased, when the latter's testimony is true. For example, the former witness must not be more inclined to contradict the latter on those occasions when the latter's testimony happens to be true, since agreement of the two testimonies would then indicate their incorrectness. So $p[R_2, R_1 \& S]$ must not be less than $p[R_2, S]$. But the other witness's testimony may make the corroborating witness more inclined to testify to what he believes to be true. True testimony is genuinely corroborative whether it springs solely from the witness's belief about the fact at issue, or is influenced also by the other witness's truth. So $p[R_2, R_1 \& S]$ could be greater than $p[R_2, S]$. Similarly, if one piece of evidence is to converge with another, the former must not reduce, but may increase, the probability of the latter when the indicated conclusion is correct. For example, a man's consumption of both barbiturates and whisky before going to bed do not converge to raise the probability that he slept well, even though either fact indicates this on its own. For, if he really consumed both, the combination might well make him ill. And it is easy to see what blocks convergence here. If the man slept well, and therefore was not ill, he is less likely to have consumed both barbiturates and whisky beforehand. That is, $p[R_2, R_1 \& S]$ is less than $p[R_2, S]$ and so convergence fails.

But a man's having a motive for killing the victim and his apparent lack of grief at the victim's death could converge to raise the probability of his being the killer, even though either fact would increase the probability of the other. For, if he was the killer, his lack of grief would confirm the strength of his motive and his motive would confirm that his apparent lack of grief was not due to concealment of his feelings. That is, even if $p[R_2, R_1 \& S]$ exceeds $p[R_2, S]$ convergence may still occur. So the second independence condition is just that $p[R_2, R_1 \& S]$ must be greater than or equal to $p[R_2, S]$. R_1 must not be unfavourably (though it may be favourably) relevant to R_2 on the assumption that S is true.

Schematically, therefore, when all the premisses in a simple case of corroboration or convergence are made explicit and expressed in terms of mathematical probability, we have two premisses about probability-raising, viz. $p_M[S, R_1] > [p_M S]$ and $p_M[S, R_2] > p_M[S]$, and two premisses about independence, viz. $p_M[R_2, \text{not-}S] \geqslant p_M[R_2, R_1 \& \text{not-}S]$ and $p_M[R_2, S] \leqslant p_M[R_2, R_1 \& S]$. From these four premisses, plus the assumption that $R_1 \& R_2$ is not self-contradictory and therefore does not have zero probability, and the assumption that $p_M[S, R_1]$ has room for increase, it is demonstrable, with the help of nothing but standard mathematical principles, that $p_M[S, R_2 \& R_1] > p_M[S, R_1]$. In other words, however the mathematical probabilities in question are measured, the formal structure of the mathematical calculus of chance ensures that corroboration or convergence takes place under appropriate conditions.

Indeed, if this were not demonstrable, the title of the mathematical calculus of chance to be interpreted as a theory of probability would be very substantially weakened, since corroboration or convergence is so important a pattern in everyday human reasonings about probabilities. Hence the demonstration deserves to be set out in detail.[6]

---

[6] I do not know of any other such demonstration. Certainly the corroboration-convergence situation cannot be represented in terms of what H. Reichenbach, *The Direction of Time* (1956), pp. 157 ff., calls the principle of the common cause. A common cause, S, is indicated for two events R_1 and R_2, according to Reichenbach, when the following four conditions are satisfied:

$$p_M[R_1 \& R_2, S] = p_M[R_1, S] \times p_M[R_2, S]$$
$$p_M[R_1 \& R_2, \text{not-}S] = p_M[R_1, \text{not-}S] \times p_M[R_2, \text{not-}S]$$
$$p_M[R_1, S] > p_M[R_1, \text{not-}S]$$
$$p_M[R_2, S] > p_M[R_2, \text{not-}S]$$

The premisses are:

1. $p_M[S,R_1] > p_M[S]$
2. $p_M[S,R_2] > p_M[S]$
3. $p_M[R_2 \& R_1] > 0$
4. $p_M[R_2,S] \leqslant p_M[R_2,R_1 \& S]$
5. $p_M[R_2, -S] \geqslant p_M[R_2,R_1 \& -S]$
6. $1 > p_M[S,R_1]$

From these premisses it is required to prove that

$$p_M[S,R_2 \& R_1] > p_M[S,R_1]$$

It will be convenient to set out the proof in algebraic form. So let us put

7. $p_M[S] = s$
8. $p_M[R_1] = r_1$
9. $p_M[R_2] = r_2$
10. $p_M[R_1 \& S] = a$
11. $p_M[R_2 \& S] = b$
12. $p_M[R_2 \& R_1] = c$
13. $p_M[R_2 \& R_1 \& S] = d$

If these four conditions are satisfied, Reichenbach shows, it is possible to infer such conclusions as that

$$p_M[R_1,R_2] > p_M[R_1] \text{ and } p_M[S,R_1] > p_M[S] < p_M[S,R_2].$$

Now the trouble is that these conditions do not always cover the crucial factors in the corroboration-convergence situation. For example let R_1 be x's being one out of just five men who had the opportunity to commit the crime, while S is x's committing the crime. Then $p_M[S,R_1] > p_M[S]$. But suppose that it is extremely rare for just five men to have had the opportunity to commit this kind of crime, when it has been committed, and much commoner for such quintets of opportunity-possessors to be found when the crime has not actually been committed. (Perhaps prospective criminals tend to be put off by the thought that only four others could be suspected on ground of opportunity.) Then $p_M[R_1,S] < p_M[R_1,\text{not-}S]$. So here a typically incriminatory piece of circumstantial evidence, R_1, is known, but the common cause analysis, by being sensitive to some rather irrelevant facts of criminological statistics, fails to represent the incriminatoriness of the evidence.

Carnap's relevance measure r also (*Logical Foundations of Probability* (1951), pp. 360 ff.) is no use for representing the corroboration—convergence situation. A Carnapian relevance function $r(i,h,e)$ represents the change in the probability of h on e by the addition of new evidence i. One theorem (ibid., p. 370) for r is that $r(i \& j,h,e) = r(i,h,e) + r(j,h,e) - r(i \lor j,h,e)$. But suppose i states the fact that witness A incriminates C, and j states the fact that witness B incriminates C, while h states that C is guilty. Then $i \lor j$ may be at least as relevant to h on the other evidence e, as is i or j, on its own, and so according to Carnap's theorem, no testimonial corroboration would take place even when two witnesses spoke quite independently of one another, if the corroboration of i by j in relation to h is construed as an increase in the relevance of $i \& j$ to h over that of i alone.

The proof will use certain standard principles of the calculus of chance, viz. 14–19:

14. $p_M[A] = 1 - p_M[-A]$

15. $p_M[B,A] = 1 - p_M[-B,A]$

16. $p_M[A \& B] = p_M[A] \times p_M[B,A] = p_M[B \& A]$

17. $p_M[B,A] = \dfrac{p_M[A \& B]}{p_M[A]}$ where $p_M[A] > 0$

18. $p_M[B,A] = \dfrac{p_M[A,B] \times p[B]}{p_M[A]}$ where $p_M[A] > 0$

19. $p_M[A \& -B] = p_M[A] - p_M[A \& B]$

We first prove

20.	$p_M[R_1] > 0 < r_1$	3, 8, 16.
21.	$p_M[R_2] > 0 < r_2$	3, 9, 16.
22.	$p_M[S] > 0 < s$	1, 7, 18, 20.
23.	$1 - p_M[S] > 0$	6, 14, 15, 18, 20.
24.	$p_M[R_1 \& S] > 0 < a$	1, 10, 16, 20, 22.
25.	$p_M[R_1 \& -S] > 0$	6, 15, 16, 20.

We next obtain algebraic expressions, along with 7–13, for all the probabilities mentioned in the premisses 1–6, as follows (26–31):

26. $p_M[S,R_1] = \dfrac{a}{r_1}$ 17, 20; 8, 10.

27. $p_M[S,R_2] = \dfrac{b}{r^2}$ 17, 21; 9, 11.

28. $p_M[R_2,S] = \dfrac{b}{s}$ 18, 22, and 7, 9, 27, give us

$$p[R_2,S] = \dfrac{\dfrac{b}{r_2} \times r_2}{s}$$

29. $p_M[R_2,R_1 \& S] = \dfrac{d}{a}$ 17, 24; 10, 13.

30. $p_M[R_2, -S] = \dfrac{r_2 - b}{1 - s}$

    i. $p_M[R_2, -S] = \dfrac{p_M[R_2] - p_M[R_2 \& S]}{1 - p_M[S]}$ 17, 19; 14, 23.

    ii. $p_M[R_2, -S] = \dfrac{r_2 - b}{1 - s}$ i, 7, 9, 11.

31. $p_M R_2, R_1 \ \& \ -S] = \dfrac{c-d}{r_1-a}$

    i. $p_M[R_2, R_1 \ \& \ -S] = \dfrac{p_M[R_2 \ \& \ R_1 \ \& \ -S]}{p_M[R_1 \ \& \ -S]}$ 17, 25.

    ii. $p_M[R_2, R_1 \ \& \ -S] = \dfrac{c-d}{r_1-a}$ i, 19; 8, 10, 12, 13.

Premisses 2–5 are reformulated in algebraic terms (32–35):

32. $\dfrac{b}{r_2} > s$ 2, 7, 27.

33. $c > 0$ 3, 12.

34. $\dfrac{b}{s} \leqslant \dfrac{d}{a}$ 4, 28, 29.

35. $\dfrac{r_2-b}{1-s} \geqslant \dfrac{c-d}{r_1-a}$ 5, 30, 31.

The proof then proceeds algebraically as follows:

36. $\dfrac{\frac{b}{s}-b}{1-s} > \dfrac{r_2-b}{1-s}$ 7, 23; 22, 32.

37. $\dfrac{\frac{b}{s}-b}{1-s} = \dfrac{b-bs}{s(1-s)} = \dfrac{b}{s}$

38. $\dfrac{d}{a} > \dfrac{r_2-b}{1-s}$ 34, 36, 37.

39. $\dfrac{d}{a} > \dfrac{c-d}{r_1-a}$ 35, 38.

40. $\dfrac{d}{a} > \dfrac{\frac{c}{a}-\frac{d}{a}}{\frac{r_1}{a}-1}$ 24, 39.

41. $\left(\dfrac{r_1}{a}-1\right) \times \dfrac{d}{a} > \dfrac{c}{a}-\dfrac{d}{a}$ 40.

42. $\dfrac{r_1}{a} \times \dfrac{d}{a} > \dfrac{c}{a}$ 41.

43. $\dfrac{d}{c} > \dfrac{a}{r_1}$ 20, 33, 42.

Finally, we translate 44 back into the language of probability in order to obtain what we set out to prove:

44. $\dfrac{d}{c} = p_M[S,R_2 \ \& \ R_1]$ 12, 13; 17, 33.

45. $p_M[S,R_2 \ \& \ R_1] > p_M[S,R_1]$ 43; 26, 44.

In fact line 1 above is a rather stronger premiss than is needed since it is required only for the establishment of lines 22 and 24 and could thus be replaced by $p_M[S,R_1] > 0$. The point that emerges, in other words, is that additional evidence, if favourable (premiss 2), normally increases the mathematical probability of a conclusion irrespectively of whether the previous evidence was favourable or unfavourable, provided that the two pieces of evidence are compossible (premiss 3) and appropriately independent (premisses 4 and 5) and provided that the previous evidence did not wholly rule out either the truth or the falsity of the conclusion (premisses 1 and 6).[7] The extent of this increase in probability, and how exactly it is determined, need not concern us here.

§36. *The legal inadmissibility of positive prior probabilities*

Nevertheless, though a mathematicist analysis of probability thus permits corroboration or convergence, the conditions under which it permits this are never legitimately obtainable in criminal courts of the English and American legal systems, for at least two reasons.

The first reason arises from what was said in §20 about the difficulty of conceiving the balance of probability in complex civil cases in terms of the difference between prior and posterior probabilities. If the probative force of evidence is to be measured not by the probability of the conclusion on the evidence but by the difference between this and the conclusion's prior proba-

---

[7] This result may be construed as an analysis, not only of testimonial corroboration and of the convergence of circumstantial evidence, but also of theory-consilience where scientific confirmation is understood in terms of favourable relevance. Specifically, where R_1 and R_2 are two lower-level generalizations and S is a higher-level theory, premiss 4 represents the (co-tenability) requirement that R_1 should not undermine R_2 on the assumption that S is true and premiss 5 represents the (independence) requirement that R_1 gives no confirmation to R_2 which does not stem from the truth of S. However, though it can thus deal adequately with the problem of consilience, there are certain other difficulties with a favourable-relevance account of scientific confirmation: cf. p. 65, n. 1 above and § 49, p. 171 below.

bility, a plaintiff is enabled sometimes to establish his over-all case on the balance of probability even if he fails to establish one or more of his component points on its own, whereas this would clash with what the courts would actually decide about his case.

The second reason for not invoking prior probabilities is because in the Anglo-American system of procedure an accused person is to be judged only on the facts before the court. Hence he does not come into court with a certain positive prior probability of guilt. But in talking about mathematical probabilities within a given domain we cannot distinguish the non-existence of a positive probability for S from the existence of certainty for not-S, any more than in talking about a well-formed formula of a complete deductive system we can distinguish its non-provability from its disprovability (cf. §10, pp. 34 ff., above). So if there is no positive probability of S, where S is the proposition that the accused committed the crime in question we have to suppose that the prior mathematical probability of not-S is 1; and, if that is the standing of not-S, no amount of evidence is going to alter it. That is, if $p_M[S] = 0$, it must also be true[8] that $p_M[S,R_1] = 0$ and $p_M[S,R_2] = 0$. So neither of the two probability-raising premisses in §35—$p_M[S,R_1] > p_M[S]$ and $p_M[S,R_2] > p_M[S]$—will then be available. It follows that, though the general nature of corroboration and convergence admits perfectly well of analysis in terms of mathematical probabilities, as we have seen in the preceding sections

---

[8] This is due to principle 18 above, viz. $p_M[B,A] = \dfrac{p_M[A,B] \times p_M[B]}{p_M[A]}$, which

follows by simple arithmetic from $p_M[A,B] \times p_M[B] = p_M[A\&B] = p_M[B,A] \times p_M[A]$ where $p_M[A] > 0$. Note that this principle obstructs a mathematicist interpretation of judicial probability because it makes us take background probabilities into account. If we confine ourselves to dyadic probability functions the principle appears in the form

$$p_M[B,A \& C] = \frac{p_M[C,A \& B] \times p_M[B,A]}{p_M[C,A]}$$

(cf. H. Reichenbach, *The Theory of Probability*, tr. E. H. Hutten and M. Reichenbach (1949), p. 91). So that unless we have to assign a positive value to $p_M[S,R_0 \& R_1]$, where R_i states a fact before the court and R_0 states facts not before the court, it should not matter that $p_M[S,R_0]$ ought to be taken as equal to zero. The trouble with the mathematicist account is that it cannot avoid requiring us to assign a positive value to $p_M[S,R_0 \& R_i]$ in these situations, since it represents one of the conditions for corroboration or convergence as being that $p_M[S,R_0 \& R_i] > p_M[S,R_0]$.

§§32–5, such an analysis is inapplicable to occurrences of corroboration and convergence in the special circumstances of English and American criminal courts. These occurrences must be analysed instead in terms of some other concept of probability, which permits them to occur even when no positive prior probabilities of guilt are admissible.

A mathematicist might try to get round this difficulty by arguing that the prior probability could be determined here in relation to some other item of evidence, R_0, which is not one of the mutually corroborating or converging premises. This would often work all right for corroboration, since there would often be other facts before the court besides the testimonies that corroborate one another. But such a legitimately non-zero prior probability would not be available, even in regard to corroboration, where the only evidence was that of two mutually corroborating witnesses. Moreover, this escape-route would not be available at all in regard to convergence. In exploiting convergence to the full one needs to amalgamate every piece of evidence that raises the probability of the desired conclusion. There is no warrant for selecting one piece of evidence to determine a base-point, or prior probability, by reference to which the probability-raising capacities of other evidential items are to be judged. Nor are there any recognized procedures whereby prosecuting or defending lawyers may justify, or juries may appraise, the selection of one piece of evidence rather than another for this purpose. Yet the use of one such base-point rather than another would often affect the extent of corroboration or convergence that is achieved on the amalgamated posterior evidence.

Another tempting escape-route for the mathematicist is to claim—despite the obvious paradox—that the normal presumption of innocence is quite compatible with assuming a very small prior probability of guilt which is uniform for everyone. A crime has been committed, it may be said, so someone is guilty, and prior to considering the facts the jury must assign equal probabilities to everyone.

It is not much use rejoining that this makes the law-abiding citizen start off with the same handicap as the habitual criminal. Such a citizen always has the right to bring evidence of good character to counteract his handicap. Nevertheless this escape-route for the mathematicist encounters a serious difficulty. How is the prior probability of guilt to be calculated? Is it determined by the ratio of convictions achieved to prosecutions launched? Does the mere appearance of a man in the dock establish, say, a ·6 probability of guilt prior to consideration of any evidence? But not only would this be flatly incompatible with the standard presumption of innocence.[9] It would also mean in practice that the same evidence was being allowed to count twice against a man. First, by persuading the police to prosecute him (or a grand jury to indict him, or a magistrate to send him for trial) the evidence against the man would establish the prior probability of guilt at his trial; and then, secondly, the evidence would all count again in determining the posterior probability of guilt at the trial. A form of double jeopardy would be incorporated into every criminal trial!

So perhaps instead the prior probabilities should be distributed evenly over all those residing under the same legal system? Or would it be fairer instead to distribute them only over those already at the age of criminal responsibility? But is it so much more difficult to prove an inhabitant of the Isle of Man guilty, because there are so few of them? Are not some crimes committed by temporary visitors from other jurisdictions? Must a jury be expected to know the current statistics of tourism? Is it really easier to prove a man guilty in the height of the tourist season, because the population is swollen and prior probabilities are correspondingly reduced? Worse still, it sometimes turns out that there was no crime after all. Perhaps the accused pleads successfully that the alleged victim's death was actually due to natural causes or that the allegedly stolen property was actually his own. So the prior probability of, say, the accused's being the killer is even more difficult to compute satisfactorily. It must be compounded from one figure for the prior probability of there having been a killing at all, and another figure for the prior probability that, if there has been a crime, any one person is guilty of it. Whichever way one turns, absurdities abound.

[9] J. B. Thayer, *A Preliminary Treatise on Evidence at the Common Law* (1898), pp. 562 f., maintaining that the statistics of successful prosecutions are irrelevant, remarks that 'the presumption of innocence forbids the consideration of such probabilities . . . and says simply this: "It is the right of this man to be convicted upon legal evidence applicable specifically to him." '

Yet another tempting escape-route for the mathematicist is to claim that any analysis of juridical proof must allow some background knowledge, or assumptions, to the jury in terms of which they assess the probabilities of proposed conclusions on the facts put before them. 'Does not this common set of background beliefs or assumptions', it may be asked, 'provide a framework within which prior probabilities may be assessed quite legitimately? Is not your own imaginary case of evidence that the criminal is a male an example of this, since no one is seriously going to suggest that a juror is transgressing some procedural rule if he assigns an approximate value of ·5 to the prior probability of a criminal's being male?'

Well, let us suppose that the accused is a male and that a witness testifies to the crime's having been committed by a male. The trouble is that the incriminatory force of this testimony, if interpreted as raising the mathematical probability of the culprit's being a male, would depend not on the prior probability of any person's being male but rather on the prior probability that a person who committed a crime of that particular type is a male. And the latter is a statistically based probability about which juries are hardly entitled to form unevidenced beliefs or make unevidenced assumptions. Indeed, even the proportion of males to females in a human population varies from time to time and place to place. The only kind of prior mathematical probabilities that would not involve factual knowledge of one kind or another would be some arbitrarily assumed figures like the range-measures of Carnapian confirmation-theory. And, as we have already seen (§29, pp. 87 f.), the arbitrariness of such measures serves to exclude them from legitimate use in judicial contexts.

Of course, when all the evidence is in, including any appropriate expert evidence about statistical probabilities the trier of fact has to assess the probability of his conclusion on this evidence without requiring any further evidence to establish his criteria of assessment. Otherwise there would be an infinite regress. But whatever background knowledge or assumption he employs here has to be of a quite general kind and universally shared in his culture. It must not be tied to particular cases or be in any way recondite or controversial.

Perhaps it may be said that these problems about calculating the prior probability are unimportant. 'The over-all prior probability of guilt will in any case be so small', the mathematicist may say, 'that its exact size does not need to be computed. It can be as small as you like, as long as it is greater than zero.' But even such a very small prior probability assumes that an accused is not to be judged wholly on the facts before the court. Other facts, relating to the proportion of real crimes to supposed crimes and to the size of a certain population, are also to be taken into account. The mathematicist theory implies the legal paradox that there would be nothing inherently improper in a judge's instructing a jury to bear these criminological and demographic facts in mind, in estimating the degree of corroboration or convergence, even though *ex hypothesi* no evidence is given in court about them and they are neither formally admitted nor judicially noticed. But such an instruction would indeed be highly improper.[10] In an adversary system of procedure natural justice requires that both parties should have an equal opportunity to prove their points and cross-examine: *audi et alteram partem*. So every individual fact to be taken into account by the jury must lie openly and challengeably before the court: statistical claims must be supported by

[10] Cf. R. Cross, *Evidence*, 3rd edn. (1967), p. 129: 'The general rule is that all the facts in issue or relevant to the issue in a given case must be proved by evidence —testimony, admissible hearsay, documents, things and relevant facts. If, in a moment of forgetfulness, the plaintiff or prosecutor fails to prove an essential fact, his opponent may succeed on a submission that there is no case to answer although the evidence was readily available, for the court has a discretion when deciding whether to allow a witness to be recalled. There are two obvious exceptions to the general rule, for no evidence need be given of facts of which judicial notice is taken or of those that are formally admitted. It is often said that no proof is required of facts which are presumed, but the basic facts of every presumption have to be proved in the ordinary way and they are tendered as proof of the presumed fact. Evidence may also be said to be unnecessary in the case of an estoppel, but, so far as the party against whom it operates is concerned, estoppel is best regarded as an exclusionary rule rendering evidence of certain facts inadmissible.'

Note that legally regulated presumptions do not constitute the positive prior probabilities that a mathematicist analysis of corroboration or convergence requires. The commoner type of presumption (R. Cross, op. cit., pp. 109 f.) is a conclusion that a fact (e.g. death) exists which may, or must, be drawn if some basic fact (e.g. absence without news for seven years, etc.) is proved or admitted. Here the basic fact has still to be proved, and the law does not assign it a positive prior probability. The other kind of presumption is a conclusion which must be drawn until the contrary is proved. But there are relatively few such presumptions, and at least one of them (the presumption of an accused's innocence) seems rather to exclude than to sustain a positive prior probability of guilt.

the testimony of experts. The impropriety of taking greater-than-zero prior probabilities into account is rooted very deeply in the nature of the Anglo-American legal system. So, if any value at all is to be properly assigned to the prior mathematical probability of an accused's guilt, that value is zero. But, since such a valuation of the prior probability renders impossible a greater-than-zero value for the mathematical probability of the accused's guilt on the evidence it is clear that the probability in terms of which this guilt is properly judged cannot conform to the principles of the mathematical calculus.

Moreover, quite apart from its incompatiblity with the Anglo-American legal tradition the notion of infinitesimally small, but non-zero, prior probabilities creates two other rather serious difficulties for the rational analysis of judicial proof.

The first difficulty is that evidence in favour of an accused person has to be very strong indeed if it is to reduce an infinitesimally small prior probability of guilt. In fact evidence that is to be favourably relevant—any piece of evidence of the kind needed by the defence for corroboration or convergence—must then be only infinitesimally short of proving innocence. So the doctrine of infinitesimal priors makes the task of defending accused persons unconscionably tough.

The second difficulty arises when we consider some of the propositions that may need to be proved as halfway stages on the way to proving an accused person's innocence. For example, suppose a man and a woman are jointly accused of a murder and each tries to put the blame on the other. Then the defence of each may set out to prove that the fatal blow was actually struck by a person of the opposite sex. But how can a jury, in assessing these proofs, assign an infinitesimally small prior probability not only to the proposition that the assailant was in fact a male but also to the proposition that the assailant was in fact a female? Obviously if prior probabilities are invoked at all here, they must instead be assigned realistic values that are complementary to one another; and that plunges the mathematicist back into all the other difficulties about there being no statistical evidence before the court to determine these values.

§37. *The method of contraposition*

Finally, there is a not uninteresting way to try and sidestep all these problems about prior probability. It may be held that the judicial probability of the accused's being the killer, on a certain premiss, is equivalent to the mathematical improbability of the premiss's being true on the assumption of the accused's not being the killer. The multiplicative conjunction principle for mathematical probability would then seem to generate corroboration and convergence quite straightforwardly. Because of that principle, for example, it might turn out to be substantially more *mathematically* improbable that the accused had both motive and opportunity on the assumption that he was not the killer, than that he had either of these alone on that assumption. Correspondingly the *judicial* probability of the accused's being the killer might be inferred to be higher on the convergent evidence of motive and opportunity than on the evidence of either alone. Moreover the conjunction principle for mathematical probability would be particularly likely to promote this desirable consequence if, in the circumstances of the case, motive and opportunity were relatively independent of one another. Schematically we should have $p_M[\text{not}(R_1 \& R_2), \text{not-}S] > p_M[\text{not-}R_1, \text{not-}S]$ because $p_M[R_1, \text{not-}S] > p_M[R_1 \& R_2, \text{not-}S]$ and therefore $1 - p_M[R_1 \& R_2, \text{not-}S] > 1 - p_M[R_1, \text{not-}S]$.

This moves seems at least to have the virtue of capturing an ordinary juror's normal repugnance to accepting an excessive level of coincidence in the alleged course of events. However, to gain that advantage you have to suppose that when judges or jurors talk about the probability of a certain conclusion S on a certain premiss R, they are not talking about $p_M[S,R]$, since $p_M[S,R]$ is not necessarily equivalent to $p_M[\text{not-}R, \text{not-}S]$.[11] So the move under discussion is not strictly compatible with the mathematicist approach. It allows that the judicial probability of S on R may after all not be equivalent to the mathematical probability of S on R.

There is also a certain contradictoriness involved in proposing this interpretation. On the one hand, since the mathe-

---

[11] A proof that this equivalence holds only under rather special conditions is given in *TIOI* p. 113.

matical probability of S on R is allowed to differ from the judicial probability of S on R, the judicial concept of probability is assumed to differ from the mathematical one. The judicial probability of S on R is not the same as the mathematical probability of S on R because it is the mathematical probability of not-R on not-S. On the other hand an appeal seems to be made to an intuitively plausible equivalence between the probability of S on R and the probability of not-R on not-S, as if only one concept of probability were being employed and no pun or equivocation was occurring.

In any case the proposed analysis generates an undesirable result in certain situations just because it has no room to take account of prior probabilities. Consider a situation where both R_1 and R_2 are intrinsically irrelevant to S, i.e. where R_1 and R_2 are about matters unconnected with S and so $p_M[S,R_1] = p_M[S] = p_M[S,R_2]$. In such a situation, if R_1 and R_2 are independent of one another, we shall still have $p_M[\text{not}(R_1 \& R_2), \text{not-S}] > p_M[\text{not-}R_1, \text{not-S}]$. So apparently corroboration or convergence can occur even when the testimony or evidence is intrinsically irrelevant!

II

The Case against a Mathematicist
Account of Judicial Probability

Summary

§38. Each of the six above anomalies in a mathematicist analysis of juridical proof might be tolerable on its own. But together they constitute a reason for preferring an analysis of juridical proof that is not confronted by such anomalies—if an analysis of this kind is available. §39. I do not dispute that a mathematicist analysis may fit the actual procedures illegitimately employed by some lawyers or triers of fact, or that it might fit the correct procedures in a suitably altered legal system. But at present the laymen who serve on juries must be presumed capable of operating with a different concept of probability than the mathematical one.

§38. *The impact of accumulated anomalies*

Various axiomatizations exist for the mathematical calculus of chance. Kolmogorov, Reichenbach, Popper, etc. have all supplied postulate-sets for the calculus, with varying degrees of abstractness.[1] But we need not concern ourselves in this context with any minor differences that may exist between those various systematizations. The paradoxes described above derive from principles—the multiplicative principle for conjunction, the complementational principle for negation, etc.—that are common to all normal formulations of the Pascalian calculus. There are certainly at least six anomalies involved in any attempt to construe Anglo-American standards of juridical proof in terms of mathematical probabilities.

What are these anomalies? No overall evaluation of outcome can be given in complex civil cases without the risk of apparent

---

[1] H. Reichenbach, 'Axiomatik der Warscheinlichkeitsrechnung', *Mathematische Zeitschrift*, 34 (1932), 568 ff.; A. Kolmogorov, 'Grundbegriffe der Warscheinlichkeitsrechnung', *Ergebnisse der Mathematik* 2. 3 (1933); and K. R. Popper *The Logic of Scientific Discovery* (1959), pp. 326 ff. Cf. also R. T. Cox, *The Algebra of Probable Inference* (1961), and p. 8, n. 3 above.

injustice (Ch. 5). Proof by inference upon inference has to be assumed subject to a mysteriously unmotivated legal constraint (Ch. 6). Another special rule, of inadmissibility, has to be postulated in relation to statistical evidence in order to avoid difficulties about complementation (Ch. 7). The normal criteria for thinking it reasonable to doubt the guilt of an accused have to be ignored (Ch. 8). None of the normal ways of evaluating mathematical probabilities seem to be applicable to evaluating the strength with which factual conclusions are proved in the courts (Ch. 9). And the logical structure of corroboration and convergence cannot be adequately elucidated without assuming some positive prior probability for any proposition to be proved thereby, which is contrary to procedural norms (Ch. 10).

One of these anomalies on its own might be tolerable, and would scarcely justify the claim that judicial probability does not admit of a mathematicist analysis. Even six anomalies might be tolerable if they were all closely connected with one another or arose only in some highly artificial context. But the accumulation of at least six widely different paradoxes is much more serious, especially when the concept of probability involved is supposed to be used by jurymen in their everyday lives as well as in the lawcourts. In philosophy as in science economy and simplicity of theoretical apparatus can be bought at too high a price in *ad hoc* assumptions and other evasive stratagems. If a differently structured concept of probability allows a smooth and paradox-free interpretation of the standards of juridical proof, that other concept deserves to be enthroned —as a coadjutor, not a rival—alongside the various concepts of probability that conform to the mathematical calculus of chance.

I am not putting forward the absurd claim, that there is something intrinsically wrong with any criteria of probability that ensure conformity to the mathematical calculus. I do not doubt that such criteria have very many important fields of employment. But there is at least one type of use for which their unsuitability is demonstrable. The special constraints that operate on juridical proof in Anglo-American lawcourts obstruct the correct use there, in any form, of a mathematicist criterion of probability, wherever the probability of a proof's conclusion on its premisses is at issue. Moreover the concept of probability that is correctly used there is supposed[2] to be the same as that which jurors and other laymen use in everyday life. So there must be quite a lot of everyday discourse about probability, outside the lawcourts, to which the mathematicist analysis is also inapplicable.

§39. *The existing standards of assessment*

When I argue that the mathematicist anslysis does not fit judicial proof in Anglo-American courts, I am contending only that it does not fit the assessment of judicial proof according to existing legal standards and procedures. I am not denying that it might fit one or both of two other types of assessment.

First, it might fit the actual procedures illegitimately employed by some lawyers or triers of fact to assess juridical proofs. Those who are prepared to disregard the normative constraints that I have been discussing could confine themselves to using a mathematical concept of probability in relation to judicial proof. Or at any rate they could do this if they could find a method of assessing mathematical probabilities that was practicable in the judicial context. But, even if there were some such people, their existence would not count against my thesis, since I am offering an account of the *de jure*, not the *de facto*, situation. Nor can there be very many such people, unless the present *de jure* situation is founded upon an erroneous factual assumption. If lay jurors are in fact, as the system assumes, able to employ their everyday concept of probability in *de jure* appropriate assessments of judicial proof, there can hardly be very many who take the trouble to employ a different concept that is *de jure* inappropriate.

Secondly, the mathematicist account could be made true, after a certain date, by changing the law. All the above-mentioned anomalies could then be avoided by altering the data to fit the theory instead of by altering the theory to fit the

[2] I ignore the small range of facts (e.g. absence without communication for seven years) to which English or American law attaches an artificial probative value in certain types of case. The need for members of an English or American jury to be specially directed on such a point, when it arises, serves to highlight their normal right and duty to rely on their own criteria of probability. They are not supposed normally to use a specifically legal abacus of proof, even though such an abacus has sometimes existed in other legal systems. Compare, for example, the old arithmetic of *plena* and *semi-plena probatio* in pre-Napoleonic French law (cf. J. Ph. Lévy, *La Hiérarchie des preuves dans le droit savant du moyen-age*, 1939).

data. Over-all evaluations of outcome could be declared otiose. Inference upon inference could be made easier. Statistical evidence could be ruled inadmissible in regard to individual acts. An appropriate measure could be ordained for mathematical probability and for the exclusion of reasonable doubt. And some assignment of positive values to prior probabilities could be legitimized by statute. I concede that such changes would be possible.[3] My point is just that they would be changes, and that the mathematicist account does not fit existing legal standards and procedures. Accordingly most of Parts III and IV is taken up with developing an account of a concept of probability that does fit those standards and procedures, and with exploring some other applications of this concept.

Perhaps, however, it will be argued against me that, so far as the existing standard of judicial proof in civil cases is not based on a mathematical concept of probability it is vitiated by intellectual error. The argument might run as follows: 'Presumably the aim of legal procedure in civil case is to ensure that a correct decision is made more often than not, or even perhaps substantially more often than not. In the long run this is bound to happen if and only if judgement is always awarded on the balance of mathematical probability. So where judgement is not awarded in accordance with that standard an injustice takes place. For example, the suit against the gate-crasher at the rodeo (cf. §24 above) ought to be successful; and in a complex case the multiplicative principle for conjunction does indeed place serious constraints on the number of component issues in the outcome or on the level of probability at which proof is required (cf. §17). The legal practices to which you appeal are therefore founded on an intellectual error about the proper way to maximize the frequency of correct decisions. You can hardly establish intellectual respectability for a non-mathematical concept of probability by appealing to such ill-founded practices.'

This objection shows a certain contempt for the natural intelligence of lawyers. Their logico-mathematical intuitions must be surprisingly widely fallacious if the objection is correct. Nor is it at all clear why their pattern of error should be so

[3] They might nevertheless be socially and politically undesirable, as argued by L. H. Tribe, 'Trial by Mathematics: Precision and Ritual in the Legal Process', 84 *Harvard L.R.* 1329–93 (1971).

self-consistent and uniform. Of course, the objection would certainly be successful for any legal system that aimed solely to discover the truth more often than not. Inquisitorial objectives would be well served by requiring proof on the balance of mathematical probability. But the advancement of truth in the long run is not necessarily the same thing as the dispensation of justice in each individual case. It bears hard on an individual like the non-gate-crasher at the rodeo if he has to lose his own particular suit in order to maintain a stochastic probability of success for the system as a whole. So if the system exists for the benefit of individual citizens, and not vice versa, the objector's argument fails. Each individual has a right to his day in court, when his interests are touched by the possibility of litigation; and the task of the court in an adversary, as distinct from an inquisitorial, system is to deal out justice between the contending parties in each suit that comes before it. If the parties disagree solely about the facts (and not about the law), judgement has to be awarded to the party that has the better case on the facts before the court. Of course, the law against perjury helps to promote the discovery of the truth. Of course, the court itself would argue only from premises that it believes to be true, and would find reason to reject a suggested premiss or conclusion that it believed to be false. However, the discovery of the truth may be obstructed not only by the production of false evidence but also by the non-production of true evidence. A conclusion that is reasonably probable on the balance of available evidence may in fact—unknown to the court—be false because too little evidence is available. The acceptance of such a possibility is implicit in an adversary, as distinct from an inquisitorial, system of justice. If the overriding aim of the court were to discover the full truth about the relevant past, the trier of fact would need to have (in addition to the powers, that already exist in certain circumstances, to compel disclosure of documents, require interrogatories to be answered on oath, etc.) a general power to summon his own witnesses and perhaps even the right to use information of his own that is not before the court. And this is just what an adversary, as distinct from an inquisitorial, system of justice does not allow, because it sees the trier of fact as an arbiter in a contest of proof-strength rather than as a research worker in the science of the past.

PART III

THE ELEMENTS OF
INDUCTIVE PROBABILITY

12

The Foundations of Inductive Logic

Summary

§40. In order to provide a rational reconstruction for the concept of inductive probability, it is necessary first to provide one for the concept of inductive support. §41. But a theory of inductive support should not aim to axiomatize its author's intuitions. Its primary data are the judgements of reputable scientists, not the intuitive deliverances of philosophers.

§40. *Inductive probability and inductive support*

Part II of this book (§§ 14–39) has been taken up with arguing that various anomalies and paradoxes arise if one interprets Anglo-American standards of judicial proof in terms of mathematical probability. Part III will be devoted to delineating another type of probability, which has a demonstrably different logical structure from that of mathematical probability. Part IV will aim to marry the two arguments together by showing that with this non-Pascalian type of probability not only can we handle all the issues that arise in judicial proof without generating any anomalies or paradoxes but we can also resolve some familiar problems that arise elsewhere.

The non-Pascalian type of probability that is now to be delineated may conveniently be termed 'inductive probability'. And it may be helpful to begin by explaining why the term 'inductive' is appropriate.

It has already been shown (§§ 1-11) that there are good reasons for accepting a general analysis of probability as degree of inferential soundness. To grade the probability of B on A is to talk qualitatively, comparatively, ordinally, or quantitatively about the degree of inferential soundness of a proof-rule that would entitle one to infer B immediately from A. But there are different types of proof-rule and correspondingly different criteria of inferential soundness. Let us consider here just those rules of inference that may be read off from generalized conditionals about the world of events. For example, the rule

(1)   From the presence of dark clouds infer imminent rain

may be read off from the generalized conditional

(2)   Any event, if an event of dark clouds' being present, is an event where rain is imminent.

Such a rule's degree of inferential soundness will obviously depend on the reliability of the corresponding generalized conditional statement. How then is the reliability of statements like (2) to be assessed? Traditionally this is the province of inductive logic, or the theory of inductive support, and I see no reason to change the terminology. So to assess the inferential soundness of a rule like (1) we must gauge how much inductive support there is for the corresponding generalization like (2).[1] The inductive probability of imminent rain, on the evidence that dark clouds are present, is equal to the grade of inductive support that appropriate observations may detect for the generalization (2).

---

[1] Some rules of inference, in some deductive systems, do not have provable conditionalizations in those (or similar) systems: cf. §9, p. 31, above. But this demonstrable truth of metamathematics does not affect the present issue at all. It should not deter anyone from attempting to gauge inductive support in any such case. For, first, it is trivially easy to write out a linguistic prescription for transforming any expression of a material rule of inference like (1) into a corresponding generalisation like (2); secondly, for any category of such generalizations about matters of fact it is possible to formulate an indefinite number of empirically corrigible hypotheses about the appropriate inductive support-function, as in §§42–9 below; and thirdly, it is not possible to prove that some such generalization belongs to no category for which there is an appropriate support-function, since to have the proof would be tantamount to having conclusive empirical evidence available that some type of event is wholly and permanently isolated from causal interaction with any other type of event in the universe—whereas there is no reason whatever even to conjecture this.

Note therefore at the outset that in discussing inductive probability one may need to refer to two quite different categories of evidence. There is the evidence on the assumption of which the probability is predicated, like the dark clouds that probabilify imminent rain, and the other evidence—whether merely observed or experimentally produced—that supports the corresponding generalization, like whatever meteorological data support (2). So, in order to give an adequate account of inductive probability, it will be necessary first to pay some attention to certain questions about inductive support. What is the normal method of assessing inductive support? What, consequently is the logical structure of statements that grade it? And can it be shown that this structure is altogether un-analysable in terms of mathematical probability? When satisfactory answers to these questions have been established, it will be possible to draw out their implications for the notion of inductive probability. That is to say, the logical structure of statements about inductive probability can then be analysed, though the question whether such statements are commonly made, or have any important roles in our intellectual culture, will be postponed for separate consideration (in Part IV).

§41. *On what foundations should a theory of inductive support be based?*

Questions about the nature of inductive support are not easily answered. The issues are highly controversial and there is not even any general agreement about the premises on which a resolution of the issues should be founded.

According to one popular type of approach a system of inductive logic is acceptable only if it axiomatizes the relevant intuitions of many or all philosophers interested in the subject, or conforms to logically specific criteria of adequacy that they find intuitively appropriate. For example, Carnap came to insist on the *a priori*, intuitive nature of the grounds for accepting a particular set of axioms in confirmation theory. He wrote:[2] 'The reasons to be given for accepting any axiom of inductive logic . . . are based upon our intuitive judgements concerning inductive validity.' A philosopher who has adopted this point of view comes quite naturally to concentrate his research on

---

[2] R. Carnap, 'Replies and Systematic Expositions', in P. A. Schilpp (ed.), *The Philosophy of Rudolf Carnap* (1963), p. 978.

the refinement of mathematical techniques for formulating such intuitive ideas and exploring their deductive liaisons. The question whether the ideas have ever played any real part in the history of science is totally neglected.[3] This quasi-Cartesian methodology now emerges curiously often in the work of philosophers who might otherwise be supposed to regard themselves as continuing the work of the Vienna Circle.[4] As their over-all objective many of them now apparently seek the systematization of their own intuitions rather than the rational reconstruction of the language of science. Moreover this widespread retreat from empiricist aims and principles seems to have been carried out with surprising *insouciance*. Those who have engaged in it have made no attempt to provide an epistemological foundation or rationale, as Cartesians and Kantians once did, for accepting the validity of the type of intuitions with which they are primarily concerned.

[3] No trace of any interest in the historical issue is to be found in the posthumously published text of the volume that Carnap planned as a continuation of his *Logical Foundations of Probability*, viz. R. Carnap and R. C. Jeffrey (eds.). *Studies in Inductive Logic and Probability*, vol. i, (1971). Yet in his earlier work Carnap was certainly ready to invoke examples from the history of science: e.g. in *The Logical Syntax of Language*, tr. A. Smeaton (1937), p. 319, when discussing the syntax of the language of physics, Carnap cited the Maxwell equations' introduction of the electric-field symbol as a primitive symbol.

[4] Examples from the work of Carnap, J. G. Kemeny, I. Scheffler, H. E. Kyburg, I. Levi, and J. Hintikka are discussed in detail, and the appeal to intuition compared with that to common sense or to ordinary language, in L. Jonathan Cohen 'How Empirical is Contemporary Logical Empiricism?' *Philosophia*, 5 (1975), 299 ff., reprinted in *Language in Focus: Foundations, Methods and Systems*, ed. A. Kasher (1976), pp. 359 ff. A rather similar methodology is employed by R. M. Chisholm, *Theory of Knowledge* (1966), and 'On the Nature of Empirical Evidence', in *Experience and Theory*, ed. L. Foster and J. W. Swanson (1970), pp. 103 ff. Chisholm proposes definitions and axioms for such notions as '*e* inductively confers evidence upon *h*', but makes no attempt to establish that these principles apply to actual patterns of reasoning in specific areas of human activity such as experimental science or judicial procedure. He is content instead with completely general claims about what any human being would think in epistemically problematic situations; and, because these global claims lack the constraints that specificity might afford, they are neither obviously true nor obviously false but tend to generate a rambling and rather sterile type of controversy. R. Ackerman, 'Some Problems of Inductive Logic' and 'Rejoinder to Skyrms and Salmon', in *Philosophical Logic*, ed. J. W. Davis, D. J. Hockney, and W. K. Wilson (1969), pp. 135–51 and 164–71, respectively, assumes not only that the basic data for inductive logic are intuitive, but also that these intuitions admit of no general methodology or rationalization. Such a nihilistic assumption surrenders the title of philosophy to propose rational reconstructions, without even waiting to see the outcome of disputes about the success of such reconstructions. It blocks the path of inquiry.

Indeed, there is a curious double contrast here between many of our latter-day practitioners of logical analysis, on the one side, and at least one Kantian, on the other—William Whewell. For though Whewell believed that the fundamental concepts of natural science did not derive from human sensations, he was a thoroughgoing empiricist in regard to the methodology of research in the philosophy of science. His theory of induction was based on a vast amount of research in the history of science and supported by a rich variety of historical examples.

In any case intuitive assent is a peculiarly unsatisfactory criterion of truth in the philosophy of science, for at least four reasons.

First, there is the obvious point that the appeal to intuition leaves no interpersonally neutral means of resolving controversy. At critical nodes it reduces philosophy of science to philosophers' intellectual autobiographies. If a thing has been genuinely observed by one person in a certain situation, it could also have been observed, *ceteris paribus*, by any other person there. But if it has been intuited by one philosopher it may very well not be intuited by another.

Secondly, to invoke intuition as an oracle of truth obscures the legitimate role of intuition as an impetus to inquiry. A natural scientist might welcome intuitive hunches as hypotheses to be investigated and tested. But he would not regard them as self-authenticating—as constituting evidence of their own validity. Why then should a philosopher of science so regard them?

Thirdly, some inductive logicians might claim that, when invoking their intuitions, they are merely reporting how they would think of inductive support if they themselves were experimental scientists. But if we are to pay any regard to intuitions here, it must surely be to the reported intuitions of professional experimentalists, not to those of inductive logicians practising armchair science. Disinterested arbitration, if available, is always worth greater respect than the verdicts of those who set up as judges in their own cause.

Fourthly, if you believe that a few intuitions can settle once and for all the fundamental criteria of support-assessment in natural science, you conceive the problem in altogether too static and homogeneous a fashion. Not surprisingly Carnap's intuitionism has helped to bring on, as a natural reaction, the current wave of anti-logicism in the philosophy of science. It is easy enough for a historian of science to show that different disciplines, and different periods in the development of a single discipline, have differed substantially from one another in regard to their methods of assessing evidential support for scientific hypotheses.[5] But this is not, as it has sometimes been claimed to be,[6] a reason for saying that inductive logic is irrelevant to science. It is rather a reason for saying that an inductive logic which is to be relevant to science must not be founded on philosophers' intuitions. Such a logic must instead show itself sensitive to empirical fact at just those nodes at which novelty or variety of fact has tended to change scientists' views about their own criteria of support-assessment.

Accordingly I shall not invoke intuition in defence of any controversial principle in the theory of inductive support to be developed here. Nor shall I count it as an objection to any such principle that some philosophers find it counter-intuitive. If they do find it counter-intuitive, and it is nevertheless other-wise defensible, then so much the worse for their intuitions. Nor shall I invoke large numbers of historical examples in order to argue that all scientific reasoning—in all disciplines and at all times—fits the framework I shall sketch. That is not my thesis. The thesis is rather that *some* important forms of reasoning, in *some* substantial disciplines, on *some* reputable occasions of research, fit the framework to be sketched. This will be a sufficient foundation for my theory of inductive probability, since I make no claims for its uniqueness as a theory of probability nor even as a theory of non-Pascalian, or non-mathematical, probability. All I need to establish is one reputable mode of inductive support-grading that generates a suitable concept of probability—viz. a concept that is not open to the difficulties confronting mathematical probability in contexts like those already discussed (§§ 14–39).

A satisfactory method of argument to establish an account of inductive support would therefore be to describe in general terms, with the help of real or imaginary examples, a method of reasoning that would be familiar to anyone *au fait* with

---

[5] Cf., e.g., S. Toulmin, *Human Understanding*, vol. i, (1972), pp. 156 f.
[6] Ibid., pp. 478 ff.

the normal practices of experimental science and then to show that this account of inductive support-assessment is implicit therein. I have used such a method of argument elsewhere[7] to develop an account of inductive support at length and in detail. I have argued there also that this account of inductive support derives considerable corroboration from its width of application. It applies to linguistic theory, to moral reasoning, to legal arguments from judicial precedent and to certain forms of mathematical reasoning,[8] for instance, just as well as to experimental science. Moreover, the same underlying structure is evident when we grade how much qualification a hypothesis needs in order to fit the evidence, as when we grade how much support its unqualified version has. This underlying structure also has claims to rationality that may be justified by systematic analogies with the structure of logical truth. A statement asserting the existence of such-or-such a grade of inductive support for 'If R, then S', and thus giving a relatively weak licence for inferring S from R, turns out to have a logical syntax precisely analogous to that of a statement which ascribes logical truth to 'If R, then S' and thus guarantees the deducibility or demonstrability of S from R.[9]

Rather than repeat any of those detailed arguments here it will be more profitable to reinforce them by adopting an even more direct appeal to empirical fact. I shall begin here by analysing one actual, historical example of experimental reasoning in order to show that in that case too the same pattern of inductive support-assessment was present. After all, as already remarked, my theory requires only that *some* reputable use has been made of the pattern in question, not that *all* scientific generalization has invoked it.

Conversely, if anyone wishes to refute this theory, it is no use for him to quote the intuitive deliverances of his inner light. Instead he must show that the cited facts are better interpreted or explained by another theory. Or, if he wishes instead just

---

[7] *TIOI*, §§5–13.
[8] In *TIOI*, p. 181, I cited G. Polya's 1954 work on inductive reasoning in mathematics. Compare also J. M. Keynes, *A Treatise on Probability* (1921), pp. 243 f.: cf. B. Russell, 'Logical Atomism', in *Contemporary British Philosophy*, First Series, ed. J. H. Muirhead (1924), p. 362, and, for Leibniz's views, cf. L. Couturat, *La Logique de Leibniz* (1901), p. 262 ff.
[9] *TIOI*, §§16–20.

to restrict the present theory's range of application, he must himself cite evidence of areas of responsible inquiry in which support for generalized conditionals is graded in some patently different way and conforms to radically different principles. Theories in the philosophy of science, like theories in science itself, have to face up to the challenge of appropriately accredited experience within their appointed domains.

On the other hand, though inductive logic and the philosophy of scientific reasoning share some common problems, neither is just a part of the other. Just as other forms of reasoning besides those of experimental science may exhibit an inductive structure, so too other considerations besides inductive support may enter into deliberations about the acceptance, rejection, or evaluation of a scientific hypothesis. I am far from wishing to claim that an inductivist analysis tells the whole story even in the case of the experimental investigations now to be examined.

13

The Grading of Inductive Support

Summary

§42. An analysis of von Frisch's reasoning about bees' colour-discrimination shows that support builds up for a hypothesis when it fails to be falsified in more and more complexly structured tests—where complexity of structure depends on the number of relevant variables manipulated in the test. §43. The results of any such test are essentially replicable, which has important consequences for detachment and the treatment of 'anomalous' test-results. §44. The series of relevant variables for testing a generalization has to be defined in a way that will ensure each variable's being non-exhaustive, and independent of every other variable, and it is also necessary to ensure a suitable ordering for the series as a whole. §45. There is a certain tension between the ontological and epistemological points of view in the philosophy of inductive support, since the former is concerned solely with the truth-conditions for support-gradings while the latter is concerned with the empirical methods by which we may establish systems of assessment for support-grades. §46. The method of relevant variables subsumes all that is sound in J. S. Mill's five canons of inductive reasoning. §47. The method of relevant variables can also be shown to apply to the grading of support for scientific theories that have considerable explanatory generality. §48. Whewell's consilience criterion, and Lakatos's distinction between progressive and degenerating problem-shifts, may be construed as representing applications of the method of relevant variables to the problem of how to determine inductive support for scientific theories. §49. Finally, the method of relevant variables copes particularly satisfactorily with the existence of anomalies that falsify accepted scientific theories, since it allows E to give some support to H in certain cases even if E contradicts H.

§42. *An example of inductive support-assessment in entomology*

Let us examine a justly famous paradigm of experimental reasoning about animals—Karl von Frisch's work on bees. Von

Frisch reported[1] an extensive series of investigations into the behavioural abilities of bees. The six main hypotheses with which he was concerned may be stated, roughly, as follows. Bees discriminate between different colours. Bees discriminate between different shapes. Bees discriminate between different odours. Bees' olfactory organs are situated in their antennae. Bees discriminate between different tastes. And bees communicate to their co-workers the existence and odour of a food-source together with its distance and direction from the hive.[2] Von Frisch's method of reasoning in each case was to eliminate alternative, antecedently not unlikely, explanations of the phenomena which his experiments (and those of others) revealed.

For example,[3] bees return again and again to a transparent source of food (sugar-water) on a piece of blue cardboard. Perhaps, however, they are colour-blind and identify their feeding-place by its shade of greyness? This explanation is eliminated by surrounding the blue card with grey cards of all shades from white to black, which carry food-containers but no food: the bees still return to the blue card. Perhaps the bees recognize the relative location of the blue card? This explanation is eliminated by rearranging the cards in many different ways. Perhaps the bees recognize the smell of the blue card? But the result is just the same if the card is covered with a plate of glass. Perhaps bees recognize no other colour than blue? But when the same experiments are repeated with other colours it turns out that they discriminate between four different colours: yellow, blue-green, blue, and ultra-violet. Perhaps bees' colour-discriminations are specially connected with their feeding activity? But a similar series of experiments with homing bees show that they can recognize their hives by the colour of the outside.

What is going on here is that the circumstances of the experiment are being varied in certain systematic ways in order to ascertain the effect of these variations on the outcome of the experiment. So far as the outcome continues to accord

---

[1] In lectures published as *Bees, Their Vision, Chemical Senses and Language* (1950), hereafter cited as *Bees*.

[2] *Bees*, pp. 4 ff., 21 ff., 25 ff., 29 ff., 38 f., and 53 ff.

[3] *Bees*, pp. 4–18.

with the initial hypothesis and alternative possible explanations
are eliminated, the initial hypothesis is thought less and less
open to reasonable doubt or query. Where the outcome fails
to accord exactly with the initial hypothesis, an appropriately
modified hypothesis is substituted so as to maintain the growing
immunity to reasonable doubt. More specifically, the hypothesis
that bee populations are colour-discriminatory survives variation in the shading of adjacent cards. That is to say, a bee
population is found in each of these circumstances that behaves
discriminatorily in relation to the coloured card. The hypothesis
also survives variations in the relative locations of the cards.
It survives variations in their smell potential. It survives
variation from a feeding situation to a homing one. But it has
to be modified in relation to the range of colours recognized.
The hypothesis that in the end von Frisch thinks reasonably
well established is that bees discriminate between yellow, blue-
green, blue, and ultra-violet.

Why are just these kinds of variation taken into account?
In each case their relevance to the inquiry is implicitly or
explicitly inferred from previous experience. Colour-blindness
occurs elsewhere.[4] Bees are known to have a good memory for
places.[5] Recognition by scent occurs elsewhere.[6] Most insects
are blind to red, though birds are especially sensitive to it.[7]
And beekeepers disagree as to whether the colouring of a hive
helps bees to recognize it.[8] But, though several relevant
variables are thus thought to be known already, important
progress is made in the study of bees' sensory discriminations
when the relevance of some further variable is discovered, like
that of variation from a broken to an unbroken shape.[9] How
was the latter variable discovered? Well, any test involving
shape discrimination tended to produce contradictory results
until the manipulation of that variable was introduced into the
explicit structure of the test. So, in general (see further § 44
below), a variable—i.e. a set of circumstance-types—may be
said to be inductively relevant to hypotheses in a given field

[4] *Bees*, p. 5.
[5] *Bees*, p. 6.
[6] *Bees*, p. 6.
[7] *Bees*, p. 9.
[8] *Bees*, pp. 13 f.
[9] *Bees*, p. 23.

of inquiry if each of its variants, or circumstance-types, suffices to falsify at least one generalization in that field. But it is reasonable to suppose that the manipulation of additional relevant variables is worth while only if the variants of any one relevant variable are substantially independent of the variants of any other. For example, so far as it seems from past experience that, whenever a certain variant V_i of a variable v_i is present, a certain variant V_j of another variable v_j has also to be present, it will suffice to include V_i in the list of variants of relevant variables manipulated and to omit its subaltern V_j.

By taking more and more of these relevant variables into account in the given order, and combining their variations in all possible ways, one can describe a series of six different tests—t_1, t_2, . . ., t_6—in cumulative order of complexity, to which in effect von Frisch submits the hypothesis that bees are colour-discriminatory. Test t_1 is the limiting-case, as in the first experiment, where no variations are deliberately introduced into the circumstances of the bees' colour-recognition. Test t_2 varies these circumstances with the shading of adjacent cards. Test t_3 combines this variation with variations in the relative location of the cards. Test t_4 combines those two variations with variation in the release of the food-carrying card's smell. Test t_5 performs this experiment for several other colours besides blue. Test t_6 combines performance of these various experiments for feeding bees, as in t_5, with performance of the same varieties of experiment for homing bees. The support that is believed to exist for the hypothesis at any one stage of the investigation may then be graded in accordance with the number of the test that the hypothesis is believed to have passed. The more complex the test it has passed, the higher the grade of support the hypothesis has attained. Moreover comparisons can be drawn not only between the different grades of support that reports of different tests thus give to the same hypothesis, but also between the different grades of support that reports of the same test give to different hypotheses. The hypothesis that wasps are colour-discriminatory, for example, may presumably also be tested in the above way, and appropriate comparisons can then be drawn between the grade of support attained by the one hypothesis and by the other.

Von Frisch's reasoning in connection with his other hypotheses follows substantially the same pattern. Bees' other discriminatory capacities and their methods of communication are established by similar sequences of experiments. So if H is a first-order generalization, like 'All bee-populations are colour-discriminatory', the support that E gives H—denoted by the dyadic functor 's[H,E]'—is to be graded in accordance with the complexity of the most complex appropriate test that, in effect, E reports H as passing. In this way, wherever the same ordered set of relevant variables is involved, we can compare $s[H,E_1]$ with $s[H,E_2]$, $s[H_1,E]$ with $s[H_2,E]$, or even $s[H_1,E_1]$ with $s[H_2,E_2]$. Indeed the function $s[\ldots,---] = /n$ may usefully be taken to map ordered pairs of propositions on to the first $n+1$ integers $\geqslant 0$, if '$s[H,E] = 0$' implies no passing even of test t_1, '$s[H,E] \geqslant 1$' implies passing the test t_1 that is too simple to contain any variations, and n different tests are appropriate because a certain ordered set of n-1 variables is considered relevant. Thus the form of support-grading that captures all we can, at best, say about how well E supports H may be written as '$s[H,E] = i/n$'. This means that E gives H the ith grade of support, where the nth is the highest possible grade, and E gives H no higher than ith grade support.

§43. *The importance of evidential replicability*

It is important to notice here that a genuine test-result is always replicable, within appropriate limits of precision. Experimental scientists always treat replicability as an essential element in the title of a test-result to constitute evidence, whether, *qua* evidence, the test-result is favourable, or unfavourable, to the hypothesis tested. If von Frisch's results were not replicable, they would not be regarded by his colleagues as having any evidential value.[10] Where replication breaks down, the operation of some hidden or undetected variable has to be inferred and the test obviously needs restructuring. I do not meant that in checking on a previous test-result experimental scientists expect to produce phenomena that are identical with some previous phenomena in all respects but spatio-temporal location. Absolute identity of this kind, as Leibniz long ago remarked, is hardly to be found in nature. Instead what experi-

[10] *Bees*, p. vi.

mentalists have a right to expect is identity in all relevant respects and within specified limits of precision.

It follows that, if E is to give H more than zero-grade support, E must not only state that the antecedent and consequent of H is satisfied on at least one occasion in each of such-and-such combinations of circumstances. E must also state grounds for inferring the replicability of the results it reports. How can this best be represented? One straightforward way is to require that, if E were fully articulate in reporting a result of test t_i, it would, for each characteristic that is a variant of any other relevant variable—i.e. other than the relevant variables manipulated in t_i, deny that it was present in the situation reported. For, if that were true, and our list of relevant variables is complete, the reported outcomes must have ensued solely as a result of the reported experimental circumstances and can be expected, so far as similar causes produce similar effects, to recur in the same circumstances, whenever all variants of other relevant variables are again absent. That is to say, in the light of our background knowledge about relevant variables, which we invoke when we assert that E gives ith grade support to H, we can infer from the results stated by E that such results are replicable.

Several important consequences follow. I shall mention two here and two more in §§ 52–3 below.

The first important consequence is that from E and $s[H,E] \geqslant i/n$ we are entitled to detach the appropriate monadic support-grading $s[H] \geqslant i/n$. If the favourable test-result reported by E is genuinely replicable, it constitutes a solid evidential fact, unshakable by other evidence, from which we can safely infer H to have a certain grade of reliability.[11] Scientists like von Frisch constantly infer the status of their hypotheses from the results of their own experiments. But sometimes they turn out later to have been mistaken in making these inferences, because

---

[11] However from E and $s[H,E] < i/n$ we cannot detach $s[H] < i/n$. For, if $s[H,E]$ is less than i/n, this may be either because E reports something sufficiently unfavourable to H or because E does not report anything sufficiently favourable. For a more detailed examination of the relations between monadic and dyadic support-gradings cf. *TIOI*, pp. 67 ff. Though the term 'support' was used in *TIOI* in relation to both monadic and dyadic gradings, the reader may find it easier to think of monadic gradings as gradings of 'reliability'.

they were mistaken about the relevance of the variables manipulated in their experiments.

The second important consequence is that even when E contradicts H we may still have s[H,E] > 0. The point is that E may report H's passing test t_i and failing test t_{i+1}, and if the achievement of passing test t_i is genuinely replicable it can hardly be allowed to be wiped off the slate, as it were, by a replicable failure to pass t_{i+1}. The grade of inductive support attributed to H represents the inability of certain complexes of relevant factors to cause H's falsification. If the introduction of a further factor does cause H's falsification, that should not be allowed to give H zero-grade support. For then H would have been put on the same level as a hypothesis that could not stand up to any test at all. H would not have been given due credit for the extent to which it is, in fact, reliable: it would not have been given due credit for the various combinations of circumstances in which it holds good. We shall see later (§ 49) how the normal treatment of so-called 'anomalies', in relation to scientific theories, bears out the possibility of having s[H,E] > 0 even when E contradicts H.

§44. *The definition of a series of inductively relevant variables*

There is a prima-facie difficulty here, which can best be examined in the form of a plausible objection. 'A hypothesis might appear to pass test t_i', the objection would run, 'and then to fail t_{i+1}. Presumably some variant of the relevant variable that is manipulated in t_{i+1} but not in t_i helps to cause the falsification. But surely it was just the absence of that variant, on the occasion when t_i was performed, that enabled the hypothesis to pass t_i. Hence if the report on the result of performing t_i claimed no hidden factors to be operating—i.e. no variant of any relevant variable other than those specifically manipulated in t_i—this report was mistaken. Correspondingly, if the report was in fact correct, the hypothesis must also pass every more complex test, since if the absence of this or that circumstance was not operative in securing the success of the successful experiment, its presence cannot help to secure failure in more complex experiments. So if s[H,E] $\geq i/n$, we also have s[H,E] $\geq i + 1/n$. In short, if the evidential report is true, it must either imply the hypothesis to have passed the most complex test or not state that it has passed any test at all. No intermediate grades of support are evidentially certifiable.'

This objection would have some point if the variants of each relevant variable were logically exhaustive, so that everything must be characterized by some variant or another of it—e.g. by the presence or absence of a specified characteristic.[12] In such a case a true evidential report would afford either the maximum grade of support or no support at all. But if the variants of a relevant variable never exhaust its domain, i.e. if there is always a non-relevant circumstance incompatible with each such variant, the objection fails. And it is in fact necessary to suppose the existence of these non-relevant circumstances (for reasons that will emerge below and in § 54). For example, where the relevant variable consists of different bands of wind-speed, a test in still air—the 'normal' situation—will exclude any variant of the relevant variable from being present. So if a hypothesis passes t_i, but is falsified in t_{i+1} by a high wind-speed, the report of the results of t_i canot be said to have been false, since no variant of the relevant variable in question (wind-speed) was present in t_i. And a test in white light will behave analogously when the relevant variable consists of variations in the colour of the lighting. Also, where tests are carried out on samples, a suitably randomized selection of each sample may count as excluding hidden factors from affecting the statistical properties at issue.[13]

A relevant variable, and a common series of relevant variables, for a particular category of first-order generalizations are therefore to be defined as follows. The definitions are a little complex, but it does not seem possible to reconstruct the concepts implicit in von Frisch's reasoning more economically.

We suppose a given category of first-order generalizations, determined by reference to the two sets of non-logical terms— m-adic predicables for any finite m—that may be used, along with quantifiers and truth-functional logical connectives, to construct the generalizations. These two sets of predicables are mutually exclusive. One of them contains only predicables that are mutually incompatible, such as 'is a bee population',

---

[12] In *TIOI*, §5, relevant variables of this type, with logically exhaustive variants, were mistakenly admitted.
[13] Cf. *TIOI*, pp. 120 f.

'is a wasp population', etc., and its members will be referred to (for reasons that will emerge shortly) as the v_1 predicables. The other predicables, such as 'discriminates colours', 'discriminates smells', etc., will be referred to as the target predicables. Each of them must be linguistically compatible with each v_1 predicable. A testable generalization, in the given category, is constructed by universal quantification over the individual variables of a truth-functionally conditional schema that is constructed according to the following two specifications. First, its antecedent is constituted by the ascription of a v_1 predicable or by a conjunction of such ascriptions. Secondly, its consequent is a truth-function of the ascriptions of one or more target predicables. For example, (x_1) (x_2) ... (x_m) $(Rx_1x_2...x_m \to Sx_1x_2...x_m)$ is a testable generalization, where 'R' stands for an m-adic v_1 predicable and 'S' for an m-adic target predicable. Similarly, (x) (y) $((R_1x \ \& \ R_2y) \to -Sxy)$ is a testable generalization, where 'R_1' and 'R_2' stand for monadic v_1 predicables and 'S' for a dyadic target predicable. Generalisations formed in other ways from the logical and non-logical terminology of the category are called non-testable ones.[14]

Note that no observability-conditions need to be imposed on the basic predicables here. Even on matters of fact[15] inductive reasoning is not confined to the objects of human sensory perception. In order to know of any evidence of inductive support for a particular generalization one has to know that the antecedent and consequent of the generalization have been satisfied in an appropriate variety of relevant circumstances. But the knowledge may be gained by observation, inference, introspection, recollection, hearsay or any other legitimate means. Hence human intentions, for example, are just as much a possible topic for inductive reasoning as are the insects' colour-discriminations and hive-recognitions that von Frisch studied.

[14] The definition of testability given here is somewhat simpler than that given in *TIOI*, pp. 96 f. For example, the logical truth of a generalization does not now exclude it from testability in the required sense: so the maximum inductive reliability that logically true generalizations possess is elucidated by their capacity to survive all possible tests. But Hempel's paradoxes are still excluded, as in *TIOI*.

[15] *TIOI*, pp. 155 ff., discusses the application of inductive reasoning to moral and legal issues—issues about what is *de jure* right rather than about what is *de facto* actual.

A circumstance is a relevant one, for the given category of generalizations, if it is not describable in the terminology of the category and its presence in an otherwise normal type of situation suffices causally to exclude at least one testable generalization belonging to the category from holding true for that type of situation, nor is there any part or feature of the circumstance that is unnecessary for this exclusion. Since a circumstance is thus relevant in virtue of its *causing* a generalization to be false, there must also be some control feature whereby we can test that the generalization would not have been falsified in any case. And typically that control would itself be either a non-relevant circumstance—a circumstance that is not relevant because relatively normal for the kind of phenomena under investigation—or alternatively a circumstance of which the relevance emerges only from its causing some other generalization to be false.

Any set of mutually co-ordinate and mutually incompatible relevant circumstances for the category is then a relevant variable for it. The circumstances that are the members of the set are the variants of the variable. Also, any two relevant variables v_i and v_j that have at least some combinable variants may be combined into a third relevant variable which has as its variants each possible combination of the variants of v_i and v_j: relevant variables of the latter type are to be termed 'compounded' and all others 'uncompounded'. There are no other relevant variables for the category.

The series of relevant variables for a particular category of generalizations may then be defined, with the help of three further terms. A relevant variable is to be termed 'maximal' if it is a set of relevant characteristics that is closed under the relationship of co-ordinate incompatibility. A relevant variable is to be termed 'non-exhaustive' if there is some non-relevant circumstance that is incompatible with any of its variants. An uncompounded relevant variable is to be termed 'more important than' another if it has greater falsificatory potential within the category.

The assessment of falsificatory potential is discussed in §45 below. But one necessary condition for having greater falsificatory potential must be mentioned here because it is quintessential for the avoidance of inconsistencies in support-grading.

If $v_1, v_2, \ldots, v_i$ are a set of relevant variables in decreasing order of falsificatory potential, then any generalization falsified by some combination of variants of $v_1, v_2, \ldots,$ and v_{i-1} must also be falsified by some combination of these variants with some variant of v_i. In other words a more important relevant variable can never have its falsificatory power wholly nullified by a less important one, and the more important it is the greater the number of other relevant variables to which it thus rises superior.

A relevant variable is a prima-facie member of the series of relevant variables for the category if and only if it is either (i) uncompounded, maximal, non-exhaustive and not equal in importance to any other such relevant variable, or (ii) compounded from two or more uncompounded, maximal and non exhaustive relevant variables that are equal in importance to one another but not to any other such variable. The prima-facie members of the series are arranged in order of decreasing relative importance, with any compounded member occupying the position of its uncompounded components.

Finally, the first real member of the series is the set of circumstances described by the v_1 predicables of the category. The other real members of the series are determined from the prima-facie members by an independence requirement. All prima-facie members are real members in the same order except that, if a prima-facie member v_j of the series $v_1, v_2, \ldots$ contains a variant that tends to be present whenever a certain variant of another prima-facie member v_i, with $j > i$, is present, or whenever a certain combination of variants of such other variables is present, then the real member that stands in place of v_j is the largest sub-set of v_j that lacks this dependent variant.

It needs to be pointed out that a support-function for generalizations of a certain category applies primarily to a sub-set of these generalizations—the testable ones. That is to say, only testable generalizations possess inductive reliability, or acquire inductive support, in virtue of the actual or causally possible co-instantiation of their antecedents and consequents. Other propositions formulated in the basic terminology of the category have whatever inductive support they do have in virtue of their logical relations (as in §§ 50–3 below) with testable generalizations that are inductively supported. This restriction represents the actual procedures of experimental research in a particular area of inquiry. But it also helps to avoid Hempel's paradoxes.[16]

§45. *Ontology versus epistemology in the philosophy of inductive support*

The appropriate series of relevant variables for generalizations of a particular category determine the series of more and more complex tests that can be constructed in the way already described (§42, pp. 129 ff.): with test t_1 manipulating variable v_1, t_2 manipulating v_1 and v_2, t_3 manipulating v_1, v_2 and v_3, and so on. But, since we may not *know* exactly which series of variables is the appropriate one, it is obvious that the matter may be looked at both from an ontological and from an epistemological point of view. The difference between these two points of view deserves more emphasis than it sometimes gets in the philosophy of inductive support.

From an ontological point of view we are discussing a mode of gradation, not a method of assessment (cf. § 1, p. 6 above). We are discussing the truth-conditions, for any C, of statements of the form $s_c[H] \gtreqless i/n$, where s_c denotes the function that grades the reliability of C-category generalizations in accordance with their ability to resist falsification in certain combinations of circumstances: when no variant of any member of the series of relevant variables is present but v_1, when no variant of any member of this series but v_1 and v_2 is present, and so on. From this ontological point of view certain variables belong, in a certain order, to the series for C-category generalizations whether or not anyone ever knows or believes it. Also, that series may have either a finite or an infinite number of members, and each of its members may have either a finite or an infinite number of variants. Similarly, a proposition of the form $s_c[H] \geqslant i/n$ may be true whether or not we know it. That is to say, the antecedent and consequent of the generalization—or of some testable generalisation implying it—may at some time be co-instantiated, or may at least be open to co-instantiation, in this or that variety of relevant circumstance, whether or not any appropriate observations are ever made.[17]

---

[16] *TIOI*, pp. 96 ff. In the ordering of relevant variables I have avoided here the unsatisfactory conventionalism of *TIOI* pp. 57 ff.

[17] On the difference between a quasi-nominalist ontology, that requires actual co-instantiation, and a realist one, that is satisfied with causally possible co-instantiation, see §92, pp. 331 ff., below.

From an epistemological point of view, however, what we have to recapture or reconstruct is the method of assessing inductive support, not its mode of gradation. We have to represent the conditions that justify us in asserting statements of the form $s_c[H] \gtrless i/n$, rather than the conditions that make such statements true. We have to represent the condition E that justifies us in detaching $s_c[H] \geqslant i/n$, say, from $s_c[H,E] \geqslant i/n$. And we have to show how such conditions can be learned. Hence we have to emphasize that the relevance of a certain variable is itself a matter for empirical investigation. Experimenters are constantly formulating hypotheses about which variables are relevant to their own particular field of study, or modifying such hypotheses in the light of experience. Moreover, if such a hypothesis is specific enough to be empirically testable, it must assume both that each variable has only a finite number of variants and also that only a finite number of relevant variables exist for the category of generalizations concerned. For, though particular test-results could never refute the claim that a particular relevant variable had an infinite number of variants, they might be able to refute the claim that a particular finite list of such variants is complete. Hence for any continuous scale of differentiation, such as temperature or velocity, it will be policy to hypothesize relatively few intervals on the scale as relevant circumstances. Similarly, though particular test-results could never refute the claim that the series of relevant variables in the field is infinite, they might be able to refute the claim that a particular finite list of such variables is complete. In this way too it is ensured that any statement of experimental evidence E, such that we have $s_c[H,E] \geqslant i/n$, is of finite length.

Moreover, empirically influenced judgements of relative importance will normally control which well-ordered set of supposedly relevant variables is chosen as the series that determines the construction of experiments and the assessment of inductive support for particular generalizations. The greater the variety of types of hypotheses that a particular relevant variable is seen to falsify, the more important it will normally be presumed to be. In practice there is generally sufficient unanimity of choice here—between different experimenters—to permit a substantial uniformity of assessment within any one field of scientific inquiry at any one time. But no uniquely correct choice is conclusively demonstrable. Every comparative or ordinal judgement of inductive support that is actually made in relation to a particular field of inquiry depends not only on corrigible beliefs or assumptions about test-results, but also on corrigible beliefs or assumptions about the most appropriately selected and ordered list of relevant variables for that field. And, just as in judging the acceptability of ordinary, first-level scientific generalizations considerations of simplicity, fruitfulness, technological utility, etc., often have to be taken into account besides considerations of evidential support, so too these other considerations have to be taken into account in judging the acceptability of second-level hypotheses about how to assess evidential support in a particular field of inquiry.

Indeed, even the delimitation of a particular field of inquiry is subject to adjustment in the light of experience. For example, we may discover that what we previously treated as a target predicable is in fact to be regarded as describing a variant of a relevant variable. Also, though no uniquely correct choice of terminological categories is ever conclusively demonstrable, it is normally appropriate in science to prefer collections of terms that are discovered to lend themselves easily to the construction of well-supported generalizations. We begin with the unsophisticated vocabulary of everyday life, which picks out—perhaps partly with the help of innate predispositions—those easily recognized similarities within our passing environment that seem to affect our day-to-day purposes. And as the superficiality of many of these similarities becomes apparent, along with the lack of exception-free correlations between any of them, we develop new vocabularies in the attempt to pick out underlying uniformities and explanations. Water, for example, is no longer the impure liquid of rain and sea and rivers, but is defined in terms of its molecular structure. It follows that, in a rational reconstruction of inductive support-assessment from an epistemological point of view, one cannot put forward criteria for the choice of initial terminology which are independent of the idea of inductive support, even though the assessment of higher than first-grade support in any area must always itself depend on a listed series of variables that are supposed relevant to generalizations in such a terminology.[18] To accept the

[18] This would be my reply to the interesting suggestion of A. C. Michalos (in

method of relevant variables is to accept that the ascertainment of natural kinds proceeds *pari passu* with the discovery of well-supported generalizations. But this does not mean that a hypothesis should never be projected unless its terms, or co-extensive ones, have already occurred in successfully projected hypotheses. If the founders of modern chemistry had followed the latter precept, we should still be talking about earth, air, fire, and water instead of about hydrogen, lithium, beryllium, boron, etc. Instead what must be insisted on is no more than that a vocabulary for hypothesis-construction should pay its way by being fruitful of hypotheses that turn out to be well supported when they are tested against the appropriate series of relevant variables.

Again, the support-functions for different categories of generalizations are largely incommensurable with one another.[19] Zero and maximal values of these functions do have the same significance for each category, betokening no resistance and full resistance, respectively, to the falsifying effects of relevant variables. But intermediate values cannot be equated because of the differences in number, complexity, importance, etc. of the relevant variables in different series. Hence a further type of useful adjustment that experience may prompt consists in the division of a previously unitary field of inquiry into two separate ones, or the combination of two previously separate fields into a single one. Neither form of adjustment has been uncommon in the history of science.

Finally it is conceivable that in some fields of inquiry some variants, or combinations of variants, of relevant variables falsify some hypotheses only when unaccompanied by any variants of certain other relevant variables, even though they are quite capable of being combined with such other variants. Examples of this are difficult to find, but if one were found the method of relevant variables would need to be adjusted appropriately in that area of inquiry, in order to maintain the cumulative falsificatory potential of the series of tests t_1, t_2, ... and t_n. So far what has been supposed is that test t_i consists

---

his review of *TIOI* in *Philosophy of Science*, 39 (1972), 306–7) that the choice of fundamental categories might usefully be regarded as a metaphysical issue.

[19] However for simplicity's sake an unsubscripted support-functor 's[ ]' is used in other sections of the text, instead of the 's_c[ ]' of the present section.

of trials under all possible combinations of variants of relevant variables v_1, v_2, . . . and v_i, and this was understood as requiring that each such combination should, if possible, include a variant of each of v_1, v_2, . . . and v_i. The latter requirement would now have to be dropped, along with the requirement (p. 139) that any generalization falsified by some combination of variants of v_1, v_2, . . ., and v_{i-1} must also be falsified by some combination of these variants with some variant of v_i. Test t_1 would remain as before. Test t_2 would consist of test t_1 together with trials under each possible combination of a variant of v_1 with a variant of v_2. Test t_3 would consist of tests t_1 and t_2, together with trials under each possible combination of a variant of v_1 with a variant of v_3 and under each possible combination of a variant of v_1 with a variant of v_2 and a variant of v_3. And so on.

§46. *The subsumption of Mill's canons under the method of relevant variables*

I call the support one proposition can give another in the above way 'inductive', since it obviously has close affinities to what has traditionally been known as 'eliminative induction' or 'induction by variation of circumstance'. Admittedly, the term 'inductivism' has sometimes been used by critics of Bacon and Mill to name those philosophers' methodology of discovery. But it is just as much a fallacy to suppose that in the history of science the normal procedure has been first to collect evidence and then to generalize, as to suppose that it has been first to form hypotheses and then to test them. In physics it has been common enough to construct or modify a piece of experimental apparatus for the specific purpose of testing a preconceived hypothesis. But in agricultural science, for example, the experimenter sometimes has very little idea beforehand about what results to expect. For example, he may have very little idea which plant-varieties are going to grow best in a given soil until he tries them. His experiments then are genuinely heuristic, even if guided by an over-all strategy of research, or contained within a constraining framework; and he has to tailor his generalizations to fit the results. So the terms 'induction', 'inductive', etc. are best anchored to their logical or quasi-logical sense, as the analogy with 'deduction', 'deductive', etc. suggests. The concept of an inductive methodology, or learning-strategy, does not imply the temporal priority of evidence-collection to hypothesis-formation, or vice versa, though one such order of procedure may be much more appropriate than the other in certain cases.

Indeed, so far as the logic of support-assessments is concerned —as distinct from the professional proprieties of experimental science—it does not even matter whether the events taken into account as evidence are the result of deliberately contrived test-performances or have occurred partially or wholly without human intervention. Nor does it matter whether the various trials that compose a complex test are performed at the same time or not. What is essential is just that the antecedent and consequent of the generalization at issue should be jointly satisfied at some time or set of times in such-and-such varieties of relevant circumstance, or that the antecedent should, and the consequent should not, be thus satisfied. Human beings cannot control the movements of planets, for example, or dispose stars into whatever initial conditions might be desirable for an experimentally contrived test-performance. Also historical records of ancient eclipses or supernovas may have to be combined with present observations in order to complete the required evidence for an astronomical hypothesis. But none of this bars astronomers from the use of inductive reasoning.

Keynes long ago remarked that the importance of Francis Bacon and J. S. Mill, in relation to induction, lay in their contribution to its logic, not in their views about the methodology of scientific discovery; and Mill himself came to insist that even if his inductive methods were not methods of discovery they nevertheless had logical value.[20] If we view Mill's canons

---

[20] Cf. J. M. Keynes, *A Treatise on Probability* (1921), p. 265, and J. S. Mill, *A System of Inductive Logic*, 8th edn. (1896), Bk. III, ch. viii. I have not yet constructed a computer-programme for inductive learning on the basis of the Baconian inductive logic developed in this book and in *TIOI*. But to construct such a programme would be an interesting exercise in the study of artificial intelligence, and might also serve to clarify, amplify, or correct the logic in ways that I naturally cannot at present predict. In addition, it would be a good way to explore questions about the temporal order in which various procedures need to occur that are essential to learning from experience; or at any rate it would be likely to issue in a somewhat less crude and over-simplified schema for this than, say, Popper's four-stage process of problem$_1$–tentative theory–error elimination–problem$_2$: cf. K. R. Popper, *Objective Knowledge* (1972), pp. 121 ff. The input to a first-order programme

accordingly—not as precepts for the discovery of causes but as criteria for the assessment of a timeless support-relation between propositions—we can see that the method of relevant variables, as described in §§ 42–5, is readily extended into being a unified and graduated systematization of whatever is sound in Mill's five canons (the core of which can be traced back before Mill's *System of Logic* to J. F. W. Herschel, Francis Bacon, and beyond).[21]

Take first Mill's Method of Agreement, viz.

If two or more instances of the phenomenon under investigation have only one circumstance in common, the circumstance in which alone all the instances agree is the cause (or effect) of the given phenomenon.

The point of this canon, as a criterion for the assessment of evidential support, is to draw attention to the extent to which, by being drawn from a variety of relevant circumstances, the evidence eliminates alternative possible explanations of a phenomenon. So presumably, the greater the relevant variety of the instances reported, the greater the support given by an evidential report to an explanatory hypothesis. In order to capture the criterion that underlies Mill's Method of Agreement we have to conceive a mode of testing hypotheses that relies on the manipulation of more and more relevant variables as in §§ 42–5.

In a very natural and obvious way the method of relevant variables can be extended to include the criterion that underlies

---

would be (i) an initial list of target predicables plus (ii) an on-going supply of sentences asserting the existence of individuals that satisfy or fail to satisfy such-or-such predicates or combinations of predicates. The output would be (i) a continuously updated list of generalized conditionals that have truth-functions of the target predicables as consequents, where each such generalized conditional is paired with a monadic grading of its reliability, plus (ii) periodical lists of questions whether individuals exist that satisfy such-or-such combinations of predicates.

[21] Cf. *TIOI*, pp. 124 ff. Mill wrote (ibid., Bk. III, ch. iv, §2, p. 213): 'The notion of Cause being the root of the whole theory of Induction, it is indispensable that this idea should, at the very outset of our inquiry, be, with the utmost practicable degree of precision, fixed and determined'. However, though Mill was right to stress the underlying importance of causation to induction about natural events, he underestimated the extent to which any clarification of the concept of cause may itself need to invoke the concept of inductive reliability: see immediately below, and also §92, p. 332.

Mill's Method of Concomitant Variations. According to that canon

> whatever phenomenon varies in any manner whenever another phenomenon varies in some particular manner, is either a cause or an effect of that phenomenon, or is connected with it through some fact of causation.

Now suppose we have to deal with a hypothesis H (involving second-order quantification) that correlates one natural variable with another, e.g. the volume of a certain substance with its temperature, or the velocity of a falling object with the period for which it has been falling. Clearly we have to test H in relation to any other variable that we know to be relevant for hypotheses of H's type. For example, such factors as wind-strength or height above sea-level might affect hypotheses about falling objects. But in addition to the other variables that are relevant for any hypothesis of H's type there will also be a variable that is necessarily relevant to H itself, viz. the variable alluded to in H's own antecedent—the 'independent variable', as it is sometimes called. For example, if H asserts the velocity of a falling object to be such-and-such a function of the period for which it has been falling, H obviously needs to be tested over an appropriate set of intervals within the continuous variable constituted by its period of fall. This set is v_1—the first member of the series of relevant variables that is appropriate for hypotheses of H's type—and we manipulate it alone in test t_1. That is, in t_1 we just manipulate the variable in the antecedent of H over an appropriate set of intervals; in t_2, we operate every one of those variants and every variant of the first of the other variables that are relevant to hypotheses of H's type, in every possible combination with one another, or singly where no such combination is possible; in t_3 we operate every possible combination of these variations with variations of the second of those other variables; and so on.[22]

---

[22] A good example of this is to be found in Newton's experimental work on the connection between spectral colours and differing degrees of refrangibility of light rays—a connection that he found to be unaffected by the position of the glass, by unevenness of the glass's thickness, by the size of the aperture through which the sun's rays enter, by the angle of these rays' incidence, and so on. Cf. the reprint of his first published paper in I. Bernard Cohen (ed.), *Isaac Newton's Papers and Letters on Natural Philosophy* (1958), pp. 47 ff.

This type of situation is to be contrasted with the type considered earlier, where the method of relevant variables is applied to a first-order generalization like 'Anything if a bee population is colour-discriminatory' and only one variant of relevant variable v_1 is operated, viz. the characteristic predicated in the antecedent of the generalisation. So the difference between Mill's Method of Concomitant Variations and his Method of Agreement may be succinctly formulated in terms of the method of relevant variables. The Method of Concomitant Variations describes an application of the method of relevant variables in test t_1 on a second-order generalization, while the Method of Agreement describes an application of that method in some test t_i, where $i > 1$.

When it is applied to causal hypotheses in test t_1, the method of relevant variables may now be seen to embody the criterion underlying Mill's Method of Difference. According to that canon

if an instance in which the phenomenon under investigation occurs, and an instance in which it does not occur, have every circumstance in common save one, that one occurring only in the former; the circumstance in which alone the two instances differ is the effect, or the cause, or an indispensable part of the cause, of the phenomenon.

This expresses the familiar requirement that in order to establish a causal hypothesis we need a control. For example, perhaps our hypothesis is not that bees discriminate certain colours but that they pollinate certain flowers. To test such a hypothesis we shall need not only trials in which these flowers are exposed to a bee population with no other insects present but also trials in a control situation where no bees are present either. Otherwise we should have no reason to suppose that bees were the pollinating agents. So the first relevant variable here perhaps contains the variants: presence of a bee population without other insects, presence of a wasp population without other insects, etc., and presence of no insect population. Only the first and last of these would be manipulated in test t_1, on the hypothesis in question.

Consequently in any test t_i on such a causal hypothesis where $i > 1$ we in effect operate the criterion underlying Mill's

Joint Method of Agreement and Difference. For what that canon claimed was that

if two or more instances in which the phenomenon occurs have only one circumstance in common while two more or instances in which it does not occur have nothing in common save the absence of that circumstance, the circumstance in which alone the two sets of instances differ is the effect, or the cause, or an indispensable part of the cause, of the phenomenon.

But instead of writing 'two or more instances' Mill should have written 'two or more relevantly varied instances'; instead of writing 'only one circumstance in common' Mill should have written 'one variant of the relevant variable for test t_1 in common'; and instead of 'nothing in common save the absence of that circumstance' he should have written 'an appropriate variant of the relevant variable for test t_1 in common'.[23]

Three other points must be noted here.

The first is that a control is needed for testing a hypothesis about one event's being a sign of another in normal (or specified) circumstances, as well as for testing causal hypotheses. Dark clouds would not be the sign of imminent rain on a summer's day if rain were always imminent on a summer's day even when there were no dark clouds.

The second point is that, if the hypothesis to be tested is about *the* cause or *the* sign of something, an adequate control is specified merely by negating the description of the hypothesized

[23] It is easy to find good examples of inductive reasoning about causal connections in the literature of ethology. N. Tinbergen and A. C. Perdeck, Cf., e.g., 'On the Stimulus Situation Releasing the Begging Response in the Newly Hatched Herring Gull Chick', *Behaviour* 3 (1950), 1–39. Here the hypothesis is that sight of a distinctive patch on the feeding gull's lower mandible releases a chick's begging response, and the hypothesis is, in effect, tested in relation to at least a dozen relevant variables, such as odour of patch, colour of bill, colour of head, shape of bill, shape of head, position of patch, direction in which bill points, height of bill above ground, distance of bill from chick, movement of bill, solidity of bill, nature of food present, and accompanying sounds. Cf. also H. F. and M. Harlow, 'Social Deprivation in Rhesus Monkeys', *Scientific American*, 207:5 (November 1962), 136–46, where the hypothesis that social deprivation in infancy affects a rhesus monkey's social adaptability in later life is tested against such relevant variables as nature of deprivation (from mother, mother-surrogate, siblings, etc.), period of deprivation, and opportunity for play.

cause or sign.[24] But if, because a plurality of possible causes or signs is envisaged, the hypothesis is just about *a* cause or *a* sign, the control must be described in terms that exclude any of these possible causes or signs. It would be wrong to conclude that throwing unextinguished cigarette stubs on to combustible material is not a cause of forest fires merely because forest fires sometimes occur even when no unextinguished cigarette stubs are thrown on to combustible material. Forest fires have a variety of causes, and only when *none* of these is present is there no fire.

The third point to be noted is that, as a consequence of what has been said, a proposition of the form

(1)   Being R is a cause (or a sign) of being S,

is true if and only if

(2)   s[Anything if R is S and also there is some characteristic incompatible with being R such that anything that has this characteristic is not S] is maximal.

Mill thought that the maximum inductive reliability which is implicit in (1) and explicit in (2) could be attained in a single step, as it were, by his Joint Method of Agreement and Difference. I am suggesting that a more graduated procedure is possible, in accordance with the method of relevant variables. But on both views asserting a proposition with the form of (1) is asserting something about corresponding expressions (of any language) that have the form of the square-bracketed generalizations in (2). Hence arises the particular type of non-extensionality that is widely attributed (cf. § 7, p. 22, above) to propositions with the form of (1). Admittedly it is often convenient to speak as if a causal proposition like (1), rather than a conjunction of generalizations like the square-bracketed expression of (2), is the hypothesis for which support is sought. Indeed it is quite natural to say that the experimental evidence gives such or such a grade of inductive support to the former rather than to the latter. But strictly speaking we should always make it

---

[24] The first member of the series of relevant variables may be extended—in dealing with causal hypotheses—to include the contradictories of v_1 predicables, without falling foul of the argument against supposing any relevant variable to be logically exhaustive which was discussed in §44, pp. 135 f. That argument has force only in regard to each relevant variable v_i where $i > 1$.

clear that experimental evidence will provide inductive support *for* (1) and *for*, say, the square-bracketed generalizations of (2) in different senses of 'for'. It will be evidence which indicates how far the latter have progressed towards attaining that maximal grade of reliability which is already implicitly assigned them in (1) and explicitly in (2). (And often that grade is not attainable except by generalizations which are prefaced by 'In normal circumstances' or some such other qualification as in §54 below.[25])

The only one of Mill's five canons that is not largely subsumable within the method of relevant variable in his Method of Residues. That canon runs:

Subduct from any phenomenon such part as is known by previous inductions to be the effect of certain antecedents, and the residue of the phenomenon is the effect of the remaining antecedents.

But consider, for example, the various functioning parts of a motor-car and its resources of energy. We may know that the lights and wipers work off the battery, but it certainly does not follow that the engine works off the petrol supply alone. Mill's Method of Residues is blatantly invalid, and the method of relevant variables loses nothing by failing to subsume it.

§47. *How the method of relevant variables applies to scientific theories*

What has been shown so far is how the method of relevant

---

[25] In these cases both what I call 'a cause' and what I call 'a sign' are what J. L. Mackie, *The Cement of the Universe* (1974), p. 62 (following a suggestion of D. C. Stove), calls an '*inus* condition'. An inus condition is defined by Mackie as an *insufficient* but *non-redundant* part of an *unnecessary* but *sufficient* condition. In my account the requirement of being an insufficient part of a sufficient but unnecessary condition is paralleled by the conception of a cause or sign as something that intrudes on normal circumstances and combines with them to form a sufficient but unnecessary condition—some kinds of events may be producible by more than one kind of cause or indicatable by more than one kind of sign—while the requirement of non-redundancy is paralleled by my insistence on the need for a control. However non-redundancy should not be taken to exclude the possibility of causal over-determination (as with death by simultaneous bullets in heart and brain) or of there being more than one sign of the same individual event. It's just that having one or more of the relevant causes or signs is indispensable—not that having only one of them is. The difference between the concept of a cause and the concept of a sign need not concern us here, though important features of it are obviously that signs have to be manifest while causes may be hidden, that causes explain while signs only indicate, and that causes normally precede or at most accompany their effects while signs often follow the events they signify.

variables determines assessments of support for quite elementary generalisations like von Frisch's, for generalisations about causes or signs, and for generalizations asserting correlations between natural variables. Indeed it is undeniable that the working of the method of relevant variables is displayed most conspicuously at this relatively humble stage of scientific endeavour. That is because, when generalizations are still relatively narrow in scope, very many of them may be needed to cover a particular field of inquiry, and so it is readily possible to acquire knowledge of relevant variables from the results of inquiries in one part of the field and then to apply this knowledge in the assessment of further results. Correspondingly Mill himself tends to choose his examples from this level of science. He illustrates his inductive logic with references to such regularities as causes of death, oscillations of pendulums, or the passage of electricity. But other writers on the logic of scientific reasoning, like Whewell or Popper, have often chosen their prime examples from a more advanced level of science. Their illustrations are from Newtonian mechanics, relativity theory, particle physics, and so on. And it will be worth while to show how the method of relevant variables applies to scientific theories of this type also. Only thus can it be shown that the foundations of statements about inductive probability lie in a method of reasoning that has a fairly wide general range of application in natural science. Admittedly, grades of inductive probability will turn out to be directly connected with grades of support for first-order generalizations, not with support for higher-order generalizations or theories. But the hard core of the method of assessing this support for first-order generalizations is equally applicable to scientific theories.

What is essential to such a theory is that it should constitute an explanation of one or more accepted regularities. If it does not do this, it has not even got off the ground, and, other things being equal, the greater the number of relatively independent regularities it explains the better it is normally regarded. Newtonian mechanics, for example, could be regarded as an explanation of the course and velocity of planetary orbitings, of the acceleration of falling bodies on Earth, and of many other regularities of motion. So, roughly speaking, the relevant variables for a theory are those accepted regularities, or groups of accepted regularities, in its field which are not special cases of, or produced or overlapped by, one another. Ideally a theory would explain all of these. But, strictly speaking, a relevant variable is a set of circumstances over which a hypothesis is to be tested. So we must say rather that each relevant variable for a scientific theory is the set of circumstances that severally compose the most thorough possible test of such an accepted generalization about a regularity in the subject matter of the theory.

But how should we envisage the form of a hypothesis that can be tested against relevant variables like these? To be in keeping with the type of procedure already discussed, a testable scientific theory must take the form of a universally quantified conditional that is in principle capable of having its antecedent and consequent co-instantiated in each possible combination of the variants of the appropriate series of relevant variables. Admittedly no normal scientific textbook contains a theory in this form, any more than it contains a full axiomatization for the theories of which it speaks. But on the assumption that any scientific theory H is in fact axiomatizable one can construct an equivalent of H that takes the form, as required, of a universally quantified conditional. An exact statement of the form this equivalent can take will be rather complicated. But, as a first approximation, what seems to be required is a statement to the effect that, if U is a universally quantified conditional which is derivable—in a sense yet to be determined—from the postulates for H, then whenever the antecedent of U is instantiated so is its consequent.

Now what is to be meant here by 'derivable from the postulates for H'? It is clear that from a bare statement of the laws of motion, for instance, as in Newton's own axioms, neither the solar orbit of Mars nor its orbital velocity is logically deducible. The premises for such a deduction must also include propositions about the masses of the sun and its planets and their distance from one another at a particular time. So, if part of the evidence for the laws of motion is to be constituted, in effect, by the observed positions of Mars at different times, we must mean by 'derivable from the postulates for H' one or other of two things. One alternative is that by 'derivable' we mean 'logically deducible'. Then for the purpose of inductive logic the postulates for our theory of motion must be conceived to include some propositions that will bridge the logical gap between the generality of the fundamental laws and the singularity of the evidence. Similarly the postulates for a theory of electro-magnetism would be conceived to include some propositions that bridged the gap between the theoretical terminology of the fundamental laws and the observational terminology of the evidential reports. The other alternative is that we conceive the postulates to include no more than the fundamental laws and that by 'derivable from the postulates' we mean 'logically deducible from the postulates with the help of accepted bridging propositions'. The former alternative produces a neater reconstruction of a scientific theory for the purposes of inductive logic, but at the cost of imputing much more content to the theory than most textbooks would attribute to it. The latter alternative sticks more closely to the textbook concept of a theory, but produces a somewhat clumsier model. I shall adopt the former alternative here, because it reflects the way in which the bridging propositions are also at risk when a theory is tested. But the method of relevant variables would be equally applicable if the latter alternative were adopted instead: the bridging propositions would then be relatively *a priori*.

Let us assume, for purposes of clarity, that the regularities to be explained by a scientific theory H are all correlations between just two variables. (Again the validity of my point would be unaffected, though its expression would become more complicated, if this restrictive assumption were abandoned.) Then the inductively testable equivalent of H will have the form

(3)   For any natural variables v_R and v_S, any dyadic second order property f, any first-order characteristic R and any individual element x, if x has R and R is a variant of v_R and the conjunction A_1 & A_2 & ... & A_m implies (logically or mathematically) that if x has R and R is a variant of v_R then there is an S such that x has S and S is a variant of v_S and $f(S,R)$, then there is an S such that x has S and S is a variant of v_S and $f(S,R)$,

where A_1, A_2, ... and A_m are the postulates for H (including appropriate bridging propositions). Though a hypothesis like (3) is a third-order proposition, a merely first-order existential proposition, asserting, say, that there is an x that has V_R and V_S and ...., will imply the co-instantiation of the antecedent and consequent of such a hypothesis, or the co-instantiation of its antecedent and of the negation of its consequent, just so long as V_R and V_S are variants of variables that have a correlation deducible from the conjunction A_1 & A_2 & ... & A_m.

People sometimes speak as if correlational generallizations themselves can support a theory. Perhaps a stated value for the acceleration of falling bodies, for instance, may be said to support Newtonian mechanics. But in an analytical reconstruction of discourse about inductive support it is preferable to suppose a theory supported by first-order statements of evidence for correlational generalizations rather than by these correlational generalizations themselves. On the former supposition we can infer from the premiss that a report of such-and-such test-results is true, to the conclusion that there is this-or-that grade of support for the theory. But on the other supposition— with the theory being supported by correlational generalizations —we can only infer this-or-that grade of support for the theory from a premiss asserting the truth of some such generalization. And then, since such a truth is in turn a matter for inductive support rather than observational verification, we shall find ourselves entitled, by the experimental evidence, to infer only that there is support for there being support for the theory— which is a rather more indirect form of support than what is normally claimed for familiar scientific theories. So (3) seems a suitable form in which to conceive of an equivalent of H that is testable against the relevant variables for theories in that field. It is no doubt largely because membership in the series of these relevant variables is determined by the set of correlational generalizations derivable from H that the latter are themselves sometimes said to support H.

What is to be said about the ordering of these relevant variables? From an ontological point of view they constitute a series in decreasing order of relative importance or falsificatory potential. So from an epistemological point of view one must suppose that scientists attach greater importance to the explanation of some regularities in a particular field of inquiry than to that of others. Anomalies—conflicts between theory and replicable evidence—may be tolerated in relatively minor matters (see §49 below). But this is only because the theory has already shown its worth by explaining some relatively major ones. No theory will be entertained seriously if it does not fit even the regularities that are central to its field.[26]

So, given an appropriate list of relevant variables, we can describe a hierarchy of tests on a theory in which more and more relevant variables are manipulated as the tests get more and more thorough. Admittedly it will very often not be physically possible to combine a variant of one such variable with a variant of another. To the extent that a theory is a generalization over a very wide range of subject matter the different types of regularity with which it deals may often be too diverse to be capable of co-instantiation. But in principle the tests are constituted in just the same way as for more elementary generalizations. Test t_1 contains a trial in every variant of the first relevant variable; test t_2 manipulates every variant of the first relevant variable and every variant of the second in every possible combination with one another, or singly where no such combination is possible; and so on. So statements reporting the results of such tests will afford evidence for grading the inductive support that exists for a theory in just the same way as for more elementary generalizations. The logical syntax of inductive support-assessments for first-order generalizations turns out to have certain features that it does not share with that of support-assessments for higher-order generalizations. In particular the uniformity principle (cf. §51, p. 170, below) does not apply to the latter, since a property that belongs to some intervals on a physical variable may not belong to all.[27] But the logical syntax of support-assessments for scientific theories is precisely the same as that for correlational generalizations, and the method of relevant variables is just as applicable to the assessment of inductive support for scientific theories as it is to the assessment of support for first- or second-

---

[26] In *TIOI*, p. 85, it was suggested that the series of relevant variables for a scientific theory might be arranged in decreasing order of their recalcitrance to explanation. What I am now saying implies the reverse: this fits the fact that a regularity may be difficult to explain without being particularly important (cf. §49, p. 163, below for examples).

[27] Cf. *TIOI*, pp. 82 ff.

order generalizations. We thus have a way of ranking or grading the inductive support for scientific theories that may fairly be said to preserve the central features of the Baconian tradition in inductive logic.

§48. *Whewell's consilience, and Lakatos's progressive problem-shift, as inductive criteria*

Not that this way of grading support for theories has lain wholly unnoticed by philosophers. Important features of it have certainly been described before now, albeit in other terms. For example, Whewell ascribed great value to what he called the 'consilience of inductions', when 'the explanation of two kinds of phenomena, distinct, and not apparently connected, leads us to the same cause.'[28] Thus in Newton's theory

the force of Universal Gravitation, which had been inferred from the *Perturbations* of the moon and planets by the sun and by each other, also accounted for the fact, apparently altogether dissimilar and remote, of the *Precession of the equinoxes.*[29]

In other words

the Consilience of Inductions takes place when an Induction, obtained from one class of facts, coincides with an Induction, obtained from another different class. This Consilience is a test of the truth of the Theory in which it occurs.[30]

But that is exactly how the method of relevant variables has been shown to build up inductive support for scientific theories.

Again, much more recently, Lakatos[31] distinguished between what he called progressive (i.e. scientific) problem-shifts and what he called degenerating (i.e. pseudo-scientific) problem-shifts. He regarded a scientific theory H_1 as being falsified only if another theory H_2 has been proposed such that (i) the supposed counter-evidence to H_1 is a corroborating instance for H_2 that is either inconsistent with or independent of H_1, and (ii) H_2 satisfactorily explains all the empirical success of

[28] W. Whewell, *The Philosophy of the Inductive Sciences*, 2nd edn. (1847), II, p. 285.
[29] Ibid., p. 66.
[30] Ibid., p. 469.
[31] Imre Lakatos, 'Falsificationism and the Methodology of Scientific Research Programmes', in *Criticism and the Growth of Knowledge*, ed. I. Lakatos and A. E. Musgrave (1970), pp. 91 ff., esp. pp. 116 ff.

H_1 and also successfully predicts hitherto unknown facts. Correspondingly he distinguished between empirically progressive problem-shifts, where a series of two or more theories have replaced one another under these two conditions, and degenerating problem-shifts, where one theory replaces another without both conditions being satisfied. Thus, on Lakatos's view,

Einstein's theory is not better than Newton's *because* Newton's theory was 'refuted' but Einstein's was not: there are many known 'anomalies' to Einsteinian theory. Einstein's theory is better than— that is, represents progress compared with—Newton's theory . . . *because* it explained everything that Newton's theory has successfully explained, and it explained also *to some extent* some known anomalies and, in addition, forbade events like transmission of light along straight lines near large masses about which Newton's theory had said nothing but which had been permitted by other well-corroborated scientific theories of the day; moreover *at least some* of the unexpected excess Einsteinian content was in fact *corroborated* (for instance, by the eclipse experiments).[32]

Lakatos pointed out that Leibniz long ago remarked on the merit of a hypothesis which predicts hitherto undiscovered phenomena,[33] while Mill denied that such a hypothesis had any special merit.[34] But Mill's view here is inconsistent with the core of soundness in his views about inductive support, and in any case Leibniz was anticipated on this point by Francis Bacon.[35] The fact is that Lakatos's preference for what he called progressive problem-shifts over what he called degenerating problem-shifts is implicitly endorsed by anyone who adopts the method of relevant variables as a system of criteria for the evaluation of scientific theories.

Suppose E_1 states nothing but the successful results of performing the most thorough tests on i relatively independent correlational generalisations $U_1, U_2, \ldots,$ and U_i in the field of a theory H_1 that has the form described in §47, p. 154. Suppose too that all these generalizations are derivable from H_1. Then, on the appropriate ordering of the relevant variables for H_1, E_1 implies the successful result of test t_i on H_1. But

---

[32] Ibid., p. 124.

[33] In his letter to Couring of 19 Mar. 1678, published in *Die philosophischen Schriften von G. W. Leibniz*, ed. C. J. Gerhardt (1965), vol. i, p. 196.

[34] *System of Logic*, 8th edn. (1896), Bk. III, ch. xiv, §6.

[35] *Novum Organum* I. ciii, cvi and cxvii.

suppose that all these correlational generalizations are also derivable from H_2, that a further correlation U_{i+1} is derivable from H_2 though not from H_1, and that E_2 reports nothing but the successful results of performing the most thorough tests on U_1, U_2, ..., U_i and U_{i+1}. Then if assessments of support are based on the method of relevant variables we have—where s is the appropriate support-function—$s[H_2,E_2] > s[H_1,E_1]$ and $s[H_2,E_2] > s[H_1,E_2]$. Indeed, if U_{i+1} is not merely not derivable from H_1 but is actually inconsistent with it, then E_2 would normally be inconsistent with H_1 also. We should then have not only $s[H_2,E_2] > s[H_1,E_1]$, but also, if E_2 is true, $s[H_2] > s[H_1]$.

Compare the typical situation that Lakatos called a degenerating problem-shift. Here there are two possibilities. Either the supposed counter-evidence to H_1 is not a corroborating instance for H_2, so that we do not have evidence from which we can infer $s[H_2] > s[H_1]$. Or H_2 does not satisfactorily explain all the empirical success of H_1 and also predict hitherto unknown facts, so that $s[H_1,E_2] \geqslant s[H_2,E_2]$. In either case H_2 is no advance on H_1, so far as inductive assessments can tell us, whereas in a progressive problem-shift the superiority of H_2 over H_1 is given either by the appropriate monadic, or by the appropriate dyadic, support-assessment.

Admittedly a progressive problem-shift involves more than just superiority of evidential support from known facts. The new theory must also predict hitherto *un*known facts. But since the relevant variables for a theory are, roughly, the main regularities in its field, to discover a new regularity is, in effect, to discover a new relevant variable and thus substantially to improve our capacity to construct inductive tests. Hence so far as the superiority of a progressive problem-shift over a degenerating one involves more than just an increase in *actually* achieved inductive support, it derives this extra merit from increasing the grade of support that our theories are *capable of* achieving. It makes, implicitly, a double contribution to human knowledge. It makes a contribution both at the ground-floor level of ordinary science and also at a higher level—the level of theories about criteria for evaluating ordinary hypotheses in that particular field of scientific research. It gives us not only a better supported scientific hypothesis in a certain problem-area, but also a better system for assessing the inductive support that such hypotheses may possess. If H_2 merely covered more of the already accepted facts than H_1 covered, it would not make this double contribution. But if besides being a hypothesis that covers U_{i+1} as well as U_1, U_2, ... and U_i, H_2 also improves our ability to evaluate our hypotheses by successfully predicting U_{i+2}, it brings us nearer to the truth on two distinct levels of human inquiry. It advances us both towards truth about phenomena and also towards truth about the comparative merits of our hypotheses. Thereby it guarantees that its greater comprehensiveness is not achieved trivially by the mere conjunction of H_1 with the already known U_{i+1}, and so guarantees that we are fully entitled to assert $s[H_2,E_2] > s[H_1,E_1]$.[36]

It should be noted too that important increases in a theory's comprehensiveness, or explanatory power, are thus to be assessed by reference to increases in the accepted list of relevant variables, and that the natural existence of such variables, and their mutual independence, are matters for empirical discovery. This jibes well with the fact that we cannot make worthwhile assessments of a theory's explanatory power—or even comparisons of its explanatory power with another theory's—without knowing what it has to explain. So when we see that a familiar theory can explain some newly discovered regularity, or when we discover the reality of some regularity that the theory predicts, we have to revise our previous opinions of the theory's explanatory power. Attempts to construct global, *a priori* measures of a theory's explanatory power—in terms of, say, the *a priori* mathematical improbability of its truth—cannot possibly come to grips with the epistemology of the problem. It is not philosophical generalists, but scientific specialists, who discover the explanatory power of a particular scientific theory.

It does not matter here if part or all of the observational reports E_1 or E_2 presupposes that certain experimental findings are to be interpreted in accordance with some other theory. Indeed we might have to accept half a dozen other theories in

---

[36] On the avoidance of merely trivial increases in comprehensiveness, which do not increase inductive support, cf. *TIOI*, pp. 87 f. But it is normally a virtue, not a vice, in a scientific explanation that the explanandum should derive from only a small fraction of the content of the explanatory theory, *pace* K. Lehrer, *Knowledge* (1974), pp. 168 ff.

order to be entitled to accept the truth of E_1 or E_2. The grade of inductive support that E_2 can give to H_2 is no more affected by this than the superiority of an empirically progressive problem-shift, as Lakatos conceived it, is affected by the possible theory-dependence of the evidence for it. It is true that the method of relevant variables does not allow us to compare the inductive support available for a theory in one field with the inductive support available for a theory in a different field. But Lakatos himself was not concerned with comparisons between theories in different fields. Similarly the method of relevant variables does not (without compounding variables) allow us to compare the grade of inductive support available for H_1 with the grade of inductive support available for H_2 if there is one relevant variable in relation to which H_1 survives testing but H_2 does not, and another relevant variable in relation to which H_2 survives but H_1 does not. But neither does Lakatos's criterion for differentiating between progressive and degenerating problem-shifts tell us what to say about this kind of case. So the operation of Lakatos's criterion is subject to the same conditions and limitations as the method of relevant variables.

Moreover, while Lakatos gives a vivid and perceptive demonstration from historical evidence *that* progressive problem-shifts are held superior to degenerating ones, he does not explain *why* they are. He answers the question *quid facti*—to borrow Kant's terminology—but not the question *quid juris*. In order to answer the latter question it is necessary to integrate Lakatos's criterion within a general theory of induction which has an answer to Hume's scepticism about the rationality of inductive reasoning. And the theory presented here meets Hume's scepticism by implying that grades of inductive reliability, evidence for which is evaluated by the method of relevant variables, are steps on a staircase that mounts towards necessity. Evaluations of inductive reliability have sufficiently systematic analogies of logical syntax with evaluations of logical truth, for one to be able to treat the latter as a limiting case of the former, or the former as a generalization of the latter.[37] Of course, to infer from the antecedent to the consequent of an inductively supported conditional is not *as* rational as inferring

[37] The detailed argument is given in *TIOI*, §§19–22.

from the antecedent to the consequent of a logically true conditional, which is Hume's paradigm of rationality. But it is a stage on the way to that perfection.

§49. *The problem of anomalies*

One further important point of similarity deserves attention. Lakatos's criterion does not bar the possibility that a research programme might remain a 'progressive' one even when confronted with facts that are anomalies for it. Though inconsistencies must be seen as problems, the discovery of an anomaly does not mean, on his view, that the development of a research programme must immediately be stopped.[38] Similarly the method of relevant variables allows a hypothesis to have greater than zero support even on evidence that contradicts it. The hypothesis can pass test t_i and fail only the more complex test, t_{i+1}. Indeed even when a new regularity in the field is discovered and the list of relevant variables is correspondingly increased, a theory can still have greater support on the new evidence than on the old if the falsifying variable—that is, the anomaly—is kept at the end of the list of relevant variables because of its relative unimportance. The extent to which anomalies have accumulated may then be assessed by the extent to which the hypothesis requires qualification (along the lines discussed in §54, p. 182 ff., below) if it is to be made consistent with all the evidence.

Furthermore, just as on Lakatos's view it is possible for wholly true hypotheses to constitute a degenerating problemshift, so too, according to my own account, a true hypothesis can have zero-grade inductive reliability. This is trivially obvious where a generalised truth-functional conditional is true because its antecedent turns out never in fact to be satisfied. Such a generalization does not thereby acquire some positive grade of inductive reliability, because its truth is accidental and not rooted in resistance to falsification by relevant variables. Symbolically, $-(\exists x)(Rx)$ does not give any inductive support to $(x)(Rx \to Sx)$. Hence logical implication is not a limiting case at the upper end of any scale of dyadic inductive support, any more than contradiction—as exemplified in anomalies—is a limiting case at the lower end.

[38] Op. cit., p. 143.

One can easily find examples of the tolerance of anomalies in the history of science. Newton's theory of gravitation was thought at first, even by Newton himself, to give a markedly incorrect value for the forward movement of the apse of the moon. It was not till 1752 that Clairaut showed how the theory could be made to produce results that agreed with the observed movements. Yet no serious thinker in the meantime either qualified or rejected Newton's theory because of its apparent failure to accord with known fact.[39] Similarly no serious thinker rejected Newton's theory because it failed to explain the movement of the perihelion of Mercury, although this movement was in the end explained only by Einstein's general relativity theory.

No doubt such anomalies are sometimes supposed to be merely apparent, in the sense that the apparently anomalous regularity is thought to be somehow reconcilable with the theory (perhaps by an appropriate alteration in the bridging assumptions) even though no one knows how to achieve this at the time. But it is not always thought so reconcilable. The perihelion of Mercury is a case in point. So the concept of anomaly is one with which any philosophical analysis of scientific reasoning has to come to terms. It plays a vital part in deliberations about which theory to accept and which to reject at a particular time. To suppose that no theory can remain acceptable once it has been confronted with counter-evidence is quite untenable. Accordingly, since a theory that is known to have zero support from the evidence is surely not a serious candidate for acceptance, it must be wrong to suppose that a theory always has zero support on any evidence that contradicts it. A method of assessing inductive support for scientific theories must be capable of doing justice to the tests they pass as well as to the tests they fail.

This is an especially desirable feature for any form of inductive reasoning that is to apply unrestrictedly to generalizations over fairly extensive domains, like scientific theories, since even when replicable kinds of counter-evidence within these

---

[39] See the remarks by Florian Cajori in the appendix to his edition of Newton's *Principia Mathematica* (1962), pp. 648 ff. Other examples are given by R. G. Swinburne, 'Falsifiability of Scientific Theories', *Mind*, LXXIII (1964), 434 ff., and I. Lakatos, op. cit., pp. 138 ff.

domains are unknown it is often obviously rash to suppose them non-existent. Scientists may well want to detach, from a report of existing evidence, the conclusion that a theory H_2 is decidedly more reliable than theory H_1—i.e. $s[H_2] > s[H_1]$— without having to imply thereby that H_2 is totally true, and has no counter-instances in time or space, within its proposed domain. And for that it is essential to be able to suppose that even if replicable counter-evidence to H_2 became known it would not refute the view that $s[H_2] > o/n$. Indeed an extended series of monadic support-gradings is quite unobtainable otherwise. For, if we were to allow a generalizations' falsity to imply its failure to attain even first-grade reliability, then by contraposition we should have to allow that where a generalization has even first-grade reliability it is true.

Perhaps the situation here can be clarified by pointing out the existence of an inconsistent quartet of theses in relation to the problem of anomalies—four theses that are not co-tenable though each has seemed plausible to many philosophers. These theses concern any dyadic function f that is most appropriate for grading or measuring the evidential support which one proposition, in a certain area of subject matter, gives to another.

Thesis I asserts that among the propositions for which evidential support can in principle be graded or measured by f are generalizations over indeterminately large, or infinite, domains. This is because many scientific theories are standardly construed as being, or including, generalizations of such a type.

Thesis II asserts that evidential support is the clue to reliability, in the sense that, where E states the total available evidence, H_1 may reasonably be taken to be more reliable than H_2 if and only if $f[H_1,E] > f[H_2,E]$. To make comparisons of this kind is commonly taken to be a principal purpose of constructing f.

Thesis III asserts that, even if it is highly reliable, a scientific theory may nevertheless not hold good universally. Anomalies are possible.

Thesis IV asserts that for any E and H, if E necessarily implies not-H, then $f[H,E] = o$. That falsification should be treated as the null-case of evidential support is a tenet not only of the Carnapian philosophy of confirmation, which holds f to be a mathematical probability, but also of the very different

Popperian conception of f as a measure of what Popper calls 'corroboration'.[40]

Any three of these theses are co-tenable, but not all four; and there are serious objections to rejecting theses I, II, or III.

The philosophers who, like Carnap and Hesse,[41] reject thesis I confine inductive logic to assessing the reliability of predictions over finite and relatively determinate intervals. But in this way they in principle exclude from evaluation the unrestricted generalizations that figure so conspicuously in the actual work of men like Newton and Einstein. And in any case they do not avoid the paradox. What made lunar movements appear anomalous in relation to Newton's theory of gravity was that the theory was taken to generate particular well-supported predictions which were observably false.

Popper in effect rejected thesis II. Because his corroboration-measure could not deal with anomalies, he developed a supplementary concept, the concept of 'verisimilitude',[42] in order to be able to arbitrate between two theories that may both be false. But the latter concept turns out to be incapable of its appointed task, as Miller has shown.[43]

Many other philosophers prefer, like J. S. Mill, to reject thesis III. If a scientific theory has counter-instances, they sometimes say, then what may be reliable is a suitably qualified version of the theory—a version which excludes such cases—or alternatively the theory may be said to be reliably applicable to any domain that excludes them. But once the degree of qualification thus introduced comes to be graded, a statement about the extent of qualification that is needed in order to maintain full reliability turns out to be necessarily equivalent

[40] K. R. Popper, *The Logic of Scientific Discovery* (1959), pp. 268 and 393, respectively.

[41] R. Carnap. *Logical Foundations of Probability* (1950), p. 572, and M. Hesse, *The Structure of Scientific Inference* (1974), pp. 198 f. On Carnap's theory of instance-confirmation cf. p. 188 f. below.

[42] K. R. Popper, *Conjectures and Refutations* (1963), pp. 233 ff. Inductive reliability has sometimes been confused with verisimilitude. But whereas verisimilitude is thought of as the measure for a hypothesised law's truth- and falsity-content, inductive reliability grades the accumulation of relevant variables that are powerless to interfere with such a law's operation.

[43] David Miller, 'Popper's Qualitative Theory of Verisimilitude' and 'On the Comparison of False Theories by their Bases', *British Journal of the Philosophy of Science* 25 (1974), 160–88. Cf. K. R. Popper, 'A note on Verisimilitude', ibid. 27 (1976), 147 ff.

to a statement about the grade of reliability pertaining to the unqualified version of the theory, as in §54, pp. 182 f., below. There is no logical difference—no difference in logical implications—between admitting that a theory does not apply to certain situations and admitting that it is less than fully reliable because of certain anomalies. So it is more difficult to reject thesis III, and its retention is correspondingly less paradoxical, than may appear.

The method of relevant variables, like Lakatos's criterion of progressive problem-shifts, rejects thesis IV. Evidential support for a generalization, and therefore the generalization's reliability, is graded by the generalization's degree of entrenchment in nature—by its degree of resistance to falsification by relevant variables. *This* kind of reliability can be very high even in the case of theories that have counter-instances in special circumstances. So the existence of anomalies can be accommodated without any paradox.

Admittedly, Lakatos's philosophy of science has sometimes encountered the objection—especially from historically minded philosophers—that certain actual sequences of events in the history of science do not quite fit the framework which Lakatos seeks to impose on it. But a good philosophical theory also, like a good scientific theory, often achieves generality only by idealization. So it is not killed by a few relatively unimportant counter-examples if there is no superior theory to take its place, as Lakatos himself emphasized.[44] For example, the history of spectroscopy between 1870 and 1900 was an anomaly from Lakatos's point of view because, while the spectra of the elements were being described with ever increasing precision, there was very little refutation going on. The fact is that Lakatos's analysis fits best the more important kind of scientific progress, which is marked by our having a deeper and deeper understanding of what is going on in some area of nature. It does not fit that kind of scientific progress which consists in our having more, or more precise, information at the same level of inquiry, as with much of spectroscopy between 1870 and 1900.

[44] Imre Lakatos, 'History of Science and its Rational Reconstructions', in *Boston Studies in the Philosophy of Science*, vol. viii, *PSA 1970*, ed. R. C. Buck and R. S. Cohen (1971), p. 118.

14

The Logical Syntax of Inductive
Support-gradings

Summary

§50. According to von Frisch's method of reasoning the conjunction of two generalizations must have the same grade of support as has the less well supported of the two or as both have if they are equally well supported. §51. Also, any substitution-instance of a generalization must have the same grade of support as the generalization, since it is equally resistant to falsification by manipulations of relevant variables. So substitution-instances conform to the same conjunction principle as generalizations. §52. The assumption of evidential replicability is crucial here and bars Carnap's confirmation-measures, or any form of enumerative induction, from applying to experimental reasoning like von Frisch's. §53. Once the correct negation principle for inductive support has been established it becomes clear how the emergence of mutually contradictory support-assessments can function as a *reductio ad absurdum* argument for the revision of a list of relevant variables. §54. A support-function for generalizations of a certain category applies not only to those propositions that are constructed out of the basic vocabulary of the category but also to those that have been constructed out of this category when it has been enriched by the addition of terms describing the variants of relevant variables. Top-grade support can than be maintained for a generalization, in the face of adverse evidence, by qualifying its antecedent appropriately. But the consequence principle must be correspondingly restricted in its application to qualified generalizations.

§50. *The conjunction principle for inductive support*

To show that inductive probability has an independent standing, and is not to be derived in any way from mathematical probabilities, it is necessary to show first that inductive support, from which inductive probability does derive, is not itself a function of mathematical probabilities. Two arguments to that effect will be given below (in §§55–7). But the second of the two arguments depends on a certain feature of inductive support-gradings which has not yet been established. So §§50–3 are devoted to the discussion of this feature and of some of its corollaries.

The feature in question is that in any particular field of inquiry the conjunction of two propositions of certain kinds turns out to have the same grade of inductive support, on the evidence of any third proposition, as has the less well supported of the two conjuncts or as both have if they are equally well supported. More specifically, where H and H' are first-order universally quantified conditionals belonging to the same category as one another, or substitution-instances of such, and E is any proposition whatever, the principle asserts

(1) If $s[H',E] \geqslant s[H,E]$, then $s[H \& H',E] = s[H,E]$

on the assumption that s is the support-function appropriate for propositions of that category.

There is a quite general argument in favour of (1) if only a finite number, n, of grades of support are possible. This argument runs as follows. If $s[H',E] = s[H,E]$, there are just three possible kinds of value for $s[H \& H',E]$, viz.

(i): $s[H \& H',E] > s[H',E]$
(ii): $s[H \& H',E] < s[H,E]$
(iii): $s[H \& H',E] = s[H',E]$

Possibility (i) is not available where $s[H',E] = n$, and possibility (ii) is not available where $s[H,E] = 0$. Possibility (iii) is available in both cases as well as where $n > s[H',E] = s[H,E] > 0$. Possibility (iii) is therefore the only one that is available for uniform application in every case. Though no similar argument is available for the inequality $s[H',E] > s[H,E]$, even this argument seems to establish a major difference from the conjunction principle for mathematical probability. The inductive reliability of a conjunction is not necessarily lower than that of a conjunct where the latter is greater than zero and less than total.

But the above argument, plausible as it may seem, rests on the assumption that only a finite number of grades of support are possible, and there is no *a priori* reason why this should in fact be true in every field of inquiry (cf. §45). The argument therefore needs to be fortified by some further consideration of what is actually involved in grading inductive support for a consistent conjunction on the basis of experimental evidence, irrespective of whether a finite or an infinite number of such grades is possible.

Let H and H' be testable first-order generalizations. Since H and H' are hypotheses in the same field of inquiry, they are open to the same series of tests as one another. For example, H might be

(2) Anything, if it is a bee-population, is taste-discriminatory

while H' was

(3) Anything, if it is a butterfly-population, is smell-discriminatory.

So a way of arguing for (1) is to say two things. First, if E implies in relation to H that it is not adversely affected by cumulatively increasing combinations of relevant variables up to v_i, and in relation to H' that it is not adversely affected up to v_j, where $j \geqslant i$, then E must imply in relation to the conjunction H & H' that it too is not adversely affected up to v_i. Secondly, if E does not imply that H passes some particular test it cannot be taken as implying that H & H' passes that test. The combination of these two arguments establishes (1) where H and H' are universally quantified conditionals.

Of course, the conjunction of H and H' is not a testable generalization, according to the definition of testability given above (in §44, p. 137). But what an inductive test establishes is the circumstances under which a generalization may be relied on, and this is what the separate tests on H and H' establish for the conjunction H & H'. So it would hardly be reasonable to prohibit the support-function which grades the reliability of H and H' separately from also grading the reliability of their conjunction, as in the case of von Hess's hypothesis that both fishes and invertebrates are colour-blind.[1]

Moreover, when H and H' conflict with one another it can easily be shown that, according to the method of relevant variables, either s[H,E] or s[H',E] or both must be equal to zero, so that by (1) s[H & H',E] is also zero.[2]

---

[1] *Bees*, p. 4. [2] Cf. *TIOI*, pp. 64 ff., and also § 53, p. 178, below.

§51. *The uniformity principle for inductive support*

But what about the cases in which H and H' are substitution-instances of one or two such generalizations? To deal with these cases I shall need two other principles as premisses.

The first of these is the equivalence principle

(4)   If H is necessarily equivalent to H' and E to E', according to some non-contingent assumptions, such as laws of logic or mathematics, then s[H,E] = s[H',E'] and s[H] = s[H'].

The basis of this principle is that no proposition can be reasonably expected to be either more, or less, reliable than its logical equivalents, nor can any proposition be reasonably expected to be at all different in evidential import from its logical equivalent. But, though reliability (inductive supportedness) is invariant over equivalence, testability (and the capacity to pass inductive tests) is not. The relevance of a relevant variable is tied to its causal impact on individuals that satisfy the antecedent clause of a testable generalization—not the antecedent clause of, say, its contrapositive. So the method of relevant variables is not hit by Hempel's paradoxes.[3]

The second principle needed here is a principle of uniformity:

(5)   For any U, P, and E, if U is a first-order universally quantified conditional that contains no reference to specific individuals and P is just a substitution-instance of U, then s[U,E] = s[P,E] and s[U] = s[P].

By calling P 'just a substitution-instance of U' I mean here that P predicates of one or more specified individuals the conditional schema quantified in U but gives no other relevant information about this individual or individuals. Otherwise it would be easy enough to construct paradoxes out of (6) in which the individual referred to by P was identified as, say, 'the best known counter-instance to U'. Moreover, a consequence of the fact that P gives no other relevant information about its referent or referents is that, where different bound variables occur in U, different individual constants are to

---

[3] Cf. *TIOI*, pp. 18 f. and 101.

occur in P. The point of this latter restriction is that if, for example, we allow sentences of the form

$$a \neq a \rightarrow (Raa \rightarrow Saa)$$

to count as substitution-instances of generalizations of the form

$$(x)(y)(x \neq y \rightarrow (Rxy \rightarrow Sxy))$$

we obtain some logically true substitution-instances for contingent generalizations. Such a substitution-instance will, in virtue of its logical truth, either have maximum support or at least be assigned always the same support-grade, while there may be different grades of support for different contingent generalizations of the form in question.[4]

Inductive support is derived ultimately from the results of experimental or observational tests on universally quantified conditionals. The problem now is to determine the way in which such support may belong to singular propositions that are the substitution instances of those conditionals. Clearly, if U were an appropriately formulated generalization about some causal connection in experimental science and P a substitution-instance of it, the equivalence principle (4) would entitle us to assert the uniformity principle (5), since P would be necessarily equivalent to U. For example, if removal of a bee's antennae genuinely sufficed to produce loss of olfactory sense in one case, it must also do so in any other case.[5] But this mode of argument from assumptions about causal uniformity is not open to us in relation to hypotheses like (2) and (3), which describe abilities rather than causal connections. If U and P in (5) could be *any* first-order universally quantified conditional and one of its substitution-instances, respectively, there is no reason to suppose that P is necessarily equivalent to U or to any other substitution-instance of U.

Nevertheless assumptions about causal uniformity can help

---

[4] In *TIOI* (pp. 20 ff.) this restriction was unfortunately omitted from the informal statement of the principles that required it; and the formal versions of the principles in *TIOI* (pp. 228 ff.) need a corresponding qualification, which is allowed for in §66, p. 236, below (in connection with criterion of theoremhood 112). The assignment of maximum inductive support to logical truths may be justified by systematic considerations of analogy: cf. *TIOI*, §§20–2, and especially p. 200. But see also p. 137, n. 14 above.

[5] *Bees*, pp. 29 ff.

us indirectly here. For, though U itself may not be a hypothesis about a causal connection, yet every experimental test on U investigates certain possible causal connections. It investigates, by the variations typical of causal enquiry (cf. §§42–6 above), whether certain combinations of circumstances suffice to cause the falsification of U. And to say this is equivalent, in virtue of appropriate assumptions about causal uniformity, to saying that if an experiment is to count as a valid piece of evidence it must be replicable: compare what was said about replicability in §43, p. 133, above. If this or that combination of relevant circumstances really suffices to cause the falsification of one substitution-instance of a particular generalization, it should suffice to falsify any other, and if it really fails to falsify one it should also fail to falsify any other. Accordingly, if inductive support is to be assessed in the light of resistance to falsification by combinations of relevant circumstances and if P is as resistant as U but no more resistant than U—i.e. if P resists in just the same combinations of relevant circumstances as U does—then it is reasonable to assign P just the same grade of inductive support as U in the light of any reports of experimental evidence. So the uniformity principle (5) follows in a relatively unrestricted form from the bearing of causal uniformity on the experimental testing of any hypotheses. We do not need to suppose that (5) is defensible only if U is itself a hypothesis about a causal connection. (Similarly where the tests are observational rather than experimental, (5) will follow from the fact that the variants of relevant variables are reliably regular signs of certain outsomes in appropriate circumstances.)

But once (5) is accepted we also have to accept (1) where H and H′ are substitution-instances of first-order quantified conditionals.[6] Consider first the case where H and H′ are

[6] It is perhaps worth pointing out that the argument given here for this conclusion does not have as one of its premisses the principle referred to in *TIOI*, pp. 19 f., as the instantial comparability principle, viz. the principle that inequality of inductive support for two first-order generalizations entails, and is entailed by, a similar inequality of support for their substitution-instances. In *TIOI* that principle was a premiss for the conclusion in question—a premiss which some critics found counter-intuitive. Here, however, the principle is itself easily derivable from (5). (In neither case can the conclusion be established for second-order generalizations which correlate variables with one another. This is because the same combination of relevant circumstances may not have the same causal impact on each variant of the independent variable. Cf. *TIOI*, pp. 82 f.)

substitution-instances of two different generalizations, U and U', respectively. There will always be a further generalization U" that stands in the same relation to the conjunction U & U' as does the generalization

> For any x and any y, if either x is a bee population or y is a butterfly population, then x is a bee population only if taste-discriminatory and y is a butterfly population only if smell-discriminatory.

to the conjunction of (2) and (3). Also there will always be a substitution-instance, H", of U" that stands in a corresponding relation to the conjunction H & H'. Now it has already been established (in §50) that if $s[U',E] \geqslant s[U,E]$, then $s[U \& U',E] = s[U,E]$. So, since according to the uniformity principle (5), where H and H' are substitution-instances of U and U' respectively, we have $s[U',E] = s[H',E]$, $s[U,E] = s[H,E]$ and $s[U'',E] = s[H'',E]$; and since, according to the equivalence principle (4), $s[U \& U',E] = s[U'',E]$ and $s[H \& H',E] = s[H'',E]$; we can conclude that, if $s[H',E] \geqslant s[H,E]$, then $s[H \& H',E] = s[H,E]$. Replacing U' by U we get the same result for the case where H and H' are substitution-instances of the same generalization.

In order for the above argument to go through, it is not necessary to premise that *all* causal connections between individual events should be treated as instances of uniformities. It is necessary to suppose only that such connections are sometimes so treated in, say, experimental entomology—which is adequately warranted. However, the case against a uniformity analysis of causation is not as strong as it is sometimes taken to be. As the topic is marginal to my present concern I shall discuss just two arguments that are sometimes put forward against such an analysis.

First, it is sometimes suggested that the uniformity analysis is an outcome of excessive reverence for Newtonian mechanics, and that in modern science

> One event is the cause of another if the appearance of the first event is followed with a high probability by the appearance of the second, and there is no third event that we can use to factor out the probability relationship between the first and second events.[7]

[7] P. Suppes, *A Probability Theory of Causality* (1970), p. 10.

On this view causal uniformities are merely the limiting case of an essentially probabilistic and Pascalian relationship. But it would be historically more correct to say that the long reign of Newtonian mechanics merely strengthened a pre-existing belief in uniform causation, since such a belief is clearly essential to Francis Bacon's inductive logic and its search for 'forms'. Of course, no one ever doubted that causal uniformities were hard to come by, in a fully determinate formulation. Hence the common use of prefixes like 'in normal circumstances . . .', 'under laboratory conditions . . .', etc. The question at issue is therefore whether one should suppose that there is always a causal uniformity to be found, if only one searches long enough, or whether instead, at a certain stage of refinement in one's investigations of a problem, one should be prepared to give up the search for uniformities altogether and rest finally content with mathematical probabilities. Short of a theory that compels one to do this in a particular area of inquiry, as in quantum physics, it is not easy to see why any philosopher of science should want to say or imply that this is in principle the right way to proceed, if adequate time and resources are available for research. No doubt statistical approximations, or generalizations restricted to 'normal circumstances', are often all that may in practice emerge. But to surrender the thesis that causal connections are, *in rerum natura*, always instances of determinate, unrestricted uniformities is to surrender the most powerful intellectual impetus to further inquiry that has ever existed in human history.

Secondly, it is sometimes claimed that certain causal connections between individual events in nature are instances of neither determinate nor approximate uniformities. For example, it may be suggested that this claim is borne out by statements like

(6)   That woman's death was caused by the contraceptive pill she took

since it is thought very uncommon for the pill to have a fatal effect. But it is a mistake to suppose, that because a statement like (6) does not specify the terms of an underlying uniformity, it therefore does not imply one to exist. For it does have this implication, though in unspecified terms. We are always

entitled to ask: why should we believe such a statement?
How would such a statement be substantiated if it were
challenged? How *could* it be substantiated except by reference
to what happens to women in the same state of health etc., if
they are not given the type of pill in question? Consequently
the implicit uniformity is that any women in that state would
survive under normal conditions if and only if not given the
pill: it is the pill that causes the death of these women.

§52. *Some consequences of evidential replicability*

Thus, so far as the conjunction principle (1) depends on the
uniformity principle (5), it is a consequence of the assumption
that any valid piece of experimental evidence—any result that
is to count as evidence at all—is replicable. And that assumption also has another important consequence. Inductive support,
as here described, cannot be obtained by what Bacon and Mill
called enumerative induction.

Specifically what is assumed in the normal discourse of
experimental science is that any statement of the form 'The
experiment described in E is evidence supporting H', or 'The
experiment described in E is evidence against H', already implies that the result of the experiment described in E will recur
whenever the initial conditions described in E are reproduced.
Hence so far as getting *more* evidence is concerned there is no
point in just repeating the same experiment. If the replicated
outcomes are again favourable to the hypothesis concerned,
this cannot be regarded as increasing the grade of support for
that hypothesis. If they are again unfavourable, this cannot
be regarded as decreasing its grade of support. Instead, if you
accept the normal assumption about replicability, you must
regard any attempt at the actual replication of such an experiment as being merely a check-up on its evidential validity. You
must regard such an attempt as being merely a crude test—at
best a t_1-type test—of whether the reported outcomes occurred
as a result of the reported experimental conditions. There may
conceivably be some contexts of human enquiry in which
enumerative induction is legitimate—i.e. in which the replicability of experimental results (or the repeatability of observational ones) is not assumed and more evidence of the same favourable kind as before is properly taken to constitute an increase

of support. But in the analysis of experimental reasoning like von Frisch's nothing is gained by confusing the question whether an alleged experimental result is replicable and therefore evidentially valid, with the question how much it would favour or disfavour a particular hypothesis if it were valid.

To avoid confusion here is particularly important if one wants to come to some conclusion about the applicability of Carnap's inductive logic. In his system it can be proved[8] (with the help of Reichenbach's convergence axiom) that the confirmation of a singular statement H_1 is increased when, in addition to original evidence stated in E, which is consistent with H_1, we accept a new observational statement H_2 which reports an instance of the same attribute as H_1: i.e. $c[H_1,H_2 \& E] > c[H_1,E]$. But the discovery of a proof for this principle, though welcomed by Carnap, was in fact a heavy blow to his claim to be explicating natural-scientific modes of discourse about inductive support. The discovery showed that this 'principle of instantial relevance', as Carnap called it, is rather deep-rooted in his confirmation-theory; and the harsh truth is that functions for which the principle is provable are cut off therewith from grading the support given by experimental evidence in any context in which an assumption of replicability operates. For in such a context, if E already reports an instance of the attribute described by hypothesis H_1, H_2 cannot be regarded as stating evidence that increases the support for H_1 merely because it describes yet another instance of the same attribute. In relation to von Frisch's type of experimental reasoning Carnapian confirmation-functions could at best provide us with crude measures for the evidential validity of experimental results, in so far as this validity depends on replicability.

Similarly it is easy to construct supposed counter-arguments to inductive principles like (1) and (5) if the error is made of taking these principles to be intended to apply to enumerative induction. For example, if the evidence reports nine observed swans to be white and one black, then the generalization that all swans are white might seem much less well supported than

---

[8] R. Carnap, 'A Basic System of Inductive Logic', in R. Carnap and R. C. Jeffrey (eds.) *Studies in Inductive Logic and Probability*, vol. i (1971), pp. 161 ff., and proofs by Jürgen Humburg and Haim Gaifman, ibid. pp. 227 ff.

some single substitution-instance of that generalization. The substitution-instance seems to have, as it were, some chance of being true, while the generalization has none. So the uniformity principle (5) seems quite untenable if support may be assessed by reference to the numbers of favourable or unfavourable instances. But once you recognize that replicability is a condition of evidential validity in relation to (5), you cannot consistently pay any regard to numbers of instances in assessing the degree of support that some piece of valid evidence affords a given hypothesis. And if enumerative induction is thus clearly distinguished from the familiar, Baconian form of inductive reasoning at present under discussion, the supposed counter-arguments all collapse.[9]

§53. *The negation principle for inductive support*

A pattern of axiomatization for the logical syntax of statements about inductive support is given below in §66. The axiom-schemata themselves and most of the main theorem-schemata have been provided with informal justifications elsewhere,[10] though further arguments for the conjunction and uniformity principles have been given in §§50–1 above. We shall find, for example, that a familiar form of consequence principle is derivable, viz.

(7) For any E, H and H', if H' is a consequence of H according to some non-contingent assumptions, such as laws of logic of mathematics, then $s[H',E] \geqslant s[H,E]$.

The concept of inductive support has in any case to be moulded into conformity with this principle because it would not be much use obtaining evidential support for a theory if one did not thereby obtain evidential support for all the propositions that are logically or mathematically implied by the theory. But at least one important principle has not yet been provided with an appropriate rationale—viz. the negation principle

(8) For any E and H, if E reports a physically possible event or conjunction or events, then, if $s[H,E] > 0/n$, $s[\text{not-H}, E] = 0/n$.

---

[9] Cf. R. G. Swinburne, 'Cohen on Evidential Support', *Mind*, LXXXI (1972), 244 ff., and L. Jonathan Cohen, 'A Reply to Swinburne', ibid., pp. 249 f.
[10] Cf. *TIOI*, p. 221.

One argument in favour of (8) might run as follows. Consider any universally quantified conditional

(9) $(x)\ (Rx \rightarrow Sx)$

that is attributed greater than zero support because of some successful test-results for it or for propositions that imply it. The negation of (9) is (or is equivalent to)

(10) $(\exists x)\ (Rx\ \&\ -Sx).$

But as (10) is not a universally quantified conditional it cannot itself be subjected to inductive tests and be attributed support therefrom. The existence of inductive support for it could be learned only indirectly from test-results for propositions which imply it. But when we consider what the latter results must be we can see that in fact the support for (10) must be zero. For example, if we had favourable test-results for both

(11) $(x)\ (Px \rightarrow Qx)$

and

(12) $(x)\ ((Px \rightarrow Qx) \rightarrow (Rx\ \&\ -Sx))$

we could infer, by the conjunction and consequence principles for inductive support – (1) and (7), respectively—that at least as high a grade of inductive support had been shown to exist for (10) as for the conjunction of (11) and (12), since (10) is logically implied by this conjunction. But every test that (12) passed (by a series of coinstantiations of its antecedent and consequent) would necessarily also be a test that (9) failed. So if in fact (9) has some grade of positive support as was supposed we could not have a physically possible combination of test-results that built up positive support for its negation (10) in this indirect way. If E states a physically possible combination of test-results (i.e. s[not-E] < n/n) and s[H,E] > o/n, then s[not-H,E] = o/n. Hence, by taking E to be a true report of the most thorough test-results, we can also derive a negation principle for monadic support-functions:

$$\text{If } s[H] > o/n, \text{ then } s[\text{not-}H] = o/n.$$

However, the above argument rests on the assumption that the definition of testability (given in §44 p.137) may be safely extended in a way that would allow testability to (12). To avoid having to make that assumption one could argue instead that one has to adopt the above negation principles if one is not to be forced by the conjunction principle into admitting the existence of inductive support, on occasions, for the truth of a self-contradictory statement. If we did have both s[H,E] > o/n and s[not-H,E] > o/n, the conjunction principle would give us s[H & not-H,E] > o/n. And then, if E were true, we could detach s[H & not-H] > o/n. To avoid that undesirable result from the consequence principle we have to suppose that for any E describing an encounterable set of events either s[H,E] or s[not-H,E] must be zero. The negation principle (8) states just this, and thus ensures, via (1), that for such an E we shall always have s[H & not-H,E] = o/n.

Someone may perhaps object at this point that a difficulty now emerges for the proposed treatment of anomalies in theoretical science (§49 above). 'Let H_1', the objection would run, 'be a theory that has greater than zero support on E, where E includes the report of evidence of an anomaly in relation to H_1. Let H_2 be a theory that explains this anomaly, together with all the other laws explained by H_1, so that H_2 has even higher support on E than H_1 has. Then H_1 and H_2 are apparently inconsistent in their consequences, so that H_2 implies not-H_1. By the consequence principle therefore we have s[not-H_1,E] ⩾ s[H_2,E] > o/n. But we also have s[H_1,E] > o/n. So we now have both s[H_1,E] > o and also s[not-H_1,E] > o even where E states perfectly respectable test-results; and that contradicts your negation principle.'

This line of reasoning is quite impeccable. But the conclusion to which it leads is not that the present philosophical account of inductive support is untenable. The conclusion should instead be that the particular method of assessing support which generates such a contradiction has to be rejected. All assessments of inductive support that are actually made, and the particular criteria by which they are made, are empirically corrigible. What has happened here is just that the emergence of apparent support for a contradiction forces us to regard one such method of support-assessment as requiring readjustment. If E indeed states a physically possible combination of circumstances, then it contains evidence arbitrating effectively between H_1 and H_2. The relevant variable thus arbitrating—call it 'v'—may therefore be taken to be the most important relevant variable so far as judgement on H_1 and H_2 are concerned; and in accordance with an appropriately readjusted list of relevant variables with v now as first member of the series, we shall have $s'[H_1,E] = o/n$. In other words the regularity that was previously regarded as an anomaly, while H_1 was the only available theory, need no longer be so regarded, because a new theory H_2 is now available to explain it. In relation to the two theories v is now to be considered the relevant variable with greatest falsificatory potential and put first in the appropriate list of relevant variables. Accordingly there is no longer any need to suppose that H_1, despite the existence of evidence refuting it, has greater than zero support, and thus no longer any apparent support for the contradiction H_1 & not-H_1.

The negation principle may therefore be viewed as enabling us to construct a *reductio ad absurdum* argument here for revising the ordering of our set of relevant variables. By the old ordering we had $s[H_1,E] > o/n$, from which the negation principle entitled us to infer $s[\text{not-}H_1,E] = o/n$ for the E in question. But we could also infer $s[\text{not-}H_1,E] > o/n$. Now these two conclusions cannot both be true, if E is true, since $s[\text{not-}H_1]$ cannot be both equal to and greater than zero. It follows that there must be something wrong with our method of assessing support. And if we have no reason to suspect the correctness and adequacy of our set of relevant variables it must be the ordering of this set that is at fault.

We must be particularly careful to keep apart here our ontological conception of inductive support from our epistemological one. Support may actually exist for a theory, though it is as yet unknown to us and unrepresented in our judgements. So major advances in science, as already remarked (§48, pp. 159 f.), proceed on at least two levels. Such advances involve not only the discovery of better theories about the world but also the discovery of better methods for assessing the reliability of these theories. The point emerged earlier in relation to the superiority of a theory that predicts hitherto unknown facts about the world, since this extends our list of relevant variables.

And the same point emerges now in relation to the superiority of a theory that eliminates anomalies. That kind of theory enables us to reorder our list of relevant variables.

Yet a third way in which the point emerges is also worth mentioning. Two theories H_1 and H_2 may have incompatible implications about which no evidence is at present available. Popper[11] cites the example of Einstein's and Newton's theories of gravitation, which lead to incompatible results for strong gravitational fields and fast-moving bodies. In such a case, where the actual evidence does not discriminate at all between the two theories and supports both equally, we again have a result, with the help of (7), that contradicts the negation principle. But here too the proper conclusion to draw is that there is something wrong with the particular method of assessing support which generates the contradiction. Specifically, the method is at fault in not including some of the relevant variables, viz. the ones that would in fact arbitrate between the two theories. The situation is that tests with these variables are at present impracticable, so they cannot be listed in our current criteria of assessment. But then we must be content to find the incompleteness of our current criteria reflected in the contradictions which are generated by the claim to adequacy that is implicit in these criteria. The evidence shows that claim not to be fully supported. That is, we have to act on a hypothesis about the proper method of assessment for our scientific theories which, because it encounters its own special kind of anomaly, has itself to be assessed—at the appropriate, higher level—as falling short of full reliability.

In short, the emergence of such contradictions is very far from being an objection to the proposed logical syntax for statements about inductive support. Rather, it enables us to elucidate how the actual progress of science in a particular field of inquiry imposes a continuing local readjustment in our criteria of evidential support. Inductive appraisal has a vitally important internal dynamic that must not be ignored. Any globally applicable analysis, like Carnap's, which supposes each derivable support-assessment to be *a priori* true for all time, inevitably obscures this dynamic.

[11] K. R. Popper, *Logic of Scientific Discovery* (1959), p. 374.

§54. *Some consequences of modifying a generalization in order to ensure reliability*

I shall assume that the logical syntax of statements about inductive support is the same for non-testable generalizations and their substitution-instances as for testable ones. This assumption is underwritten partly by the equivalence principle (4), and partly by considerations of systematic analogy. But it should be noticed that a support-function for hypotheses of a certain category applies also to certain other propositions besides those testable and non-testable ones that are constructed out of the basic vocabulary of the category. Specifically, it applies also to those propositions that are constructed out of this vocabulary when it has been enriched by the addition of one or more predicables describing variants of v_2, v_3, . . . or v_n in the series of relevant variables. And the reason is that any member of the series of relevant variables must also be relevant to some generalizations constructed out of the enriched vocabulary.

Suppose that the series includes variable v_j as well as variable v_i. Then the mutual independence of relevant variables implies that each variant of v_j falsifies some generalization which is not falsified by any variant of v_i. So, *a fortiori*, each variant of v_j would falsify some of the generalizations it does falsify even if they were qualified in their antecedents so as to apply only to this or that variant of v_i—provided that the qualification did not in fact protect the generalizations against such falsification. And, where it did protect them, each variant of v_j would falsify some of the generalizations it does falsify when they were qualified in their antecedents so as to apply only when this or that variant of v_i was absent. The variable v_j is therefore relevant to propositions formulated in the basic vocabulary enriched by the terms of v_i, for just the same kind of reason as it is relevant to propositions formulated in the basic vocabulary alone.

It follows that, whenever a testable generalization passes all tests up to t_1 but fails t_{i+1}, we can always modify it so as to produce a generalization implicit in the original one which will in fact pass t_{i+1} and therefore has just as good a claim to be called 'testable'. We can do this in either of two ways, and such modified propositions will hereafter also be regarded as testable.

One way is to specify some particular circumstance in the antecedent that excludes the falsifying variant. For example, if the original generalization were

(13)   Anything, if it is R, is S

and the falsifying variant of relevant variable v_{i+1} were V^1_{i+1}, then the generalization that would survive test t_{i+1} might specify some other variant of v_{i+1}, as in

(14)   Anything, if it is R and V^2_{i+1}, is S.

Essentially this was von Frisch's move when he discovered that bees did not discriminate all colours.

The other way of buying support for a generalization at the cost of weakening it is to restrict its range of application. This may be achieved by specifying in the antecedent that no variant at all of a certain relevant variable is present. For example, we might replace (13) not by (14) but by

Anything, if it is R and not V^1_{i+1} and not V^2_{i+1}, is S

where V^1_{i+1} and V^2_{i+1} are all the variants of v_{i+1}. In other words we would replace (13) by

(15)   Anything, if it is R and not characterized by any variant of v_{i+1}, is S.

Such a move is always possible because no member of a series of inductively relevant variables is logically exhaustive (cf §44, p. 136, above) and therefore there is always—for each relevant variable in the series—some non-relevant circumstance that excludes any variant of the relevant variable from being present. For example, it might be that certain adverse weather conditions, such as rain, hail, or snow, affects some insects' sensitivity to colour. So a hypothesis on this subject might need to be restricted, on the model of (15) to normal weather conditions.

The qualification of causal generalizations proceeds analogously. To assert that anything's being R is a cause or a sign of its being S is tantamount, as we have seen (§46, p. 150), to asserting that the conjunction of (13) with an appropriate statement about a control for R is maximally reliable. So if a causal generalization is qualified by adding one or more specified variants of relevant variables to the causal conditions, then the conjunction to which maximal reliability is ascribed must include not only a qualified conditional generalization, like (14), but also appropriate statements about controls for each of these specified variants as well as for R itself. But if instead— as is also very common—a causal generalization is qualified negatively, like (15), the situation is somewhat different. To assert that, when not characterized by any variant of v_{i+1}, anything's being R is a cause or a sign of its being S, is tantamount to asserting just that the conjunction of (15) with a similarly qualified statement about a control for R is maximally reliable.

Indeed the expression 'in normal circumstances', which is so often used in practice to qualify hypothesised generalizations, may be interpreted as a comprehensive, collective restriction of the type present in (15) or in an analogously qualified causal generalization. So may *ceteris paribus*, 'under laboratory conditions', and similar phrases. Accordingly the introduction of non-exhaustive relevant variables into a theory of inductive support is not just an *ad hoc* dodge to get round the objection mentioned above (in §44, p. 135). Rather, it is essential if we want to be able to precisify the common proviso 'in normal circumstances' and elucidate its role in inductive reasoning. A non-relevant circumstance that is co-ordinate but incompatible with each variant of a particular relevant variable is a safe or 'normal' circumstance because, *qua* non-relevant, it does not exclude any generalisation (that belongs to the category concerned) from operating. Hence this concept of 'normal circumstances' also plays an important role in hypothetical or counterfactual inference. When we discuss what would have happened if the match had been struck in the oil refinery, we have to make some assumption about the other circumstances in this hypothetical or counterfactual situation. And the most appropriate assumption is that, so far as they are unstated, they are normal. That ensures that the generalization which covers our inference would have operated.[12]

---

[12] This problem is discussed at greater length by N. Goodman, *Fact, Fiction and Forecast* (1954), pp. 17 ff., and by N. Rescher, *Hypothetical Reasoning* (1964). The solution proposed here meets all the difficulties discussed by Goodman and Rescher.

The value of operating with relevant variables that are not logically exhaustive is thus that however low-grade the test our hypothesis has actually passed we can always claim that something has been fully established. If a hypothesis like (13) is reported to have passed test t_i but failed t_{i+1}, for example, we can legitimately claim that the hypothesis

(16)   Anything, if it is R and not characterized by any variant of v_{i+1}, v_{i+2} ... or v_n, is S

is fully supported according to the list of relevant variables with which we are operating. (Remember that a report of test-results E, in order to state a premiss for inferring their replicability, was supposed to deny that any variant of a relevant variable was present that was not a variant of the relevant variables manipulated in the test.) Admittedly, if i in (16) is too low, nothing of much importance for science has been established, just as when the word 'normal' in the qualifying phrase 'in normal circumstances' has to be construed too loosely. But for the theory of inductive probability it is quite crucial to recognize the existence of a necessary equivalence between a statement assigning ith grade support to a generalization like (13) and a statement assigning top-grade support to a generalization like (16). To put the same point another way, the threshold of abnormality for fully supported generalizations like

(17)   In normal circumstances, anything if it is R is S

varies directly with the grade of support for unqualified generalizations like (13). Similarly, if we know (or think we know) a safe variant, V_k, for each relevant variable, we can purchase (or think we purchase) full support for our hypothesis by specifying these variants in the antecedent, as in

(18)   Anything, if it is R and V^k_{i+1} and V^k_{i+2} and ... and V^k_n, is S

Or we can combine the method of (16) and (18) as in

(19)   Anything, if it is R and V^k_{i+1} and V^k_{i+2} and ... and V^k_j and not characterized by any variant of v_{j+1}, ... or v_n, is S

It will turn out that, for the rational reconstruction of statements about inductive probability, all these methods of qualification or modification are important.

But what should be said where a hypothesis like (13) is modified by a variant of v_{i+1} as in (14) and the modification is disadvantageous rather than advantageous? That is, what should be said when the circumstances described in the antecedent of the modified version suffice to exclude the truth of the consequent, and the generalization is therefore false? Clearly no other support-grading than zero is appropriate for the modified version: this version does not resist falsification under any test.[13] But the unmodified version, (13), may have greater than zero reliability because it manages to pass some of the simpler tests. It follows that, since the unmodified version logically implies the modified one, the consequence principle mentioned in §53 cannot apply unrestrictedly to hypotheses like (14) or (18).[14] We cannot say that such a hypothesis will always have at least as much inductive support as any hypothesis of which it is a logical consequence. So what principle is operative here?

Obviously the essence of the consequence principle is that a proposition is exposed to any source and extent of falsification to which any consequence of it is exposed. Hence the principle applies only where whatever exposes the consequence to falsification also exposes the premiss. So the restricted consequence principle, which can apply not only to propositions in the basic terminology of a particular category but also to appropriately modified versions of such propositions, will be

For any propositions E, H, and H′, such that H′ is a con-

---

[13] This is because tests $t_1, t_2, \ldots t_i$ would be inapplicable, since a variant of v_{i+1} would be present in each (cf. p. 134), and tests $t_{i+2}, t_{i+3}, \ldots t_n$ would falsify the generalization, since the series of relevant variables is so ordered that a more important relevant variable can never have its falsificatory potential wholly nullified by a less important one (cf. p. 139).

[14] The need to restrict the consequence principle was not recognized in *TIOI*, pp. 148–9, because the only modifications considered there were advantageous ones and the concept of an ith grade version was applied not only to modifications of the type exemplified by (14) and (18) but also to those of the type exemplified by (15) and (16)—which in any case create no special problem.
This restriction of the consequence principle for inductive support turns out to be rather important for the possibility of developing a concept of inductive probability: cf. §63, p. 218 f., below.

sequence of H according to some non-contingent assumptions such as laws of logic or mathematics, if either

  (i) no variant of a relevant variable is mentioned in H', or
  (ii) each of H and H' is a testable generalization or a substitution-instance of one, and for any variant V of a relevant variable, if H' states its consequent to be conditional on the presence of V, H also states its consequent to be conditional on the presence of V,

then $s[H',E] \geqslant s[H,E]$ and $s[H'] \geqslant s[H]$.

It is worth noting, finally, that a testable generalization could be modified not only by addition but also by subtraction. Instead of adding the presence of further variants to the circumstances upon which the consequent of (13) is conditional —as in (14), (18) or (19)—we might also subtract the existing antecedent R, which is a variant of v_1 in the series of relevant variables. This kind of modification would produce from (13) the generalization

(20)   Anything is S

which could be attributed first-grade inductive support if it survived testing under every variant of v_1 and then ith grade support if it survived test t_i. Indeed, it would be neater and more systematic to rewrite our philosophical reconstruction of inductive reasoning so as to treat (13) as a modified version of (20), rather than vice versa. Perhaps we cannot subject the discourse of modern experimental science to this degree of regimentation without distorting it out of sufficiently easy recognition. But the conception of (20) as the most primitive form of scientific generalization might be held to have achieved at least one historical realization. At the beginning of Greek science Thales' theory that everything is water, and Anaximenes' that everything is air, could be regarded as over-simplified generalizations that needed to be modified in order to avoid falsification.

15

The Incommensurability of Inductive
Support and Mathematical Probability

Summary

§55. If inductive support-grading is to allow for the existence of anomalies it cannot depend on the mathematical probabilites involved. §56. A second argument for the incommensurability of inductive support with mathematical probability may be built up on the basis of the conjunction principle for inductive support. If $s[H,E]$ conforms to this principle, the actual value of $p_M[H]$ must be irrelevant to that of $s[H,E]$ unless intolerable constraints are to restrict the mathematical probability of one conjunct on another. §57. Since the actual value of $p_M[E,H]$ must also be irrelevant to that of $s[H,E]$, and $s[H,E]$ cannot possibly be a function of $p_M[E]$ alone, it follows that $s[H,E]$ cannot be a function of the mathematical probabilities involved.

§55. *The argument from the possibility of anomalies*

It is integral to reasoning about inductive support, as we have seen (§43, pp. 135 f., and §49, pp. 162 ff.), that $s[H,E]$ may be greater than zero even where E contradicts H. The concept of anomaly has an important part to play in the scientific assessment of scientific theories. It follows from this at least, if from nothing else, that a dyadic support-functor $s[\ldots,---]$ does not have the same logical syntax as a dyadic mathematical probability-functor $p_M[\ldots,---]$.

Perhaps someone will object, however, that Carnap's concept of instance-confirmation is not hit by this difficulty. Carnap[1] equates the instance-confirmation of a law with the ordinary degree of confirmation for the hypothesis that a new individual, not mentioned in the evidence, satisfies the law. So the instance-confirmation of a law need not be zero on evidence that contradicts the law. However this objection will not stand. Its weakness is that not only laws, but also the predictions derivable

[1] R. Carnap, *Logical Foundations of Probability* (1950), pp. 572 ff.

from them, need to admit of being regarded as well supported though false. What made lunar movements appear anomalous in relation to Newton's theory of gravity was that the theory was taken to generate well-supported predictions which were observably false. No doubt Carnap could have developed a further concept—call it 'particularized instance-confirmation' —whereby any substitution-instance of a law is assigned a degree of particularized instance-confirmation equal to the law's degree of instance-confirmation. But, if we were to regard such particularized instance-confirmation as the correct mode of appraisal for singular statements, we should thereby undermine the foundation on which (via the concept of instance-confirmation) this mode of appraisal ultimately rests. For that foundation is the thesis that the correct mode of appraisal for singular statements is one of Carnap's ordinary confirmation measures, which are all measures of mathematical probability.

Indeed it is possible to demonstrate that any concept of inductive support that accommodates anomalies appropriately is not merely not a mathematical probability itself but is not even any function of the mathematical probabilities that might be supposed to be concerned. This is true even if the support-function were to *measure* evidential support, and not just *rank* it. The logical syntax of the concept of inductive support (or of the progressiveness of a Lakatosian problem-shift) cannot be mapped in any way on to the mathematical calculus of probabilities. The demonstration runs as follows.

If the value of s[H,E] were a function of the mathematical probabilities involved, it would be a function of those probabilities relating to H and E that are expressable in the calculus of mathematical probability. Specifically, since mathematical probability functions take the elements of a Boolean algebra as their arguments, it would be a function of the probability of some truth-function of H and E, of the probability of some truth-function of H on some truth-function of E, or the probability of some truth-function of E on some truth-function of H. But it can easily be shown that, for any E and H, $p_M[E,H]$, $p_M[H]$ and $p_M[E]$ are the only mathematical probabilities with which, in relation to s[H,E], we need concern ourselves when, as normally, $1 > p_M[E] > 0$. For first, though negation and conjunction are represented (*qua* Boolean operations) in the formalism of the calculus of mathematical probability, $p_M[\text{not-}H,E]$ and $p_M[\text{not-}H]$ are functions of $p_M[H,E]$ and $p_M[H]$, respectively, while $p_M[H \ \& \ E,E]$ is a function of $p_M[H,E]$, $p_M[H \ \& \ E,H]$ is a function of $p_M[E,H]$, and $p_M[H \ \& \ E]$ of $p_M[H]$ and $p_M[E,H]$. Secondly, the calculus gives us, when $p_M[E] > 0$

$$p_M[H,E] = \frac{p_M[E,H] \times p_M[H]}{p_M[E]}$$

So $p_M[H,E]$ is a function of $p_M[E,H]$, $p_M[H]$ and $p_M[E]$, when $p_M[E] > 0$. Similarly $p_M[H, \text{not-}E]$ is a function of $p_M[E,H]$, $p_M[H]$ and $p_M[E]$ when $p_M[\text{not-}E] > 0$. Thirdly, $p_M[H,H \ \& \ E]$ $= p_M[E,H \ \& \ E] = 1$. Hence for any E and H, since all other truth-functions are definable in terms of negation and conjunction, $p_M[E,H]$, $p_M[H]$ and $p_M[E]$ are the only mathematical probabilities with which we need concern ourselves here in relation to $s[H,E]$ if $1 > p_M[E] > 0$.

Now consider two logically independent generalizations U and U', such that $p_M[U] = p_M[U']$. Let E report, as it might well do, an unfavourable result of test t_i on U, plus a favourable result of test t_i on U' and an unfavourable result of test t_j on U', where $j > i$. So $1 > p_M[E] > 0$. We shall then have $s[U',E] > s[U,E]$, as in §42 above. But at the same time we have $p_M[E,U]$ $= p_M[E,U'] = 0$, because E condradicts both U and U', and also $p_M[U] = p_M[U']$, as given. So here is a by no means abnormal type of case in which the grades of inductive support are different for two generalizations while each pair of mathematical probabilities concerned is identical. It follows that $s[H,E]$ cannot, for every H and E such that $1 > p_M[E] > 0$, be a function of just $p_M[E,H]$, $p_M[H]$ and $p_M[E]$. Inductive support is quite incommensurable with mathematical probability.

To avoid being hit by this argument a mathematicist account of inductive support would have either to require every proposition to have a different prior probability from every other, which seems rather capricious, or to abandon any attempt to reckon seriously with the existence of anomalies in the way that the method of relevant variables does.

§56. *The argument from the conjunction principle: first stage*

In addition to the argument of the preceding section there is also another argument, founded on the conjunction principle for inductive support, which leads to the same conclusion. It is in any case obvious that this conjunction principle does not allow a dyadic support-functor s[..., ---] to have the same logical syntax as a dyadic mathematical-probability-functor p[..., ---]. This is because the multiplicative nature of the conjunction principle for mathematical probability ensures that the mathematical probability of a conjunction will often be less than that of either conjunct, whereas the conjunction principle for inductive support guarantees that the support for the conjunction is never less than that for one of the two conjuncts. But it can also be shown that if inductive support obeys such a conjunction principle it is not merely not a mathematical probability itself but is not even any function of the mathematical probabilities involved. That is, the conclusion is again to be that the logical syntax of such support-gradings cannot be mapped on to the mathematical calculus of chance in any way. The argument will proceed by showing that, if such support-gradings did have a syntax mappable on to the mathematical calculus of chance, they would for that reason have other features that were unacceptable.[2]

The conjunction principle for inductive support implies at least (cf. §50) that, where H and H' are first-order universally quantified conditionals belonging to the same category as one another, or substitution-instances of such, and E is any proposition whatever,

$$\text{If } s[H'E] \geqslant s[H,E], \text{ then } s[H \& H',E] = s[H,E].$$

It follows directly from this, since either $s[H',E] \geqslant s[H,E]$ or $s[H,E] \geqslant s[H',E]$, that for all H, H' and E concerned either

[2] Some earlier formulations of this argument have been too terse to escape the accusation of invalidity from a few critics who were apparently not prepared to investigate whether they could expand the argument satisfactorily for themselves. So the argument here is considerably expanded, and its structure elucidated.

Up to a point we do not need the argument of §§56–7 as well as that of §55. Both arguments are conclusive and so either would suffice. But there are two reasons for giving both arguments here. One reason is to show just how deeply rooted is the resistance of inductive reasoning to a mathematicist analysis. No minor change would undermine this resistance, because the argument of §§56–7 is based on other features of inductive reasoning than those on which the argument of §55 is based. And the second reason for giving the longer and more complex argument of §§56–7, as well as the rather short and simple argument of §55, is that only the former has an analogue for inductive probability (cf. §65, below).

(1) $s[H,E] = s[H \ \& \ H',E]$

or

(2) $s[H',E] = s[H \ \& \ H',E]$

or both (1) and (2) are true. Let us confine attention to those propositions H, H', and E for which at least (1) is true, since this will certainly be a sufficiently wide range of cases for our purposes.

Now it has already been shown (in §55) that, if the value of $s[H,E]$ were a function of any or all of these mathematical probabilities, it would be a function, where $1 > p_M[E] > 0$, of just $p_M[E,H]$, $p_M[H]$ and $p_M[E]$. So, in virtue of (1), the value of the two-place function on propositions $s[H,E]$ would always be equal to that of a three-place function on numbers f such that where $1 > p_M[E] > 0$,

(3) $f(p_M[E,H],p_M[H],p_M[E]) =$
$\qquad f(p_M[E,H \ \& \ H'],p_M[H] \times p_M[H',H],p_M[E]).$

Next, we can make a helpful transformation of (3) by means of the principle[3] that, where $p_M[H',H] > 0$,

(4) $$p_M[E,H \ \& \ H'] = \frac{p_M[E,H] \times p_M[H',H \ \& \ E]}{p_M[H',H]}$$

We then obtain that our three-place function f must be such that, where $1 > p_M[E] > 0$ and $p_M[H',H] > 0$

(5) $f(p_M[E,H],p_M[H],p_M[E]) =$
$\qquad f\left(\dfrac{p_M[E,H] \times p_M[H',H \ \& \ E]}{p_M[H',H]}, \ p_M[H] \times p_M[H',H],p_M[E] \right)$

Consider the cases where E does not increase or decrease the mathematical probability of H' on H. That is, consider the cases where

---

[3] The multiplicative principle for conjunction gives us
$$p_M[H',H] \times p_M[E,H \ \& \ H'] = p_M[E \ \& \ H',H] =$$
$$p_M[E,H] \times p_M[H',H \ \& \ E]$$

and thus

$$p_M[E,H \ \& \ H'] = \frac{p_M[E,H] \times p_M[H',H \ \& \ E]}{p_M[H',H]}$$

where $p_M[H',H] > 0$.

(6) $p_M[H'H \& E] = p_M[H',H].$

In all those cases we find, by transforming (5) with the aid of (6), that our function f must be such that, where $1 > p_M[E] > 0$ and $p_M[H',H] > 0$,

(7) $f(p_M[E,H], p_M[H], p_M[E]) =$
$$f(p_M[E,H], p_M[H] \times p_M[H',H], p_M[E]).$$

Obviously the truth of (7) would be trivial where $p_M[H',H] = 1$. But there might be indefinitely many cases where $1 > p_M[H',H] > 0$. For example, H and H' might be logically independent universal hypotheses, or substitution-instances of these, or they might be substitution-instances of a generalization that was not of the type (to which causal generalizations belong) where, on a strict interpretation, every substitution-instance necessarily implies every other. Moreover, in these cases $p_M[H',H]$ might presumably have any value n, such that $1 > n > 0$. After all, universal hypotheses make each other plausible, and presumably therefore probable, to very varying degrees. Also the extent to which the substitution-instances of a non-causal generalization make each other plausible must surely vary with the nature and/or domain-size of the generalization. So the three-place function on numbers f must be so constructed, apparently, that in all these cases, whatever the value of $p_M[H',H]$ within these limits, (7) remains true.

But what kind of function on numbers can this f be? What we have shown is that f would have just the same value if its second argument were not $p_M[H]$ itself but any proper fraction of $p_M[H]$—specifically $p_M[H] \times p_M[H',H]$. For any H and any E, if $1 > p_M[E] > 0$ and $p_M[H',H] > 0$, then for any H' such that $p_M[H',H] = p_M[H',H \& E]$ the function f has to have just the same value whether its second argument is $P_M[H]$ or $p_M[H] \times p_M[H',H]$. Now, when $p_M[H]$ is very small this conclusion is rather unimportant. But as $p_M[H]$ gets bigger the conclusion obviously gets more important, since the range of possible values for $p_M[H] \times p_M[H',H]$ gets wider. Where the conclusion can be shown to hold for a sufficiently large $p_M[H]$, it follows that to compute the value of f, which is equal to the value of $s[H,E]$, we need apparently take no serious account of the functor's second argument-place. But in what cases can this be shown? We must bear in mind that when $p_M[H]$ is close to 1, then if $p_M[E]$ is also close to 1 so is $p_M[E,H]$. And the conclusion would be rather uninteresting if it held only when a fairly heavy constraint was imposed on $p_M[E]$ and $p_M[E,H]$, e.g. if it held only when if $p_M[E]$ is large so is $p_M[E,H]$.

Assume instead, therefore, for the moment that we are concerned only with support-metrics that apply only to propositions that have prior mathematical probabilities of less than ·5. This covers most practical needs. Normally in scientific research there is in fact a choice between two or more alternative universal hypotheses H, so that $p_M[H] \leqslant ·5$. And the whole point of carrying out experimental tests is that any particular outcome for them—reported by E—also has a low prior probability, so that $p_M[E] < ·5$. Of course, certain disjunctions of such low probability propositions, or negations of them, might have high prior probabilities. But in practice the inductive support available to or from such a high-probability disjunction or negation is rarely of interest. We hypothesize fairly narrowly, albeit in universal terms, and we want to discover exactly what the evidence is. So choose an H that will give $p_M[H] < ·5$. It is then in principle possible to choose at the same time a range of E's that will give you any combination of values you like for $p_M[E,H]$ and $p_M[E]$, within the limits $1 \geqslant p_M[E,H] \geqslant 0$ and $·5 > p_m[E] > 0$. For example, you could choose an E that gave a relatively large $p_M[E]$ with a small $p_M[E,H]$, or a large $p_M[E]$ and large $p_M[E,H]$, or small $p_M[E]$ and small $p_M[E,H]$, or small $p_M[E]$ and large $p_M[E,H]$. But whatever choice of E you add to your initial choice of H, with $p_M[H] < ·5$, you still have (7). That is, f still has to have the same value whether its second argument is $p_M[H]$ itself or any proper fraction of $p_M[H]$. Hence, on the above assumption, if the value of s[H,E] is a function of the mathematical probabilities involved and also conforms to the conjunction principle for inductive support, then it may be treated as being equal to the value of a two-place function on the numbers $p_M[E,H]$ and $p_M[E]$.

Under what conditions could this conclusion be avoided? Only, it seems, if the range of arguments for the two-place function on propositions, s, were heavily restricted.

Suppose that this range were restricted to propositions H_1, H_2, H_3, ... and E such that $p_M[H_i, H_j] = 1$ or $p_M[H_i,H_j] =$

0 or $p_M[H_i,H_j] \neq p_M[H_i,H_j \, \& \, E]$. Then the above line of reasoning would not go through. But such a restriction would deprive the function of any serious utility.

Or suppose the function applied only to propositions H_1, H_2, H_3, . . . and E such that, wherever $p_M[H_i,H_j = p_M[H_i,H_j \, \& \, E]$, E was wholly immaterial to H_i. We should then have established our conclusion only for a rather uninteresting range of cases where $s[H_i,E] = 0/n$ and, in virtue of (1), $s[H_i \, \& \, H_j,E] = 0/n$. But there is no need whatever to suppose (6) restricted to such cases. So long as E contains appropriate reports of favourable test-results, we can have $s[H_i,E] > 0/n < s[H_i \, \& \, H_j,E]$ even when at the same time E also contains, conjoined with these reports some other propositions (e.g. other hypotheses) that adversely affect the mathematical probability of H_i on E.[4] Hence if the other propositions balance the test-result reports so as to make (6) true, we can have (6) true where $s[H \, \& \, H',E] \geqslant i/n$ for any possible $i > 0$.

In general, therefore, our argument loses force in accordance with the strength of the restriction placed on $p_M[H_i,H_j]$ where H_1, H_2, H_3 . . . are the hypotheses to which our support-function applies. But a strong restriction on $p_M[H_i,H_j]$ would deprive the function of any serious utility. As already remarked, universal hypotheses make each other plausible, and therefore presumably probable, to very varying degrees; and it is reasonable to assume that the extent to which the substitution-instances of a non-causal generalization make each other mathematically probable must vary with the nature and/or domain-size of the generalization. Consider here, for example, such a range of hypotheses as 'All insects are taste-discriminatory', 'All butterflies and female moths are taste-discriminatory', 'All spiders are taste-discriminatory', 'All ants are either taste-discriminatory or smell-discriminatory', 'All ants are incapable of discriminating sour from bitter', 'All ants are capable of distinguishing flower-smells but not animal-smells', 'All pear sawflies are capable of distinguishing sweet from bitter but not from sour', and so on.

---

[4] Cf. the consequence principle for evidential propositions (*TIOI* p. 62): for any E, F, and H, if F is a consequence of E according to some non-contingent assumptions, such as laws of logic or mathematics, then $s[H,E] \geqslant s[H,F]$.

§57. *The argument from the conjunction principle: second stage*

It is therefore reasonable to accept that, if for any H and any E (that are subject to the assumed constraints $p_M[H] < \cdot 5$ and $0 < p_M[E] < \cdot 5$) the value of s[H,E] is a function of the mathematical probabilities involved and conforms to the conjunction principle for inductive support, then the value of s[H,E] is always equal to that of a two-place function on the numbers $p_M[E,H]$ and $p_M[E]$. Hence in virtue of (1) above we should have a function on numbers f' such that

(8) $f'(p_M[E,H],p_M[E]) = f'(p_M[E,H \ \& \ H'],p_M[E])$

But what kind of a function can this f' be? It apparently has the same value whether we take as its first argument $p_M[E,H]$ or $p_M[E,H \ \& \ H']$, whatever H′ may be (so long as s[H′,E] $\geqslant$ s[H,E]). So either the two-place function on propositions p_M is very unresponsive to variations in its second argument-place or the two-place function on numbers f' that gives us the value of s[H,E] is very unresponsive to variations in its first argument-place. Or, to put the point another way, the more we allow $p_M[E,H \ \& \ H']$ to differ from $p_M[E,H]$, the more we approach the situation in which we can treat the actual value of $p_M[E,H]$ as irrelevant when we compute the value of f' that is equivalent to s[H,E] for chosen H and E. s[H,E] comes to depend on $p_M[E]$ alone.

The same conclusion emerges if, where $p_M[H',H] > 0$, we transform (8) with the aid of (4) into

(9) $f'(p_M[E,H],p_M[E]) =$
$$f'\frac{(p_M[E,H] \times p_M[H',H \ \& \ E],}{p_M[H',H]} \ p_M[E])$$

Unless, for any such H,H′ and E, some undesirable constraint is imposed to restrict variations in the ratio of $p_M[H',H \ \& \ E]$ to $p_M[H',H]$ we learn from (9) that using f' to compute the value of s[H,E], we need apparently take no serious account of the filler for f''s first argument-place. And the reason for this is that f' would have just the same value here whether its first argument was in fact $p_M[E,H]$ or was instead the product of $p_M[E,H]$ and the ratio of $p_M[H',H \ \& \ E]$ to $p_M[H',H]$.

Someone might be tempted to object here as follows: 'In the first stage of your proof you establish f's equivalence to a two-place function f' by assuming the truth of (6). But in the second stage you in effect establish this two-place function's equivalence to a one-place function by assuming the falsehood of (6), i.e. by assuming that $p_M[H',H] \neq p_M[H',H \& E]$. So the second stage rejects an assumption of the first. It is therefore not entitled to take the conclusion of the first stage as one of its premisses, though it needs to do this in order to go through. The proof as a whole collapses.'

However, such an objector would have misunderstood the nature of my reasoning. The first stage proceeds by considering what kind of a function f must be, as the measure of s[H,E] for any H and any E of a certain kind, if it is to accommodate the fact that, for each such H and E, there may be a vast variety of other propositions H' such that (6) is true. The second stage proceeds by absorbing this consideration and then considering what kind of a function f must be if it is also to accommodate the fact that, for each H and E, there may be a vast variety of other propositions H' such that (6) is false. So there is nothing incompatible between the premisses of the first stage and the premisses of the second. For any H and E there may well be a vast variety of both kinds of other proposition.

Perhaps it would be helpful to summarize at this point the general structure of the above reasoning.

I am investigating the nature of a three-place function on numbers f that determines the value of a two-place function on propositions s, when s conforms to (1) and the arguments of f are in fact the mathematical probabilities determined by the propositions that are the arguments of s. The initial move is to establish that, for all numbers n_1, n_2, n_3, n_4, and n_5, if $1 \geqslant n_1 \geqslant 0$, $\cdot 5 > n_2 \geqslant 0$, $\cdot 5 > n_3 > 0$, $1 \geqslant n_4 > 0$, and $1 \geqslant n_5 > 0$, then there may be propositions H, H', and E such that $n_1 = p_M[E,H]$, $n_2 = p_M[H]$, $n_3 = p_M[E]$, $n_4 = p_M[H',H]$, $n_5 = p_M[H',H \& E]$, and (5) and (6) are true. From this the conclusion is drawn that, for all numbers n_1, n_2, n_3, and n_4 in the specified intervals, $f(n_1, n_2, n_3) = f(n_1, n_2 \times n_4, n_3)$, as in (7). Thence the further conclusion is drawn that there is an f' such that, for all numbers n_1, n_2, and n_3 in the specified intervals, $f(n_1, n_2, n_3) = f'(n_1, n_3)$. Next we infer in relation to this f' that, for all numbers n_1, n_3,

n_4 and n_5 in the specified intervals, $f'(n_1,n_3) = f'\left(\dfrac{n_1 \times n_5}{n_4},\ n_3\right)$

as in (9), and hence that there is an f'' such that, for all numbers n_1 and n_3 in the specified intervals, $f'(n_1,n_3) = f''(n_3)$. So there is an f'' such that, for all numbers n_1, n_2 and n_3 in the specified intervals, $f(n_1,n_2,n_3) = f''(n_3)$.

The upshot is thus that the value of a support-function which conforms to the conjunction principle for inductive support cannot be equal to the value of a function of the mathematical probabilities concerned unless the support-function is either intolerably restricted in its application or assigned a value that is measured by the probability of the evidential proposition alone. But, if the probability of the evidential proposition alone is the measure, any two hypotheses would have the same support on given evidence, which is absurd.

Admittedly this conclusion has been reached on the assumption that our support-function is concerned only with the important sub-set of propositions that have a prior mathematical probability less than ·5. But the conclusion remains valid even when that assumption is discarded. Any method of mapping each ordered pair of propositions on to a number must also provide a method of mapping each member of any sub-set of propositions on to a number. So, if it has been shown that no satisfactory method of doing the latter is obtainable in the case of a certain critically important sub-set, then no satisfactory method of doing the former is obtainable either. I conclude finally, therefore, that there is no seriously viable support-function that both conforms to the conjunction principle for inductive support and has a logical syntax that can be mapped on to the mathematical calculus of probabilities A proposition's inductive support on given evidence has nothing to do with mathematical probability.

16

The Grading of Inductive Probability

Summary

§58. The inductive probability that a particular thing is S on the premiss that it is R is equal to the reliability-grade of the generalization that anything, if it is S, is R. Hence, just as a higher grade of inductive support may sometimes be bought for a generalization at the cost of inserting a qualification into its antecedent, so too a higher grade of inductive probability may sometimes be bought for an inference by enriching its premiss. §59. In the assessment of an inductive probability favourable and unfavourable circumstances may be balanced off against one another. A tree-structure simile is available. §60. Uncounteracted favourable evidence raises the inductive probability of a proposition, but uncounteracted unfavourable evidence reduces it to zero—which is not at all the same as making the proposition's negation certain. §61. A statement of the inductive probability of S on R may be construed as grading the informativeness (what Keynes called the weight) of R in favour of S. §62. If R states all the relevant evidence we know and the inductive probability of S on R is high enough, it may be reasonable to believe that S is true, but we cannot detach here a monadic, unconditional grading for the inductive probability of S.

§58. *The relation between inductive support and inductive probability*

I argued in §§1–9 that the reason why the principles of the mathematical calculus of chance often have a bearing on what we call 'probability' in science, industry, commerce, or everyday life is because they control gradations of inferential soundness when these gradations are determined by certain familiar types of criteria. Fundamentally it was that fact which entitled Bernoulli, Leibniz, and others to start interpreting the mathematical calculus of chance in terms of a concept of probability. It follows that if there are yet other modes of grading the inferential soundness of a proof-rule—modes of gradation that may even be quite resistant to the principles of the calculus of chance—these other modes of grading inferential soundness must also be taken to generate criteria of probability.

Now a monadic grading of inductive support—a grading of inductive reliability—for the first-order generalization that anything if it is R is S is also a grading of the soundness of a rule of inference entitling us to prove from a particular thing's being R that it is also S. So for any particulars a_1, a_2, ... a_m we can derive a grading of inductive probability from the grading of the corresponding generalization, by virtue of the uniformity principle (5) of §51 (p. 170). Roughly speaking, we can say that inductive probability stands to inductive reliability as deducibility stands to logical truth. More specifically, where s is the monadic support-function appropriate to such generalizations and p_I the inductive probability-function, what we shall have is that $p_I[Sa_1, Ra_1] = i/n$ is true if and only if $s[Sa_1 \rightarrow Ra_1] = i/n$ is true. A theory of inductive support thus necessarily generates a concept of inductive probability.

From an epistemological point of view, however, monadic assessments of inductive support are obtainable only by detachment from dyadic ones on the basis of whatever experimental, observational, or inferred evidence we have and in reliance on some accepted list of relevant variables. It follows that, just as these monadic assessments of inductive support are empirically corrigible in various ways, so too—correspondingly—are any assessments of inductive probability.

Should one primarily think of inductive logic (for a first-order language) as the study of the principles involved in evaluating the reliability of generalized conditionals or as a study of the principles involved in evaluating the probability of such a conditional's consequent on its antecedent? This is like asking whether inductive logic should acknowledge its closest formal-logical analogue in the theory of logical truth or in the theory of natural deduction. And the answer can only be, as in formal logic, that since both approaches are possible both need to be explored.

It is also necessary to recall here (from §54) that a certain grade of inductive support may be maintained for the substance of a generalization even in the face of unfavourable evidence that appears to reduce the generalization's grade of support. We achieve this by qualifying the generalization in such a way as to protect it against falsification by the threatening evidence. Our generalization can then keep a higher grade of inductive support than it would otherwise manage to do, at the cost of losing a little of its simplicity. For example, the hypothesis

Any bee population can discriminate one colour from another

turns out to be falsified, as we have seen (§42), by a test complex enough to incorporate different pairs of colours in the experimental situation. But this type of test does not falsify the more qualified hypothesis

Where only the colours yellow, blue-green, blue, and ultraviolet are at issue, any bee population can discriminate one colour from another.

Nor does it make any logical difference if in such circumstances, instead of talking about qualifying a generalization, we prefer to describe what we do as restricting its range of application. In other words, suppose that, in order to avoid falsification, a generalization like

(1)   Anything that is R is S

has to be qualified into

(2)   Anything that is R and V is S

Then the generalization like (1) may be said to be well supported only in its application to things that are V. Or V-type circumstances may be said to be favourable to, or normal for, applying that generalization, to the extent that the generalization is guaranteed a certain grade of support—i.e. survival in tests of a certain level of complexity—if it is construed, like (2), as concerning only V-type situations. Of course, on fundamental issues scientists typically seek the most comprehensive theories (cf. §48 above) and are inclined to accept qualified generalizations only with some reluctance. But much of our everyday vocabulary has been developed to describe the complexly diverse surface features of our everyday experience, and the terms of this vocabulary do not readily line up one-to-one with one another in the construction of well-supported first-order generalizations. Human conduct, plant and animal life, the weather—all these are fields for which we have a rich descriptive vocabulary. But we can rarely construct well-supported generalizations about these fields in terms of our everyday vocabulary without introducing several qualifications into the antecedents of the generalizations. That is why theoretical science, in its search for more comprehensive understanding, has often to develop a new vocabulary that will help to pick out the underlying uniformities.

This point is particularly important for the assessment of inductive probabilities. The better supported the generalization, the higher the probability derivable from it. So, if higher support for the generalization has to be bought at the cost of inserting substantial qualification into its antecedent (as it often has to be in generalizations about human affairs, for example), the probability of a's being S will be raised only on the assumption that a itself satisfies those further conditions. At the same time it must be remembered (see §54, p. 185, above) that, even though the generalization is then better supported, it may nevertheless apply with complete reliability only in the case of anything that is not characterized by any variant or combination of variants of any other relevant variables. So a completely safe inference to a's being S can be drawn only on the assumption, not just that a is R and V_2 and V_3 and . . . and V_i, but also that a is not characterized by a variant or combination of variants of relevant variables v_{i+1}, v_{i+2}, . . . or v_n. That is, a completely safe inference requires the additional assumption that all the other relevant circumstances are normal.

§59. *The balancing off of favourable and unfavourable circumstances in the assessment of an inductive probability*

Let us look a little more closely at the way in which inductive probabilities are determined within a field of inquiry, like human conduct or British weather, in which surface uniformities are very rare and most well-supported generalizations are heavily qualified.

Assume some appropriate domain of discourse, such as weather situations in an oceanic climate. Then, if R states just that dark clouds are looming up at a particular time and place and S that rain is imminent there, we may have $p_i[S,R] > 0$, because there is some inductive support for the generalization that dark clouds are followed by rain.

That is to say, suppose that in normal circumstances dark clouds are followed by rain. The generalization that dark clouds portend rain may therefore be said to pass its inductive test t_1. (Test t_1 for a generalization like (1), it will be remembered from §42, was the limiting case of an inductive test, where no variants of relevant variables are present except the factor described by the antecedent of the generalization.) So, if in fact there is at least first grade support for the generalization, then $p_I[S,R] \geqslant 1/n$, where n is the total number of relevant variables.

But the presence of an offshore wind (V_2) tends to falsify the generalization that dark clouds are followed by rain. That is, in normal circumstances dark clouds and an offshore wind are not followed by rain. Therefore the generalization that dark clouds are followed by rain fails test t_2, if the direction of the wind is supposed to be the second relevant variable. Hence $p_I[S,R] < 2/n$, and, more precisely, $p_I[S,R] = 1$. Or we can talk instead about the generalization that dark clouds and an offshore wind are followed by rain. This generalization has zero reliability, because it has an unfavourable variant of the second relevant variable—wind-direction—built into it and is falsified by every test (cf. §54, p. 186). Hence $p_I[S,R \ \& \ V_2] = 0$. What emerges then is that $p_I[S,R \ \& \ V_2] < p_I[S,R]$. That is, rain is less probable on the evidence of dark clouds and an offshore wind than on the evidence of dark clouds alone: an offshore wind is unfavourably relevant to the probability of rain on the evidence of dark clouds.

Note, however, that the term 'evidence' has a different reference here from what it had in §§42–57. The typical evidence for an inductive probability is not—as it is for inductive support—the results of experimental or observational tests on a generalization under suitably varied conditions. Instead it is the satisfaction of the antecedent of an appropriate generalization in a particular case covered by that generalization. Similarly what is primarily evidenced by this is the satisfaction of the consequent of the same covering generalization in the same case, not a purely general statement that makes no mention of particular cases. Valid evidence for a grading of inductive *support* is in principle replicable or repeatable: the report of some observed regularity is said to support some rather more comprehensive generalization, because of what we think we know about relevant variables. But in regard to inductive *probability* one singular proposition is said to provide evidence for another because of what we think we know about inductive support.

Now perhaps when the barometer is falling (V_3) an offshore wind tends not to falsify the generalization that dark clouds portend rain. So the generalization that dark clouds with an offshore wind and falling barometer are followed by rain may be rather better supported, because more protected against falsification, than the unqualified generalisation that dark clouds *simpliciter* are followed by rain. More precisely, if decreasing barometric pressure tends to prevent the presence of an offshore wind from falsifying the generalization that dark clouds are followed by rain, what we must accept is that, *if* no other relevant circumstances are present, dark clouds with an offshore wind and falling barometer are followed by rain. Hence the generalization that dark clouds with an offshore wind and falling barometer are followed by rain passes test t_3, if barometric pressure is supposed to be the third relevant variable. Therefore $p_I[S,R \& V_2 \& V_3] \geqslant 3/n$, and $p_I[S,R \& V_2 \& V_3] > p_I[S,R]$. That is, rain is more probable on the evidence of dark clouds, offshore wind and falling barometer, than on the evidence of dark clouds alone.

Again, perhaps even our relatively well-qualified generalization tends not to hold good in the height of summer (V_4). So, if the season of year is assumed to be our fourth relevant variable, the generalization that in the height of summer dark clouds, offshore wind, and falling barometer are followed by rain will fail to pass test t_4, and has zero reliability, because it has an unfavourable variant of the fourth relevant variable built into it. Hence $p_I[S,R \& V_2 \& V_3 \& V_4] = 0$. That is, V_4 tends to counteract the probabilifying force of the combination of other factors. But perhaps there is an exception to this when heavy thunder is audible (V_5). Correspondingly $p_I[S,R \& V_2 \& V_3 \& V_4 \& V_5] \geqslant 5/n$.

What is happening here is that the relevant circumstances of the situation are being divided into two classes—those that favour applying the generalization 'Dark clouds are followed by rain' and those that do not. These favourable and unfavourable circumstances are then balanced off against one another, and the probability is determined accordingly. If we could safely assume that, apart from the factor mentioned in the antecedent of the original generalization, there were only four relevant variables (wind-direction, barometric pressure, season, and atmospheric electricity), we could safely claim maximum inductive probability. The thunder would have said the last word, as it were, and rain would be certain on the evidence described. But if there were other relevant factors in a particular situation that we had not detected, or did not know to look for, it would be wrong to claim certainty of rain for that situation even on the evidence described, though the probability might be high. The imminence of rain would not be beyond reasonable doubt. Indeed it might in the end turn out that, when the evidence of *all* the relevant circumstances at the particular time and place was taken into account the imminence of rain had only a zero probability.

Of course, favourable and unfavourable circumstances need not alternate with one another as they do in the example just described. There might be a long run of the one type of circumstance, or of the other. So another way to look at such an example of inductive probabilification is *via* the following simile.

The circumstances of test t_1 for a universally quantified, but unqualified, truth-functional conditional may be viewed as the primary level trunk of a tree that divides into a secondary level of branches, one for each of the variants of relevant variable v_2 that enters into test t_2, plus one for the circumstances that are non-relevant, in relation to v^2, and are thus normal for test t_1. The latter branch goes straight to the top of the tree but is as weak as it is long. The other branches are stouter and much shorter, but divide further at a tertiary level, so as to make up at this level, when all the new branchings are taken into account, the various possible combinations of relevant circumstances manipulated in test t_3 plus one for the circumstances that are normal in relation to t_2; and here too the latter branch goes straight to the top but is as weak as it is long, while the others are stouter and shorter but divide again. And so on, until a level is reached from which no further branchings take off. The proliferation of branches at each level corresponds to the progressively increasing complexity of the tests, while the number of the level corresponds to the number of different relevant variables that combine to constitute the various distinct combinations of relevant circumstances at that level. At the top of the tree some of the branches bear a fruit and some do not. So if a short, stout branch at level i bears a fruit (which it may do only if level i is at the top) or leads to a long, weak branch at level $i + 1$ that bears a fruit, then that short and stout branch corresponds to an advantageous variant, while if it neither bears a fruit itself, nor leads to a long and weak branch that does, it corresponds to a disadvantageous variant. At each particular node more than one (perhaps every) short, stout branch may be advantageous and more than one (perhaps every) such branch may be disadvantageous. But for any level i at which there is a disadvantageous branch—or trunk—there is also a disadvantageous branch at level $i + 1$, in order to allow for the ordering of relevant variables according to their relevant importance (as in §44, pp. 139 f.).

Assigning a non-zero inductive probability on given evidence is like discerning how many levels of short, stout branching, including the trunk, are ascended from the bottom by a given route (which is described only for these levels), where the topmost branch mentioned is an advantageous one. Assigning a zero probability on given evidence is like discerning that the topmost branch mentioned in a given route is a disadvantageous one or that no route of any kind has been given (i.e. the evidence is irrelevant). That is to say, the route is the evidence, and the further the route goes advantageously on short, stout branches, the greater is the weight of evidence and therefore the higher the probability. If the route extends on short, stout branches only as far as level i, after which the climber has to take his chances on a long, weak branch, then the probability is ith grade. In an actual situation, however, when we acquire another piece of evidence, what previously seemed probable might come to seem improbable. And this would be like extending a climber's route on to a short, stout branch that was disadvantageous, from the node at which he leaves his last advantageous one.

It emerges clearly then that, if dark clouds are followed by rain under all, or almost all, relevant circumstances whatever,

R would not need to be conjoined with reports about the presence of certain variants of relevant variables in order to achieve a high inductive probability for S. The level of $p_I[S,R]$ depends on the grade of inductive support that exists for the generalization entitling us to take the truth of R as evidence for the truth of S; and if this grade were high even when the generalization was relatively unqualified so too would be the level of $p_I[S,R]$. The second, evidential argument of an inductive probability-function does not need to be a long conjunction of propositions in order for the function to have a high value. Or, to put the point in terms of the tree simile, you may have a quite low-level node on your tree from which all, or almost all, subsequent branches are favourable to finding fruit at the top. But in regard to any matter, like human conduct or British weather, about which rather simple generalizations are usually false, high inductive probabilities can be expected to be obtainable only on the evidence of a fairly long conjunction. On *those* trees you may have to climb rather high before you find a node from which all, or almost all, subsequent branches are favourable.[1]

§60. *The asymmetric effects of favourable and unfavourable evidence*

One feature of the above mode of assessing probabilities may at first sight seem somewhat surprising. There is a marked asymmetry between the way in which an assessment is affected by uncounteracted favourable evidence and the way in which it is affected by uncounteracted unfavourable evidence. As the evidence taken into account increases, the inductive probability of a particular outcome is raised further by each relevant circumstance of the situation that both favours this outcome by excluding the presence of some unfavourable circumstance and also is not itself counteracted by the presence of another unfavourable circumstance. But an uncounteracted unfavourable circumstance always has the same effect. It gives the outcome

---

[1] A computer-programme for inductive learning, of the kind mentioned in n. 20, p. 145, could presumably be extended to represent the formation of inductive probability judgements. It would take as additional input sentences asserting that this or that named individual satisfies such-or-such a combination of predicables; and it would deliver as additional output sentences specifying, according to the current state of inductive learning, the grade of probability on the available evidence, that the given individual satisfies such-or-such a target predicable.

a zero probability. The point can also be made in terms of the tree simile of §59. If your route takes you to a short, stout branch from which a fruiting branch leads off, your probability of climbing successfully right up to the fruit gets greater at higher levels, as the length of this fruiting branch decreases and its safety increases. But if there is no fruit at all at the top of the long and weak branch that leads off from your short and stout one, then your probability of obtaining some fruit by trying to climb it is always zero, at whatever level you are.

This asymmetry is deeply rooted in the nature of inductive gradation. It arises because inductive probability varies with the inductive reliability of an appropriately applicable generalization. Uncounteracted favourable evidence for the probability of a proposition may mean that just one level of potential difficulty has been surmounted, which might have closed off the way to such a generalization's being applicable. Or it may mean that several such levels have been surmounted. But uncounteracted unfavourable evidence establishes just that one such level has not been surmounted and the generalization is inapplicable. A disadvantageously modified version of a hypothesis has zero reliability (§54, p. 186).

To put the point another way we can say that the function $p_I[S,R]$ grades the weight of evidence which is stated by R and which is on balance—i.e. when all the various interacting factors have exerted their influence—in favour of S. There may be more, or less, of this evidence, if the balance is indeed in favour of S. But there is none at all of it if the balance is not in favour of S.

One possible source of surprise at the above-mentioned asymmetry is a failure to distinguish adequately between two different probability-judgements. On the one hand we have the judgement that S has zero-grade probability on R, which may be true irrespective of the grade of probability that not-S has on R. For we can even have $p_I[S,R] = o/n = p_I[\text{not-}S,R]$, where R is neither favourably nor unfavourably relevant. On the other hand we have the judgement that not-S has maximum probability on R. The former judgement means that there is no positive level of probability at which S may be inferred from R, the latter that not-S may be inferred from R with certainty. So it would be quite wrong to construe an assignment of zero-grade probability to S on R as equivalent to a judgement that not-S is certain on R. Such an equivalence holds for mathematical probability, because of the complementational negation principle $p_M[\text{not-}S, R] = 1 - p_M[S, R]$. But it does not hold for inductive probability, which turns out (as we shall see in §64) to have a non-complementational negation principle.

This fact throws some light on the asymmetry we have been considering, and should make it appear somewhat less startling. Each piece of uncounteracted favourable evidence, we saw, raises the inductive probability of an outcome one grade further, while an uncounteracted unfavourable circumstance reduces the inductive probability of the outcome at once to zero. But that does not at all imply that a single uncounteracted unfavourable circumstance makes the denial of the outcome certain. It means merely that the inference to S cannot be made with any degree of reliability at all, not that the inference to not-S can be made with complete reliability.

We may compare here the difference, in ordinary language, between

(3)   It is wrong to think it probable, on the evidence, that it will rain

and

(4)   It is probable, on the evidence, that it will not rain

or its equivalent

(5)   It is improbable, on the evidence, that it will rain.

This difference is obscured in ordinary language when we replace (3) by

(6)   It is not probable on the evidence that it will rain,

since (6) may easily be thought an equivalent of (4) or (5), not of (3), just as

I do not believe that it will rain

is a common equivalent of

I believe it will not rain.

But strictly we should treat 'probable' as a modal term like 'necessary' or 'provable'.[2] So (4) is no more an equivalent of (6) than

> It is necessary that you do not lie to him

is an equivalent of

> It is not necessary that you lie to him,

or than

> It is provable in Newtonian mechanics that angels do not have wings

is an equivalent of

> It is not provable in Newtonian mechanics that angels have wings.

Again, (5) is not an equivalent of (6), because the improbability of so-and-so's being the case is the same thing as the probability of its not being the case, and quite different from the non-probability of its being the case. Improbabilities have gradations, and it makes sense to ask about (5): 'How improbable is rain?' But the denial that something is probable is a flat assertion. You cannot ask about (6): 'How not probable is rain?' Thus 'improbable' is not related to 'probable' in the way that 'impossible' is to 'possible'. The impossibility of S is not the fact that not-S is possible, while the improbability of S *is* the probability of not-S. The negation principle for mathematical probability elides the disanalogy between impossibility and improbability by putting the probability of not-S equal to the complement of the probability of S.

In this respect, therefore, the usage of natural language approximates more closely to the principles of inductive probability than to those of mathematical probability. But I point that out here only in order to dispel any suspicion of paradox that may attach to the asymmetry between the way in which uncounteracted favourable evidence affects inductive probabilities and the way in which uncounteracted unfavour-

[2] Cf. C. L. Hamblin, 'The Modal "Probably"', *Mind*, LXVIII (1959), 237. There are some interesting similarities between Hamblin's system and the logic of inductive probability. However, Hamblin is concerned with a non-Pascalian concept of probability that is basically monadic, rather than dyadic, and basically qualitative, rather than comparative or ordinal.

able evidence affects them. I do not claim that the point has much force against the mathematicist position, since most systematic analyses or reconstructions of a pattern of human reasoning are on some points obliged to put considerations of simplicity—in notation, postulates, or proof procedures— before those of representational fidelity to ordinary language. The strong arguments against the mathematicist position are arguments like those of §§14–39, which are based on substantive norms of judicial proof in Anglo-American courts, not just on the lexical and morphological quirks of this or that natural language or group of languages.

§61. *Inductive probability as a grading of evidential informativeness*

It was remarked earlier (in §54, p. 185) that for any statement ascribing ith grade inductive support to a hypothesis of the form

Anything, if it is R, is S

there is a necessarily equivalent statement ascribing full support to a hypothesis of the form

Anything, if it is R and not characterized by any variant of v_{i+1}, v_{i+2}, . . . or v_n, is S.

So it will also be the case that for any statement ascribing ith grade support to a hypothesis of the form

Anything, if it is R and V_j and V_{j+1} and V_{j+2} and . . . and V_i, is S

there is a necessarily equivalent statement ascribing full support to a hypothesis of the form

Anything, if it is R and V_j and V_{j+1} and V_{j+2} and . . . and V_i and not characterised by any variant of v_{i+1}, v_{i+2}, . . . or v_n, is S.

And a hypothesis of the latter form may be taken as a precisified analysans for a hypothesis of the everyday form

In normal circumstances anything, if it is R and V_j and V_{j+1} and . . . and V_i, is S.

when the threshold of abnormality is of ith grade height.

Transpose this now into the idiom of inductive probability. What you get is that wherever, say, $p_I[S,R\ \&\ V_2\ \&\ V_3] \geqslant 3/n$, we can infer S with certainty from R & V_2 & V_3 on the assumption that no variant of $v_4, v_5, \ldots$ or v_n is present in the situation concerned. Or, in more familiar terms, we can infer S with certainty from the available evidence on the assumption that all the other circumstances of the situation are quite normal. An assignment of non-zero inductive probability may therefore be construed as assessing the weakness of this assumption. The higher the grade of probability, the weaker the *ceteris paribus* assumption can be—i.e. the less the content that needs to be packed into this assumption, because the evidential statement itself says more. So low favourable probabilities rest on a shortage of relevant evidence, rather than on a preponderance of unfavourable evidence. If $p_I[S,R]$ is greater than zero but not at all high, then R is to be regarded as relatively uninformative about S, not as relatively unfavourable to S.

In terms of the tree-climbing simile of §59 we have to think of the man who achieves his conclusion by means of a *ceteris paribus* assumption as being like a climber who, at some particular level that happens to be favourable, stops trying to find his way up the maze of short, stout branches and instead tries to climb up a long, weak one to the fruit that he sees at the top. The higher the level he is on, the shorter his final climb, and the greater his chance of success. The length of this final, rather risky climb corresponds to the extent of relevant ignorance of the man who has to rely on a *ceteris paribus* assumption in order to prove his conclusion with certainty.

A rather deep difference emerges here between the mathematical probability of propositions, on the one side, and their inductive probability, on the other. The function $p_M[S,R]$ grades how favourable the evidence of R is to S, on the assumption that R alone is to be considered, irrespectively of how large or small a portion R manages to report of the total relevant facts. But $p_I[S,R]$ grades the actual extent of that portion of the total relevant facts which is on balance favourable to S and is what R reports.

This remains true even when the fairly high inductive probability of S on R springs from the applicability of a relatively unqualified generalization. In such a case $p_I[,SR]$ is fairly high despite R's not being the conjunction of many independent items of evidence. But even here R must be a fairly large portion of the total *relevant* evidence, since $p_I[S,R]$ always varies inversely with the strength of the *ceteris paribus* assumption that has to be conjoined with R for S to be inferable with certainty from their conjunction. The most accurate gauge of the informativeness of an evidential statement is the fewness of the assumptions that need to be made in answer to relevant questions which the statement omits to answer. So R can be highly informative in relation to S even though its semantic content is relatively slight. This is like when you are describing a route up a tree and, between certain levels, do not need to specify which branch to take at each node because all branches are advantageous.

It follows that inductive probability is concerned with that dimension of appraisal which Keynes referred to as the 'weight' of evidence. As we have already seen (in §11, pp. 36 f.) Keynes held that

One argument has more *weight* than another if it is based on a greater amount of relevant evidence . . . It has a greater *probability* [i.e. mathematical probability] than another if the balance in its favour, of what evidence there is, is greater than the balance in favour of the argument with which we compare it.

Such a dimension of appraisal, we saw, constituted a gradation of inferential soundness that was analogous to proof-criteria in an incomplete deductive system. And in keeping with that analogy the appropriate negation principle for such a dimension of appraisal was seen (§§10–11) to be a non-complementational one, such that, if the truth of A is possible and $p[B,A] > 0$, then $p[not\text{-}B,A] = 0$. It is fitting therefore that the negation principle for inductive probability should turn out (cf. §64, p. 221, below) to be of this form.

§62. *The presumption of total evidence*

We have noticed (in §61) that the magnitude of $p_I[S,R]$ varies inversely with the strength of the *ceteris paribus* assumption that has to be conjoined with R for S to be inferable with certainty from their conjunction: the probability rises as the content of the assumption gets slighter. But this *ceteris paribus* assumption should not be confused with the presumption raised by anyone who utters an elliptical judgement of probability—a judgement that elides mention of the evidence because it is unnecessary. Noting the dark clouds, the east wind, and the falling barometer, for example, a man might intelligibly claim

(7)   There's a good (inductive) probability of rain.

He would thereby raise the presumption that he had taken into account all the facts that he knew and thought relevant, because his utterance would be taken to be elliptical for

(8)   On the available evidence there's a good probability of rain.

Anyone who thinks that (7) is true without making appropriate efforts to inform himself about relevant facts would normally be jumping to conclusions; and anyone who asserted (7) without taking into account all the facts that he knows and thinks relevant would normally be misleading his audience. But such faults are just faults in the procedure of forming or uttering elliptical probability-judgements. Hence even when we learn that the presumption raised by an utterance of (7) is correct we can infer only that the author of the utterance has behaved correctly. It is not at all like learning the truth of the *ceteris paribus* assumption. It is not at all like learning that, after all, there are no other relevant facts in the present case than the dark clouds, the east wind, and the falling barometer, and therefore that the appropriate prediction, which we thought to be only probable, is certain to be true.

Nor should a judgement like (7), which is elliptical for a dyadic judgement of probability like (8), be confused with a genuinely monadic judgement of inductive probability. We can in fact define a monadic function $p_I[S]$ to have the same value for any first-order proposition S as the dyadic function $p_I[S,R]$ where R is tautological. It then turns out to be demonstrable—cf. §66, p. 237, below—that, for any first-order proposition S, $p_I[S] = s[S]$. That is, a monadic or 'prior' inductive probability is, as one might expect, just the same thing as a monadic grading of inductive support. An inductive probability that is 'prior', in the sense of not being relative to evidence, is one that is given unconditionally by our knowledge about inductive reliability. For example, if the appropriate dyadic function assigns ith grade inductive probability, on the present evidence of dark clouds, to the proposition that it will rain, the corresponding monadic function assigns ith grade probability (support, reliability) to the proposition that dark clouds will be followed by rain.

So the relation between monadic and dyadic judgements of inductive probability is not analogous to that between monadic and dyadic judgements of inductive support. From the dyadic judgement that certain replicable test-results would provide ith grade support for the generalization

Anything, if it is R, is S

it is possible, if we are given these test-results, to detach the monadic judgement that the generalization has ith grade reliability. This form of detachment is common in science, as has already been remarked (§43, p. 134). But from the dyadic judgement that a particular thing's being R gives it an ith grade inductive probability of being S, it is not possible, even if we know that the thing is R, to detach the monadic judgement that it has an ith grade inductive probability, *simpliciter*, of being S. In this respect inductive probability resembles mathematical probability. Just as R & $p_M[S,R] = \cdot6$ does not entail $p_M[S] = \cdot6$, so too R & $p_I[S,R] = 6/n$ does not entail $p_I[S] = 6/n$.[3] For any particular category of proposition, however, we can stipulate a threshold, i, such that, for any two propositions of that category, R and S, if we know the truth of R and of $p_I[S,R] \geqslant i/n$, and R is all the relevant evidence we know, then we may regard it as reasonable to believe, or accept, the truth of S. This is fundamentally because inductive probability grades the weight of evidence and, if we are to make up our minds at all, there must be some stage at which we take sufficient evidence to be already available. The difficulties that beset the concept of such an acceptance-threshold for mathematical probability will turn out (see §89, p. 319, below) not to affect inductive probability.

In the case of mathematical probability the situation is particularly confusing because we have there two distinct but

[3] See p. 30, n. 21, above and theorem-schemas 702 and 703, p. 238.

easily confounded considerations about relevant evidence. First, we have a presumption—similar to that discussed in the case of inductive probability—which is raised by anyone who utters an elliptical judgement of probability. Any speaker is standardly presumed to have tried to acquaint himself with all the reasonably available facts that are relevant to the truth of what he says, whether he is speaking about probability, as in (8), or anything else. But there is more to the matter than this: otherwise the requirement of total evidence, as Carnap called it, would hardly have figured so prominently in the literature of probability.[4] The second consideration is that a mathematical probability-function evaluates the soundness of inferring S as a conclusion from R only on the assumption that R does contain all the relevant premisses. Ultimately this is because criteria of mathematical probability, with their complementational negation-principle, can always be conceived as a generalization on the proof-rules of a deductive system that is *complete* as to provability (cf. §10, p. 34, above). Hence anyone who asserts an elliptical judgement of mathematical probability analogous to (7) without trying to acquaint himself with all the available evidence has committed a double offence, as it were. He has not only failed to live up to what is standardly expected from any speaker on any topic. He has also failed to do his best to ensure the applicability—for his case— of the assumption implicit in any detachment of a monadic from a dyadic evaluation of mathematical probability. For it is only because mathematical probabilities grade inferential soundness in a complete system that, so far as a man (who knows the truth of R) is entitled to claim that R states all the facts relevant to S, he is also entitled to detach $p_M[S] = r$ from $p_M[S,R] = r$. No analogous detachment of $p_I[S] = i/n$ from $p_I[S,R] = i/n$ is available, because inductive probability-functions do not *assume* the completeness of the evidence—they grade it, and so, if i is sufficiently high, they allow the detachment of S itself.

[4] Cf. R. Carnap, *Logical Foundations of Probability* (1950), pp. 211 f.

17

The Logical Syntax of Inductive Probability-gradings

Summary

§63. Inductive probability-gradings conform to logical principles that are rather like those for mathematical probability in regard to symmetry between individuals; in regard to logical consequence; and also in regard to the value of $p_1[S,R]$ where R implies S. §64. But inductive probability-gradings conform to quite different principles from those for mathematical probability in regard to contraposition; in regard to the relation between prior and posterior probabilities; in regard to a proposition's conjunction with other propositions; and in regard to its negation. In terms of inductive probability it is possible to describe a generalized form of *reductio ad absurdum* argument. §65. The logical structure of inductive probability cannot be mapped on to the calculus of mathematical probability. Indeed, because inductive support does not seem to be additive, inductive probabilities do not seem to be measurable—though they are rankable. §66. The logical syntax of inductive probability may be deployed axiomatically within a modal logic that generalizes on Lewis's system S4.

§63. *Some logical similarities between inductive and mathematical probability*

One principle that the logic of inductive probability shares in effect both with the logic of mathematical probability and with that of inductive support is the principle of symmetry. It will be remembered that according to the uniformity principle for dyadic inductive support (§51, above) s[P,E] = s[U,E], where E is any proposition whatever, U is any first-order universally quantified conditional and P any substitution-instance of U. It follows, when we take E to be a true statement of the results of the most thorough possible test on U, that we can also derive a uniformity principle for monadic support-functions, viz.

$s[P] = s[U]$. Hence, if P_1 and P_2 are two different substitution-instances of the same generalization U, $s[P_1] = s[U] = s[P_2]$. Correspondingly assessments of inductive probability are invariant under all uniform transformations of their references to individuals. That is to say, $p_I[Sa,Ra] = p_I[Sb,Rb]$, where 'a' and 'b' are place-holders for different expressions that refer to the same or different individuals. A similar principle of symmetry seems to hold for all plausible criteria of mathematical probability on any interpretation of the mathematical calculus that makes propositions the arguments for its functions, as Carnap pointed out.[1] And, though the principle is not derivable from the unenriched axioms of the mathematical calculus when so interpreted, it jibes well with the fact that when the calculus is interpreted as a theory about sets instead of propositions probabilities are predicated collectively but not distributively. Differences between individuals are below such a theory's level of attention.

Note, however, that a principle of symmetry is available for inductive probability-functions only so long as we confine the arguments of these functions to first-order propositions about individuals. The point is that there is no uniformity principle for inductive support in regard to higher than first-order generalizations.[2] So, if we did try to derive an assessment of inductive probability from the support-assessment for some higher-order generalization, it would not conform to any analogous principle of symmetry. Indeed, though the consequence principle would place a lower limit on such a probability, it is not at all clear, in the absence of a uniformity principle, how any upper limit could be determined from the support-assessment for the generalization. A theory of inductive probability is therefore developed here only for first-order propositions.

Another area of resemblance between inductive and mathematical probability is in regard to the relation between $p[S,R]$ and $p[S',R]$ where S' is a consequence of S according to some non-contingent assumptions. This is because even the restricted consequence principle for inductive support (which was given in §54, p. 187) ensures, where S' is a necessary consequence of

[1] Op. cit., pp. 483 ff.
[2] Cf. p. 172, n. 6, above.

S, and no variant of a relevant variable is mentioned in S',and H and H' are the covering generalizations for $p_I[S,R]$ and $p_I[S',R]$, respectively, that we must have $s[H'] \geqslant s[H]$ and therefore $p_I[S',R] \geqslant p_I[S,R]$. Thus R's probabilification of S is not to be confused with R's being weak, moderate, or strong evidence that S is true, in one familiar sense of 'evidence'. In this sense R could be evidence that Smith's murderer was left-handed without also being evidence of the necessary consequence that Smith was murdered. 'R is (weak, moderate, or strong) evidence that S is true' is then equivalent to something like 'Knowledge of R (weakly, moderately, or strongly) justifies anyone who also knows the other relevant evidence in believing that S is true'. The theory of inductive probability sets up a sharply explicit paradigm, by comparison with which this familiar concept of evidential justification appears somewhat loose or elliptical.

Again, consider the probability of S on R where R logically implies S. A logically true generalization cannot be falsified by any combination of relevant circumstances; and this non-falsifiability, as a matter of necessary truth, is necessarily implied by any statement of experimental test-results. Hence a logically true generalization may be said to be given full inductive support by any such statement, and therefore has maximal inductive reliability. So $p_I[S,R] = n/n$, just as $p_M[S,R] = 1$, where R necessarily implies S. And here the dyadic inductive probability-functor obeys a different principle from a dyadic inductive support-functor, since $s[H,E]$ may be zero even when E logically implies S (see §49, p. 162).

§64. *Some logical differences between inductive and mathematical probability*

An important difference in logical syntax between a dyadic mathematical probability-function or a dyadic inductive support-function, on the one side, and a dyadic inductive probability-function, on the other, is that though the former are not invariant in value under contraposition of their arguments,[3] the latter is. Since $(x)\ (Rx \rightarrow Sx)$ is logically

---

[3] For the reasoning behind this assertion cf. *TIOI*, p. 113 and pp. 194 f., respectively.

equivalent to $(x)(-Sx \rightarrow -Rx)$, and equivalent propositions have the same grade of inductive reliability as one another, it follows that the reliability of the covering generalizations for inductive probability-functions is invariant under contraposition. So one must accept, for any S and R, $p_I[S,R] = p_I[\text{not-R, not-S}]$.

Another important difference between inductive and mathematical probability lies in the relations that exist between monadic and dyadic functions in each case. Because of the consequence principle for inductive support (§53, p. 177) we have $s[(x)(Rx \rightarrow Sx)] \geqslant s[(x)(-Rx)]$ and also $s[(x)(Rx \rightarrow Sx)] \geqslant s[(x)(Sx)]$. Hence analogues appear for the so-called paradoxes of truth-functional implication. We have $p_I[S,R] \geqslant p_I[-R]$ and also $p_I[S,R] \geqslant p_I[S]$. However, though these principles of inductive probability do not have counterparts for mathematical probability or inductive support, they are scarcely paradoxical. For, first, a generalization of the form $(x)(Rx)$ is not testable, according to the criteria stipulated in §44. So such a generalization cannot acquire inductive support in the normal way, and only in rather special circumstances[4] will it acquire support in virtue of its logical relationship to other generalizations. Normally, therefore, we should expect to have $p_I[-R] = 0$ and so to learn nothing about the value of $p_I[S,R]$ from the principle $p_I[S,R] \geqslant p_I[-R]$. Secondly, what the principle $p_I[S,R] \geqslant p_I[S]$ tells us, in virtue of the equation $p_I[S] = s[S]$, is that, if S in any case has a certain grade of inductive support (which we could learn about from appropriate experimental or observational research), then S has at least that grade of inductive probability on any relevant evidence—which is scarcely objectionable. But though, where $p_M[R] > 0$, $p_M[S] = 0$ implies $p_M[S,R] = 0$, no counterpart principle exists for inductive probability (or for inductive support). This is because $p_I[S] = 0$ implies just the non-existence of prior inductive reasons for believing S, not also the existence of prior inductive reasons for believing not-S. If we need a particular reason to expect S on inductive grounds we may well have $p_I[S] = 0$ and $p_I[S,R] > 0$.

Again, inductive probability differs from mathematical probability in regard to conjunction. Instead of a multiplicative principle for the probability of a conjunction what we have is

(1)   If $p_i[S',R] \geqslant p_i[S,R]$, then $p_i[S \& S',R] = p_i[S,R]$.

This principle follows quite straightforwardly from the conjunction principle for monadic support-functions, viz.

(2)   If $s[H'] \geqslant s[H]$, then $s[H \& H'] = s[H_1]$,

which may be obtained from the conjunction principle for dyadic support-functions (cf. §50, p. 168) by taking E in the latter to be a true report of the most complex possible tests on H and H'. Let us take H to be the covering generalization for $p_i[S,R]$ and H' for $p_i[S',R]$. Then, if $p_i[S',R] \geqslant p_i[S,R]$, $s[H'] \geqslant s[H]$ and, by (2), $s[H \& H'] = [H]$. But H & H' is logically equivalent to the covering generalization for $p_i[S \& S',R]$; so that, by the equivalence principle for inductive support, the latter generalization must have the same grade of support as H & H'. Therefore, if $p_i[S',R] \geqslant p_i[S,R]$, the covering generalization for $p_i[S \& S',R]$ has the same grade of inductive support as H has; and so $p_i[S \& S',R] = p_i[S,R]$—as in (1).

Moreover we can now obtain a non-complementational negation principle, which establishes yet another respect in which the logic of inductive probability differs from that of mathematical probability. Consider a case in which S and S' are mutually contradictory even though $p_i[S',R] \geqslant p_i[S,R] > 0$. It will follow from what has just been said about conjunction that in this case R gives some non-zero grade probability to the truth of a self-contradictory conjunction. Since such a conjunction cannot possibly be true and its negation is tautologous, there is (by contraposition) a prior probability—of just the same strength as $p_i[S \& S',R]$—that R is false. In short, one thing that follows is

(3)   If $p_i[S,R] \geqslant i/n$ and $p_i[\text{not-}S,R] \geqslant i/n$, then $p_i[\text{not-}R] \geqslant i/n$.

Then from (3)—with $i = 1$—we obtain the negation principle for inductive probability,

(4)   If $p_i[S,R] > 0$ and $p_i[\text{not-}R] = 0$, then $p_i[\text{not-}S,R] = 0$.

This is rather like the negation principle for inductive support obtained earlier (in §53, p. 177). It is also just the principle that was to be expected from any conception of probability as the gradation of provability in an incomplete system: cf. §11, p. 37, above.

Indeed we could have obtained (4) also be considering the covering generalizations for $p_i[S,R]$ and $p_i[\text{not-}S,R]$ plus the fact that, if the covering generalization for $p_i[S,R]$ replicably passes test t_1, the covering generalization for $p_i[\text{not-}S,R]$ must fail that test. For, if two generalizations have the same antecedent and contradictory consequents, the only condition under which they could both be regularly (albeit trivially) true is if their antecedents were regularly unsatisfied, which would generate $p_i[\text{not-}R] > 0$.

Perhaps someone will think it a mark against any concept of inductive probability that on certain kinds of evidence there can be a non-zero inductive probability for a self-contradictory proposition. 'What cannot conceivably be true', such an objector may urge, 'cannot be probable either. So inductive probability is gravely inferior to mathematical probability as an instrument of human reasoning, since a self-contradictory proposition has zero mathematical probability on any evidence.'

But this objection would be quite mistaken. For, first, the *prior* inductive probability of a self-contradictory proposition is certainly zero, just as is the inductive reliability of such a proposition. But in inductive logic, unlike the Pascalian calculus of chance, a zero prior probability does not compel a zero posterior probability, because inductive probability-functions evaluate the weight of evidence. Secondly, what emerges here, in the logic of posterior, or dyadic, inductive probability, is just a generalized form of the principle of argument by *reductio ad absurdum*. When Euclid proved that if you suppose a highest prime number to exist you can derive a contradiction, he proved it to be untrue that a highest prime number exists. But what should be said if the contradiction is not *demonstrable*, or *certain*, on the premiss but only *probable*? The answer to this question must surely be that the premiss has not been demonstrated not to be true, but only that there is at least as much probability of the premiss's not being true as there is, on its evidence, that something self-contradictory is true. And this is exactly the position with which the logic of inductive probability presents us in (3).

The position here is further clarified if we remember that a statement of the inductive probability of S on R may always be viewed as assessing the weakness of the *ceteris paribus* assumption that would be necessary for us to be able to infer S from R with certainty (cf. §61, p. 212, above). For, if the covering generalization has ith grade support, we can infer S with certainty from R on the assumption that no variant of the relevant variables $v_{i+1}, v_{i+2}, \ldots$ or v_n is present in the situation concerned. So, if T is this assumption and S is a conjunction of contradictories, what we can be certain about is that R and T are not both true. If the assumption T is true and therefore R covers all the kinds of evidence that are pertinent in the situation, R must misreport some of this evidence. But if R is true throughout, then T is false and therefore R does not cover all the pertinent kinds of evidence. If more evidence were collected, the favourable evidence for one of the two contradictory conjuncts in S might well be counteracted while the favourable evidence for the other was strengthened. This is rather like the situation in a *reductio ad absurdum* proof where a contradiction has been shown to follow from certain premises but rather than reject the premises you choose to reject one of the rules of inference employed in the proof. For, if mutually contradictory conclusions seem to follow with non-zero probability from certain indisputably true premises, then one or both of the generalizations you have invoked to license your inference is ultimately inapplicable to the situation. This inapplicability, if your premises are true as far as they go, must be due to the fact that your premises are incomplete. That is, the situation has further relevant characteristics, not described in your premises, that render your rule or rules of inference inapplicable.

Here perhaps someone will object that, if the evidence must be incomplete whenever what is inductively probable fails to occur, then the discovery of all the evidence would always enable us to make predictions that are certain to be correct. 'Thus inductive probability presupposes Laplacean determinism', runs the objection, 'whereas the characteristic aim of probabilistic reasoning is to deal with the problems that arise when a deterministic framework of prediction is inapposite.'

The premiss of this objection—that inductive probability presupposes a kind of Laplacean determinism—must be granted, provided that it is qualified in two important respects. First, what is presupposed is not a single, global determinism, but a set of local determinisms. To hypothesize a series of relevant variables for a particular category of generalizations is undoubtedly to conceive the subject matter of those generalizations within a Laplacean framework. But nothing is thereby implied about other subject matters, which may well resist the imposition of such a framework. Secondly, though the series of relevant variables hypothesized must always be a finite one, in order that the hypothesis may be corrigible (as remarked in §45, p. 141), the actual number of different relevant variables might in fact be infinite. Where this was the case, any human claim to have enough evidence for predictive certainty would always in fact be false, though its falsehood might not always be easy to discover.

However, once the premiss of the objection has been qualified in these two ways, that premiss seems far too innocuous to generate a serious paradox. No doubt mathematical probability offers a pattern of reasoning which does not rely at any point on covering generalizations or assumptions of causal uniformity. But that is not a reason for supposing that any other concept of probability must be equally non-deterministic. If the heart of probability lies in the gradation of inferential soundness, as argued in §§1—11, there is nothing particularly paradoxical about proposing a criterion of probability that is applicable only where knowledge of all the relevant facts, if we ever had it, would permit certainly correct predictions. Indeed this requirement is intrinsic to any criterion that grades inferential soundness by reference to the weight of evidence.

§65. *The incommensurability of inductive and mathematical probability*

Since inductive probability grades the weight of *relevant* evidence, there must be at least some connection between criteria of inductive and of mathematical probability, respectively. What is favourable evidence according to an inductive probability-function will normally, though not necessarily, be favourably relevant according to a mathematical one. Normally, that is to say, if $p_I[S,R] > 0$, then $p_M[S,R] > p_M[S]$. Also, if $p_I[S,R]$ is high, $p_M[S,R]$ will normally, though not necessarily, be high.

But this is just about as far as the connection does go, because to grade the weight or extent of the relevant evidence is not at all the same thing as grading its degree of relevance in terms of the difference between prior and posterior mathematical probabilities. A small piece of the evidence may be very favourably relevant in mathematicist terms, while a larger chunk may be much less so. For example, the evidence that a man is a thirty-years-old professional philosopher may be highly favourable—in terms of the difference between prior and posterior mathematical probabilities—for his survival till the age of seventy. But the weight of this evidence is rather low, and when we know more about his present health, his parents' age of death, his hobby of rock-climbing, his smoking habits, his driving-record, etc., the picture may alter considerably. Also, the operation of a certain causal law, which generates a substantial inductive probability, may in practice be so often impeded by an accidentally intruding factor, that a very low mathematical probability arises. For example, perhaps very few *kinds* of relevant circumstance prevent contact with an infected person from causing smallpox. But some of these kinds of circumstance—in particular, vaccination—may now occur so frequently that contact spreads infection in relatively few instances. So here we have a case where $p_I[S,R]$ is by no means insignificant but $p_M[S,R]$ is negligible, if R reports the contact and S reports the infection. The difference is hardly surprising if we bear in mind that judgements of inductive probability relate to the probability of an individual event in the light of evidence directly bearing on that particular event, while judgements of mathematical probability must relate also to extraneous considerations—to the probability of a particular event within a coherent set of such probabilities, or to the frequency of a particular type of event within a reference class, or to the set of possible worlds in which both premiss and conclusion are true, or to a propensity that is to be estimated from samples of such events, etc.

Indeed, since the grade of inductive support for a generalization is not a function of any of the mathematical probabilities connected with it (as was shown in §§55–7), it is evident that the value of an inductive probability is at least not a function of any of the mathematical probabilities connected with its covering generalization. This does not exclude the possibility that $p_I[S,R]$ may instead be some function of $p_M[R,S]$, $p_M[S]$, and $p_M[R]$. But a further argument is available to exclude even that possibility.

Clearly there can be no anti-mathematicist argument for inductive probability that is analogous to the argument of §55 for inductive support. The argument of §55 was based on the fact that $s[H,E]$ may be greater than zero even when E reports an anomaly and contradicts H. But $p_I[S,R]$, like $p_M[S,R]$, is normally equal to zero when R contradicts S. This is because where R necessarily implies not-S we have $p_I[\text{not-}S,R] = n/n$ (§63, p. 219), and also therefore, if $p_I[\text{not-}R] = 0$, $p_I[S,R] = 0$ (by the negation principle of §64). However, the anti-mathematicist argument of §§56–7 was based instead on the conjunction principle for inductive support; and, since the conjunction principle for inductive probability is precisely isomorphic with that for inductive support (cf. §51, p. 168, and §64, p. 221), it is reasonable to expect that a corresponding argument can be constructed on its basis. In fact the same argument goes through quite smoothly, *mutatis mutandis*. What emerges is that, if $p_I[S,R]$ conforms to (1), its value cannot be equal to the value of a function of $p_M[R,S]$, $p_M[S]$ and $p_M[R]$, unless an inductive probability-function is either intolerably restricted in its application or assigned a value that is a function of the mathematical probability of the evidential proposition alone (i.e. $p_M[R]$). A proposition's inductive probability on given evidence, therefore, has no feasible representation in terms of mathematical probability.

Such a conclusion may be reinforced by the consideration that mathematical probabilities are countably additive and measurable, while inductive probabilities about matters of fact are only rankable. But this restriction to rankability is of a somewhat different nature from the previous argument. It rests not so much on the method of relevant variables itself, but rather on certain general features of our universe which that method seems to reveal when it issues in judgements about the relative importance of different relevant variables and their variants.

As Campbell long ago made clear, the difference between those orderable physical properties that can be measured in their own right, like weight, and those that cannot, like colour, arises from the possibility or impossibility of finding in connection with these properties a physical significance for the process of addition.[5] For example, two bodies of equal weight can be combined with one another to make an object of twice that weight. Similarly, we can double the ratio of red balls in an urn so as to double the mathematical probability that a ball picked at random from it (and replaced) will be red. So if inductive probability is to be measurable there must either be some analogously appropriate operation of addition *in rerum natura*, or inductive probability must be definable in terms of other properties for which such operations do exist. And this means, in effect, that such an operation must exist for inductive support, since gradings of inductive probability derive in the end, as we have seen, from gradings of inductive support.

Now several fairly obvious conditions must be satisfied by any operation that is to count as addition in regard to a particular property.[6] First, the system produced by adding one possessor of the property to another must have a greater quantity than either has separately. Secondly, the sums of equals must be equal. Hence the magnitude of the resultant system must depend only on the separate magnitudes of what are added and not on anything else, such as the order of addition or an interaction between the elements added. And no doubt there are other necessary conditions also, such as

[5] N. R. Campbell, *Physics, the Elements* (1920), pp. 277 ff. Campbell is speaking here of fundamental measurement, i.e. of the measurement of a property without reliance on the measurements of other properties.

[6] N. R. Campbell, op. cit., listed only the first two of these conditions. But cf. his *An Account of the Principles of Measurement and Calculation* (1928), pp. 2 ff.; P. Suppes, 'A Set of Independent Axioms for Extensive Quantities', *Portugaliae Mathematica* 10 (1951), 163 ff.; and B. Ellis, *Basic Concepts of Measurement* (1968), pp. 74 ff. Suppes recognizes, op. cit., p. 172 that in any case the statement of formal conditions for natural additivity may represent a somewhat idealized version of what it is in practice possible to ensure: e.g. if the relation of 'longer than' is taken to be perfectly transitive we should need equally perfect senses to detect what is longer than what.

associativity. But it is unnecessary to state any further conditions here since the only operation that seems eligible for the role of addition in regard to inductive support is already ruled out by the second condition stated.

Clearly, if such an operation exists, it must pertain, from an epistemological point of view, to the construction of the tests on which assessments of inductive support are based. It must be concerned with the introduction of a further relevant variable into a test in which one or more other relevant variables are already playing a part. Indeed, since this is the process by which, if the test is successful, a higher grade of inductive support is attained, it looks as though the first of the two above mentioned necessary conditions for additivity must always be satisfied. A successful test in which an additional relevant variable has been manipulated always gives a higher grade of inductive support to a hypothesis.

But the second condition for additivity is not normally satisfied by this process of toughening, or enriching the structure of, a test. For in this process the magnitude of the resultant system does not depend solely on the separate magnitudes of what are added. It depends also in fact on the order or method of their addition. We cannot ensure comparability between the various grades of inductive support that exist for different hypotheses unless we assess that support in terms of results from a single series of cumulatively more and more complex tests. And such a series of tests presupposes some accepted well-ordering for the set of relevant variables. One reason for this is that different relevant variables *may* in fact be of unequal importance in nature. Hence, if the above mentioned comparability is to be ensured, we cannot just select and combine any one, two, or more relevant variables at will (out of our accepted ordered set) so as to form the test to which a given hypothesis is to be subjected—the test that is to determine its grade of inductive support. Indeed, we could not safely select and combine relevant variables at will even if we could safely assume that every relevant variable was of equal importance. Nature has so arranged things, in many areas, that the combination of a certain variant of one variable with a certain variant of another is in fact of much greater causal efficacy, in regard to the falsification of hypotheses, than the combination of any two variants of two other relevant variables. For example, in testing the safety of a drug the volume of the dose and the body-weight of the patient may constitute a much more important combination of relevant factors than do the patient's sex and occupation, even if dosage, body-weight, sex, and occupation are all of equal importance on their own.

I conclude that the toughness of an experimental test is not an additive property of it. Hence there is no process of addition in *rerum natura* that could justify ascribing additivity to objectively determined grades of support. Any allowable system for grading inductive support objectively—in relation to hypotheses about matters of fact—must map pairs of propositions on to integers functioning as ordinals, not on to real or rational numbers. In this sense inductive support, and with it inductive probability, are in principle unmeasurable. Nor is their unmeasurability due to merely practical difficulties, like the unmeasurability of the volume of water on the surface of the Earth at a given time. It is due to the intrinsic nature of inductive reliability and the variety of causal processes. But this is not too serious a disadvantage. In many a field of inquiry there is more use for a non-quantitative grading of inductive support that applies quite empirically to hypotheses about measurable physical quantities within that field (as in §46, p. 147, above), than for a quantitative measure of inductive support, like Carnap's or Hintikka's, that is itself unable to measure support for hypotheses about physical quantities and treats its applicability to the actual world as an *a priori* truth.

§66. *A formal axiomatization for the logical syntax of inductive probability*

In order to establish the main conclusions of this book, and in particular to resolve the problems about judicial probability that were discussed in §§14–39, it is unnecessary to enumerate more of the structural principles that control gradings of inductive probability. What has been said already provides an adequate basis for the later sections (§§67–91) where I shall explore some of the ways in which the concept of inductive probability operates in contemporary human culture.

[7] Cf. *TIOI*, pp. 207–9. Readers uninterested in the details of formalization may wish to proceed directly to §67.

But for the usual reasons[7] it is unsatisfactory to leave these principles wholly unaxiomatized and their formal structure unexplored. Indeed, even from what has been said already in the present chapter it should be clear that, though inductive probability is not a measurable quantity, it nevertheless has a quite determinate logical structure. It would be a great mistake to suppose that because inductive probability is not measurable it is therefore hazy, unstructured or incapable of formal analysis.

More specifically, the core logic of inductive probability, as of inductive support, is a generalized modal logic. Its key idea is that grades of monadic inductive support, or reliability, are steps that mount towards the level of natural necessity and are therefore structurally analogous, *mutatis mutandis*, to the modality of necessity: they obey the same conjunction principle, the same uniformity principle, etc., as that modality. Indeed, one cannot believe that a proposition states a law of nature, or that its truth has this type of necessity, without implicitly believing that it has maximum inductive reliability according to the appropriate criteria for grading such reliability.

The formal structure of inductive support for unmodified propositions may be deployed axiomatically within a modal logic that generalizes on C. I. Lewis's system S4. Those features of the system that are basic to the analysis of inductive probability for first-order propositions, are set out in the following paragraphs.[8]

The formalism developed here is not intended to bear an

[8] A much fuller development of the system, though without the theory of probability, is given in *TIOI*, §§21–2. The numbering of formulas in the present book is continuous with that in *TIOI*. A consistency proof is given in *TIOI*, pp. 236–7.

The main differences between the theory of inductive support presented in the present book, and the theory in *TIOI*, are noted at appropriate places in the text. They are:

1. The definition of testability (§44, p. 137).
2. The requirement that relevant variables should be non-exhaustive (§44, p. 136).
3. The mode of ordering relevant variables (§44, p. 139, and §45, p. 142).
4. The restriction on the rule of substitution for multiply quantified generalizations (§51, p. 171, and §66, p. 236).
5. The provision for an infinite series of relevant variables (§45, p. 140, and §66, p. 233).

So far as informal exposition goes, there is also the difference specified in n. 14, p. 187 above, viz. the restriction on the consequence principle for modified versions.

interpretation that would allow it to articulate the logic of support-gradings or probability-gradings for propositions that mention variants of relevant variables. But the additions and alterations that would be necessary if the formalism were to admit of such an interpretation are sketched at the end of the section. That is to say, the formal structure of the simpler type of statement is developed in some detail, because it reveals clearly all the main syntactic features of inductive probability. But the formal structure of the more complex statements is sketched much more briefly, since its full-scale development has little of interest to add that would justify the technical complications involved.

The logic is developed in a syntactical meta-language which describes formation-rules and criteria of theoremhood for each of any number of object-languages of a specified kind indifferently. These object-languages are intended to correspond to different fields of intellectual inquiry, for which different series of relevant variables, and correspondingly different support-functions and probability-functions, are appropriate. The various object-languages may therefore differ from one another in the number and nature of their non-logical terms and in the number of grades of support or probability they can express. But they all have the same logical terminology and conform to the same logical principles, which can be described in a single syntactical meta-language.

The symbolism of the syntactical meta-language is as follows:

'x', 'y', or 'z', represents an individual symbol in the object-language, occurrences of which, if unbound, are assumed to denote without describing. 'Q', 'R', or 'S', represents a first-order predicate symbol, occurrences of which, if unbound, are assumed to describe a characteristic in the field of inquiry (like the v_1 predicables and target predicables of §44, p. 137).

Additional metalinguistic symbols of these two types are generated by appending numerical subscripts.

Brackets, dash, ampersand, and existential quantifier are self-representing. Dashes and ampersands in the object-language are assumed to have their usual interpretations as signs of negation and conjunction, respectively. Quantification is to be given a substitutional, not an objectual, interpretation.[9] No representations of second-order predicate-symbols are needed, because the theory of inductive probability is developed only for first-order propositions.

Squares represent modal operator-constants and operator-variables. The operator-constants in any one object-language are squares that are differentiated from one another by numerical superscripts. '$\Box^d$' in the meta-language represents a designated object-language square—the one with the highest superscript. The number denoted by this superscript is referred to by 'd'. $\Box^d$ . . . is intended to have the interpretation 'it is logically or analytically true that . . .' '$\Box^e$' represents the square with the superscript denoting the number that is closest to d, and 'e' refers to this number. $\Box^e$ . . . is intended to have the interpretation 'there is complete inductive reliability for the proposition that . . .' (i.e. 'it is inductively established that . . .'). '$\Box^i$' or '$\Box^j$' represents any primitive modal operator-constant indifferently, unless otherwise stated, and 'i' or 'j', as the case may be, refers to the number denoted by the superscript of the square so represented.

$\Box^i$ . . ., where $e > i$, is intended to have an interpretation that ascribes a certain grade of less than complete inductive reliability to a specified proposition. But, in order to state just what grade of reliability it does ascribe, one has to bear in mind that there may be either a finite or an infinite number of such grades in the field of inquiry covered by the object-language in question. So as to maximize corrigibility, every working hypothesis about the appropriate method of assessing inductive support in a particular field of inquiry should specify a determinate, finite list of relevant variables. But from an ontological point of view (cf. §45, p. 14, above) it must always remain logically possible that the actual number of relevant variables is denumerably infinite. So among the object-languages to be described we must suppose that there are some with the capacity to express only a finite number of different grades of support and some with the capacity to express a denumerably infinite number.

Various different kinds of notational device are available for this purpose. Here I shall assume that $d = 2$; that $e = 1$; that

the primitive modal operator-constant with the lowest superscript has the superscript '$\frac{1}{2}$'; and that, if there is a modal
operator-constant with a superscript denoting the number
$\frac{r}{r+1}$, there is also one with a superscript denoting the number
$\frac{r+1}{r+2}$, up to any desired number of modal operator-constants
ascribing less than complete support. If these modal operator-
constants, with superscripts denoting numbers less than 1, are
arranged in order of magnitude of superscript—$\Box^{\frac{1}{2}}$, $\Box^{\frac{2}{3}}$, $\Box^{\frac{3}{4}}$,
. . .— the first will signify the existence of at least first-grade
inductive reliability for the proposition within its scope, the
second will signify the existence of at least second-grade reliability, and so on. The grade of reliability signified is thus sufficiently indicated by the numerator of the superscript fraction.
The number, n, of relevant variables and positive support-grades
is indicated by the denominator of the highest superscript fraction, if there is one, or is ∞ if there is no highest superscript
fraction. So these fractional superscripts do not measure quantities or ratios of any kind. They function merely as convenient
notational devices for ordering the primitive modal operator-
constants in such a way that an object-language may contain
either a finite or an infinite well-ordered series of those constants
with superscripts denoting numbers less than e—the number
signifying complete reliability.

Modal operator-variables are represented by '$\Box^x$' and '$\Box^y$'.
If an object-language had only a finite number of modal
operator-constants and was therefore capable of ascribing
only a finite number of different grades of inductive reliability,
it could have integer superscripts for its modal operator-
constants and dispense altogether with modal operator-
variables (by a device to be described shortly).[10] But since
some object-languages are to be supposed in possession of a
denumerably infinite number of such constants it is convenient
to construct the logic of all these object-languages uniformly
and build modal operator-variables into each of them.

Individual and predicate symbols, and modal operator-

---

[10] At the cost of longer formulas in primitive notation, and longer proofs, modal
operator variables could have been dispensed with, for this reason, in the system
described in *TIOI*.

variables, are also represented indifferently, unless otherwise specified, by u and w.

$Rx_1x_2 \ldots x_n$ is a well-formed formula (wff) where R is n-adic. If A and B are wff, so are $-A$, $(A \& B)$, $\square^i A$, $(\exists x)A$ and $(\exists R)A$. If A is a wff, and B differs from A only in having an occurrence of $\square^x$ in one or more places in which A has an occurrence of $\square^i$, then $(\exists \square^x)B$ is a wff. Henceforth 'E', 'F', 'G', 'H', 'I', or 'J' represent wff.

The definition-schemata (metalinguistic statements describing permissible alternative ways of writing wff) include the following:

1. $(H \rightarrow I)$ for $-(H \& -I)$.
2. $(u)H$ for $-(\exists u) - H$.
3. $(H \leftrightarrow I)$ for $((H \rightarrow I) \& (I \rightarrow H))$.
4. $(H \text{ v } I)$ for $(-H \rightarrow I)$.
5. $(H \rightarrow^i I)$ for $\square^i (H \rightarrow I)$.
6. $(H \leftrightarrow^i I)$ for $((H \rightarrow^i I) \& (I \rightarrow^i H))$.
7. $\Diamond^i H$ for $-\square^i - H$.
8. $\square^o H$ for $\square^{\frac{1}{2}} H \text{ v} - \square^{\frac{1}{2}} H$.

Hereafter '$\square^i$' and '$\square^j$' represent any primitive modal operator-constant, or '$\square^o$', indifferently.

Monadic and dyadic support-functors, s[ ] and s[,], may be introduced contextually and self-representingly. Where there are n grades of inductive reliability and $e \geqslant i \geqslant 0$, contextual definition-schemata for s[ ] are:

9. $s[H] \geqslant i/n$ for $\square^i H$.
10. $s[H] < i/n$ for $-s[H] \geqslant i/e$.
11. $s[H] \leqslant i/n$ for $-\square^j H$ where $i = 0$ only if $j = \frac{1}{2}$,

    $e > i = \dfrac{r}{r+1}$ only if $j = \dfrac{r+1}{r+2}$, and $i = e$ only if $j = d$.

    That is to say: we assert that the reliability of H is no higher than a certain grade, by denying the applicability of the modal operator-constant with next higher superscript.

12. $s[H] > i/n$ for $-s[H] \leqslant i/n$.
13. $s[H] = i/n$ for $s[H] \geqslant i/n \& s[H] \leqslant i/n$. Hereafter i/n will be written as i, and brackets will sometimes be omitted under the usual convention.

14. $s[H] \geqslant s[I]$ for $(\square^x)(\square^x I \to \square^x H)$. In an object-language with a finite number n of modal operator-constants it would be possible to replace the definiens here by an appropriate finite conjunction $((s[I] \geqslant 0 \to s[H] \geqslant 0) \ \& \ (s[I] \geqslant \frac{1}{2} \to s[H] \geqslant \frac{1}{2}) \ \& \ (s[I] \geqslant \frac{2}{3} \to s[H] \geqslant \frac{2}{3}) \ \& \ \dots \ \& \ (s[I] \geqslant \dfrac{n-1}{n} \to s[H] \geqslant \dfrac{n-1}{n}) \ \& \ (s[I] \geqslant e \to s[H] \geqslant e))$.

15. $s[H] > s[I]$ for $-s[I] \geqslant s[H]$.
16. $s[H] = s[I]$ for $s[H] \geqslant s[I] \ \& \ s[I] \geqslant s[H]$.

The theory of dyadic support-functors[11] will be omitted here. It is based essentially on the idea that $s[H,E] \geqslant i$ abbreviates $E \to^e \square^i H$, so that $s[H,E] < i$ may be distinguished, as $-(E \to^e \square^i H)$, from $E \to^e s[H] < i$, which abbreviates $E \to^e - \square^i H$.

Dyadic probability-functors will now be introduced. Henceforth 'R' ('R$_1$', 'R$_2$', . . .) and 'S' ('S$_1$', 'S$_2$', . . .) are to represent wff in which no square or quantifier occurs, and in 34–41 the wff they represent are such that any individual symbol has one or more occurrences in R(R$_1$, R$_2$, . . .)if and only if it also has one or more occurrences in S(S$_1$, S$_2$, . . .).

34. $p[S,R] \geqslant i$ for $s[R \to S] \geqslant i$.
35. $p[S,R] < i$ for $-p[S,R] \geqslant i$.
36. $p[S,R] \leqslant i$ for $-p[S,R] \geqslant j$ where $i = 0$ only if $j = \frac{1}{2}$,

$e > i = \dfrac{r}{r+1}$ only if $j = \dfrac{r+1}{r+2}$, and $i = e$ only if $j = d$.

37. $p[S,R] > i$ for $-p[S,R] \leqslant i$.
38. $p[S,R] = i$ for $p[S,R] \geqslant i \ \& \ p[S,R] \leqslant i$.
39. $p[S_1,R_1] \geqslant p[S_2,R_2]$ for $s[R_1 \to S_1] \geqslant s[R_2 \to S_2]$.
40. $p[S_1,R_1] > p[S_2,R_2]$ for $-p[S_2,R_2] \geqslant p[S_1,R_1]$.
41. $p[S_1,R_1] = p[S_2,R_2]$ for $p[S_1,R_1] \geqslant p[S_2,R_2] \ \& \ p[S_2,R_2] \geqslant p[S_1,R_1]$.

Monadic probability-functors can now be introduced as well:

42. $p[S] \geqslant i$ for $p[S,Sv-S] \geqslant i$.
43. $p[S] < i$ for $-p[S] \geqslant i$.

[11] It is given in *TIOI*, pp. 220 and 229 ff.

44. $p[S] \leqslant i$ for $p[S, Sv - S] \leqslant i$.
45. $p[S] > i$ for $-p[S] \leqslant i$.
46. $p[S] = i$ for $p[S] \geqslant i$ & $p[S] \leqslant i$.
47. $p[S_1] \geqslant p[S_2]$ for $p[S_1, S_1v - S_1] \geqslant p[S_2, S_2v - S_2]$.
48. $p[S_1] > p[S_2]$ for $-p[S_2] \geqslant p[S_1]$.
49. $p[S_1] = p[S_2]$ for $p[S_1] \geqslant p[S_2]$ & $p[S_2] \geqslant p[S_1]$.

A theorem-schema is an assertion in the syntactical meta-language that has the form 'H is a theorem'. It may be abbreviated to '⊢H'.

The following criteria of theoremhood are needed:[12]

101. If H is a truth-functional tautology, then ⊢H.
102. If ⊢H and ⊢H→I, then ⊢I.
103. If ⊢H, then ⊢□^{d}H.
104. If ⊢H, then ⊢◇^{i}H where $e > i > 0$.
105. $\vdash (H \to {}^i I) \to (\Box^i H \to {}^i \Box^i I)$ where $i > 0$.
106. $\vdash (H \to {}^i I) \to (\Box^i H \to \Box^i I)$ where $e > i > 0$.
107. $\vdash \Box^j H \to \Box^i H$ where $j > i$.
108. $\vdash \Box^e H \to H$.
109. $\vdash \Box^i H \to \Box^i (x) H$ where $i > 0$.
111. $\vdash H \to (u) H$ where u has no free occurrence in H.
112. $\vdash (u) A \to H$ if (1) H is like A except for having free occurrences of y or R or occurrences of $\Box^i$ (with $e \geqslant i > 0$), wherever A has free occurrences of u, and (2) when any free occurrence of x in A is in a part of A of the form $\Box^i G$ or $\Box^x G$, then free occurrences of y in those places in H where A has free occurrences of x are occurrences of an individual symbol that is distinct from any symbol having a free occurrence in $(x) A$.
113. $\vdash (u)(A \to B) \to ((u) A \to (u) B)$.

---

[12] On the rationale of these criteria cf. *TIOI*, p. 221. Condition (2) of 112 is needed—though it was not laid down in *TIOI* p. 221—in order to ensure that, on the intended interpretation, the system does not have undesirable consequences of the kind mentioned in §51, p. 172 (cf. p. 230, n. 4). Correspondingly theorem-schemas 357–60 and 475–81, in *TIOI*, pp. 228 f. and 233 f. respectively, now hold only under the additional condition that y_i is distinct from y_j if and only if x_i is distinct from x_j. Note that in *TIOI* the numeral superscripts for modal operator-constants denoted integers, while here they mostly denote fractions in order to allow a denumerable infinity of such constants. Also in *TIOI* some of these superscripts could denote numbers i such that $d > i > e$, whereas here (for the sake of simplicity) that is not allowed.

114. If ⊢H, then ⊢(x)I, where I is like H except for having free occurrences of x wherever H has free occurrences of y.

115. If ⊢H, then ⊢(R)I, where I is like H except for having free occurrences of R wherever H has free occurrences of S.

116. If ⊢H, and $\Box^i$ (with $e \geqslant i > 0$) occurs in H, and if, for some places in which $\Box^i$ occurs in H and for any superscribed number j such that $e \geqslant j > 0$, ⊢G where G is like H except for having free occurrences of $\Box^j$ in these places, then⊢ $(\Box^x)$A where A is like H except for having free occurrences of $\Box^x$ in these places. That is, if '⊢ . . .' is a theorem-schema and '$\Box^i$' occurs in one or more places in '. . .', with no restriction on i other than '$e \geqslant i > 0$', then '$(\Box^x)$---' is a theorem-schema, if '---' is like '. . .' except for having '$\Box^x$' where, and only where, '$\Box^i$' occurs in '. . .').

A considerable number of theorem-schemas are easily provable in these terms. They reveal the logical structure of inductive probability rather more concisely than informal exposition permits. Let us begin with some theorem-schemas affecting monadic probability-functors:

601. ⊢p[S] $\geqslant i \leftrightarrow$ s[S] $\geqslant i$.
Proof[13]:

   i. ⊢$((Sv - S) \to S) \to {}^d S$ 101, 103, 5.
  ii. ⊢$((Sv - S) \to {}^i S) \to \Box^i S$ i, 208, 102.
 iii. ⊢$\Box^i S \to ((Sv - S) \to {}^i S)$ 215.
 iv. ⊢p[S] $\geqslant i \leftrightarrow$ s[S] $\geqslant i$ ii, iii, 118, 3, 9, 42.

602. ⊢p[S] $\geqslant 0$.   301, 601.
603. ⊢$\Box^d S \to$ p[S] $\geqslant e$.   107, 601.
604. ⊢$\Box^d - S \to$ p[S] $= 0$.   319, 601.
605. ⊢p[S] $> 0 \to$ p[$-S$] $= 0$.   306, 601.
                               (The negation principle)

---

[13] After this theorem-schema only sketches of proofs are given. Theorem-schemas cited with numbers below 600 are to be found in *TIOI*, pp. 222 ff., along with their proofs from 101–16 (where these proofs are not obvious).

606. $\vdash p[-S] \geqslant p[S] \rightarrow p[S] = o.$ 310, 601.

607. $\vdash (S_1 \rightarrow {}^e S_2) \rightarrow p[S_2] \geqslant p[S_1].$ 344, 601.

608. $\vdash p[S_1 \text{ v } S_2] \geqslant p[S_1].$ 349, 601.

609. $\vdash p[S_2] \geqslant p[S_1] \rightarrow p[S_1 \text{ \& } S_2] = p[S_1].$ 351, 601. (The conjunction principle)

610. $\vdash p[S] \geqslant i \text{ v } p[S] \leqslant i.$ 323, 601.

611. $\vdash p[S_1] \geqslant p[S_2] \text{ v } p[S_2] \geqslant p[S_1].$ 324, 601.

612. $\vdash (p[S_1] \geqslant p[S_2] \text{ \& } p[S_2] \geqslant p[S_3]) \rightarrow$ $p[S_1] \geqslant p[S_3].$ 331, 601.

613. $\vdash p[S_1] = p[S_2]$ where S_1 differs from S_2 only in having x_1 where S_2 has y_1, x_2 where S_2 has y_2, ... and x_m where S_2 has y_m, and x_i is distinct from x_j if and only if y_i is distinct from y_j. 359^{14}, 601.

614. $\vdash p[S \text{ \& } -S] = o.$ 604.

615. $\vdash p[S_1] > p[S_2] \rightarrow p[S_1] > o.$ 601, 315.

We now pass to some theorem-schemas affecting dyadic probability-functors:

701. $\vdash p[S,R] = i \leftrightarrow p[R \rightarrow S] = i.$ 601, 38, 46

702. $\vdash p[R] \geqslant i \rightarrow (p[S,R] \geqslant i \leftrightarrow p[S] \geqslant i).$ 601, 208, 215, 34, 42.

703. $\vdash \square^d R \rightarrow (p[S,R] \geqslant i \leftrightarrow p[S] \geqslant i).$ 107, 208, 215, 34, 42.

704. $\vdash p[-R] \geqslant i \rightarrow p[S,R] \geqslant i.$ 216, 34, 42.

705. $\vdash \square^d -R \rightarrow p[S,R] \geqslant e.$ 107, 216, 34.

706. $\vdash p[S] \geqslant i \rightarrow p[S,R] \geqslant i.$ 215, 34, 42.

707. $\vdash \square^d S \rightarrow p[S,R] \geqslant e.$ 107, 215, 34.

708. $\vdash p[-S] > o \rightarrow (p[-R] = o \rightarrow$ $p[S,R] = o).$ 601, 706, 356, 38, 45, 46.

709. $\vdash \square^d -S \rightarrow (p[-R] = o \rightarrow$ $p[S,R] = o.$ 107, 708, 38.

710. $\vdash (p[R_2,R_1] \geqslant i \text{ \& } p[S,R_2] \geqslant i) \rightarrow$ $p[S,R_1] \geqslant i.$ 211, 34.

[14] Theorem-schema 359 has to be read with the qualification mentioned in n. 12 on p. 236 above.

711. $\vdash p[S,R] = p[-R,-S]$.   210, 41.

712. $\vdash (S_1 \to {}^c S_2) \to p[S_2,R] \geqslant p[S_1,R]$ 106, 39.

713. $\vdash p[S_1 \ \& \ S_2,R] \geqslant i \to p[S_1,R] \geqslant i$.   101, 103, 107, 712, 34.

714. $\vdash p[S_1,R_1] = p[S_2,R_2]$ where S_1 differs from S_2, and R_1 from R_2, in the same way as S_1 differs from S_2 in 613.   359, 38, 34.

715. $\vdash p[S_1,R_1] > p[S_2,R_2] \to p[S_1,R_1] > 0$.   315, 34, 40.

716. $\vdash p[S,R] \geqslant i \ v \ p[S,R] \leqslant i$.   323.

717. $\vdash p[S_1,R_1] \geqslant p[S_2,R_2] \ v \ p[S_2,R_2] \geqslant p[S_1,R_1]$.   324.

718. $\vdash (p[S_1,R_1] \geqslant p[S_2,R_2] \ \& \ p[S_2,R_2] \geqslant p[S_3,R_3]) \to p[S_1,R_1] \geqslant p[S_3,R_3]$.   331.

719. $\vdash (p[S_1,R_1] > p[S_2,R_2] \ \& \ p[S_2,R_2] > p[S_3,R_3]) \to p[S_1,R_1] > p[S_3,R_3]$.   335.

720. $\vdash (p[S_1,R_1] > p[S_2,R_2] \ \& \ p[S_2,R_2] \geqslant p[S_3,R_3]) \to p[S_1,R_1] > p[S_3,R_3]$.   342.

721. $\vdash (p[S_1,R_1] \geqslant p[S_2,R_2] \ \& \ p[S_2,R_2] > p[S_3,R_3]) \to p[S_1,R_1] > p[S_3,R_3]$.   343.

722. $\vdash p[S_1,R] \geqslant p[S_2,R] \to p[S_1 \ \& \ S_2,R] = p[S_2,R]$.   351.

723. $\vdash p[S_1,R] = 0 \to p[S_1 \ \& \ S_2,R] = 0$.   316.

724. $\vdash p[S_1 v S_2,R] \geqslant p[S_1,R]$.   712.

725. $\vdash (p[S_1,R] > p[S_2,R] \ \& \ p[S_1,R] > p[S_3,R]) \to p[S_1,R] > p[S_2 \ \& \ S_3,R]$.   717, 722, 720.

726. $\vdash (p[S_1,R] > p[S_3,R] \ \& \ p[S_2,R] > p[S_3,R] \to p[S_1 \ \& \ S_2,R] > p[S_3,R]$.   717, 722, 721.

727. $\vdash (p[S_1,R] > p[S_3,R] \ \& \ p[S_2,R] > p[S_4,R]) \to p[S_1 \ \& \ S_2,R] > p[S_3 \ \& \ S_4,R]$.   717, 722, 720, 721.

728. $\vdash (R \to {}^d S) \to p[S,R] \geqslant e$.   107.

729. $\vdash (R \to {}^d -S) \to (p[-R] = 0 \to p[S,R] = 0)$.   356, 601.

730. $\vdash (R \to {}^d -S) \to (p[R] > 0 \to p[S,R] = 0)$.   306, 356, 601.

731. $\vdash (p[S,R] > 0 \ \& \ p[-R] = 0) \to p[-S,R] = 0$.   356, 601.

732. $\vdash (p[S,R] > 0 \ \& \ p[R] > 0 \to p[-S,R] = 0$.   306, 356, 601.

733. $\vdash(p[S,R] \geqslant i \; \& \; p[-S,R] \geqslant i) \to$
$\qquad p[-R] \geqslant i.$ 731.

734. $\vdash p[S,R] \geqslant p[-S,R] \to (p[-R] = o \to$
$\qquad p[-S,R] = o).$ 731.

735. $\vdash p[S \; \& \; -S,R] \geqslant i \to p[-R] \geqslant i.$ 713, 733.

736. $\vdash(p[S_1,R] > p[-S_1,R] \; \& \; p[S_2,R] >$
$\qquad p[-S_2,R]) \to (p[-R] = o \to$
$\qquad p[S_1 \; \& \; S_2,R] > p[-(S_1 \; \& \; S_2),R]).$ 734, 722, 715.

737. $\vdash(p[S_1,R] > p[-S_1,R] \; \& \; p[-S_2,R] >$
$\qquad p[S_2,R]) \to p[-(S_1 \; \& \; S_2),R] \geqslant$
$\qquad p[S_1 \; \& \; S_2,R].$ 712, 722.

738. $\vdash \square^d((R_1 \leftrightarrow R_2) \; \& \; (S_1 \leftrightarrow S_2)) \to$
$\qquad p[S_1,R_1] = p[S_2,R_2].$ 248, 41.

739. $\vdash \square^d(R \leftrightarrow S) \to p[S,R] = p[R,S].$ 738, 41.

740. $\vdash(p[S_1,R] > p[S_2,R] \; \& \; p[-R] = o) \to$
$\qquad p[-S_1,R] = o.$ 715, 731.

A model-theoretic semantics that exploited the idea of alternative possible worlds could presumably be constructed for any object-language of the above kind, in addition to a natural-language interpretation like that proposed above (pp. 231 f.). Such a semantics would afford a certain basis for comparison with other systems of inductive logic. In informal outline the part of this semantics that was concerned with wff in which squares occur would run as follows, for any particular category of v_1 and target predicables with n relevant variables.

A logically possible world, W_1, could be said to be 'subject to the uniformities of' another, W_2, if and only if (i) every testable generalization that is true and instantiated in W_2 is also true, whether vacuously or by instantiation, in W_1, and (ii) every testable generalization that is vacuously true in W_2 is also vacuously true in W_1. A logically possible world would be termed 'physically possible' if and only if it is subject to the uniformities of the actual world. The complete definition of the series of relevant variables need not be reconstructed here, but a circumstance C, which is not describable in the terminology of v_1 and target predicables, would be termed 'relevant' if and only if there is a testable generalization H that is false in some and every physically possible world in which C and the antecedent of H are jointly instantiated, and is true in at least some physically possible word in which the antecedent of H is instantiated but C is not. A physically possible world would be termed a 't_1' world if and only if every variant of variable v_1, and no variant of any other relevant variable, is instantiated in it. A physically possible world W would be termed a 't_2' world if and only if every t_2 world is subject to the uniformities of W and every admissible combination of a variant of v_1 with zero or more variants of relevant variable v_2, and no variant of any other relevant variable, is instantiated in W. And, in general, a physically possible world W would be termed a $t_{\frac{r}{i}}$ world if and only if every $t_{\frac{r-1}{i}}$ world is subject to the uniformities of W and every admissible combination of a variant of v_1 with zero or more variants of relevant variables v_2, v_3, . . . v_r $(r < n)$, and no variant of any other relevant variable, is instantiated in W. The actual, and each t_n, world would thus contain a plenitude of events, whereby every physically possible combination of a variant of v_1 with zero or more variants of relevant variables is instantiated in it. And, for all i and j, each t_i world is subject to the uniformities of each t_j world, where $j \geqslant i$, as well as to the uniformities of the actual world.

Where H is to be interpreted as a testable generalization or as a conjunction of testable generalizations, $\square^i$H (with $i < e$) would be true if and only if H is true (whether vacuously or by instantiation) in all t_i worlds; $\square^e$H would be true if and only if H is true in the actual world as well as in all t_i worlds where $i < e$; and $\square^d$H would be true if and only if H is true in all logically possible worlds. Where H is not to be interpreted as a testable generalization or conjunction of such, $\square^i$H would be said to be true if and only if there is a wff I such that $\square^i$I is true and H is true in all logically possible worlds in which I is true.

Hence the *prior* inductive probability (which equals the inductive reliability) of a testable generalization could be viewed as a ranking of inductive range, by contrast with Carnap's conception of the prior mathematical probability of a proposition as a measure of its logical range.[15] The inductive range of a generalization would be ranked by the fullest kind of physically possible world—highest grade of relevantly

[15] Cf. R. Carnap, *Logical Foundations of Probability* (1950), pp. 79 f.

eventful world—in which the generalization always holds good, while the logical range of a proposition is measured by reference to the sum of the values severally assigned to each logically possible world in which the proposition holds good.

Note also how the characteristic conjunction principle would emerge for inductive reliability. Since a t_i world is subject to the uniformities of a t_j world where $j \geqslant i$, it follows that if one generalization holds good in all t_i worlds and another in all t_j worlds, their conjunction must hold good in all t_i worlds. Similarly a high grade of inductive reliability is compatible with the existence of anomalies, since a generalization may hold good in all t_i worlds where $i < e$ even though falsified in our actual world: the relation of being 'subject to the uniformities of' is not symmetrical. Indeed an experimental test, as a set of circumstances to be contrived, could be thought of as a simulated minimal t_i world; and the idealized domain to which some scientific generalizations apply[16]—e.g. the domain of bodies moving in a vacuum—could also be thought of as a t_i world for some appropriate i.

Finally the relation of being 'subject to the uniformities of' would constitute a relation of inductive accessibility or knowability that holds between some possible worlds in the model and not others. Since this relation is transitive and reflexive but not symmetrical, the appropriate formalization could be expected[17] to be a suitable generalization of C. I. Lewis's modal system S4, as in the text,[18] and not of any other Lewis system.

But unfortunately the idea of alternative possible worlds is no more than a metaphysical metaphor, which cannot afford a firm foundation for reasoning about the nature of probability, even though—as above—it may help to illuminate a network of principles that are independently attestable. The metaphor is to treat 'world' as a sortal concept, when the world involved is not a continent, or even a galaxy, but a totality of facts. And

---

[16] Cf. *TIOI*, p. 144.

[17] Cf. G. E. Hughes and M. J. Cresswell, *An Introduction to Modal Logic* (1968), pp. 75 ff.

[18] Cf. *TIOI*, pp. 223 f. If relevant variables were logically exhaustive—which they are in fact not allowed to be (cf. §44, p. 136 above)—the scale of reliability-grades would collapse and the only physically possible world would be the actual one. The relation of inductive accessibility would then be symmetrical, and the logic of inductive gradings would be analogous to S5.

logicians have sometimes tended to overlook the point that this can be no more than a metaphor. The classical example is the dream of Theodorus in Leibniz's *Essais de Theodicée*.[19] To describe the world might perhaps be to give a complete description of the assignment of persons, objects, events, etc. to sorts, but such a description would not include any assignment of the world itself to a sort. To take the world for an entity of a certain sort in this way, or to talk about functions from names to possible worlds, is a typically metaphysical manoeuvre, of the kind that Kant characterized as taking what he called a 'regulative' idea for what he called a 'constitutive' one. And the antinomies inevitably generated by such manoeuvres, according to Kant, are exemplified in the present case by the currently fashionable controversy about whether the same individual can exist in more than one possible world. Indeed for one kind of determinist (e.g. Spinoza) the idea of alternative possible worlds is self-contradictory; and, if the meaning or intension of a term is said to be given by a rule that regulates its extension in all possible worlds, then such a determinist— who admits only one possible world—is being deprived of any title to distinguish between intension and extension, between meaning and reference. So to construct a semantics for modal logic in terms of possible worlds—literally understood—is to construct a house of cards which collapses at the first blast of anti-metaphysical criticism. Of course, a purely linguistic account of possible worlds, which treats sentences about them as material-mode equivalents of formal-mode sentences about state-descriptions, escapes this criticism. But such a semantics achieves no more than the mapping of one formal language on to another. The Kantian criticism can also be side-stepped if a hierarchy of 'world'-types is postulated. But the Leibnizian flavour of such a semantics has then been very much diluted; and, if the hierarchy of 'world'-types is not to appear as a purely *ad hoc* device that has been adopted in order to avoid a specific criticism, it will need a fairly elaborate argument to give it a rationale. (Perhaps the hierarchy of levels of inductively

---

[19] *Philosophischen Schriften*, ed. C. J. Gerhardt, vol. vi (1885), pp. 362–5. More recent examples are to be found in D. Lewis, *Counterfactuals* (1973), and R. Montague, *Formal Philosophy* (1974), *passim*. Leibniz's, and certain other, principles of plenitude are discussed in §94, p. 339 ff. below.

relevant variables, mentioned in §45, p. 142 above and §97, p. 350 below, would help here, but only so far as physical possibility was concerned.)

It should be remembered that in the formalization developed above predicate letters are not intended to be interpreted as describing variants of relevant variables. If you want some of the predicate letters to bear that interpretation, you must restrict criteria of theoremhood 105 and 106 above, along with all the theorem-schemas deriving from them, similarly to the way in which the consequence principle was restricted in the informal exposition (§54, p. 187).

However, if such a step were to be taken at all, it might be as well to establish certain distinct families of predicate letters—one family for each relevant variable. This would assist, where the numbers of relevant variables and their variants were finite, in capturing the point (cf. §61, p. 212) that every statement of inductive probability has a corresponding statement of inductive certainty that is equivalent to it. For example, if Sx has ith grade inductive probability on the evidence Rx, then Sx would be inductively certain on the evidence of Rx plus the evidence that x was not characterized by any variant of relevant variables $v_{i+1}, v_{i+2}, \ldots$ If an appropriate criterion of theoremhood were added, embodying that principle, one would be able to derive further theorem-schemas corresponding to such principles as that, if something which is probable on available evidence does not happen, the evidence must be incomplete, or that, if something does not happen which is probable on a statement covering all the relevant issues, some element in this statement must be false. This further criterion of theoremhood would thus be relatively easy to spell out in the syntactical metalanguage if the numbers of relevant variables and of their variants were both assumed always to be finite. Without that assumption an infinite series of predicate-letters—$Q_1, Q_2, Q_3, \ldots$—would have to be postulated in some object-languages, with each Q_i to be interpreted as signifying the absence of any variant of a relevant variable other than v_1, $v_2, \ldots$ or v_i.

PART IV

SOME APPLICATIONS OF INDUCTIVE PROBABILITY

18

The Assessment of Judicial Proof

Summary

§67. It has now to be shown that the concept of inductive probability, as derived from the concept of inductive support for covering generalizations, plays an important part in human reasoning. §68. Our inferences about the behaviour of others normally rest on the large stock of rough generalizations about human behaviour that we carry in our heads. So it is possible to construe proof beyond reasonable doubt as proof at a maximum level of inductive probability. §69. Proof of S on the preponderance of evidence may then be construed as proof at a higher grade of inductive probability than that at which not-S is proved; and other standards of proof are also intelligible in these terms. §70. Contextual clues are normally available to determine whether a given statement of probability is to be evaluated in accordance with mathematical or with inductive criteria, though experimental psychologists have not always recognized this. In fact experimental data confirm the thesis that normal intuitive judgements of probability are often inductive rather than mathematical.

§67. *Are there any uses for the concept of inductive probability?*

In the last two chapters I have constructed an account of that concept of inductive probability which may be developed out of an analysis of Baconian reasoning about inductive support. If you grant that the characteristic procedures of eliminative induction—the procedures that Mill sought to represent by his

Method of Agreement and Method of Difference and that I have entitled collectively 'the method of relevant variables'—can be used to grade support for first-order universal statements in a particular field of enquiry, you must also grant that for each such field an inductive probability-function is obtainable that maps ordered pairs of propositions on to a sequence of natural numbers $\geqslant 0$. In whatever fields the method of relevant variables can be used to grade inductive reliability it generates, as a natural corollary, a function for ranking probabilities.

The logical structure of such functions has now been explored in sufficient detail for present purposes. But does this notion of probability have any important role to play in human reasoning? It is one thing to construct a system for ranking probabilities, quite another to show that the system actually has a use. I suggested in §§1–9 that instead of supposing there to be just one appropriate semantics for the calculus of mathematical probability we should rather seek to determine the various types of task for which the different possible interpretations of the mathematical calculus might be severally appropriate. An analogous question now arises here. To what domains of human reasoning is an analysis in terms of inductive probability applicable?

I propose to begin the answer to this question by reverting to the topic of juridical proof, which was discussed in §§14–39. It would be quite out of place for me here to attempt the vast task of an exhaustive analysis of the structure of juridical proof—an analysis in which many detailed questions about *onus probandi*, proof of causal responsibility, proof of identity, proof of intention, etc., would have to be tackled. My purpose is much more limited. I aim to show in §§67–76 only that the concept of inductive probability has *some* regular use in relation to juridical proof. Anglo-American standards of juridical proof can be systematically analysed, or reconstructed, in the vocabulary of inductive probability. So here is at least one important role for a non-Pascalian probability. But juridical proof in Anglo-American courts is by no means the only domain of application for the theory of inductive probability; and §§77–91 will be devoted to exploring four other common patterns of reasoning in which inductive probability-functions are implicitly invoked.

§68. *Proof beyond reasonable doubt*

If you saw a pedestrian step straight off the curb in a city street, you would normally infer that he was intending to cross the highway. If challenged for your title to make such an inference, the safest reply would be that this is normally what people are intending to do if they step straight off the curb. You would then be invoking a universally acceptable generalization about human intentions in order to license your inference from a particular instance of its antecedent to a particular instance of its consequent. But the generalization would only be universally acceptable because you had qualified it by the word 'normally' and thus left open the possibility that it did not apply to the situation in hand. In fact, over a lifetime, most people tacitly invoke enormous numbers of such generalizations about human intentions, attitudes, emotions, or actions, and about numerous other matters, since they make so many such inferences from singular proposition to singular proposition. Typically these generalizations are not statable as exact and fully determinate correlations, like Newton's laws of motion, because the level of phenomena with which they deal is altogether too variegated and complex. They function instead as common-sense presumptions, which state what is normally to be expected but are rebuttable in their applications to a particular situation if it can be shown to be abnormal in some relevant respect. If there are any statistical patterns, or underlying uniformities, in the areas with which our common-sense generalizations deal, they are still unknown to most of us. In everyday life we normally content ourselves with roughly qualified generalizations or rebuttable presumptions.

Perhaps someone will say: 'If *I* were challenged for my title to infer that the man intends to cross the road, I should reply instead that there was a high mathematical probability of a man's intending this if he steps straight off the curb.' But such a reply would not account for two important facts. First, you normally infer that he *is* intending to cross the road, not that he is probably intending to cross the road. Secondly, there are times—the abnormal cases—when you do not infer at all that he intends to cross the road but perhaps that he intends stepping out to talk to a car-driver who has just hailed him.

So what allows your inference when it occurs, and occasionally forbids it, must be a rough awareness of the circumstances where a certain kind of inference is permissible, which is tantamount to a rough awareness of the circumstances where a certain kind of inference-licensing generalization is applicable. A rough awareness of the high level of a certain mathematical probability is undoubtedly useful for some people on some occasions. But it is useful for them only where they do not think they can distinguish in practice between the circumstances to which the corresponding generalization applies and the circumstances to which it does not. In fact most people think they can do this, up to a sufficient level of accuracy, for a very wide range of generalizations about human affairs and the human environment.

This is therefore the intellectual equipment with which the lay juryman enters on his duties. Correspondingly it is in these terms, as many legal philosophers have seen, that judicial proofs are normally constructed, within the framework established by the vast number of specific legal rules about admissibility of evidence, burden of proof, etc. As Sir James Stephen, for example, put it in this connection:[1]

The rules relating to human conduct . . . are usually expressed with little precision and stand in need of many exceptions and qualifications, but they are of greater practical use than rough generalisations of the same kind about physical nature, because the personal experience of those by whom they are used readily supplies the qualifications and exceptions which they require.

Perhaps a policeman swears, and defending counsel accepts, that the accused was found at 3 a.m. in the garden of a house which had just been burgled, and also that the stolen jewels were then in his pocket. The conclusion proposed by the prosecution is that the accused was the burglar. The rough generalization tacitly invoked as a licence for this inference might be that normally, if an object has been moved from its usual place and a man is found nearby immediately afterwards

[1] J. F. Stephen, *The Indian Evidence Act with an Introduction on the Principles of Judicial Evidence*, (1872), p. 31. Cf. J. H. Wigmore, *A Treatise on the Anglo-American System of Evidence in Trials at Common Law*, 3rd edn. (1940), vol. i, §30, pp. 416 ff. Cf. also J. Bentham, *Works*, ed. J. Bowring (1843), vol. vii, pp. 4–56, for a detailing of some of the generalizations that are relevant to the establishment of criminality.

in possession of the object, then he deliberately removed it himself. So the defence has to try to prove, in effect, that this generalization is inapplicable to the situation in question. Perhaps, for example, the defence can produce testimony alleging that some other stranger also was in the garden immediately after the burglary and that the defendant merely picked up, with the intention of returning, what the other man had dropped. Clearly the presence of one or more other people is one relevant variable for such generalizations as that tacitly invoked by the prosecution. (Even if you were unwilling to admit that this presence sometimes *causes* the falsehood of these generalizations, at least you would have to admit that in certain circumstances the presence of other people always makes certain kinds of inference unreliable—i.e. is a sign that such an inference cannot be trusted—and so long as there are such underlying uniformities the method of relevant variables can come to grips with the issue.) So the prosecution, in order to remove any element of reasonable doubt, would need to destroy the force of the defence's testimony in some way, either directly by showing that no one else was in the garden or indirectly by showing, as a disproof of honest intention, that, say, when the accused was first seen he was running away from the house.

Accordingly, if the defence challenges the prosecution's argument at every possible point, what the prosecution has to do, in effect, is to establish that every relevant feature of the situation is one of those that are favourable, or not abnormal, for the generalization invoked: e.g. that no other person was in the vicinity, that the accused was in full possession of his senses and knew what he was doing, etc., etc. In a relatively uncomplicated case proof beyond reasonable doubt—i.e. an inductive probability that amounts to virtual certainty—is achieved when every let-out of this nature is eliminated, either by oral, documentary, or other evidence, or by reference to facts that the defence admits or the court is prepared to notice. For then the situation has been shown in effect to satisfy the antecedent of a fully supported (because appropriately qualified) generalization of which the consequent in effect declares the defendant's guilt. If every relevant feature of a is favourable for applying the generalization

Anything that is R_1 is also S

and the relevant features of a are R_2, R_3, . . . and R_n, then a satisfies the antecedent of the fully supported generalization

Anything that is R_1 & R_2 & R_3 & . . . & R_n is also S.

Correspondingly (cf. §59) we can make the assessment

$$p_I[Sa, R_1a \ \& \ R_2a \ \& \ . . . \ \& \ R_na] \geqslant n/n.$$

In more complicated cases, however, a great deal of argument may be needed even to establish such facts as the reliability of a certain witness or the ownership of the objects allegedly stolen. Also, more than one inductively supported generalization may be invoked in the attempt to establish a required conclusion. For example, perhaps a man is accused of knowingly possessing stolen property, because some stolen jewels are found in his shanty. The prosecution may then need to invoke, tacitly, such generalizations as that, normally, people who live in shanties cannot afford to buy valuable objects and do not have friends to give them expensive presents, and also that, normally, people who find valuable articles and do not intend to keep them, either return them to the owner immediately or hand them over immediately to the police. For by the first generalization a trier of fact would be licensed to infer that the accused did not buy the jewels and was not given them, and by the second that if he found the jewels he did not intend to return them or hand them over to the police. But, however complicated the structure of the proof in a criminal case, the requisite level of inductive certainty is always achieved in the same way. Every relevant reason for doubt has to be excluded.

A merely fanciful possibility, however, is not a ground for reasonable doubt. In effect, when juries are discouraged from taking such possibilities into account, they are being warned to neglect variables that are inductively irrelevant to reasoning about the generalizations tacitly invoked. For example, it might conceivably be suggested that an insomniac jackdaw could have abstracted the jewels and dropped them into the accused's pocket at 3 a.m. But the activity of insomniac jackdaws is not acceptable as a relevant variable for generalizations about changes in the possession of objects, because no such generalizations are commonly known to have been falsified by it.

Nor is the need to invoke inductively supported generalizations confined to cases of circumstantial evidence, i.e. to cases where evidence produced in court provides the premises from which (along with admitted or judicially noticed facts) the desired conclusion may be inferred in accordance with the licence afforded by appropriate generalizations. A generalization is also tacitly invoked even in cases of direct evidence, where someone testifies to having perceived the very event that has to be proved. For in these, and indeed in all other cases, the reliability of any testimony produced is implicitly or explicitly at issue. The trier of fact has to decide the level of reliability that is indicated by the demeanour of the witnesses, the internal consistency and plausibility of what they say, the coherence of their testimony with other items of evidence, and the facts that emerge about their lives, reputations, abilities, and involvement in the case; and he has to decide this in relation to the actual type of situation that the case instantiates. Everybody, or almost everybody, has some types of occasion on which he tells the truth and some on which he tells lies or makes mistakes or misinterpretations. The normal presumption, that a sworn witness is veridical, lies open to rebuttal in various ways. Some witnesses may be relied on to tell the truth about strangers, for example, but not about friends, relations, or neighbours. Others may perhaps have quite good eyesight in the day-time, but rather poor vision at night. Yet others may be both intellectually honest and visually acute, but prone to misinterpret what they see as being more like what they have seen before than it actually is. So what the trier of fact has to decide, in gauging the reliability of testimony, is the strength of inductive support which exists for the prediction that the circumstances of the witness, in the circumstances of the case, are such as to produce veridical testimony. In other words, the probability that a witness is telling the truth is also to be regarded as an inductive probability, not a mathematical one. No statistics of truth-telling are taken into account here. If the probability is thought to be higher than was at first supposed, this happens in a characteristically inductive fashion, as a larger and larger range of relevant circumstances are seen to be favourable: the witness spoke forthrightly and without evasions, he never contradicted himself, what he said tallied with what others said, his reputation for honesty was unchallenged, and so on.

§69. *Proof on the preponderance of evidence*

So far we have been considering only proof beyond reasonable doubt. But other legal standards or proof may also be readily construed in terms of inductive probability. Let us now consider the standard in civil cases, where a plaintiff has to prove his case, not necessarily beyond reasonable doubt, but at least on the preponderance of evidence or balance of probability.

Suppose the defendant is being sued for breach of contract to build the plaintiff a factory by a certain date, whereby the plaintiff suffered financial loss in his business. Suppose it is argued between the parties that no factory was built and that the plaintiff would have gained £100,000 if a factory had been built by the date in question. But it is disputed whether a contract was in fact ever concluded. The plaintiff produces evidence that such a contract was proposed and that on several occasions the defendant expressed an active interest in it. This evidence (R_1) might give some initial probability to the conclusion (S) that the defendant accepted the proposal, but for the fact (R_2), stressed by the defence, that the plaintiff can produce no documentary evidence of acceptance. Here the generalization initially invoked by the plaintiff is that, normally, if a contract is proposed to a man and he expresses an active interest in it on several occasions, he will eventually accept it. Then the non-existence of documentary evidence is taken to be a presumably unfavourable circumstance for applying this generalization. So the plaintiff strengthens his case by showing (R_3) that a substantial sum of money passed from him to the defendant, allegedly as a down-payment. But the defendant counters by showing (R_4) that the plaintiff owed him money on another account. The plaintiff also proves (R_5) that the defendant assembled suitable building materials, as if he intended to build the factory. But the defendant counters again by showing (R_6) that he needed such materials for another operation. At this point, perhaps, there might be no more facts brought to the attention of the jury. The plaintiff would then have failed to prove his case on the preponderance of evidence, or balance of probability.

What is happening here is analogous to the balancing out of probabilificatory evidence in the example discussed in §59, where the presence of dark clouds gave some probability to the imminence of rain. I do not mean, of course, that the balancing out is a temporal process, unless perhaps in the deliberations of ideally rational jurors. Procedural rules require that in the normal case all the plaintiff's evidence be introduced first, and all the defendant's postponed till after this has been completed. But the metaphor of a balance, which seems quite deeply entrenched in legal terminology here, is not inapposite to the logical structure of the situation. The plaintiff in the case considered seeks to establish the applicability of a generalization entitling him to infer S: the defendant seeks to establish the applicability of a generalization entitling him to infer not-S. When a relevant feature is found favouring the former generalization the probability of S on the evidence is increased, and that of not-S relapses to zero, while when a feature is found favouring the other generalization the probability of not-S is increased and that of S relapses to zero. First, one part of the balance is weighed down and the other is carried away, and then vice versa. Schematically, in accordance with the method of assessing inductive probabilities that was described in §59, what we have is the following:

$p_I[S,R] = 1$, and $p_I(\text{not-}S,R_1] = 0$, so
$\quad p_I[S,R] > p_I[\text{not-}S,R_1]$
$p_I[S,R_1 \& R_2] = 0$, and $p_I[\text{not-}S,R_1 \& R_2] = 2$, so
$\quad p_I[S,R_1 \& R_2] < p_I[\text{not-}S,R_1 \& R_2]$
$p_I[S,R_1 \& R_2 \& R_3] = 3$, and $p_I[\text{not-}S,R_1 \& R_2 \& R_3]$
$\quad = 0$, so $p_I[S,R_1 \& R_2 \& R_3] > p_I[\text{not-}S,R_1 \& R_2 \& R_3]$
$p_I[S,R_1 \& \ldots \& R_4] = 0$, and $p_I[\text{not-}S,R_1 \& \ldots \& R_4]$
$\quad = 4$, so $p_I[S,R_1 \& \ldots \& R_4] < p_I[\text{not-}S,R_1 \& \ldots \& R_4]$

So if the plaintiff can throw one or more other pieces of evidence into the scales of justice—if he can establish one or more other relevant facts that favour his case—the balance would be weighed down on his side again. But if he cannot he loses.

In short, the winner does not need to prove his case beyond reasonable doubt. But he does need to have the preponderance of evidence on his side. And the more evidence that is taken into consideration the greater the margin by which the inductive probability of the winner's case may exceed that of the loser's. Decisions based on a greater total weight of evidence come out as being sounder, even if the actual truth of the matter is not beyond reasonable doubt. Indeed, if one wanted to put in a nutshell what was essentially wrong with the mathematical analysis of judicial proof, one would have to say just that it cannot represent this central feature of judicial proof. Mathematical probability, as Keynes long ago pointed out (cf. §11, p. 36, above), does not measure the weight of evidence, and weight is what determines a balance. But the better informed the jury is about the relevant facts, the more probably correct is the conclusion that ought ideally to emerge from the jury's deliberations. And, if both sides in a suit are allowed—subject to certain legal restrictions on admissibility—to lead all the evidence that they think is important, then, in relation to any one issue, the jury should normally be well informed enough to pronounce a verdict on the balance of probabilities that springs from there being a reasonable high inductive probability for the truth of the contention put forward by the winning side. An adversary system of procedure is thus particularly well suited to the task of establishing such a probability.

The example I have sketched is a deliberately crude and over-simplified one, in order that the underlying method of assessment should stand out as clearly as possible. For instance, in my imaginary case the arguments of plaintiff and defendant were closely meshed together, so that if the probability of the one's contention on the evidence was greater than zero the probability of the other's reduced to zero. But it would be quite possible for the arguments to proceed rather more independently of one another, so that on the total evidence actually produced in court both contentions have a greater than zero probability even though one is more probable than the other. Perhaps the plaintiff produces documents, allegedly from his office files, to show that a contract was concluded and the defendant produces other documents to show that it was not.

And then a jury could infer, by a probabilistic *reductio ad absurdum* as in §64, p. 222f., that the evidence presented was probably incomplete (perhaps yet further documents would be needed in order to clarify the position) or that at least some of the evidence was probably false (perhaps some witnesses committed perjury). But a verdict could still be given. Basing itself on those facts that it thought reliable the jury could decide which way the balance of probability lay and how weighty were the facts determining this balance.

Again, in an actual case there may be several component issues in dispute, not just one. Also the facts that one side wishes to treat as its premises may be disputed by the other side. For, even if a certain proposition is asserted by a sworn witness, and regarded by the court as legally admissible evidence, it does not necessarily state evidence in the logical sense of that word. It is not necessarily an incontestable premiss for further inference. Lawyers sometimes prove an opposing witness unreliable. Similarly affidavits may have been perjured or documents forged. Nevertheless the same logical structure is always apparent in the mode of assessment for proofs in ordinary civil cases. The cardinal question to be settled by the trier of fact may always be construed as this: on the facts before the court, is the conclusion to be proved by the plaintiff more inductively probable than its negation? For to ask this question, as §61 above makes clear, is precisely equivalent to asking: is there a greater weight of evidence for the former conclusion than for the latter?

It is clear, however, that if my account is correct proof on the preponderance of evidence does not *need* to be proof at a particularly high level of inductive probability. If the defendant's case is rather weakly evidenced, the plaintiff's case need not reach a high level of inductive probability in order to prevail. Hence there is obviously room for a higher standard of proof in certain types of civil case, if courts or legislatures wish to have one. Such a standard will force out more of the relevant facts—a greater weight of evidence. For example, where proof on 'clear, strong and cogent evidence' is required, as sometimes in American courts,[2] one can appropriately suppose that a conclusion must have a high level of probability on all the

[2] Cf. R. Cross, *Evidence*, 3rd edn. (1967), p. 90.

facts before the court, though its proof need not wholly exclude reasonable doubt.

At the other end of the scale a theory of inductive probability can also comprehend those 'reasonable grounds for suspicion' which are sometimes needed to make an arrest legally justifiable. If a stranger is seen trespassing at night in the garden of a rich man's house, there is undeniably a slight inductive probability, on just that evidence, that he intends to commit some crime. When we say this, we tacitly invoke the common-sense generalization that night-time trespassers in rich men's gardens normally have dishonest intentions. Perhaps, when we learn more, relevant circumstances might turn out not to favour the application of such a generalization. The man might have been chasing his puppy or too drunk to tell one garden from another. Then we can say that though there were reasonable grounds for suspicion the suspicion turned out in the end not to be correct. Or perhaps sometimes there is absolutely no relevant circumstance of an accused person that brings him under a suitable generalization—i.e. under a generalization licensing inference to the truth of the accusation. Then there is nothing at all to counteract the presumption that he is innocent. So he has 'no case to answer', as it is commonly put. On the known facts his innocence is not open to any doubt, and his guilt has zero inductive probability.

Finally, unlike a mathematicist one an inductivist analysis has no difficulty at all in accounting for the tendency already remarked (§37, p. 114, above) to suppose that the probability of a man's having dishonest intentions, say, on the evidence of his night-time trespass is not importantly distinguishable from the improbability of his night-time trespass on the assumption that his intentions are honest. For on an inductivist analysis, though not on a mathematicist one, this supposition is correct. The value of an inductive probability-function is invariant under contraposition of its arguments: $p_I[S,R] = p_I[\text{not-}R, \text{not-}S]$.

§70. *Contextual clues to the disambiguation of probability-sentences*

Notoriously philosophers are sometimes tempted by the apparent simplicity of what was described in §1 as a mono-criterial theory of probability. Under the influence of such a temptation a critic may well object to the thesis that the concept of inductive probability is used in the appraisal of proofs in Anglo-American courts. 'You cannot deny that the concept of mathematical probability is sometimes invoked', he may say, 'even in the courts. So how is one supposed to know that on certain occasions the word "probability" means one thing, and on other occasions another? If the word were really as ambiguous as you are suggesting, surely we should long since have adopted the practice of disambiguating it, where this is appropriate, by prefixing some such modifiers as your own terms "mathematical" and "inductive"?'

The answer to this objection is that the context in which the word 'probability' is used normally provides sufficient clues to determine whether the appropriate criteria of probability are mathematical or inductive. For example, where determinately identified individual events are under discussion and no ratio or real number is given as the probability-value, the normal presumption seems to be that criteria of inductive probability are applicable, since the individual event in question can be treated as instantiating some inductively supported generalization. But that presumption would cease to operate in certain circumstances, as when the individual event in question is Excalibur's winning the 3.30 at Newmarket and the event's probability is discussed in relation to betting-odds. Again, where only the *kind* of event concerned is specified, and it does not matter at all which particular instance of the specified kind is considered, the normal presumption seems to be that the appropriate criterion of probability is a mathematical one, since the underlying relationship seems to lie between the sizes (cardinalities) of certain classes of events. But that presumption would cease to operate if the kind of event in question were specified so narrowly that no relevant statistical data could reasonably be expected to be available. Thus the following would naturally be taken, in effect, as a judgement of inductive probability:[3]

It is more probable than not that a man is a burglar, if he

---

[3] We can bring such judgements within the analytical scope of the formal system developed in §66 by interpreting free occurrences of one of the system's individual letters as occurrences of an individual constant of unspecified denotation—an arbitrary name.

is arrested at 3 a.m. with stolen jewels in his pocket in the garden of a house that has just been burgled and he claims to be chasing his puppy, though there is no evidence that he owns a dog.

The situation here is quite analogous, as remarked in §9, to what happens with other evaluative terms, like 'good' or 'beautiful'. We have to tell from the linguistic or non-linguistic context of the word's occurrence how to judge the correctness with which it is predicated. We have to tell whether to judge goodness by the criteria of a good pen, say, or those of a good gardener. But for the most part we do not need to prefix modifiers to guide us in this task. We do not need to speak of 'calligraphic goodness' or 'horticultural goodness'. Analogously we have to tell from the context of occurrence how to judge the correctness with which the phrase 'highly probable' has been used.

However, in the highly artificial and restricted context of a psychological experiment disambiguation may be rather difficult and confusions can easily arise. Hence especial care is needed in interpreting some recent important results of experimental investigations by Kahneman and Tversky.[4] In investigating the probabilities intuitively assigned by their subjects to certain outcomes Kahneman and Tversky assume throughout that the only type of probability which can possibly be at issue is one that conforms to the mathematical calculus. Correspondingly they assume that standard norms of statistical analysis determine correct procedures for resolving the conundrums about probability which they pose to their experimental subjects. When a subject does not obey these norms, therefore, they describe him as committing a fallacy. But in fact, so far as at least some of their results are concerned, no fallacy at all is demonstrable if the subjects are interpreted to be making judgements of inductive, not mathematical, probability.

In a typical experiment the character of a certain person, Tom W., is sketched; and, while one group of student subjects

---

[4] D. Kahneman and A. Tversky, 'On the Psychology of Prediction', *Psychological Review*, 80 (1973), 237–51; 'Subjective Probability: A Judgment of Representativeness' in *The Concept of Probability in Psychological Experiments*, ed. C.-A. S. Staël von Holstein (1974), pp. 25–48; 'Judgment under Uncertainty: Heuristics and Biases', *Science*, 185 (1974), 1124–31.

is asked to rank his similarity to their stereotype of a graduate
student in each of nine fields of specialization, another group is
asked to predict which is likely to be his actual field of graduate specialization. Because a very high positive correlation occurs
between the similarity-rankings and the predicted likelihoods,
irrespective of the well-known fact that there are many more
graduates in some fields than in others, Kahneman and
Tversky interpret their experiment as showing that their
subjects ignored prior probabilities. The subjects are supposed
to have fallaciously preferred judging by the extent to which
an outcome is 'representative' of the evidence rather than by
the outcome's probability. According to Kahneman and
Tversky[5]

A fundamental rule of statistical prediction is that expected accuracy
controls the relative weights assigned to specific evidence and to
prior information. When expected accuracy decreases, predictions
should become more regressive, that is, closer to the expectations
based on prior information. In the case of Tom W., expected
accuracy was low, and prior probabilities should have been weighted
heavily. Instead, our subjects predicted by representativeness, that
is, they ordered outcomes by their similarity to the specific evidence,
with no regard for prior probabilities.

But it might be more charitable to suppose that the subjects
made straightforward judgements of inductive probability on
the basis of heavily qualified generalizations about what kinds
of students specialize in the various subjects. After all, they
were asked to make predictions about a particular individual,
Tom W., whose character was described in detail—not about
any student of a certain kind taken at random. It would be as
much of a muddle for them to introduce prior mathematical
probabilities into the judgement of this inductive probability,
as it would be for a jury to introduce prior mathematical
probabilities of masculine criminality into assessing a proof
that Tom X. is guilty of the crime of which he stands accused.
If a fallacy has been committed here, it seems to have been
committed not by the subjects, but by the experimenters, in

[5] 'On the Psychology of Prediction', loc. cit., p. 239.

failing to perceive the irrelevance of prior mathematical probabilities to judgements of inductive probability.

In another experiment Kahneman and Tversky told their subjects about a certain town that has both a large and a small hospital, with about forty-five babies born each day in the former and fifteen in the latter. For a period of one year each hospital was said to have recorded the days on which more than 60 per cent of the babies born were boys, as against a 50-per-cent over-all rate in the long run. On being asked which hospital recorded more such days most of the subjects judged that there was no difference between the two. Kahneman and Tversky interpret this result as showing that their subjects were insensitive to sample size in judging probabilities, since a larger sample is less likely to stray far from the over-all rate. Considerations of representativeness, they claim, have obstructed correct judgement. But again the error seems to lie more with the experimenters than with their subjects. The subjects were asked to make a judgement about birth figures in a particular pair of hospitals for a particular year, not about any two sample hospital-years selected at random. They therefore quite reasonably ignored the size of the hospitals as being causally irrelevant to the proportion of male births, and gave the inductively probable answer.

Of course, if these subjects kept on being asked the same question about other pairs of large and small hospitals, and kept on giving the same answer, they would in the long run give an incorrect answer more often than a correct one—at least if the size of the hospital is indeed causally irrelevant to the proportion of male births. So, if they bet on the correctness of each answer at even odds, they would lose money in the long run. But to fault their first answer on that account would be a *petitio principii*. That is to say, instead of evaluating the subjects' performance by mathematicist standards, it would be fairer to use inductivist ones. We should evaluate the particular judgement, not the class of judgements which it instantiates (cf. §39, p. 120). And as, in order to do this, we learn more and more about the two particular hospital-years involved, is there any reason to expect that the lesser size of the smaller hospital will turn out to have influenced the ratio of male births? If not, most of the subjects made the correct judgement on the evidence before them. They made a correct assessment of whether any of the circumstances known to them were of a kind to cause changes in the proportion of male births.

In yet other experiments Kahneman and Tversky have undoubtedly exposed some sources of error in intuitive judgements of probability.[6] But over all they have not exposed as many such errors as they suppose. Their mistake is to assume that wherever judgements of probability fail to conform to the principles of the mathematical calculus a fallacy has been committed. They impute to their subjects the same mathematical concept of probability as that which they themselves have learned to employ within scientific inquiry, and then infer that the subjects have not learned to employ this concept properly in certain contexts. Presumably Kahneman and

[6] Cf. what they say about biases of 'availability' and 'anchoring' in 'Judgment under Uncertainty: Heuristics and Biases', loc. cit., pp. 1127–8. I am rather doubtful, however, whether subjects are altogether wrong to have greater confidence in predictions of students' future grade-point averages from consistent aptitude profiles—where the input variables are highly correlated—as Kahneman and Tversky argue in 'On the Psychology of Prediction', loc. cit., p. 249. Admittedly the relevant variables for inductive judgement should be causally independent of one another. But perhaps a subject may be construed as arguing to himself: 'Will the student have a high (low) grade point average? An inconsistent profile makes this inductively less probable than a consistent profile does. Hence I should be less confident in predicting from it.' Correspondingly it is hardly surprising that subjects predict both outstanding achievement and utter failure with greater confidence than they predict mediocre performance.

Two other experiments of which Tverksy's interpretation is somewhat doubtful were reported by him in a discussion recorded in *Journal of the Royal Statistical Society Series B (Methodological)* 36, 2 (1974), 187. In one experiment the light on the right of a subject is lit in two-thirds of the trials and the light on the left in one-third. The subject is instructed to make as many correct predictions as he can and is rewarded for his correct predictions. Most subjects apparently predict the right light on two-thirds of the trials and left light on one-third, contrary to what Tversky calls the optimal policy of predicting the right light in every trial. But Tversky's policy would not be optimal for a subject who wanted a chance of winning a reward for more than two-thirds of his predictions. Again, fighter-pilots in the Pacific during World War II encountered situations requiring incendiary shells about one-third of the time and armour-piercing shells about two-thirds of the time. When left to their own devices, pilots armed themselves with incendiary and armour-piercing shells in the proportion of 1 to 2. Tversky argues that, since there was no general procedure for predicting on every mission which type of shells would be required, the optimal policy was to use armour-piercing shells on every mission, and that thus the pilots reasoned fallaciously even when their own lives were at stake. But did they reason fallaciously? A pilot might well think that Tversky's policy was, in the long run, a recipe for certain suicide while the other policy offered at least some chance of personal survival—of having the right shells on each occasion—even if it was less likely to win the war.

Tversky would also have to construe the arguments of §§17–39 above as showing that the Anglo-American law of proof is founded on a systematic fallacy—a fallacy very similar to that of their own experimental subjects.

But, once the mathematicist prejudice is discarded, Kahneman and Tversky's important experimental results about judgements of so-called 'representativeness' are open to a different interpretation, which is preferable not only for the reasons already given but also because it does not imply such widespread and evolutionarily valueless stupidity among lawyers and other non-psychologists. What those results reveal instead is a widespread human tendency to make judgements of *inductive* probability in appropriate contexts. Such judgements are not only possible, as argued in §§58–66, and conventional in Anglo-American judicial contexts, as argued in §§68–9 and 71–6. They have now also been shown experimentally to be the normal intuitive[7] mode of judging the probabilities of individual events. And this experimental finding confirms, and is confirmed by, the fact that the lay juries of the Anglo-American legal system are *de jure* supposed capable of operating with standards of proof that are—implicitly—formulated in terms of inductive probability. Or, to put it another way, the experimental finding about the normal

---

[7] There are other reasons for supposing the innateness of inductive (Baconian) mechanisms. These are connected in particular with the problem of explaining how an infant can learn the syntax and semantics of its native language in such a relatively short period, cf. L. Jonathan Cohen, 'Some Applications of Inductive Logic to the Theory of Language', *American Philosophical Quarterly*, 7 (1970), 299 ff. These arguments are criticized by N. Chomsky, 'Problems and Mysteries in the Study of Human Language', in *Language in Focus: Foundations, Methods and Systems* (Essays in Memory of Yehoshua Bar-Hillel), ed. A. Kasher (1976), pp. 331–9, reprinted with revisions in N. Chomsky, *Reflections on Language* (1976), pp. 204–14. The substance of the criticism is that an inductivist account of language-learning does not allow for the existence of innate constraints on admissible hypotheses about syntactic structure. But some innate constraints on admissible hypotheses must be supposed by any theory of initial learning by induction, and the most economical theory would be one that assumed the constraints operating in syntax-learning to be the same as those operating in one or more other fields of infantile learning. Cf. L. Jonathan Cohen, 'Is contemporary linguistics value-free?', *Social Science Information*, xii. 3 (1973), 59 f. For example, Chomsky postulates a principle of structure-dependence, whereby transformation rules operate only on elements of grammatical structure. But all inductive hypotheses generalize only over a relevantly characterized manifold: cf.§44 above. A full reply to Chomsky must wait on the construction of computer-programmes for Baconian learning, of the kind proposed in n. 20, p. 145, above.

intuitive way of judging individual probabilities explains why a legal system might hold it appropriate for lay juries to operate with such standards.

At least that seems to be a reasonable conclusion from the arguments of this book. But I do not wish to claim that Kahneman and Tversky's own interpretation of their results about 'representativeness' has been decisively and conclusively refuted here. There are no knock-down arguments in philosophy any more than in science, except within a framework of selective assumptions; and when appropriate assumptions are varied any apparently knock-down argument can be undermined. Kahneman and Tversky's interpretation is refuted only if other reasons are accepted for supposing the legitimacy, and common use, of a non-Pascalian concept of probability. So if you reject the argument of §11, about degree of provability within an incomplete system, and the arguments of §§14–39, about legal standards of proof, your way is open to accept Kahneman and Tversky's own interpretation of their results. But you must be prepared to pay the price for this. You must be willing to saddle yourself with the otherwise unmotivated doctrine that degree of provability in an incomplete system cannot be regarded as a probability; you must regard the existing norms of proof in British and American courts as needing a variety of corrections or clarifications, for which there is no other justification than the fact that Pascalian principles require them. Indeed, from your point of view the institution of lay juries now becomes intellectually indefensible, because you must take it to have been experimentally demonstrated that laymen are commonly inclined to commit very serious fallacies in their judgements about probabilities. From your point of view a diploma in statistical method should be a minimum qualification for jury service in a civilized country.

In other words, even if the theory of inductive probability serves no other purpose, it does provide a coherent rationale for retaining the institution of lay juries in face of experimental results like those achieved by Kahneman and Tversky.

Perhaps, finally, it will be objected that no-one else has ever recognized an everyday, non-forensic use of the term 'probability' in accordance with Baconian rather than Pascalian principles. Hence, it may be argued, I am not entitled to assume that Kahneman and Tversky's laboratory subjects might have given that term a Baconian interpretation.

However, the use of 'probability' to express what Kahneman and Tversky call 'representativeness', or 'similarity to specific evidence' is at least as old as Hume's *Treatise*. Hume clearly recognized this as one distinct usage alongside others, such as that expressing the Pascalian probability of chance, when he wrote:[8]

I have accounted for that species of probability, deriv'd from analogy, where we transfer our experience in past instances to objects which are resembling, but are not exactly the same with those concerning which we have had experience. In proportion as the resemblance decays, the probability diminishes; but still has some force as long as there remain any traces of the resemblance.

It was the object of §§40–66 to show that there is nothing intrinsically fallacious about this mode of reasoning, so long as the resemblances involved are inductively relevant ones.

[8] *A Treatise of Human Nature* (1739), Bk. I, Pt. III, §XIII: Selby-Bigge ed. (1888), p. 147.

Kahneman and Tversky, 'Judgement under Uncertainty: Heuristics and Biases', loc. cit. p. 1129, also remark on the tendency of subjects to overestimate the probability of conjunctive events and to underestimate the probability of disjunctive ones. But this result may again be due at least in some cases to a mistaken assumption that the probabilities involved are mathematical ones. An interpretation of the data in terms of inductive probability can account for them without imputing systematic error to subjects, since a conjunctive event always has as high an inductive probability as the less probable of its conjuncts and a disjunctive event need have no higher an inductive probability than the more probable of its disjuncts (cf. theorem-schemas 722 and 724 on p. 239 above).

Finally, in a paper 'Causal Thinking in Judgment under Uncertainty', which is forthcoming in the Proceedings of the 5th International Congress of Logic, Methodology and Philosophy of Science, Kahneman and Tversky accuse their subjects of systematically underestimating probabilities that are not dependent on causal connections: the subjects do not estimate non-causal posterior probabilities to exceed prior ones even where the evidence seems to have positive Pascalian relevance. But this is exactly how one would expect inductive probability-judgments to behave. The monadic function $p_I[S]$ evaluates the strength of Nature's potential for bringing S about. So, if the covering generalisation for $p_I[S,R]$ is a causal law, then R implies absence of some possible impediment to the actualisation of this potential. If, however, the covering generalisation for $p_I[S,R]$ is not a causal law, then R does not, as it were, assist Nature to bring S about, and $p_I[S,R]$ may be no higher than $p_I[S]$.

19

Resolution of Six Difficulties for a Mathematicist Account of Judicial Proof

Summary

§ 1. The inductivist analysis entails that, if the probability of a plaintiff's over-all case may properly be evaluated, he proves it on the balance of probability if, and only if, he proves each of his component points on the balance of probability. The analysis thus eliminates the difficulty about conjunction. § 2. The inductivist analysis also denies transitivity to proof on the balance of probability in appropriate cases, thus eliminating the difficulty about inference upon inference. §73. The non-complementational negation-principle for inductive probability ensures that, on an inductivist account, the standard of proof in civil cases does not officially condone a positive probability of injustice. §74. Proof beyond reasonable doubt is proof at the level of inductive certainty. §75. The inductivist analysis elucidates why ordinary juries are competent to assess judicial proofs. §76. Convergence and corroboration, and their appropriate independence conditions, can be readily explained in terms of inductive probability, with no difficulty arising about prior probabilities.

§71. *The difficulty about conjunction*

In §14–39 I pointed out that there were at least six serious difficulties facing any attempt to interpret Anglo-American standards of juridical proof in terms of mathematical probability. None of the difficulties was utterly insurmountable, but none of the issues could be handled smoothly or straightforwardly by a mathematicist analysis. Together they constituted an accumulation of anomalies that made an acceptable mathematicist analysis of proof seem scarcely possible. In the present section I shall argue that all these anomalies disappear if judicial proof is analysed, as in §§68–9, in terms of inductive probability.

The first difficulty arose (§§17–21) in relation to the standard of proof in civil cases. What is to happen when the plaintiff's contention conjoins several component points, as it normally does? If the standard of proof is construed as implying that the plaintiff's case *as a whole* should have a higher mathematical probability of being true than its denial has, the multiplicative nature of the conjunction principle for mathematical probability imposes a rather severe constraint on the number of independent points that can be conjoined to compose the plaintiff's case or on the level of probability at which each point must be proved. But no such constraint is recognized by the courts. And, though mathematicist analysis in terms of positive relevance escapes this difficulty, it allows a plaintiff's case as a whole to be better than the defendant's even if the plaintiff has lost at least one of his points.

The inductivist analysis, however, has no difficulty in dealing with complex civil cases. Either the probabilities of the component elements are incommensurable, in which case no probability-value can plausibly be assigned to their conjunction and separate assignments to each must suffice. Or alternatively the conjunction principle for inductive probability gives a quite satisfactory and paradox-free result. The conjunction of two or more propositions about the same category of subject-matter, as we saw in §64, p. 221, has the same inductive probability on given evidence as each conjunct, if the conjuncts are equally probable on that evidence, or as the least probable of them, if they are not. That is to say, we have the principle

(1) If $p_I[S_1,R] \geqslant p[S_2,R]$ & $p_I[S_2,R] \geqslant p_I[S_3,R]$
& . . . & $p_I[S_{n-1},R] \geqslant p_I[S_n,R]$,
then $p_I[S_1 \ \& \ S_2 \ \& \ . . . \ \& \ S_n,R] = p_I[S_n,R]$.

Accordingly, if for each contention, S_i, which is put at issue by the plaintiff in a civil lawsuit, the jury accepts that $p_I[S_i,R] > p[\text{not-}S_i,R]$, the jury can deduce

(2) $p_I[S_1 \ \& \ S_2 \ \& \ . . . \ \& \ S_n,R] > p_I[\text{not-}S_1 \ \& \ \text{not-}S_2 \ \& \ . . . \ \& \ \text{not-}S_n,R]$.

But by the negation principle for inductive probability (§63, p. 221) we know that, if $p_I[S,R] > 0$ and $p_I[\text{not-}R] = 0$, then $p_I[\text{not-}S,R] = 0$ and therefore $p_I[S,R] > p_I[\text{not-}S,R]$. Moreover, the jury could hardly consider that the balance of prior probability favours the falsehood of the premiss R on which it in fact bases its argument: in other words, it must[1] assume $p_I[\text{not-}R] = o$. Hence from (2) the jury is entitled to deduce

(3) $p_I[S, \& \ S_2 \& \ldots \& \ S_n, R] > p_I[\text{not-}(S_1 \& \ S_2 \& \ldots \& \ S_n), R]$.

So on the inductivist analysis, if the plaintiff gains each of his points on the balance of probability, he can be regarded as gaining his case as a whole on that balance, as in (3), without any constraint's being thereby imposed on the number of independent points in his case or on the level of probability at which each must be won.

If instead the plaintiff loses even one of his points, S_k, the position is quite different. In such a case what we have is that $p_I[\text{not-}S_k, R] \geqslant p_I[S_k, R]$. Now according to (1), $p_I[S_1 \& \ S_2 \& \ldots \& \ S_n, R]$ cannot be higher than $p_I[S_k, R]$, while, according to the consequence principle for inductive probability (§63, p. 218) $p[\text{not-}(S_1 \& \ S_2 \& \ldots \& \ S_n), R]$ must be at least as high as $p_I[\text{not-}S_k, R]$. The jury must therefore now infer not (3) but its negation: $p[\text{not-}(S_1 \& \ S_2 \& \ldots \& \ S_n), R]$ must be at least as high as $p[S_1 \& \ S_2 \& \ldots \& \ S_n, R]$. In other words if there is at least one point that the plaintiff fails to win against the defendant he cannot win on the over-all balance of probability (cf. §66, p. 240 above, theorem-schema 737).

In sum, the plaintiff proves his over-all case on the balance of probability if, and only if, he thus proves each of his component points. The inductivist analysis produces precisely the principle that accords with our normal conceptions of justice. Moreover, it does this quite smoothly and straightforwardly, and without any *ad hoc* suppositions of law or implausible reinterpretations of familiar norms.

§72. *The difficulty about inference upon inference*

The second difficulty in the mathematicist analysis was discussed in §§22-3. It arose in relation to what lawyers call inference upon inference. Whereas the conjunction principle for mathematical probability seemed excessively severe on proofs involving a number of co-ordinate components, it seemed excessively liberal in regard to proofs that have one stage dependent on another. It allowed some proofs of the

[1] Cf. theorem-schema 606, p. 238 above.

latter kind to be valid on the balance of probability even if not all stages prior to the final one are proved beyond reasonable doubt. However, courtroom procedures do not recognize this validity. So supporters of the mathematicist analysis have to claim that the non-transitivity of proof on the balance of probability is a purely legal matter—an additional restriction that is logically supererogatory but imposed by the courts out of some abundance of legal caution. Also, the mathematicist theory is powerless to elucidate why legal caution should have abounded in this particular way. It cannot elucidate, for example, why proof beyond reasonable doubt should be required for every stage prior to the last, rather than for every stage subsequent to the first.

But, if the standards of judicial proof are interpreted in terms of inductive probability, a reason is immediately apparent why proof on the balance of probability cannot be assumed to be transitive. More than one stage of proof would not be needed if more than one type of connection were not involved. But, if more than one type of connection is involved, more than one category of covering generalization determines the inductive probabilities. A different inductive support-function is there-fore applicable to the covering generalization for each stage; and, as different support-functions are incommensurable with one another except in respect of their limiting values (cf. §45, p. 143, above), so too are the probability-functions they generate. It follows that, even if R is proved on the balance of inductive probability from Q, and S from R, we cannot be sure on those grounds that S is provable on the balance of inductive probability from Q.

The point can be clarified by fleshing it out in a simplified version of one of the examples that Wigmore took from North American case records[2] in order to substantiate his discussion of the subject. Suppose the evidence established, on the balance of inductive probability, that A's finger injury was accidental (and not deliberate), and the accidentalness of A's finger injury also establishes, on balance, that A's death was accidental (and not due to medical negligence). Does it follow that the evidence establishes, on balance, that A's death was

[2] J. H. Wigmore, *A Treatise on the Anglo-American System of Evidence in Trials at Common Law*, 3rd edn. (1940), vol. i, §41, pp. 435 ff.

accidental? The trouble is that the first stage of the proof is concerned with the everyday causation of bodily injuries, the latter with their effects under medical treatment. Different sets of factors are therefore relevant at each stage, and the inductive probabilities involved must be separately evaluated. But from such mutually incommensurable probabilities no transitive inference emerges. Inductive probability-functions evaluate the weight of relevant evidence, and what is relatively weighty for one type of conclusion may not be nearly so weighty for another.

'Why then', it may perhaps be asked, 'is there such an important difference, in judicial proof by inference upon inference, between, on the one side, having $p_I[R,Q]$ maximal and $p_I[S,R]$ rather lower, though greater than $p_I[\text{not-}S,R]$, and, on the other side, having $p_I[S,R]$ maximal and $p_I[R,Q]$ rather lower? Why should the judges' requirement be that in a many-stage proof on the balance of probabilities every stage prior to the final one must put its conclusion beyond reasonable doubt, not that every stage subsequent to the first must do this?'

The answer to this is that anything seen to be reasonably certain on known or accepted facts may itself be detached as a known or accepted fact which can provide a premise for further proof; whereas the evidence that is relevant to a first-stage conclusion on the balance of probability may seem scarcely relevant at all to later-stage conclusions. Correspondingly a judicial proof on the balance of probability sets out to show that the ultimately derived conclusion is probable on known facts, not to show that it is knowable from probable facts. With $p_I[R,Q]$ maximal and $p_I[S,R]$ at an intermediate level this objective is achieved, when Q is given. For R then becomes a fully established, known fact on which a firm argument for the probability, on balance, of S can be built. But with $p_I[R,Q]$ at an intermediate level and $p_I[S,R]$ maximal, S is not probabilified, on balance, by the known facts even when Q is given. All that can be said then about S is that its truth would be a matter of knowledge if R were certain and not, as it actually is, merely probable.[3]

[3] Of course, if R logically implies S, then the consequence principle for inductive probability ensures that if $p_I[R,Q] \geqslant i$ then $p_I[S,Q] \geqslant i$. But it does not follow from this that where R logically implies S a man who testifies to the truth of R may also be described as testifying to the truth of S, since witnesses' grasp of logical implications may vary considerably.

§73. *The difficulty about negation*

I turn now to the third difficulty for a mathematicist analysis of juridical proof. This was (cf. §§24–6, pp. 74, above) that the complementational principle for negation, in the theory of mathematical probability, makes the merit of the loser's case vary inversely with that of the winner's. Hence on the mathematicist analysis an apparent injustice would be officially countenanced by the legal system whenever a man's relevant circumstances tended to place him on the majority side of some critical statistical division even though he actually belonged with the minority, unless some *ad hoc* rule of exclusion is postulated. The honest man at the rodeo (cf. §24, p. 75) would perhaps lose his case unless statistical evidence is declared inadmissible for proving the mathematical probability of a voluntary act.

But, if the probability that triers of fact are trying to balance is an inductive and not a mathematical one, this difficulty disappears altogether. Since the negation principle for inductive probability is not complementational (cf. §64, p. 221), the level of probability attained by the plaintiff's case does not vary inversely with that attained by the defendant's. If the balance of probability is said to have swung in favour of the plaintiff to such-or-such an extent, all that is implied about the defence is that the balance has swung against it. Whether on the facts accepted by the jury there is a very large, a substantial, or only a moderate inductive probability that the winner's contention is true, the loser can have only zero inductive probability on his side. On the inductivist interpretation litigants take part in a contest of case weight, as befits the Anglo-American adversary system of procedure, rather than in the division of a determinate quantity of case merit. The plaintiff may win by a greater or lesser margin, but if he wins on all the facts in court the defendant just loses. Hence no injustice is officially countenanced by allowing proof on the balance of probability.

Admittedly even a jury that weighs quite properly all the facts before the court can still make a decision that is *de facto* unjust. This might happen not only if some of the testimony was incorrect but also if one of the litigants did not succeed in getting put before the court all the facts that stood in his favour. For, though the jury are legally obliged to take the facts before the court as the only premises that are *de jure* relevant, there may well be other facts that are *de facto* relevant. Hence, though a jury in a civil case is entitled to detach S as a proven conclusion, if $p_I[S,R] > p_I[\text{not-}S,R]$, this could lead to injustice on a particular occasion if not all the *de facto* relevant facts were before the court. But that kind of injustice would be the fault or bad luck of the litigant who suffers from it: perhaps his advisers are incompetent or his witnesses reluctant to testify. No injustice would be attributable to the standard of proof, in the way that the mathematicist interpretation seems to permit.

Indeed on an inductivist interpretation there can be no case against the man at the rodeo in the circumstances described. If there is no evidence specifically against *him*, he cannot be brought under any inductively supported generalization from which it could be inferred that he did not pay for admission. Hence in order to elucidate why there can be no case against him we do not need to resort to some *ad hoc* stratagem. We do not need to postulate a legal rule ordaining some specific inadmissibility of evidence, such as the inadmissibility of statistical evidence in relation to voluntary acts. The heart of the matter is that there just is no inductive evidence against that particular man. So, if inductive probabilities are at issue, we can say quite simply that there is no evidence against him.

In sum, when all questions of law are correctly determined and the trier of fact, in accordance with accepted inductive standards, correctly assesses the balance of probabilities on the facts before the court, the inductivist analysis implies that injustice may be done—in the sense that victory may go to the party that is actually in the wrong—only because some of the evidence is incorrect, or because some of the relevant circumstances have not been put before the court, or (much more rarely) because some commonly accepted generalization is just a popular fallacy, like the old belief that having an area of skin insensitive to pain is a sign of having had concourse with the Devil. The trouble with the mathematicist theory is that it allows there to be, officially, a by no means negligible probability that the loser really deserved to win even when all the evidence is correct, all the relevant circumstances have been put before the court and no commonly accepted belief is fallacious.

§74. *The difficulty about proof beyond reasonable doubt*

The fourth difficulty for a mathematicist analysis of juridical proof was connected with the standard of proof in criminal prosecutions. We are more inclined to hold that a proposed conclusion falls short of certainty because there is a particular, specifiable reason for doubting it, than to hold that it is reasonable to doubt the conclusion because it falls short of certainty. What makes it reasonable to doubt the guilt of the accused is the absence of any evidence of motive, say, rather than the fact that the mathematical probability of his guilt has somehow been ascertained to be not higher than ·95. So, even if a scale of mathematical probability could be used for assessing how close a particular conclusion was to certainty, its assessments would very often be quite superfluous as reasons for doubting guilt. The proof's degree of validity could be judged without regard to the scale of mathematical probability. The scale would be otiose.

In an assessment of inductive probability, however, we have just the right direction of dependence between reasons for doubt, on the one hand, and absence of certainty, on the other. If $p_I[S,R]$ is not maximal, this must be because the generalization under which the desired conclusion, S, is derivable from R has less than full inductive support. And this in turn implies that the generalization is not qualified in relation to every relevant variable in a way that ensures its avoiding falsification. In other words there is some relevant variable v such that either R leaves it open which variant of v is actually present in the situation, where at least one variant would be unfavourable to the applicability of the generalization invoked, or perhaps R even states the presence of some specified uncounteracted unfavourable variant of v. For example, the facts before the court may not suffice to establish whether the defendant had a motive for committing the murder of which he is accused, and he can hardly be convicted on circumstantial evidence if there is no known motive. Or perhaps an essential witness for the prosecution has a shifty demeanour throughout his testimony and gives evasive responses when cross-examined, so that one of the key propositions relied on by the prosecution looks false. In the former case what we have is that $p_I[S,R]$ is not maximal, though greater than zero, in the latter—perhaps—that $p_I[S,R] = 0$. In neither case, of course, do we obtain certainty of innocence, i.e. in neither case do we obtain that $p_I[\text{not-}S,R]$ is maximal (§60, p. 208). But in both cases the reasons for doubting that S is true, when R is accepted, are just the facts that keep $p_I[S,R]$ below certainty, viz. no known motive, or a perjured witness. As was remarked in §27, what is needed in practice for assessment of proof in a criminal trial is a list of the various points that all have to be established, and of the various let-outs that all have to be barred, in relation to each element in the crime, if guilt is to be proved beyond reasonable doubt. It now emerges that this is identical with a list of the circumstances that are relevant for applying the generalizations invoked in reaching an inductively certain conclusion. The discrete stages of inductive probability-grading are much better adapted to the proof of criminal guilt than is the continuum of mathematical probability. If a high mathematical probability is required at some point in a proof beyond reasonable doubt, it is because this high mathematical probability is a variant of a relevant variable that needs to be present for a particular generalization to be applicable. In proving that the accused was the author of the threatening letter in the example of §28, pp. 84 f., one relevant fact is the high probability of typewriter-identity.

Admittedly even if we judge a proof by the best standards of evidence we have, these standards may well be inadequate. The inductive support-function which we judge best from an epistemological point of view may nevertheless not be the ontologically correct one, as was remarked in §45. In particular we may not know all the inductively relevant variables. So what *seems* inductively certain may not *be* inductively certain. But the criminal courts require only that further doubt of the accused's guilt be unreasonable, and presumably reasonableness here is to be determined by the best prevailing standards of evidence.

§75. *The difficulty about a criterion*

The fifth difficulty for a mathematicist analysis of the standards of juridical proof was discussed in §§29–31. It consists in the fact that each of the more familiar methods of assigning values to mathematical probability functions seems in principle inappropriate to the assessment of juridical proofs. Statistical probabilities, so far as they are relevant, may constitute some of the premises upholding the conclusion of a proof (as in §28). But they cannot measure the strength with which the premises support the conclusion. Range-theoretical probabilities are also unsuitable for this purpose, because an infinite number of different range-measures are available. Nor are betting odds, within a coherent betting policy, a possible basis for assessing probabilities here. A juryman is not in the position of being able to wager on the truth of a proposition of which the truth-value is independently discoverable. Nor is he in a position to adjust the odds he will accept to the stake he is prepared to risk. Nor are analogies from physical theory, or from games of chance, of any value here. In short the mathematicist analysis assumes the possibility of a mode of measurement that satisfies certain rather restrictive conditions. But it cannot describe how this mode of measurement operates even in principle, let alone in practice.

The inductivist analysis, however, has no difficulty at all here. It presupposes only that when a juryman takes up his office his mind is already adult and stocked with a vast number of commonplace generalizations about human acts, attitudes, intentions, etc., about the more familiar features of the human environment, and about the interactions between these two kinds of factor, together with an awareness of many of the kinds of circumstances that are favourable or unfavourable to the application of each such generalization. Without this stock of information in everyday life he could understand very little about his neighbours, his colleagues, his business competitors, or his wife. He would be greatly handicapped in explaining their past actions or predicting their future ones. But with this information he has the only kind of background data he needs in practice for the assessment of inductive probabilities in the jury-room. He does not need to have tacitly ingested a mass of quantitative or numerical statistics for this purpose. Nor does he need implicitly to remember some sophisticated mathematical algorithm in order to compute the probabilities from the data. The inductive probability of the proposed conclusion on the facts before the court depends just on the extent to which the facts are favourable to some commonplace generalizations that connect them to the conclusion.

Not that jurymen are incapable of disagreeing with one another in their assessment of the probability with which a proposed conclusion has been proved from undisputed facts. But on any rational reconstruction of their disagreement (when prejudice, personal sympathy, sectional spite, and other irrational factors may be disregarded) the disagreement must normally be due to differences of opinion about the kinds of circumstances that are favourable or unfavourable to the application of some particular commonsense generalization. The main commonplace generalizations themselves are for the most part too essential a part of our culture for there to be any serious disagreement about them. They are learned from shared experiences, or taught by proverb, myth, legend, history, literature, drama, parental advice, and the mass media. When people ceased to believe that those who had insensitive areas of skin were in commerce with the Devil, it was symptomatic of a major cultural change. Similarly, so long as the jurymen at a criminal trial are the accused's peers his case has a reasonable chance of being judged correctly by them, while if they belong to a different culture they are more likely to misjudge it even when trying to be fair. But there is still room for occasional disagreement, even within the same culture, about the kinds of circumstance that are favourable or unfavourable to the application of some particular commonsense generalization. That is how the typical hung jury may be understood, when several jurors give reasons for dissenting from the conclusions of their fellows and their reasons are not acceptable to the latter. No one disagrees, for example, with the generalization that witnesses who have taken the oath normally tell the truth so far as they know it. But it is relatively easy to disagree about what kinds of grimace, posture, or evasiveness in a witness tend to indicate that this generalization does not apply to him. So an inductivist analysis does not imply that each ordinary citizen is happily equipped to assess correctly any judicial proof whatever that is put before him. Rather, the analysis explains why the ordinary citizen is competent to assess most of these proofs as well as anyone else, and why nevertheless disagreements may still arise in the jury-room.

Someone may now be tempted to object that assessments of inductive probability are also open to disagreement on more important grounds. 'You reject any range-theoretical analysis of juridical probability', he may say, 'on the ground that jurymen cannot be expected to be unanimous about the selection of a suitable range-measure from the continuum of available range-measures. You argue that therefore they cannot justifiably be expected to be unanimous about the range-theoretical probability of one proposition on another. Yet you yourself must admit that different orderings in the list of relevant variables for a particular field of inductive assessment can result in assigning very different grades of inductive support to one proposition on the evidence of another. That is presumably why you pay so much attention to the epistemology of this ordering in §§44–5 and §§47–9. Correspondingly you must admit that the members of a jury should not be expected to be unanimous about inductive probabilities either. Indeed it is ultimately the same difficulty that confronts both your theory of inductive probability and Carnap's range-theoretical conception of mathematical probability. Neither can assign a non-arbitrary measure for the importance of particular predicates or families of predicates.'

But the situation is not as bad for my theory as for Carnap's.

First, the question about which variables are relevant, and in what order, is on my account an empirical issue and has to be determined separately in each field of inquiry. Hence any assessment of the inductive probability of one proposition on another makes an empirical claim, since it presupposes that a particular ordered set of variables is relevant to that type of proposition. On Carnap's account the corresponding question— about which families of predicates to admit, and how to measure their ranges—has to be settled *a priori*, whether by convention or intuition. According to my analysis, if a jury disagrees about the probability of a litigant's case on the facts before the court, someone on the jury has made a factual, empirical error, in ranking or comparing certain non-quantitative, non-measurable values. But, according to any Carnapian analysis of the situation, he has made a logical, *a priori*, computational error. So on my view a jury should, ideally, contain only men and women of the local culture, with a wide experience of life and a good capacity for learning from it, though not necessarily with any special computational skills. On Carnap's view it should ideally contain only logicians or mathematicians, and a mathematically sophisticated child would be better than an experienced but non-mathematical adult. However, so far as any restrictions on jury-eligibility are of acknowledged value they tend to favour my view, not Carnap's. A certain minimum age may be thought desirable, and perhaps a certain representativeness of the adult population at large; and foreigners, madmen, etc., should not be eligible. But no one has ever seriously advocated that eligibility for jury-service should be restricted to those who have passed a qualifying course in logic or mathematics, irrespective of citizenship or experience.

Secondly, the difficulty about the ordering of relevant variables does not normally hinder applications of the two main standards of proof with which we are here concerned. So far as proof beyond reasonable doubt is concerned, the order of relevant variables is immaterial, since each component of the alleged crime needs to be attributed conclusively to the accused, i.e. attributed to him by arguments that take all the relevant circumstances into account. And, so far as proof on the balance of probability is concerned, we must in practice always be prepared to work towards formulating our list of relevant variables in a way that ensures unanimity of assessment (as in §45). A hung jury is quite at home discussing whether one particular kind of evidential item has more weight than another—whether, for instance, demeanour is more important than reputation as evidence for the truthfulness of a certain kind of witness.

§76. *The difficulty about corroboration and convergence*

The sixth difficulty for a mathematicist analysis was discussed in §§32–7. It arises from the need to elucidate the force of corroboration and convergence in the assessment of judicial proof. When one witness corroborates another, or two items of circumstantial evidence converge, the probability of a party's case may be substantially increased. In an appropriate non-judicial context the formal structure of the mathematical calculus guarantees quite adequately that corroboration and convergence will take place, under right conditions of independence for the corroborating or converging items. But it achieves this guarantee at the cost of assuming a greater than zero prior probability for the proposition to be proved, and it implies that one has to take the level of this prior probability into account in assessing the probative force of the proposition's posterior probability—the proposition's probability on the evidence. So a mathematicist analysis of corroboration and convergence in judicial proof runs into a serious paradox. Such an analysis implies that there would be nothing inherently improper in a judge's instructing his jury to discover for itself (since they would not be put in evidence) whatever criminological and demographic facts determine the prior probability of the accused's guilt. Yet juries are constantly exhorted to base their verdicts on no other relevant facts than those actually put in evidence, plus those recognized by the judge or admitted by the opposing parties.

Consider instead what the inductivist analysis implies. Corroboration and convergence now appear just as two different ways in which probabilities are raised by the favourableness of inductively relevant circumstances. Alongside such factors as a witness's willingness to take an oath, or his demeanour in the witness-box, or his reputed character, one relevant variable for the truth of his testimony is its coherence with other testimony. That is, degree of coherence with other testimony is one relevant variable for the generalization that anything a sworn witness says is true. So, in assessing the inductive probability that a particular sworn witness has spoken the truth, one relevant circumstance is the extent to which what he has said agrees with what other witnesses have said. The probability of his having spoken the truth is raised by extensive agreement, and the probability of his having spoken falsely is raised by extensive disagreement. Similarly possession of a better or worse opportunity is one relevant variable for the generalization that anyone with a motive for murdering a man tends to murder him. So, if we are assessing the inductive probability that a particular man with a motive for murdering the victim was actually the murderer, one relevant circumstance that raises the probability is the fact that this man had a good opportunity to commit the crime.

Schematically, where S is the desired conclusion and R_2 is a premiss that corroborates, or converges with, another premiss R_1 so as to raise the probability of S, the inductivist analysis implies that we are given $p_I[S,R_1] > 0$ and $p_I[S,R_2] > 0$, plus certain independence conditions. From these premisses the inductivist analysis implies that $p_I[S,R_1 \ \& \ R_2] > p[S,R_1]$ is deducible. In the first place, the relevance of R_1-type situations to issues of the S/not-S type is given by $p_I[S,R_1] > 0$, which implies that at least one generalization about a sufficient condition for the absence of S-type situations is normally falsified by an R_1-type situation; and similarly the relevance of R_2-type situations to these issues is given by $p_I[S,R_2] > 0$. Secondly, since neither corroboration nor convergence can take place, as we saw in §35, unless there is a certain level of independence between the corroborating testimonies, or the converging facts, the other main constraints imposed by the method of relevant variables are also satisfied. The independence conditions specify $p[R_2,S] \leqslant p[R_2,R_1 \ \& \ S]$ and $p[R_2, \text{not-S}] \geqslant p[R_2,R_1 \ \& \ \text{not-S}]$. And if we interpret these conditions as stating relations between inductive probabilities, they can be seen as a special case of the independence and combinability requirements that all variants of inductively relevant variables must satisfy.

The independence requirement is that, if v_i and v_j $(j > i)$ are included as distinct items in a list of relevant variables for a particular hypothesis, no variant V_j of v_j should tend to be present whenever a certain variant V_i of v_i is present (cf. §44, p. 139). The relevant variables must all be capable of varying independently of one another. This is because the incorporation of one more variable into a particular test has to produce a stiffer, more complex test and so underwrite, where test-results are successful, the assignment of a higher grade of support. Hence, where relevance is being established by the falsification of a hypothesis the presence of V_i must not raise the inductive probability that V_j is present also. More specifically, in the present type of case, $p_I[R_2,R_1 \ \& \ \text{not-S}]$ must not be greater than $p_I[R_2,\text{not-S}]$.

Thus the independence requirement for variants of relevant

variables takes care of the condition $p[R_2, \text{not-S}] \geqslant p[R_2, R_1 \ \&$ not-S]. But there was a further element in what we found to be the independence conditions for converging, or mutually corroborating, premisses. It was also necessary that $p[R_2, R_1 \ \&$ S] $\geqslant p[R_2, S]$. And this condition too has an obvious rationale when we interpret the situation in terms of inductive probability. Any two variants, V_i and V_j, of different relevant variables that are present in a test on a particular hypothesis, and are both to enter favourably into a contingent version of the hypothesis, must satisfy not only an independence requirement, but also a combinability one (§54, p. 183). They have to be capable of co-occurrence in achieving a successful result from a test on the modified hypothesis. It is not essential that they should be capable of co-occurrence in the execution of an unsuccessful test, since the inclusion of v_i in the list of relevant variables is justified if each of its variants separately is a potential falsifier. But the possibility of co-occurrence in the execution of a successful test is indispensable, since only in this way, by passing a stiffer, more complex test can a hypothesis raise its grade of support. Hence, where the hypothesis is in fact being verified, the presence of V_i must not reduce the inductive probability that V_j is present also. More specifically, in the present type of case, $p_1[R_2, S]$ must not be greater than $p_1[R_2, R_1 \ \&$ S].

It follows that corroboration and convergence are completely intelligible within the theory of inductive probability. They are just two different ways in which inductive probabilities are raised by the favourableness of relevant circumstances, and the independence conditions that are necessary for corroboration and convergence flow from necessary constraints on the method of relevant variables—the characteristic method of assessing inductive support and inductive probability.

Thus far an inductivist analysis does at least as well as a mathematicist one. But when we come to the question of prior probability an inductivist analysis does much better than a mathematicist one. An inductivist analysis does not require (cf. §§64, p. 220) that the prior probability of a desired conclusion S, should be greater than zero in order that R_2 should be capable of raising the probability of S on R_1. So an inductivist analysis permits the jury to have a completely open mind initially on any issue that might affect the guilt of the accused person. On any such issue, Q, the jury can initially accept $p_I[Q] = 0$, because this expresses the non-existence of prior inductive reasons for believing Q, rather than—as $p_M[Q] = 0$ does—the existence of prior reasons for believing not-Q.

I conclude that if the standards of juridical proof are analysed in terms of inductive probability the main difficulties that obstruct a mathematicist analysis are not encountered.[4] Moreover, the genesis of all these difficulties is now apparent. They arise because an attempt is being made to map a certain pattern of inductive (Baconian) probabilification on to the mathematical (Pascalian) calculus. But, if proofs of fact in Anglo-American courts are constructed primarily in terms of inductive probabilities, it will just not be possible to give a completely satisfactory account of them in terms of mathematical probabilities. For, as we saw in §65, the principles of inductive probability are intrinsically resistant to mapping on to the theorems of the mathematical calculus. So to attempt such a mapping, in relation to juridical proof, inevitably generates anomalies, paradoxes, *ad hoc* stratagems, or other symptoms of theoretical misfit.

[4] For implicit anticipations of the view that juridical probabilities are inductive it is interesting to look at the account of 'degrees of legal evidence', and their balancing, in J. Glassford, *An Essay on the Principles of Evidence and their Application to Subjects of Judicial Enquiry* (1820), pp. 638–80, and at J. H. Wigmore's remark, in *The Principles of Judicial Proof*, 2nd edn. (1931), p. 244, that the difference between a possibility, tendency, probability, and certainty is that 'in the highest degree we think of the sequence as occurring under any and every combination of other circumstances, but in the middle degrees under the ordinary combinations only, and in the lowest degrees under rare combinations only.'
William Whewell, *The Philosophy of Inductive Sciences* Part II, 2nd edn. (1847), pp. 284 f., claimed that testimonial corroboration, and convergence of circumstantial evidence, were closely connected with what he called the 'consilience of inductions' in theoretical science. He was right. All three (cf. §§48 and 76) may be elucidated in terms of the method of relevant variables.

20

Criteria of Merit for Explanations
of Individual Events

Summary

§77. There are other fields besides that of judicial proof in which
the concept of inductive probability may be seen to operate:
Hempel's theory of explanation for individual events needs supple-
menting in this respect. §78. Such explanations invoke the same set
of covering laws about human behaviour as judicial proofs invoke.
§79. Apart from various forms of incompleteness that do not necessarily invalidate what Hempel calls deductive-nomological explanation, there is also a kind of insufficiency in the statement of explanatory conditions that according to Hempel renders an attempt at
such explanation merely programmatic. But this is paradoxical
and the paradox can be avoided by recognizing that the adequacy
of the explanation varies with its inductive probability. §80. In
explaining individual events we do not need to aim at maximum
comprehensiveness in the covering laws invoked, as when we
explain uniformities: rather, the more adequate the explanation,
the more heavily qualified the covering law is likely to be.

§77. *Hempel's theory of explanation for individual events*

If the concept of inductive probability were used in no other
context than that of juridical and everyday proofs of individual
facts, it would still be of quite considerable importance. It
would have a much narrower range of application than the
concept of mathematical probability, though a by no means
unimportant one. However, proofs of individual facts are far
from constituting the only context in which we reason in terms
of inductive probabilities. In this and the following three
chapters I shall discuss several other such contexts, in order to
indicate how wide a range of application the concept of inductive probability really has. I am not pursuing some absurdly
monocriterial or one-sided vision, according to which all

probabilities have to obey a single favoured set of principles. It would be ridiculous to dispute the central and indispensable role of Pascalian principles in the study of statistical data of all kinds, and in the theories of signal transmission, quality control, sub-atomic particles, games of chance, and innumerable other matters. I just want to show that the concept of inductive probability also plays a substantial part in human reasoning.

Consider first what Hempel once said about explanation.[1] On his view 'general laws have quite analogous functions in history and in the natural sciences.' Both in natural science and in history explanation 'aims at showing that the event in question . . . was to be expected in view of certain antecedent or simultaneous conditions.' So, in brief, the scientific or historical explanation of an event E consists in a set of statements asserting the occurrence of certain causal events C_1, . . . C_n at certain times and places, plus a set of universal hypotheses, such that both sets of statements are reasonably well confirmed by empirical evidence and from the two sets of statements an assertion of E's occurrence is logically deducible. Later[2] Hempel substantially expanded his account of explanation. He distinguished carefully between the explanation of individual events, like the cracking of a particular motor-car's radiator, and the explanation of uniformities, like the fact that any cannon operates at its maximum range when elevated at an angle of $45°$. He developed a class of measures for the explanatory power of a theory in relation to given data. And he distinguished also between explanations that invoke universal hypotheses and explanations that invoke statistical probabilities.

But Hempel's philosophy of explanation is vitiated in two major respects by a failure to notice the part played in scientific and historical explanation by the concepts of inductive support and inductive probability. In the present chapter (§§77–80) I shall discuss this issue in relation to an important difference between the explanation of individual events, and the explanation of uniformities, by subsumption under laws.

[1] C. G. Hempel, 'The Function of General Laws in History', *Journal of Philosophy* xxxix (1942), 35 ff., as reprinted, with modifications in C. G. Hempel, *Aspects of Scientific Explanation* (1965), pp. 231 ff.

[2] In his 'Studies in the Logic of Explanation', *Philosophy of Science* 15 (1948), 135 ff., as reprinted, with modifications in his *Aspects of Scientific Explanation*, pp. 245 ff.; and in new material in the latter book, pp. 333 ff.

In the following chapter (§§81–5) I shall discuss some important problems about statistical explanation which Hempel was unable to resolve satisfactorily.

§78. *Covering laws for both proofs and explanations*

There has been a lot of controversy about the question whether Hempel was right to claim that historians use a form of explanation for individual events that implicitly subsumes them under covering generalizations. For example, Runciman[3] describes how at the critical battle of the Yarmuk in A.D. 636.

(1) The Ghassanid prince and 12,000 Christian Arabs went over to the enemy. They were Monophysites and hated Heraclius; and their pay was many months overdue.

If this is what Hempel called a 'deductive-nomological' explanation, the generalization invoked describes the effect of theological differences and arrears of pay on an army's loyalty to its commander-in-chief. Presumably no one would doubt the truth of such a generalization, if formulated in suitably qualified terms, and the explanation is achieved by describing features of the situation that satisfy the antecedent of the generalization. This description is the explanans, and the explanation is achieved if the truth of the explanandum may then be inferred.

It would be a merely trivial objection to this account of (1) that what is invoked is not a generalization but a general rule of causal inference, since every causal generalization has a counterpart rule of inference and every general rule of inference has, in some language, a counterpart generalization. The more serious objection is that human relations are far too diverse, heterogeneous and wilful, to be brought under any network of laws, and so what is invoked is neither a generalization nor a rule of inference, but the empathetic understanding of the reader. However, if the analysis of juridical proof that was offered in §§67–76 above is correct, there is certainly no shortage of generalizations about human conduct that are widely regarded as true in specifiable circumstances, even if there are very few true in all circumstances. So it would be wrong to regard the historian as being forced into an appeal

---

[3] S. Runciman, *A History of the Crusades*, vol. i (1951), p. 16.

to empathy because he has no accepted generalizations to invoke. Possibly R. G. Collingwood's famous comparison of the work of a historian to that of a detective[4] may suggest that if the empathetic method can be used by historians it can also be used by a jury. But we have to distinguish what goes on in the detective's or juryman's mind from what justifies his conclusions. We have to distinguish the phenomenology of heuristics from the logic of proof. A judicial proof must be capable of dissection, element by element, so that it becomes completely clear what are the premises, what are the conclusions, why the latter are supposed to follow from the former, and with roughly how much probability they so follow. It is not possible to construct a Collingwoodian account of judicial proof that would come anywhere near satisfying this requirement. Correspondingly, we have to suppose that very many accepted generalizations about human affairs are available to historians and therefore that, however else historians explain things, there is no reason at all why they should not occasionally use the so-called 'covering-law' pattern of explanation. So I shall assume that (1), and similar cases, are examples of this pattern.

But the nub of my thesis would not be refuted even if Collingwood was right. Since my concern is with the explanation of individual events, and not with historical explanations as such, I could just as well take all my examples from the explanation of individual events in nature (the Lisbon earthquake of 1755, the death of the College hibiscus last year, and so on).

§79. *The grading of explanatory completeness*

Hempel[5] notes several ways in which a covering-law explanation of an individual event can be, or appear to be, incomplete, though none of these constitute criteria within the main dimension of appraisal for such explanations.

First, a proposed explanation may be elliptically formulated. For example, if we say that a lump of butter melted because it was put into a hot frying pan, we omit to mention the covering law that applies. Such an ellipse is relatively common in

---

[4] In his *Idea of History* (1946), p. 268.
[5] Op. cit., pp. 415 ff.

stating nomological explanations of individual events, since the law to be applied is normally indicated by the individual fact cited as cause. But obviously this type of incompleteness is not an important flaw in an explanation, since it would be pedantic for a speaker or writer to state explicitly what the hearer or reader can so easily supply for himself.

Secondly only part of the explanandum may be accounted for. Hempel cites an example of this from Freud, who explained his insertion of an incorrect date into his diary by reference to a subconscious wish to start his professional work again as soon as possible after returning from a holiday.[6] Hempel points out that Freud's proposed explanation is incomplete, in the sense that it does not explain why his subconscious wish took the particular form it did. But at least something, if Freud is right, has been adequately explained, viz. the fact that Freud did something as if he were starting work sooner than he was.

Thirdly, an event can be overdetermined if two or more alternative explanations with non-equivalent explanans-sets are available for it. For example, perhaps a copper rod has been both heated and subjected to longitudinal stress. Either fact can be cited to explain why there has been *some* increase in the rod's length. But either fact alone would be incomplete as an explanation of the actual measure of increase.

Fourthly, if an individual event is specified by a name or definite description, such as 'the Lisbon earthquake disaster of 1755', it may be understood to have indefinitely many aspects—the nature, strength, and location of the seismic disturbances, the extent of the damage to each building, the injuries inflicted on each person, etc., etc. No explanation could ever claim completeness if it had to explain every feature of such a concrete individual. But it is easy enough to specify an individual event instead as a particular instance of a given kind of event—as, say, the occurrence of an earthquake at Lisbon in 1755. When an individual event is specified in this way there is no such bar to its complete explanation.

Fifthly, every fact cited in a nomological explanation could itself call for explanation. But to worry about this kind of incompleteness would be absurd, since to seek completeness here would be to seek to complete an infinite regress.

---

[6] S. Freud, *Psychopathology of Everyday Life* (1951), p. 64.

In sum, incompleteness, in any of these five respects, does not necessarily invalidate a covering-law explanation. But there is another dimension of appraisal which is rather more crucial. As Hempel remarks,[7] the event cited as the cause of a given explanandum may in fact have been only one of a number of circumstances and events which jointly sufficed to satisfy the antecedent of a law predicting events of the kind instantiated by the explanandum. So he says

> To the extent that a statement of individual causation leaves the relevant antecedent conditions, and thus also the requisite explanatory laws, indefinite it is like a note saying that there is a treasure hidden somewhere. Its significance and utility will increase as the location of the treasure is more narrowly circumscribed, as the relevant conditions and the corresponding covering laws are made increasingly explicit. In some cases, this can be done quite satisfactorily; the covering-law structure then emerges, and the statement of individual causal connection becomes amenable to test. When, on the other hand, the relevant conditions or laws remain largely indefinite, a statement of causal connection is rather in the nature of a program, or of a sketch, for an explanation in terms of causal laws; it might also be viewed as a 'working hypothesis' which may prove its worth by giving new, and fruitful, direction to further research.

Thus for Hempel, if there is no serious doubt about the law or laws invoked, the achievement of a covering-law explanation is a matter of all-or-nothing. Either we have explained a given event E by citing the occurrence of certain events $C_1, \ldots C_n$ from which accepted generalizations enable us to infer the occurrence of E, or we have not achieved an explanation at all but only an explanation-programme or explanation-sketch. But, if this is so, very few covering-law explanations of individual events are ever achieved, and hardly any at all in the normal writing of human history.

Consider (1) above, for example. It does not seem too bad an explanation of the Ghassanid prince's desertion, with 12,000 of his followers. No doubt their theological differences from Heraclius would not explain their desertion very well, since they were already Monophysite, and he Monothelite,

[7] Op. cit., pp. 348 ff.

when they joined his cause. No doubt arrears of pay would hardly explain desertion in an age in which religious affinities and oppositions counted for so much. But the two factors combine to constitute a fairly plausible explanation, since each blocks a hole in the other, as it were. The arrears of pay were a new source of discontent, supervening on theological differences of longer standing, and the theological differences meant that religion could hardly replace money as a prop to loyalty. Nevertheless it would be rather rash to suppose, without qualification, that any commander-in-chief is deserted by his troops as soon as several months' arrears of pay are added to theological differences. Fear of a common enemy, expectation of loot, ingrained habits of military discipline, and respect for the personal qualities of the commander, are just four of the many factors that might counteract the tendency to desert in these circumstances. Hence (1) is incomplete as an explanation, in a way that very many explanations of individual events are incomplete. It does not say enough about antecedent or attendant circumstances to invoke a covering law that would be accepted as having universal validity. Yet it seems rather paradoxical to deny that it is an explanation at all and insist that it is merely an explanation-sketch or explanation-programme. If instead of (1) Runciman had written

(2)   The Ghassanid prince and 12,000 Christian Arabs went over to the enemy. Their reasons for deserting were partly to do with religion, partly to do with money, and partly to do with other matters,

he would indeed have provided merely an explanation-sketch or explanation-programme. But statements like (1) have counted as historical explanations for nearly two and a half thousand years—from Herodotus' time to the present day—and nothing but paradox is produced by setting up a philosophical criterion of explanatoriness, like Hempel's, that excludes them all.

We do not call a scientific theory merely a theory-sketch or theory-programme if not enough experimental evidence is yet available to give it full support: a theory-sketch or theory-programme is something quite different from a partially supported theory. Analogously we should not confuse an evidentially incomplete explanation of an individual event with an explanation-sketch or explanation-programme.

The problem is resolved by recognizing that all such explanations may, at least in principle, be located on a scale of completeness in accordance with the range of relevant circumstances, in the situation of the explanandum, that they take into account. Almost all well-supported generalizations about human conduct are highly complex and qualified, as has already been remarked in connection with the covering-laws for judicial proof (§68, p. 247). Or if the laws are formulated as simple, sweeping generalizations we have to admit strong restrictions on their domain of application—which amounts to very much the same thing (§54, pp. 183 ff.). It follows that where an explanation invokes covering laws such as these it must be correspondingly complex in order to be complete, and to the extent that it is incomplete, in virtue of taking no account of certain relevant circumstances, it must be construed as invoking some less qualified covering law that is correspondingly less well supported. Degree of completeness here is therefore a matter of weight and must be identified with the grade of inductive probability that the explanans gives to the explanandum. No doubt it is reasonable to regard some historical explanations as being complete, in the sense that the explanans inductively certifies the explanandum. But the discovery that very many of them are, and perhaps must always remain, more or less incomplete should no more surprise or shock us than the discovery that very many predictions about human conduct are, and perhaps must always remain, probable rather than certain.

In the light of all this it becomes possible to elucidate the meaning of such locutions as 'what probably explains . . . is ---', '. . . very probably happened because ---', or 'it is much more probable that . . . happened because --- than because -.-.-,' in contexts where no statistics, betting quotients or other indices of mathematical probability are mentioned. The probability of the explanation is the inductive probability with which the explanandum may be inferred from the explanatory statement of antecedent or attendant circumstances. Admittedly the generalization invoked in historical explanation sometimes seems to be a fairly simple, sweeping presumption or law that every adult member of the historian's culture fully accepts as holding in normal human circumstances. But an element of inductive probability creeps in as soon as we press the question: how well does this law apply to the given situation? So the more relevant facts a historian knows about the situation, the more probable is the explanation that he is in a position to produce. The best explanation of the Ghassanid prince's desertion is the one that explicitly balances off any circumstances tending to reinforce his loyalty with all those tending to undermine it. As well as stating whatever features of the situation initially favoured his desertion, it would also make clear what counteracted the features opposed to this if there were any such. Similarly, if a historian is concerned to show why the price of tea came down in the 1780s, he has not only to explain this directly by reference to Pitt's Commutation Act which reduced the import duty on tea. He has also to explain why the powerful groups opposed to price reduction were unsuccessful in their attempts to prevent it.[8] Or again, it may be necessary to make clear the qualifications and limitations with which some covering law applies to the given situation. So Powicke, having described various ways in which the loss of Normandy under King John was a crucial factor in strengthening the English nation-state, sees the necessity of explaining why it did not also promote the further conquest of Ireland and the Scottish Lowlands.[9]

Also, as with hung juries (§75, p. 275), it is easy to see how the possibility of controversy arises here. There may well be general agreement about many laws of human behaviour, when these laws are formulated with the rather imprecise qualification 'In normal circumstances . . .'. But opinions may differ very much about which circumstances actually are normal for each law. Unanimity about the truth of the laws is often bought at the cost of admitting vagueness in their formulation, and the fires of controversy that were damped down on the arena of truth may be rekindled on the arena of precisification. For example, were Cromwell's dealings with Charles X of Sweden primarily motivated by confessional

---

[8] C. Hoh-Cheung and L. H. Mei, 'William Pitt and the Enforcement of the Commutation Act, 1784–1788', *English Historical Review*, 76 (1961), 447 ff.

[9] F. M. Powicke, *The Loss of Normandy* (1913), pp. 444–8.

solidarity, by commercial antagonism to the Dutch, or by fear of the Stuarts, or by some combination of these factors?[10] Each of these explanations invokes a covering-law that most people would accept as holding in normal circumstances. But there might be much dispute about the precise nature of the circumstances that are normal for each such covering law. And this could lead to a dispute, in the particular case of Cromwell's dealings with Charles X, about the question whether the religious, the economic, or the political explanation has greater probability.

So Hempel's analysis tends to obscure the nature of the problem that normally confronts the historian. In terms of Hempel's analysis, whenever the covering laws that are implicitly invoked are acceptable, and the reports of antecedent or attendant circumstances are true, there is *either* an explanation *or* only an explanation-sketch or explanation-programme. But in fact, even when the laws are accepted by everyone and the circumstantial reports are true, there is still a great deal of room for the adequacy of the explanation to vary without its degenerating into a mere explanation-sketch or explanation-programme.

§80. *The merit of the explanation tends to vary inversely with the generality of the covering law*

Correspondingly Hempel's analysis obscures a very important dimension of difference between covering-law explanations of individual events and covering-law explanations of uniformities. In natural science one theory is normally said to offer a better explanation of a certain uniformity than another does if it explains a greater variety of accepted uniformities and even predicts some hitherto undetected ones. As we have already seen (§47), this means that the better explanatory theory not only has greater inductive support but also obtains this grade of support without having to suffer corresponding qualifications. On the other hand in historiography, or wherever else individual events have to be explained, the best covering-law explanation is the one that cites antecedent or attendant circumstances which give the explanandum the greatest probability of occurrence. And here it does not matter at all if in order to

[10] Cf. M. Roberts, 'Cromwell and the Baltic', *English Historical Review* 76 (1961) 402 ff.

achieve this high probability the covering laws invoked are heavily qualified and have therefore only a very narrow scope of application.

Perhaps it will be objected that if we had an adequate theory of human motivation we should not be able to suppose that covering-law explanations of individual events can be satisfactory when they invoke laws of quite restricted generality. 'To regard explanations of the latter kind as being satisfactory', it may be said, 'is merely to demonstrate our inability to explain human behaviour scientifically. If we had an appropriate scientific theory, that gave us a deep and comprehensive understanding of the characteristic patterns of human behaviour, it would be applicable also to each individual event in human history.' And perhaps some objectors of this type might add that in fact we already have such a theory, through the genius of Karl Marx, say, or of Sigmund Freud.

But even if we did already have such a comprehensive scientific theory of human behaviour explanations of individual events would still differ from explanations of uniformities in the way described. Consider Cromwell's dealings with Charles X of Sweden, for example, and suppose it is true that one government's dealings with another are normally to be explained in terms of the dialectic of class conflict. Then it has to be shown that Cromwell's dealings are subsumable under one of the patterns that are so explicable. For example, perhaps they may be said to have been motivated by the pressure of British trade interests. Accordingly the question that arises, in relation to the individual event (or series of events), is this: how probable is it, in the circumstances of the time, that Cromwell was pushed or motivated by the British trading situation? If a high probability can be demonstrated, there is a correspondingly high probability that Marxist theory applies here. But the demonstration of the probability may legitimately invoke a covering law of very restricted generality, connecting the current trade rivalry with the Dutch—despite their anti-Catholicism, the current state of the ship-building industry, etc.—with Cromwell's political negotiations. Just the same is true when your car's radiator cracks in a hard frost. No doubt a high-level scientific explanation is to be found in the kinetic theory of gases for why frozen water expands with sufficient pressure to crack this or that type of metal. But to be sure that this has anything to do with your radiator's cracking you need first to establish that in the actual situation it was frost that caused the crack, because, say, the anti-freeze was rather diluted, there was no fault in the radiator's manufacture, no one hit it with a hammer, there was a very hard frost, and so on. So the explanation of the individual event achieves a high probability by invoking a covering law of very restricted generality. But this rather elementary covering law is just one instance of a type of uniformity that may in turn be explicable, if our science has progressed thus far, in terms of a much more comprehensive theory or group of theories.

In short it is undoubtedly a merit in the explanation of an individual event if it brings the event under a type of uniformity which in turn is explicable by some rather deep and wide-ranging theory. But to be sure that the event falls under some particular generalization of the type in question we may need to know a great deal about the event's circumstances, in case any of these serve to thrust it over the generalization's threshold of abnormality. The theory achieves its comprehensiveness by concerning itself exclusively with certain idealized correlations, which are alleged to hold good in the 'normal' case. By abstracting these from the tangle of complexly interconnected phenomena which fill the actual world, it achieves a degree of generality which would otherwise be unattainable. But to be sure that an individual event is a normal case, for these purposes, or at any rate fairly close to being one, we may need to know quite a lot about the concrete detail of its circumstances. So it remains a mistake to suppose that comprehensiveness of covering law is equally appropriate for covering-law explanations of individual events and covering-law explanations of uniformities. As the weight of evidence for an explanation of the former type increases, the covering law invoked may get less and less comprehensive.

A rather different argument, however, might also be advanced in favour of this supposition. It might be pointed out that, if anything that is R_1 is S, so too must anything that is R_1 and R_2 be S. If all unpaid and religiously disaffected troops desert, so do all unpaid and religiously disaffected troops who are armed with swords and spears. So if generality and comprehensiveness were of no importance for the covering law invoked, there would be nothing to choose between (1) and

(3)   The Ghassanid prince and 12,000 Christian Arabs went over to the enemy. They were Monophysites and hated Heroclius; their pay was many months overdue; and they were armed with swords and spears.

Yet it could well be completely wrong to imply that the nature of the Chassanids' arms had anything at all to do with their desertion. It might therefore be argued that even in the explanation of individual events the covering law invoked is always the most comprehensive one that applies, since this is the inevitable corollary of avoiding the attribution of explanatory force to inoperative circumstances as well as to operative ones.

But the trouble with this argument is that it assumes the covering law invoked in a historical explanation to be just a universally quantified conditional—a generalization asserting merely that, say, anything that is R is S. In fact it is normally a causal generalization of some kind, which asserts that being R is a cause of a thing's becoming S. We want to know what *caused* the Ghassanid desertion or Cromwell's Baltic policy— not just how to classify it. Such a generalization acquires inductive support initially from a test on 'Anything if R is S' where the variable of which R is a variant is manipulated, as in what Mill called the Method of Difference (cf. §46, p. 148). And the Ghassanids' arms were not part of the cause of their desertion, because the result of such a test here would normally be negative. That is to say, troops that are not as well-armed as their technology permits are even more prone to desert. Hence it is not the need for maximum comprehensiveness in his implicitly invoked covering-law that makes a historian prefer (1) to (3). It is rather the fact that he needs to invoke a causal generalization which has passed test t_1 in the method of relevant variables. Beyond that point anything that is said in the explanation to increase its probability, such as a specification of further relevant circumstances, would certainly make the covering law invoked less comprehensive. But the crucial fact is that the mention of further relevant circumstances would also imply appropriate statements about controls (as in §54, p. 183 f.) which would not be available for inoperative circumstances like the swords and spears of (3).

21

Statistical Explanation

Summary

§81. Hempel proposed to deal with the problem of epistemic ambiguity in statistical explanation by a requirement of maximal specificity in the reference-class. §82. But, as Salmon has shown, the reference-class needs to be narrowed only in statistically relevant ways. Also it needs to be homogeneous. Both requirements seek, in effect, to maximize inductive probability. §83. So successful statistical explanations do not need to invoke high statistical probabilities, but favourably relevant ones that have high inductive probability. §84. Salmon's arguments for saying that even favourable relevance is unnecessary rest on a failure to distinguish between explanations how a certain event was possible and explanations why it occurred. §85. The mathematical probabilities involved in statistical explanation are not amenable to interpretation as relative frequencies, and must be given a propensity interpretation.

§81. *Hempel's account of statistical explanation*

Hempel has argued that explanations of individual events divide into two main categories, which he calls the 'deductive-nomological' and 'inductive-statistical', respectively. The explanations that belong to the former of these two categories are those that invoke covering laws. They have been discussed in the preceding chapter (§§77–80), and it is clear that the concept of inductive probability is integral to their proper evaluation where the explananda are individual events. But what about Hempel's other main category? Has the concept of inductive probability anything to do with statistical explanation? It will turn out that it has, but the problem is a complicated one and needs careful statement. What I shall argue here is that Hempel's own account of 'inductive-statistical' explanation suffered from several important defects, which have been substantially remedied by Wesley Salmon and others. But the account of statistical explanation that then emerges is one which incorporates several Baconian features, and the concept of inductive probability is intrinsically involved.

Hempel began his account[1] of what he called 'inductive-statistical explanation' with a simple example.

As an explanation of why patient John Jones recovered from a streptococcus infection, we might be told that Jones had been given penicillin. But if we try to amplify this explanatory claim by indicating a general connection between penicillin treatment and the subsiding of a streptococcus infection we cannot justifiably invoke a general law to the effect that in all cases of such infection, administration of penicillin will lead to recovery. What can be asserted, and what surely is taken for granted here, is only that penicillin will effect a cure in a high percentage of cases, or with a high statistical probability.

So in such statistical explanation, according to Hempel, a high mathematical probability is invoked rather than a universal generalization, and correspondingly the explanans probabilifies, but does not imply, the explanandum. But a problem then arises about 'epistemic ambiguity', as Hempel calls it. Suppose that in fact Jones's illness is known to be streptococcal infection of the penicillin-resistant variety, where the mathematical probability of recovery among randomly chosen patients is very low. Then in addition to the argument for Jones's having a high probability of recovery we seem also to have another argument for his having a high probability of non-recovery. And, as Hempel pointed out, any statistical explanation for the occurrence of an event must seem suspect if a probabilistic account of its non-occurrence is equally possible.

Hempel concluded that a decision on the acceptability of a proposed statistical explanation will have to be made in the light of all the relevant information at our disposal. But to apply Carnap's requirement of *total* evidence here would be to employ the same explanans in all statistical explanations acceptable at any one time. So Hempel suggested instead a requirement of maximal specificity. An acceptable explanation, he held, must be based on a statistical probability statement pertaining to the narrowest reference class of which, according to our total

[1] Op. cit., pp. 381 ff.

information, the particular occurrence under consideration is a member. For explanations that meet this requirement the problem of epistemic ambiguity no longer arises.

§82. *The need to maximize inductive probability for the appositeness of the reference-class*

Salmon[2] has demonstrated two important flaws in Hempel's account of statistical explanation. Hempel's conditions for such explanation turn out to be neither sufficient nor necessary.

Take the question of sufficiency first and consider, for example,

(1)   Jones was almost certain to recover from his cold within a week, because he took vitamin C, and almost all colds clear up within a week after administration of vitamin C.

If we know no more about Jones than that he had a cold and took vitamin C, it is clear that (1) conforms with Hempel's criteria for statistical explanation. But the trouble is, as Salmon points out, that colds tend to clear up within a week regardless of the medication administered and controlled tests indicate that the percentage of recoveries is unaffected by the use of vitamin C. So we have a counterpart here of the difficulty that was noted at the end of the previous chapter (§80) in regard to covering-law explanation. If the covering law invoked was allowed to be a universally quantified conditional, this failed to bar the introduction of all sorts of irrelevant facts into the explananans. If anything that is R_1 is S, so too must anything that is R_1 and R_2 be S. In order to deal with this difficulty we had to require that the covering law invoked should be a causal one, so that an application to it of test t_1 in the method of relevant variables—i.e. roughly, an application of Mill's Method of Difference—could be presumed to bar the introduction of irrelevant facts into the explanans. The arms that the Ghassanid soldiers carried were not a contributory factor in causing their desertion, because without them they might have been even more ready to desert. A corresponding requirement

---

[2] In Wesley C. Salmon, *Statistical Explanation and Statistical Relevance* (1970), pp. 29 ff. Somewhat similar accounts of statistical explanation, by Richard C. Jeffrey and James G. Greeno, are published in the same book, on pp. 19 ff. and 89 ff. respectively.

seems therefore to be appropriate in the corresponding form of statistical explanation. Instead of Hempel's requirement of maximum specificity for the reference-class cited we need to require that the reference class be narrowed only in statistically relevant ways. A requirement of statistical relevance is the counterpart here of applying the Method of Difference.

This can easily be shown. For in Salmon's sense membership in a class R is said to be 'statistically relevant' to S within Q if and only if $p_M[S,Q \ \& \ R] \neq p_M[S,Q]$. Now $p_M[S,Q \ \& \ R]$ will avoid equality with $p_M[S,Q]$ if and only if it avoids equality with $p_M[S,Q \ \& \ \text{not-}R]$.[3] So R is statistically relevant to S within Q if and only if variation from R to not-R alters the mathematical probability of a Q thing's being S. And if we were generalizing about the effect of R on this probability in any randomly selected sequence of Qs, variation from R to not-R would be an application of the Method of Difference.

But the required reference class cannot be characterized merely as the class that is determined by a statistically relevant property, since there may be many such properties and some of them may contain irrelevant components. Accordingly Salmon sets out to define the concept of a homogeneous reference-class. For this purpose he makes use of Richard von Mises's notion of a place selection. According to von Mises

By a place selection we mean the selection of a partial sequence in such a way that we decide whether an element should or should not be included without making use of the attribute of the element.[4]

If every place selection is irrelevant to a given attribute in a given sequence, von Mises called the sequence 'random'. Similarly, if every property that determines a place selection is statistically irrelevant to S in R, Salmon terms R a 'homogeneous reference class' for S. His rule for selecting the reference class for the statistical explanation of an individual event is then: choose the broadest homogeneous reference-class to which the event belongs. This will ensure that no statistically irrelevant factors are cited in the explanans, and at the same time allow the largest suitable population for sampling. If,

---

[3] Cf. H. Reichenbach, *The Theory of Probability*, tr. E. H. Hutten and M Reichenbach (1949), p. 79.

[4] R. von Mises, *Probability, Statistics and Truth*, 2nd edn. (1957), p. 25.

say, the class of people with colds is homogeneous in relation to recovery within a week, there is no need to narrow the class further by citing Jones's having taken vitamin C, as in (1). Also by aiming at homogeneity in the reference class we may reasonably hope to screen off factors that are effects or symptoms, rather than causes, in relation to the explanandum. The class of days on which our barometer suddenly falls may not be homogeneous in relation to the occurrence of storms, since the barometer may be malfunctioning or there may be a local decrease of atmospheric pressure within the house. But the class of days on which there is a sudden decrease of atmospheric pressure in the garden may well be homogeneous in relation to the occurrence of storms. So by invoking that reference-class, according to Salmon, we can hope to avoid the mistake of explaining the occurrence of a storm by citing one of its effects or symptoms.

Now Salmon does not discuss the structure of the reasoning by which we may justify the belief that we have found the broadest homogeneous reference class. Admittedly, he proposes a measure for degree of inhomogeneity in a reference-class.[5] But the measure is based on statistical variance. So in order to discover—by this measure—exactly how inhomogeneous a suggested reference-class is in relation to a particular attribute one must know beforehand what the mathematical probability of the attribute is within a homogeneous partition of the universe of discourse. Salmon's measure of inhomogeneity is therefore in no way a substitute for some method of assessing the strength of hypotheses about homogeneity.

Specifically the question that arises here is this. How are we to be sure that we have not done too much partitioning of the original heterogeneous population, or too little? Perhaps genetic inheritance is statistically relevant to recovery from colds, or perhaps age is, or climate. Perhaps eye-colour, like taking vitamin C, is not. But even eye-colour and vitamin C absorption affect recovery from other illnesses (pigmentation and deficiency diseases, respectively). So what this means is that we have a hypothesis to test, and if necessary, modify, against an appropriate list of inductively relevant variables. The initial hypothesis is that in any randomly selected sub-set

[5] Op. cit., pp. 51 f.

of Q (the original population), the mathematical probability of membership in S is the same. This hypothesis needs to be modified in relation to any variant of a relevant variable that is statistically relevant to S within Q. But when sufficient modifications have been made the hypothesis should survive all further tests by manipulation of inductively relevant variables. It will then assert that, say, in any randomly selected sub-set of Q that is included in R, the mathematical probability of membership in S is the same. What Salmon calls a homogeneous reference-class—the intersection of Q and R—is thus determined, so far as we can determine it, by a characteristically inductive process of reasoning. We seek the simplest—least qualified—hypothesis that survives tests against inductively relevant variables: the merit of our hypothesis is to be gauged in terms of the inductive support that exists for it.

In sum, if we combine what was said earlier about applying the Method of Difference to secure relevance, with what has now been said about inductive modification in order to secure homogeneity, we can see that the reference-class for a statistical explanation must be chosen by a typically inductive process of reasoning. It must give the highest available inductive probability to the appositeness of the stated statistical probability. Subject to this requirement it can then be made as broad as possible in order to secure an adequate quantity of statistical data.

§83. *The need for favourable relevance rather than a high mathematical probability*

I have been discussing Salmon's remedy for Hempel's failure to determine *sufficient* conditions for statistical explanation, and I have argued that the remedy—the requirement of homogeneous relevance in the reference-class—is essentially the same as requiring that the explanatory statistical probability should be applicable to the circumstances of the explanandum with the highest available grade of inductive probability. I turn now to Salmon's other important criticism of Hempel's account. This is, in effect, that Hempel fails to determine correctly the *necessary* conditions for statistical explanation, since he requires that the explanatory statistical probability should in every case be a high one. Salmon's primary counter-example is the well-known explanation of paresis.[6] No one ever contracts paresis unless he has had latent syphilis which has gone untreated, but only a small percentage of victims of untreated latent syphilis develop paresis. So, though the best available explanation of an individual's developing paresis is that he has had untreated latent syphilis (since the reference-class of untreated latent syphilitics is, so far as we know, homogeneous), nevertheless the explanatory statistical probability is a rather low one.

Salmon rightly points out that what is crucial to the explanation in such cases is that, though the mathematical probability of an event of the explanandum's type in the reference-class is small, it is nevertheless greater than the prior probability of such an event. Paresis is very rare in the population at large, but not quite so rare among untreated latent syphilitics. So it looks as though Hempel's mistake was not merely to suppose that a high statistical probability needed to be mentioned in the explanans but also to suppose that a single probability on its own can be explanatory here. For at heart a statistical explanation why something is such-or-such must be that the probability of the explanandum in a cited reference-class is greater than its prior probability.

Of course, in their everyday modes of expression this feature of statistical explanations is often blurred or elided. But wherever that kind of ellipse is common it is all the more important for philosophical analysis to reveal the implicit or underlying structure. Indeed the full parallelism between covering-law explanation and statistical explanation-why is now revealed. Just as the explanatory principle for the former has to be a causal law and not an elementary generalization, so too the explanatory principle for the latter has to be a favourable statistical relevance and not a high statistical probability. In covering-law explanation the occurrence of the explanandum is explained by citing circumstances that cause it. In statistical explanation-why the occurrence of the explanandum is explained by citing circumstances that are statistically favourable to it. In both types of explanation some use of the Method of Difference is presupposed, in order to establish what happens when the alleged cause is not present or

---

[6] References to various philosophical discussions of this explanation are given by Salmon, op. cit., p. 86, n. 55.

what statistical probability holds within other reference-classes. And in both types of explanation some use of the Method of Agreement is presupposed, in order to eliminate rival possible causes or establish a homogeneous reference-class. So both types of explanation are to be evaluated by the method of relevant variables and are meritorious to the extent that this evaluation generates high inductive probabilities for them.

As a further parallelism, in Baconian terms, between causal-law explanation and statistical explanation-why, one may note how the well-known difficulties about plurality of causes have their counterparts in what Salmon[7] calls 'multiple homogeneity'. Ideally, in a statistical explanation why something is such-or-such, both the reference-class and its complement should be homogeneous. But sometimes the universe under discussion cannot be partitioned appropriately into less than n homogeneous classes, where $n > 2$. For example, although the reference-class of samples of table salt is completely homogeneous for water-solubility, the complementary class is not. That is, we can make further partitions in the class of samples of substances other than table salt which are statistically relevant to water-solubility. Samples of sand, wood, and gold are never water-soluble: samples of baking soda, sugar and rock salt are. Hence, as Salmon puts it, if we explain why this sample dissolves in water by pointing out that it is table salt and all table salt is water-soluble, we may feel that the explanation is somewhat inadequate. If we therefore seek some more general explanation, we shall be dealing with multiple homogeneity here in exactly the same way as we should deal with situations where the Method of Difference lends support to the existence of a plurality of causes (cf. §46, p. 150).

Since a high inductive probability is thus requisite for a good statistical explanation, it is possible to see how the belief that all probabilities are mathematical ones could easily lead to Hempel's error. Anyone who feels intuitively that a high probability is requisite, and then supposes mistakenly that all probabilities are mathematical, will be inclined to conclude, mistakenly, that a high mathematical probability is requisite. The (inductive) probability of homogeneity in the cited

[7] Op. cit., pp. 58 ff.

reference class, membership of which is (statistically) favourably relevant to the explanandum, is confused with the (mathematical) probability of the explanandum in the reference-class. And confusion of this kind is made substantially easier by the fact that where we feel unsure that maximum (inductive) probability has been achieved—i.e. that our reference-class is maximally homogeneous—we may be inclined to require a greater margin of (statistically) favourable relevance. Otherwise the margin might perhaps disappear altogether if the reference-class had to be further narrowed.

§84. *Salmon's rejection of the relevance requirement*

Curiously, after making out a good case for replacing Hempel's requirement of high statistical probability, in statistical explanation, by a requirement of favourable statistical relevance, Salmon himself rejects the latter requirement.[8] To substantiate this rejection he cites three further examples purporting to show that the posterior probability of the explanandum may be lower than, or equal to, its prior probability. So that, on Salmon's view, the fact cited in the explanans may, in terms of statistical probability, be either favourably or unfavourably relevant, or quite irrelevant, to the explanandum.

This seems to me to represent an oversimplification of the structure of statistical explanation. Nor is the need for it borne out in fact by Salmon's examples. Let us consider these examples.

First, suppose that a game of heads and tails is being played with two crooked pennies, and that these pennies are brought in and out of play in some irregular manner (e.g. by the toss of a third coin, which is unbiased). One penny is biased for heads to the extent that 90 per cent of the tosses with it yield heads. The other penny is similarly biased for tails. Furthermore, the two pennies are used with equal frequency in the game, so that the over-all probability of heads is one-half. Suppose a play of this game results in a head, which is an event that has a prior probability of ·5. Then if the toss were made with the penny biased for tails it has a posterior probability, in relation to a fully homogeneous reference class, of ·1.

[8] Op. cit., pp. 62 ff. Cf. also Wesley C. Salmon, 'Theoretical Explanation' in *Explanation*, ed. Stephan Körner (1975), pp. 118 ff.

Despite the fact that the posterior is less than the prior Salmon claims the result of the toss is to be explained by assigning the coin to its correct reference class:

Any event, regardless of its probability, is amenable to explanation. In the case of improbable events, the correct explanation is that they are highly improbable occurrences which happen, nevertheless, with a certain definite frequency. If the reference class is actually homogeneous, there are no other circumstances with respect to which they are probable. No further explanation can be required or can be given.

But Salmon fails to distinguish between two different types of explanation here. Just as we can ask not only why a particular event did happen, but also how it was possible for the event to happen, so too we can seek to explain not only why the event did happen but also how it could happen. By assigning a particular coin-toss to a reference-class where it has a posterior probability of ·1 we explain how it *could* occur. For this purpose we can use any applicable reference-class in every randomly selected sequence of which the explanandum has a non-zero mathematical probability of occurrence. But to explain why such an event *did* occur, we should need to assign it to a homogeneous reference-class in which it had a favourably relevant probability of occurrence—e.g. to the class of tosses by skilled defeaters of coin-biases. If we know of no such reference-class, then we just have no explanation of why it (actually) happened, only of how it could (possibly) happen.

Salmon's other two examples may be interpreted in the same way.

Suppose a mixture of uranium 238 atoms, that have a very long half-life, and polonium 214 atoms, that have a very short one. And suppose an atom in the mixture disintegrates, which turns out to be a uranium 238 atom. Here, according to Salmon, we have another example of a statistical explanation in which the posterior probability of the explanandum, when assigned to its appropriate reference-class, is less than its prior probability. But again the explanation offered is only of how the atom could disintegrate so soon, not of why it did. According to some philosophers of physics we ought not to hope for an explanation of the latter kind. According to others such an explanation could conceivably be forthcoming one day. But whoever is right on this issue it remains wrong to suppose that when we have an explanation of how a thing could happen we already know why it did happen.

Similarly, if we added an unbiased coin to the two biased ones in Salmon's game, the prior probability of any coin's falling heads is still a half. So if a coin that falls heads turns out to be the unbiased one the posterior probability of this occurrence is equal to the prior one. But by assigning the coin to its appropriate reference-class we still achieve an explanation only of how the toss could have this result, not of why it did. The situation is quite different from what it would be like if the coin that fell heads turned out to be the one biased for heads. For then we should have learned something relevant to the explanandum.

My point is not that explaining why a thing actually occurs is somehow a 'genuine' explanation, while explaining how it can occur is not. Explaining how, what, when, where, who, which, why, etc., are all legitimate forms of explanation. But the substantival phrase 'the explanation of S' is certainly more often used to refer to explaining *why* a thing is S than to refer to any other type of explaining. So my criticism of Salmon is that by rejecting the requirement of favourable relevance in statistical explanation he equates all statistical explanation with one of its less commonly recognized forms, and passes over the distinctive feature of statistical explanation-why that makes it analogous to causal explanation.

We normally expect things to carry on in the same way as they have been doing, with accustomed frequencies of occurrence. When the occurrence of an individual event of familiar type seems to require explaining, it is normally because the event has occurred at a time, or in a place, where it was relatively unexpected. But the event was relatively unexpected then, or there, because it was classified under a description which gave it a relatively low mathematical probability of occurrence. Hence we move a bit towards explaining why it occurred by reclassifying the event under a description which gives it a higher mathematical probability of occurrence. Recovery from streptococcal infection (in human history as a whole) has not been as common as we should like. But recovery from it after treatment with penicillin is much commoner. Analogously, when we seek the causal explanation of an event, we are looking for something that has diverted the stream of events from its otherwise-to-be-expected course. When an army deserts its general, we look for causes of disaffection. When a noise is heard from a normally silent cupboard, we look for the mouse.

§85. *The need for a propensity interpretation*

Finally, a word needs to be said about the nature of the mathematical probabilities involved in statistical explanations-why.

Hempel construed the mathematical probabilities involved in what he called 'inductive-statistical' explanations as Carnapian degrees of confirmation. Against this Salmon has three arguments. First, it is not clear how the statistical generalizations demanded by Hempel's schemata are to be obtained within a Carnapian system. Secondly, it is not clear why such generalizations should be needed when a Carnapian system of inductive logic is assumed, since within a system of this kind confirmation-functions can normally take singular hypotheses and singular evidential statements as arguments. Thirdly, Carnapian inductive logic is not concerned with establishing conclusions from premises, though Hempel holds that in any statistical explanation an assertion of the explanandum's occurrence is treated as a conclusion to be drawn (at an appropriate level of probability) from certain specified premises. Accordingly Salmon himself prefers a frequency interpretation here, which treats any probability involved as the limit of the relative frequency of an attribute in an infinite sequence of events. But he thinks[9] that everything he says about the problem of the single case for the frequency interpretation can be made directly applicable to the propensity interpretation by a simple translation. Wherever he speaks 'of the problem of selecting the appropriate reference class' in connection with the frequency interpretation, the reader is to understand 'the problem of specifying the nature of the chance set-up' in reference to the propensity interpretation.

However, it may well be that the propensity interpretation

[9] Op. cit., pp. 39 f.

can be applied with fewer difficulties here than the frequency interpretation. There are at least four reasons for thinking this.

First, so far as we know, the reference-classes involved are often finite in size. The number of people who take vitamin C in the history of the universe may be very large, but it is quite likely to be finite.

Secondly, even though it may be possible to treat some mathematical probabilities in finite classes as relative frequencies, the propensity interpretation has the advantage of allowing distributive predication of probabilities. The propensity of having a certain probability of recovering, say, is predicated distributively of each member of the class determined by the chance set-up of having a cold, instead of being predicated collectively of the class as a whole. So the explanation of an individual event falls readily within the scope of such a generalized predication: the explanandum occurred because the object or event involved was characterized by a set-up with the appropriate propensity. Relative frequencies in samples may well be the primary *evidence* on which we base our statements about statistical probabilities. But the *meaning* of such statements seems best given by a propensity interpretation, if the statements are to be used in the explanation of individual events.

Thirdly, as we have already seen (§7) a propensity interpretation makes probability functors non-extensional in their logic of substitutivity, like causal generalizations. So a propensity interpretation here maintains the parallelism between causal and statistical explanation-why which has already been noticed.

Fourthly, the parallelism between causal and statistical explanations is further sustained by the type of subjunctive conditional that derives from them. One has to distinguish in this connection between an ampliative and a non-ampliative subjunctive conditional. An ampliative one states what would be the case even if the condition predicated in its antecedent were satisfied by some specified additional entity over and above the entities that actually satisfy it, like

(2)   If you were to cross the road without looking, you would be run over.

The assertion of such a subjunctive conditional implies the corresponding truth-functional conditional to have a substantial level of inductive reliability—i.e. to resist falsification by quite a range of relevant factors, but[10] perhaps not by all. (Compare the account of causal hypotheses in §46, p. 151.) A non-ampliative subjunctive conditional, on the other hand, does not raise the possibility that the condition predicated in its antecedent may be satisfied by some specified additional entity. Smith might say, for example, in reply to the query whether the dog that has just come into the garden belongs to him,

> If it were one of my dogs, it would be white.

Such a conditional derives typically from an accidentally true generalization, not from an inductively well-supported one. Now, causal explanations notoriously sustain ampliative subjunctive conditionals. In particular they often provide a foundation in this way for prudential action. Such is the connection, for example—mediated by the uniformity principle—between support for

> Smith was run over because he crossed the road without looking

and support for (2). And statistical explanations must also be taken to sustain ampliative subjunctive conditionals. So far as the explanation of Jones's recovery from his streptococcal infection lies in the fact that anyone who has this infection has his chance of recovery increased by taking appropriate doses of penicillin, it follows that, other things being equal, if Brown were to take appropriate doses of penicillin *he* would increase *his* chance of recovery from *his* streptococcal infection. If such a subjunctive conditional were not ampliative, we could not entertain the possibility, in hypothesizing the antecedent of the conditional, that the reference-class of streptococcal patients who take appropriate doses of penicillin might have one more member than it actually has.

However, if the mathematical probabilities compared in the consequent of such an ampliative subjunctive conditional were

---

[10] The risk of falsification in the instant case is excluded by an assumption of normality, as in §54, p. 184.

relative frequencies in finite classes, we should get involved in a characteristic kind of inconsistency every time we asserted the conditional. We could not avoid supposing first, in hypothesizing the antecedent, that the reference-class of streptococcal penicillin-takers might have one more member than it actually has, at just the same time as we implied, secondly, in stating the consequent, that the relative frequency in this class would be unaltered thereby. Hence if statistical explanations were ever concerned with relative frequencies in finite classes, only non-ampliative subjunctive conditionals would be derivable from them and an important guide for prudential action would cease to be available. Yet very many biological classes, at least, seem to be of finite size. So a relative-frequency interpretation here confronts a dilemma between inconsistency and inutility. It is not inconsistent to use relative frequencies as the *evidence* for statistical explanations. But the statement about mathematical probabilities that constitutes the major premiss of the explanans must not itself be interpreted in terms of relative frequencies, on pain of depriving the explanation of its practical utility.

An interpretation in terms of propensities will therefore escape through the horns of the dilemma. Where a probability-function that maps pairs of predicables on to real numbers is extensional, it is inevitable that the exact extensions imputed to the predicables should matter for the evaluation of the function. If the exact extensions imputed to the predicables are not to matter, the probability-function must be non-extensional.

22

Criteria of Rational Belief

Summary

§86. The study of criteria for rational belief is very largely the study of the detachment conditions for dyadic judgements of probability. §87. The deductive closure condition and the logical consistency condition present difficulties for any acceptance-rule formulated in in terms of mathematical probability. §88. The proposals for dealing with these difficulties that have been put forward by Hintikka and Hilpinen, by Kyburg, by Levi, and by Lehrer, are all, for different reasons, unsatisfactory. §89. But a rule of acceptance formulated in terms of inductive probability does not encounter any of these difficulties. Mathematical probability can provide a basis for decision-theoretic strategies, but not for rational belief.

§86. *The problem of the detachment conditions for dyadic judgements of probability*

If all the relevant evidence available makes it probable that there will be a snow-storm tomorrow, and you know this, it is irrational for you to believe that there will not be a snow-storm. Indeed, if the probability is high enough, it is irrational for you not to believe that there will be one. Admittedly in certain areas of economic activity, such as gambling, commercial strategy or economic policy-making, it may sometimes be prudent not to form beliefs at all but to act in accordance with an appropriate decision-theoretic strategy.[1] For example, if, under some suitable partitioning of the possibilities, we can measure the gain to be achieved by each possible course of action in each possible state of the world, and can determine a mathematical probability for each possible state of the world, we may perhaps be prudent just to adopt that course of action for which the product of gain and probability is maximal. But where mathematical expectations cannot be calculated and decision-theoretic techniques are inapplicable, we may be

---

[1] Cf. R. C. Jeffrey, *The Logic of Decision* (1965), for a general account of this.

prudent instead to act on our rational beliefs. Moreover, it is often possible to form rational beliefs about issues which do not call for any kind of action, and are not associated with the realization of any generally accepted utility other than the formation of well-grounded beliefs. Some historical inquiry, for example, may be motivated merely by scholarly curiosity, so that the beliefs to which it leads are not associated with actions that can produce gain or loss.

It follows that one field for exploring the applicability of a concept of probability is in relation to the criteria of rational belief about singular matters of fact. Not that knowledge of what is probable on available evidence is the only possible kind of justification for belief. If one sees the cat on the mat, for example, one is justified in believing it to be there without any consideration of probabilities whatever. Or, if one has a visual sensation of tabby-colouredness, one is justified in believing that one has such a sensation without further consideration. But one can do very little in life without forming some beliefs about things that are not currently under one's nose or a matter of immediate sensation. And the justification of these beliefs inevitably raises questions of probability.

Clearly some attitudes on singular factual issues are weaker than others. Sometimes it may be quite sensible to have a slight suspicion that your neighbour's dog has been in your garden when it would be rather silly to be convinced that it has. But however weakly you believe that p you ought in honesty to accept it as true that p if you believe at all that p. Or at any rate, even if there were one sense of 'belief' in which very weak beliefs that p do not promote accepting it to be true that p, we should still need some threshold sense of 'belief' which did entail such acceptance. This is not only because we often have to act on our beliefs and desires rather than on decision-theoretic strategies, but also, and just as importantly, because a man who asserts that p is standardly presumed to believe that p to the extent of accepting it as true that p. At the very least we need a threshold concept of belief in order to elucidate the nature of assertion.

So the problem of relating probability to belief can usefully be viewed as the problem of relating probability, which is a matter of degree, to acceptance, which is a matter of all-or-nothing. More specifically, the problem for a particular theory of probability is this: what constraints does it impose on a set of rules, in relation to any propositions S and R, for accepting or not accepting S, if knowledge of the probability of S on R is to be the sole consideration determining when S is or is not to be accepted if R is known to be true? The study of rational belief is thus, at least in part, the study of justification-conditions for detaching categorical conclusions from dyadic judgements of probability.

But any attempt to set up detachment-conditions for mathematical probabilities encounters major difficulties, which have been much discussed. I shall briefly review these difficulties, and then show that the theory of inductive probability is not affected by them at all.

§87. *Difficulties for the formulation of an acceptance-rule in terms of mathematical probability*

First, it must presumably be granted that a rational man may accept more than one proposition at a particular time and that it would be quite rational for a man to accept any logical consequences of any set of propositions he accepts. Thus, if he accepts both S_1 and S_2, for example, it would be rational for him also to accept their conjunction S_1 & S_2, and if he accepts both S_1 and the proposition that if S_1 is true so is S_2, then it would be rational for him also to accept S_2. This is conveniently termed the deductive closure condition (for acceptance).

Secondly, it must also presumably be granted that a fully rational man may not accept any proposition which is logically inconsistent with any set of propositions he accepts. Consistency seems an unquestionable attribute of rationality. So let us call this the logical consistency condition (for acceptance).

But it is not at all easy to base acceptance on degree of mathematical probability in a way that permits conformity to these two Hempelian conditions.[2]

So far as the deductive closure condition is concerned we have already come up against the nub of the difficulty in §17. If the threshold of acceptance is set at a definite interval, ϵ,

---

[2] Cf. C. G. Hempel, 'Deductive-Nomological Vs Statistical Explanation', in H. Feigl and G. Maxwell (eds.), *Minnesota Studies in the Philosophy of Science* vol. iii (1962), pp. 150 f.

short of 1, the multiplicative nature of the conjunction principle for mathematical probability is liable to bring the probability of a conjunction down below $1 - \epsilon$, even when each of the conjuncts has at least that degree of probability on the evidence. It is not possible always to conform to the deductive closure condition if your rule of acceptance says

(1) For any singular proposition S about the individual or individuals a_1, a_2, . . . and a_n, accept S if for some R you know that R states all the relevant evidence available about a_1, a_2, . . . and a_n and that $p_M[S,R] \geqslant 1 - \epsilon$.

However small you make ϵ, your attempts to conform both to (1) and to the deductive closure condition will be frustrated when S is a conjunction of too many mutually independent propositions that all deserve acceptance on their own.

Perhaps some readers may doubt whether this is a real difficulty for a theory of rational belief, on the ground that the deductive closure condition is too strict a criterion of rationality. Perhaps they think it rational for a man to accept only what he believes to be the logical consequences of any set of propositions he accepts, and not necessarily everything that is actually a consequence of what he accepts. But it would scarcely be rational not to believe that, say, the two premisses S_1 and S_2 have as their joint logical consequence the conjunction S_1 & S_2, or not to believe that the premiss S_1, and the premiss that if S_1 is true so is S_2, have as their joint logical consequence the conclusion that S_2 is true. In other words it would scarcely be rational not to accept even the elementary logical consequences of what one accepts. And in fact it would quite suffice, for the purpose of developing the present paradoxes, if the deductive closure condition were understood to apply only to elementary logical consequences, so as not to make excessive demands on the concept of rationality. We do not have to suppose that a rational man must be logically omniscient, but only that he must apply a quite elementary logical competence to the determination of what he accepts and what he does not accept.

So far as the logical consistency condition is concerned, the difficulty (for a mathematicist rule of acceptance) is revealed by the lottery paradox, and here again we have already come up against the nub of the difficulty (in §24). Imagine a lottery with

n tickets, each of which has a fair and equal chance to win as far as the relevant evidence R tells us. S_1 states that ticket no. 1 will win, S_2 that ticket no. 2 will win, and so on. Then however small ϵ is in (1), we can make n large enough to ensure that $p_M[\text{not-}S_1,R] \geqslant 1 - \epsilon$, $p_M[\text{not-}S_2,R] \geqslant 1 - \epsilon$, and so on right up to $p_M[\text{not-}S_n,R] \geqslant 1 - \epsilon$. So our set of accepted sentences according to (1) should include not-S_1, not-S_2, . . . and not-S_n. On the other hand R implies that either S_1 or S_2 or . . . or S_n is true. So $p_M[S_1\text{-or-}S_2\text{-or} . . . \text{or-}S_n,R] \geqslant 1 - \epsilon$, and our set of accepted sentences according to (1) should include S_1-or-S_2-or . . . or-S_n. But if our set of accepted propositions includes not-S_1, not-S_2, . . . and not-S_n, it cannot consistently include also S_1-or-S_2-or . . . or-S_n. That is, for suitable values of ϵ and n you cannot conform to the consistency condition if you also conform to (1).

§88. *Four unsatisfactory proposals for resolving the difficulties*

Various strategies have been proposed for dealing with the above two difficulties. But none of them seems to possess any other title to adoption than their ability to circumvent these particular difficulties. They are all *ad hoc* and unprincipled, and correspondingly unconvincing.

For example, Hintikka and Hilpinen[3] adopt in place of (1) two rather different rules of acceptance. The first has the effect of permitting the acceptance of a generalization only if we also accept that in the whole universe there are only such kinds of individuals as are already instantiated in experience. Their second rule of acceptance permits the acceptance of a singular hypothesis only if it is a substitution-instance of an acceptable generalization. These rules have the merit of permitting conformity to the deductive closure and logical consistency conditions, when the probabilities are sufficiently high and the evidence sufficiently weighty. The authors admit that their solution of the detachment-problem has only been developed for a very simple first-order language with monadic predicates, and they are not sure whether it can be extended to cover richer

---

[3] J. Hintikka and R. Hilpinen, 'Knowledge, Acceptance, and Inductive Logic' in J. Hintikka and P. Suppes (eds.), *Aspects of Inductive Logic* (1966), pp. 1 ff. Cf. Risto Hilpinen, *Rules of Acceptance and Inductive Logic*, Acta Philosophica Fennica, xii (1968).

languages. But in fact their solution is quite inadequate even for the very simple languages to which it is applicable. One trouble is that it bars a man from accepting anything unless he also accepts that there is nothing new under the sun—nothing of a kind not already exemplified in the evidence.[4] Why shouldn't he accept a generalization about insects' behaviour even if he thinks that new kinds of insect, say, may yet be discovered? The recent discovery of quasars shows how risky it is to accept any generalization about mosquitoes, if Hintikka and Hilpinen are right. Nor could an acceptable generalization ever lead to new kinds of knowledge, in the way that scientists and philosophers of science have normally thought so important.[5] Indeed, if Hintikka and Hilpinen are right no ordinary mortal who has even a trace of an intellectual conscience would ever accept any monadic first-order generalization at all, since he can hardly think he knows enough to exclude the possibility of novel occurrences in every field of experience whatsoever. Nor would he accept, apparently, even the singular proposition that it will rain tomorrow without accepting that it will rain for all eternity, since he cannot accept any singular proposition unless he also accepts the corresponding generalization.[6]

This proposed solution of the difficulty is so obviously inadequate, if applied to any real-life situations, that it may seem scarcely worth the labour of description. But it serves to illustrate the strength of conviction with which some philosophers are apparently committed to the doctrine that the conditions of rational belief are to be interpreted in terms of mathematical probability. So strongly are they convinced of this doctrine that to preserve its integrity they are prepared to advocate an account of rational belief that is utterly divorced from the needs of contemporary culture.

Similarly Kyburg[7] offers what he describes as 'another

---

[4] J. Hintikka and R. Hilpinen, op. cit., pp. 8 f. Cf. what was said above (§45, p. 143) about the importance of being able to project a hypothesis even if its terms are not co-extensive with any terms occurring in hypotheses that have already been successfully projected.

[5] Cf. nn. 6 and 7, p. 10, and §48, p. 158, above.

[6] J. Hintikka and R. Hilpinen, op. cit., p. 18: however, Hintikka and Hilpinen recognize the paradoxicality of *this* feature.

[7] H. E. Kyburg, 'Probability, Rationality and a Rule of Detachment', in Y.

interpretation' of Hempel's conditions—the deductive closure and logical consistency conditions. This description of his proposal suggests that he has found a way of reconciling those apparently unexceptionable conditions of rational belief with a rule of acceptance that is formulated in terms of mathematical probabilities. But what in fact Kyburg proposes is a different pair of conditions—substantially weaker than Hempel's. Where K is the class of propositions that satisfy the rules of acceptance, then every logical consequence of each single element of K is to belong to K, but not every logical consequence of the conjunction of these elements. Also, for any proposition S, K is not to contain both S and not-S, but it may include any number of pairs of propositions that are logically inconsistent with one another. And to substitute these conditions for Hempel's is tantamount to surrendering the doctrine that mathematical probabilities can provide a basis for rational belief. For now it becomes irrational to put two and two together, as we say— i.e. to treat accepted beliefs as combinable premises for drawing further conclusions. But it might become quite rational to believe both that a given shape is round and that it is square!

Not all attempts to impose a solution on the problem have been as wide of the mark as these. Rather than reject Hempel's conditions, or an acceptance-rule like (1), Levi proposes[8] to limit the application of such an acceptance-rule to the propositions composing an ultimate-partition of the domain of assessment, such as 'Ticket number one will win' and 'Ticket number one will not win', so that the lottery paradox cannot be constructed. But while this may well be a suitable stratagem to avoid paradoxes about lotteries it is a stratagem that seems to lack any other motivation or rationale than this. And it is just as unsatisfactory and implausible to meet counter-examples to an acceptance-rule with *ad hoc* qualifications, as it is to meet counter-examples to a theoretical hypothesis in natural science in this way. For in fact Levi's acceptance-rule is too restrictive

---

Bar-Hillel (ed.), *Logic, Methodology and Philosophy of Science, Proceedings of the 1964 International Conference* (1965), pp. 307 f.

    [8] I. Levi, *Gambling with Truth* (1967), p. 92 f. Levi does, however, adopt (p. 124) a conception of degree of belief that obeys the same conjunction principle as does inductive probability.

to permit the construction of an adequate account of rational belief about other topics. Suppose you are on holiday with your family in a mountain chalet in winter in a foreign country and you run out of bread. You have reasons to think each of the following things probable: your car has enough petrol to take you down to the nearest village, the road will not be blocked by snow, the village has a shop that sells bread, the shop will be open, and the shop will honour a traveller's cheque. In order for you to believe that you can drive down and buy some bread you have to accept the conjunction of these propositions, not just each of them on its own. In the indefinitely variegated situations of everyday life we need to be able, at any one time, to combine and recombine our unit beliefs in different ways. We cannot be expected, even in relation to a single intellectual problem, to confine our current beliefs to the unit-elements of any single ultimate partition.

Lehrer also has proposed to replace (1) by a more restrictive acceptance-rule, which permits conformity to the deductive closure and logical consistency conditions. Lehrer's rule, in essence, is that evidence R entitles us to accept S if, first, S is logically consistent with R and, secondly, any S' other than a proposition deducible from R & S has a lower mathematical probability on R than S has. We can then go on to accept, also, according to Lehrer, any proposition that is acceptable according to this rule on the basis of the conjunction of the evidence we have with any proposition already accepted in accordance with this rule. But the trouble with Lehrer's rule is not only that, like Levi's, it seems to lack any other rationale than its ability to resolve the paradoxes at issue. It also produces a complete impasse, or calls for arbitrary supplementation, whenever we have propositions of high but equal probability. We might well wish to avoid accepting two such propositions that were alternative answers to the same question. But a rule is altogether too restrictive if it bars us from accepting two such propositions that are answers to different questions. Perhaps it will be said that the rule may be modified so as to permit accepting two propositions that are answers to different questions. But it is not easy to see how the appropriate degree of difference can be satisfactorily defined. For example, in order to exclude the lottery paradox it might be stipulated that two propositions would count as answers to the same question if and only if each raised or lowered the mathematical probability of some single touchstone hypothesis. Yet the questions 'What is Mrs. Smith doing today?' and 'What is Mrs. Smith doing tomorrow?' seem to be different questions to which two equally probable answers might both be acceptable, even though each answer raises or lowers the probability of the single hypothesis 'Mr. Smith is a rich man'. Nor would it be satisfactory to require that all such questions be compounded, so that one could only answer them all at once. One often wants to be able to accept answers to some of them and just not bother about the others, like 'What did Mrs. Smith do last Tuesday fortnight?' Perhaps it will be suggested that this could be achieved if disjunctions of complete answer-sets were available for acceptance. For then—if, say, just two questions were at issue—a proposition of the form 'A-and-B or A-and-not-B' could stand in for a single answer 'A'. But now the old difficulty reappears. What is to be done when the disjunctive stand-ins for answers to two different questions are equally probable? In short, it seems that Lehrer's rule faces a dilemma. Its application is either liable to be frustrated by equi-probabilities or too restrictive to fit the actual needs of human culture.[9]

Thus any satisfactory account of rational belief in terms of mathematical probability looks like being very difficult to reconcile with Hempel's deductive closure and logical consistency conditions.

§89. *The advantages of formulating an acceptance-rule in terms of inductive probability*

The root of the trouble with mathematical probability, as the foundation for a rule of acceptance, is that unlike inductive probability it does not measure the informativeness, completeness or 'weight' of the premises. To be justified in accepting a prediction about tomorrow's weather we need to know most of the relevant facts, or at least the more important ones. It would

---

[9] Lehrer's original rule is given in K. Lehrer, 'Induction, Reason and Consistency', *British Journal of the Philosophy of Science* 21 (1970), 106 ff. Modifications are to be found in K. Lehrer, 'Truth, Evidence and Inference', *American Philosophical Quarterly*, xi (1974), 79–92.

be of very little value to have some small quantity of information, on which rain was highly probable, if additional information might radically change the picture.

The general situation is thus very similar to that which we have already (§§67–76) seen to exist in regard to the special case of judicial proof. A jury's verdict is more soundly based if it takes into account more of the relevant facts. So higher inductive probabilities are what are sought, not higher mathematical ones. Accordingly a satisfactory rule of acceptance, conformity to which would make a belief rational, will be

(2) For any singular proposition S about the individual or individuals a_1, a_2, . . . and a_n, accept S if and only if for some R you know that R states all the relevant evidence available about a_1, a_2, . . . and a_n and that $p_I[S,R] \geqslant k$.

where k has to be greater than zero but its more precise level is to be determined in accordance with the nature of the subject-matter and the best available list of relevant variables for tests on generalizations about that subject matter. Presumably we should need a rather higher k for most kinds of propositions about human actions, say, than for most kinds of propositions about the behaviour of animals that have a relatively low intelligence and can be subjected fairly easily to laboratory experiments.

The deductive closure condition is easily seen to be satisfied by (2)—so long as the proposition accepted does not mention a variant of any relevant variable (which would normally be the case). According to the conjunction principle for inductive probability (§64, p. 221), if we have $p_I[S_1,R] \geqslant k$ and $p_I[S_2, R] \geqslant k$, we should then have $p_I[S_1 \& S_2,R] \geqslant k$; and also then by the consequence principle for inductive probability (§63, p. 218), if S_3 is deducible from $S_1 \& S_2$, we shall have $p_I[S_3,R] \geqslant k$. So whatever the grade of inductive probability at which we find our threshold of acceptance, every logical consequence of one or more acceptable propositions must also be acceptable.

The logical consistency condition too is easily seen to be satisfied by (2). The negation principle for inductive probability (§64, p. 221) gives us

If $p_I[\text{not-}R] = 0$ and $p_I[S,R] > 0$, then $p_I[\text{not-}S,R] = 0$.
Moreover, since not-S follows necessarily from anything

inconsistent with S, the consequence principle for inductive probability ensures that anything inconsistent with S has an inductive probability which is no greater than that of not-S. And if you *know* the truth of R there cannot be any positive inductive grounds for accepting not-R: so $p_i[\text{not-R}] = 0$. It follows, according to (2), that for any S_1 and S_2, if S_2 is inconsistent with S_1, and S_1 is acceptable, S_2 is unacceptable. A set of propositions accepted in conformity with (2) must be consistent.

But two possible objections need to be considered here.

The first objection might run as follows: 'Since (1) requires R to state *all* the relevant evidence available, it is pointless to replace (1) by a rule like (2) that bases acceptability on a probability-function that grades the extent to which R comprises all the relevant evidence. Mathematicists have always recognized the need for some requirement of total evidence in the present kind of context, since on selected bits of evidence anything might be provable. And once a requirement of total evidence is admitted there is no room, and therefore no need, for a measure of evidential weight.'

This objection confuses together two totalities that were distinguished from one another in §62, pp. 214 ff., above—the totality of facts relevant to the issue and the totality of facts relevant to the issue that are available to the person presumed to be judging the probability. No doubt different standards of availability may be appropriate to different contexts. The juror has to come to his conclusion on the facts before the court, while the admiral needs to come to his conclusion in the immediacies of battle. Neither can look as far as he might like for his evidence, though for different reasons. On the other hand the biographer of a famous politician may need to search quite widely for hitherto uncatalogued letters and memoranda as well as making use of already familiar ones. Nevertheless everyone's resources of time and assistance are limited in some way. So the totality of relevant evidence that is actually available to a person will very often not be as extensive as the totality of inductively relevant facts. If a man knows all the latter, he can expect to arrive at an inductively certain conclusion. But to the extent that his available evidence falls short of this he is confined to an inductively probable one. So even when we are given a mathematical probability on the total available evidence the question still arises: how many of the relevant facts are available? Even if we did want to use a rule of acceptance like (1) we should still need to specify some level of weight or informativeness that the total available evidence must have whenever we are to attach any importance to a high level of mathematical probability on that evidence.

Secondly, perhaps someone will now object that the paradoxes can be restated in a form that prevents them from being side-stepped by the substitution of (2) for (1). 'Whatever other rules of acceptance we admit', the objection might run, 'we surely have to admit

(3)   Accept S if for some R you know that R states the totality of relevant facts and that $p_M[S,R] \geqslant 1 - \epsilon$

where ϵ is as small as we care to make it. If the requirement stated in (3) is satisfied, maximum weight is assured. Yet the deductive closure, and logical consistency conditions still create just the same paradoxes as before.'

But these paradoxes continue to arise only if (3) is admitted— that is, only if a high degree of mathematical probability is taken to be a ground for rational belief. What I have been arguing, however, is that some appropriately high grade of inductive probability is a ground for rational belief, while a high degree of mathematical probability is not. If you know that R states all the relevant facts and that $p_M[S,R] = 1 - \epsilon$, then you can be certain that the mathematical probability of S on all the relevant facts is $1 - \epsilon$. But you have no justification for believing that S is true.

In the lottery situation this may seem particularly implausible. Suppose a lottery with a million tickets and only one prize. You may feel inclined to say: 'I have a ticket but I believe I shall not win.' Perhaps, even, that would be what most people would quite sincerely feel inclined to say. But would such a belief be rational? Certainly it would be rational for you not to have the belief that you will win. But that is a different matter (even though 'I do not believe that p' is sometimes synonymous with 'I believe that not-p'). If it were also rational for you to believe that you will not win, that would surely be because you knew some further evidence—

say. a plan to rig the draw in someone else's favour. If it is rational to believe a prediction about a particular ticket, you must have evidence for or against that particular ticket.[10]

Again, it might be either rational or irrational for you to buy a ticket if you knew just that you had a one-in-a-million chance of winning. That would depend on the size of the prize, the state of your pocket, your attitude to gambling, and other factors affecting appropriate decision-theoretic strategies. But the rationality, or irrationality, of buying a ticket is not the same as the rationality of believing that you will, or will not, win. More specifically, in a very large lottery, with a rather small prize, and no other incentives to participate, it might be rather rational not to buy a ticket. And it is tempting to paraphrase this as 'rather rational to accept that you will not win'. But we have to bear in mind here that, while acceptance is typically a matter for conscious decision, belief is not. People are victims, not agents, of wishful thinking.[11] Hence so far as rules of acceptance are intended to operate as criteria of rational belief we are debarred from exploiting the possibility of treating acceptance as being itself a suitable subject-matter for decision-theoretic strategies. If acceptance is to be judged on purely epistemological grounds, the utilities involved are quite irrelevant,[12] and it may not be rational either to accept (i.e. believe) that you will win or to accept that you will not win.

In short, the position is that if you want to adopt a rule of acceptance based on mathematical probability, you must be prepared either to modify or forego the deductive closure, and logical consistency, conditions, or to replace (1) by some more

[10] Cf. the need to judge a given litigant's contention on the evidence for or against that particular contention (§39, p. 120, and §73, p. 271) and the need to predict a given hospital's performance on the evidence about that particular hospital (§70, p. 260).

[11] On the extent to which beliefs are voluntary cf. H. H. Price, *Belief* (1969), pp. 221 ff. Unfortunately even philosophers who are not decision-theorists often confuse 'belief' with 'acceptance': e.g. R. Chisholm, 'Knowledge and Belief: "De Dicto" and "De Re"', *Philosophical Studies* 29 (1976), 1–20 passim.

[12] This remains true even when the utilities are of the so-called epistemic variety as in Keith Lehrer, 'Belief and Error', in *The Ontological Turn*, ed. M. S. Gram and E. D. Klemke (1974), pp. 216 ff., esp. p. 226: there is nothing particularly rational about believing a proposition that has a relatively rich content, though it may often be more useful to know the truth of such a proposition as distinct from one of poorer content.

restrictive rule. Such a notion of acceptance will in either case have only some rather narrow, technical and specialized range of application. If you want instead to have a rule that both allows acceptance on the basis of relatively high probabilities and also conforms to the deductive closure, and logical consistency, conditions, you must replace (1) by (2). Inductive probability affords a foundation for a rule of acceptance that has a quite general and unspecialized application.

23

Dispositions

Summary

§90. The truth-functional analysis of dispositional statements encounters difficulties that neither Quine's nor Carnap's proposal overcomes. §91. Every dispositional statement encapsulates a statement about an inductive, not a mathematical probability. §92. But statements about inductive support or inductive probability are open to both a nominalist and a realist interpretation. §93. The difference between an Austinian and a Blackstonian interpretation of legal reasoning from precedent is analogous, but adopting an anti-realist position on one such issue does not necessarily commit a philosopher to adopting this position on another, analogous issue. §94. The nominalist interpretation is not superior on grounds of ontological economy, because—from a realist point of view—it involves a principle of plenitude. But it has greater epistemological coherence. So the analysis of dispositions in terms of inductive probabilities does not necessitate any retreat from anti-realism.

§90. *Some difficulties in current truth-functional analyses of dispositions*

The logical structure of dispositional predicables, like 'friendly' or 'fragile', has an obvious resistance to straightforward analysis in truth-functional terms. If a fragile object is one that would break if struck, and if—as a truth-functional analysis implies—all singular conditionals with false antecedents are true, any unstruck object can apparently be said with equal truth to be both fragile and unbreakable. Some ingenious attempts have been made to circumvent this difficulty by proposing rather more complex truth-functional analyses. But the root of the matter turns out to be that a dispositional statement—i.e. a statement ascribing a dispositional predicate—is a statement about an inductive probability, and so far as the latter type of statement resists analysis in truth-functional terms the former must do so also.

Let us first examine two well-known attempts at a truth-functional analysis, in order to clarify the nature of the problem. In particular we must be careful not to overlook, as people often do, the ontological assumptions to which such truth-functional analyses may be committed. Despite its Ockhamian pretensions to economy truth-functionalism is often as extravagant in one ontological dimension as the doctrines it opposes are in others.

Quine[1] has recently proposed an analysis for those subjunctive conditionals that help to articulate dispositional statements, in the way that

(1)   If x were put in water, x would dissolve

articulates

(2) x is soluble in water.

Quine suggests that such a subjunctive conditional, with the structure of

(3)   If x were an R, x would be an S,

should be understood as being equivalent to a generalized truth-functional conditional with the structure of

(4)   Each natural kind that embraces all the Rs that are Ss embraces x.

And he then suggests that any statement about a natural kind could and should be reduced to a statement about the class of those objects that are similar to one another in virtue of certain matching parts. For example, statements about a chemical element reduce to statements about the class of objects that have certain matching pairs of molecules.

But Quine's truth-functional conception of natural kinds is not without its difficulties. It assumes, in effect, the infinite divisibility of matter. For example, in order to accommodate the subjunctive conditionals that can be asserted about different kinds of sub-atomic particles—about the mathematical probabilities of their behaviour under certain experimentally achievable conditions of acceleration, etc.—Quine presumably has to suppose that any two neutrons, say, are

---

[1] W. V. Quine, *Ontological Relativity and Other Essays* (1969), pp. 131 ff.

similar to one another in virtue of certain matching parts. Well, perhaps even neutrons have parts, and perhaps matter is in fact infinitely divisible. But it might be preferable not to rest one's analysis of the logic of subjunctive conditionals on such a speculative assumption.

A rather different kind of ontological assumption is implicit in an analysis once proposed by Carnap.[2] Carnap suggested that to give the meaning of a dispositional predicate like 'fragile' one should specify the truth of a sentence that has a structure like

(5)   For any object x and any time t, if x is struck at t, then x is fragile if and only if x is broken at t,

where the conditionals are all to be understood as being truth-functional. But unfortunately, ingenious though it is in avoiding the more obvious difficulties, such an analysis does not alto-gether avoid paradox. In particular it can give no proper account of dispositions that are not actualized in any of the things that have them. In a world in which nothing were ever struck, for example,

(6)   For any object x and any time t, if x is struck at t, then x is fragile if and only if x is not broken at t

would be just as true as (5).

Perhaps it will be said that in a world in which nothing is ever struck it does not matter what meaning we give to the dispositional term 'fragile'. But an engineer may well wish to design into his artefacts a type of disposition that he hopes will never be actualized anywhere—a fail-safe device, perhaps, in an atomic generator or a mega-death potential in a hydrogen bomb. On Carnap's analysis, if the disposition is unactualized, its structure could equally well be like that displayed in (5), or like that displayed in (6). And engineers cannot plan so frivolously for very serious contingencies. Even if the contingency never actually materializes it has to be allowed for, and therefore provision for it must be made amenable to discussion in quite specific and unambiguous terms.

Perhaps it will be objected now that all artificially constructed dispositions must consist of complexes of natural ones, and that

[2] R. Carnap, 'Testability and Meaning', *Philosophy of Science*, 3 (1936), 419 ff.

these basic physical, chemical, or biological properties are never unactualized. So if Carnap's analysis of dispositional terms is applied only to terms describing basic natural dispositions it is not exposed to the above-mentioned difficulty.

Against such a defence of Carnap's analysis two points can be made. The first is that from a non-truth-functional point of view it appears to rely on a very strong ontological assumption. For the defence to work, every basic natural possibility has to be actualized at some time and place. And in thus assuming that every basic natural property has some existing instances the defence assumes what Arthur Lovejoy once called a principle of plenitude, of the kind to which Spinoza and Leibniz, for example, can both be shown to be committed.[3] I shall have more to say about this kind of principle very shortly (§94). But, even if it is acceptable, there is another and quite different point to be made against any attempt to defend Carnap's analysis in this way. The analysis assumes that for any disposition, like fragility and friendliness, we can always specify a determinate set of conditions upon which the actualization of the disposition ensues. Yet this is by no means always the case. Even a fragile object does not always break if struck. Sometimes we have lucky escapes—for example, when the object is struck by a rather soft substance or along a buttressed axis. And we certainly do not feel we need to know every single circumstance in which an object will *not* break in order to be justified in calling it fragile. It suffices to know that it *will* break if struck in any of quite a range of normal circumstances.

§91. *The inductive probability implicit in a dispositional statement*

What therefore emerges from this last criticism of Carnap is that every dispositional statement encapsulates a statement about an inductive probability. Sometimes, as perhaps with (2), this probability may be a very high one. Sometimes it is a little lower, as perhaps in the case of

x is fragile.

But in either type of case it is clear that the correct analysans of a dispositional statement must be something like

[3] A. O. Lovejoy, *The Great Chain of Being* (1936), pp. 52, 151 ff., and 171 ff.

There is some characteristic that x has such that on the evidence of x's having this characteristic and being struck (put in water) it is inductively at least quite probable that x will break (dissolve).

And it is no use objecting to this type of analysis, as some philosophers have been inclined to do, that we often understand a statement about x's disposition without knowing anything about x's structure or nature. No doubt we often do. A dispositional statement implies x merely to have *some* characteristic that can help to generate the appropriate probability: it does not state what characteristic this is.

Some philosophers—Arthur Pap,[4] for example—have grasped that dispositions are essentially probabilistic in character, but have assumed that the probabilities involved must be mathematical ones. This assumption has rather paradoxical consequences. For suppose you do describe your dog as having a friendly disposition. What you imply is that it will show some signs of friendliness to a visitor if it is not ill, or asleep, or over-excited by the children, and so on. You can hardly be taken to imply, as would follow on the mathematicist assumption, that in more than half of its encounters with strangers the dog has behaved in a friendly way, since this may well be false: the dog may well have been handled wrongly on too many occasions. Indeed the statistics of dog-behaviour, if there were any, might even show that friendly dogs behave in an unfriendly way on more than half the occasions on which they encounter strangers: perhaps most people have still not learned to handle dogs correctly.

But it is not just that dispositions do not always jibe with statistical probabilities. Also the logical structure of dispositional statements is not the same as that of statements about mathematical probabilities. Consider the conjunction problem. If a dog has a friendly disposition and also has a greedy disposition, it is disposed to be both friendly and greedy. This does not mean that it will probably show signs of both friendliness and greed on any occasion on which it shows signs of either. It will show signs of both dispositions only if the appropriate activating conditions are both present. We can describe a man as being

---

[4] A. Pap, *An Introduction to the Philosophy of Science* (1963), pp. 286 ff.

of a solitary but courteous disposition, even though he clearly cannot exercise his courtesy while he is enjoying his solitude. But the important point to note is that, however many known dispositions come together more or less independently to constitute his character, the prediction we can make about his behaviour in a known set of circumstances need not have any less probability. If he does have a compound disposition, the whole of the compound will be activated in appropriate circumstances, and the same is true of the dog that is both friendly and greedy. If the constituent dispositions were construed as more or less independent mathematical probabilities, however, the multiplicative principle for the mathematical probability of a conjunction would force us to the paradoxical conclusion that most dispositions were uncompoundable. The product of the mathematical probabilities that are supposed to be implicit in the constituent dispositions might well fall below the threshold at which a disposition is said to exist. Analysis in terms of inductive probability avoids this paradox because the conjunction principle for inductive probability fits in with our ordinary views about the compounding of dispositions. The inductive probability of a conjunction is no lower than that of its least probable conjunct.

Perhaps it will be objected that dispositions might be thought of as consisting not in mathematical probabilities that are substantially greater than ·5, but in increments over prior mathematical probabilities. If the prior probability that my dog will behave in a friendly way to strangers is ·2, and the evidence of its past conduct gives this friendly behaviour a probability of ·4, then the dog might be said to have a friendly disposition even if it barked at more than half the strangers it met. But this idea runs into the same difficulty as does the corresponding attempt to defend a mathematicist analysis for the proofs involved in complex law-suits (cf. §20, p. 64, above). Paradoxical results can ensue when we come to compound the probabilities. Suppose the prior mathematical probability of deliberate solitariness in a certain population is ·1, and the evidence shows that Smith prefers to be solitary on ·9 of the occasions when he has a choice. Then presumably, on the theory under examination, Smith would be said to have a solitary disposition. Suppose also that the prior mathematical probability of cheerful behaviour, on appropriate occasions, is ·8 in this population, while the evidence shows Smith to behave cheerfully on only ·2 of such occasions. Presumably Smith would therefore be said to have an uncheerful disposition. If we compound these mathematical probabilities on the assumption that they are independent, we find that the prior probability of Smith's being cheerful but solitary is ·08 while the posterior probability of his being cheerful but solitary is ·18. So apparently Smith could be said to be of a cheerful but solitary disposition even though he has an uncheerful disposition—which is absurd. Statements about behavioural dispositions are obviously not open to this form of analysis.

It is helpful here to notice some of the differences between dispositions and tendencies. In particular, tendencies can be predicated of classes of things both collectively and distributively, while dispositions can be predicated only distributively. We can say that old houses have a tendency to be cold and mean either that the class of old houses exhibits this tendency or that each member of it does—either that a lot of old houses are cold or that every old house is cold a lot of the time. But, if we remark that spaniels have a friendly disposition, we mean that every normal spaniel has such a disposition. Otherwise we should have remarked, say, that spaniels tend to have friendly dispositions. Correspondingly statements about tendencies are more amenable to analysis in terms of mathematical probabilities. Admittedly such a statement may sometimes be used loosely to describe a disposition. Also, if in a judicial proof, say, a particular piece of evidence R is said to tend to show that a certain conclusion S is true, then the inductive probability of S on R is implied to be substantially greater than zero. But while dispositions are activated by appropriate conditions or actualized on appropriate occasions, tendencies are just exemplified from time to time; and, though many dispositions are never actualized, all tendencies must show a substantial degree of exemplification. A man cannot tend to be late for his appointments unless he is in fact late for a substantial proportion of them. Statements about tendencies seem mostly to be concerned with long-run relative frequencies, and therefore with mathematical probabilities; while dispositional statements are concerned with what happens in certain circumstances and therefore with inductive probabilities.

§92. *Nominalism versus realism in the philosophy of inductive support*

The conclusion we have to accept therefore about dispositional statements is in keeping with the position previously taken about ampliative subjunctive conditionals (§85 above). In place of a crude truth-functional analysis, or of a more sophisticated form of truth-functional analysis like Quine's or Carnap's, we have to recognize that any such statement implies the corresponding truth-functional conditional to have a substantial level of inductive reliability.

But though this clarifies the logical structure of dispositionals and subjunctive conditionals to a certain extent it would be a mistake to suppose that the issue has been decided wholly in favour of a realist account of natural laws. I call a philosophical account of natural laws a 'realist' one if and only if it holds natural laws to be principles of necessitation which are at least as much a part of nature as are individual events, so that the question whether any uninstantiated natural laws exist becomes a question of fact, not of philosophical analysis. And the correctness of such a realism is by no means an inevitable consequence of what has been said in §§90–1. Rather, the hard core of the problem has just been pushed back into the analysis of statements about inductive reliability. Admittedly it is convenient to employ a generalized modal logic for the purpose of representing the logical liaisons of statements about inductive support and inductive probability, as in §66. But there do not seem to be conclusive arguments against a quasi-nominalist interpretation of statements about the inductive reliability of such-or-such a proposition.

In sum two rather different interpretations of such statements are possible. I shall call one of these the 'quasi-nominalist' interpretation, and the other the 'realist'. On both views all empirical assessments of inductive support for factual propositions derive fundamentally from assessments of support for universally quantified truth-functional conditionals of a certain testable type. Both views agree about the way in which we should in practice assess support for such propositions, and they thus agree about the justification-conditions for asserting these assessments. But they differ about the truth-conditions for such assessments.

On the quasi-nominalist view to say that a certain universally quantified truth-functional conditional H has at least ith grade reliability is equivalent to saying that H's antecedent and consequent are actually co-instantiated in an ith grade variety of relevant circumstances or that a more comprehensive generalization which entails H has this kind of reliability. Hence to say that H does not have ith grade reliability is equivalent to saying that there is neither a more comprehensive generalization from which this grade of support for H is derivable nor are H's antecedent and consequent appropriately co-instantiated (either because the antecedent itself is never instantiated in the appropriate variety of circumstances or because in some such instantiation of it the consequent is not instantiated). Moreover, if the terms 'inductive support' or 'inductive reliability' are interpreted in this quasi-nominalist way, it is reasonable to suppose that the term 'relevance' should be interpreted analogously: the semantics of 'relevance' also must relate to what actually occurs. That is, to call a circumstance relevant to any generalization in a particular field of inquiry must be taken to be equivalent to saying that it has caused, or helped to cause, or will cause, or help to cause, the falsification of some generalization in that field of inquiry.

There is a certain kind of circularity here because, as we have already seen (§46), every statement about a causal uniformity implies that the corresponding truth-functional statement has full inductive reliability in normal circumstances. But one just has to accept that some families of terms are ineradicably interconnected in meaning, like the names for kinship-relations or days of the week. What is more significant here than the existence of this circularity is the existence of a certain regress. The correctness of a list of relevant variables—i.e. its appropriateness for the given category of propositions—has to have its inductive reliability evaluated by reference to some higher-level list or function. This kind of regress is an inevitable feature of inductive reasoning. The regress is normally interrupted in practice in a particular field of enquiry by an *assumption* that a certain list of relevant variables is correct for that field. But the regress reasserts itself, as it were, whenever the reliability of such an assumption is brought into question by adverse experience. So the interpretation can be only a *quasi*-nominalist one. Nevertheless this interpretation does require actual instantiations, of the appropriate kind, wherever there is any level of inductive reliability. Also statements about inductive relevance, on the quasi-nominalist view, are true if and only if the requisite instantiations occur. It is not enough for a circumstance to be merely *capable* of falsifying a generalization of the category concerned. It must actually do so.

Note that even on this quasi-nominalist interpretation the inductive reliability of a proposition is not something that depends at a particular time on someone's having got certain results from testing that proposition, or logically connected ones, at a previous time, or even on someone's knowing that the antecedent and consequent of the proposition have been or will be appropriately co-instantiated. It depends solely on the occurrence of such a co-instantiation. No doubt we often think that the grade of support that exists for a certain proposition is just what can be inferred from what we believe to be the results of tests already carried out. But we can also often be mistaken about this. The tests may have been rather less thorough and complex than they might have been, the actual results of the tests may have been different from what we believe them to be, or the correct ordered list of relevant variables may be different from what we take it to be. Even the quasi-nominalist interpretation allows us to conceive this much of a possible discrepancy between our subjective inductive assessments, on the one hand, and the objectively existing network of inductive reliability on the other. Assertion of such assessments is justified if and only if we believe that the appropriate co-instantiations have occurred. But the assessments are true if and only if such co-instantiations have occurred or will occur. Moreover even on the quasi-nominalist interpretation there is still an empirical, non-analytic connection between a report of canonical test-results and the monadic claim that H has at least, or at most, a certain grade of inductive support or reliability. For, whereas each item in the test-report asserts a co-instantiation, or failure of co-instantiation, in certain *specified* circumstances, the monadic support-claim asserts such an event to occur in this or that grade of cumulative combination of *relevant* circumstances, where relevance is an independent causal fact and even the ordering of relevant variables is largely a matter for empirical discovery.

On the realist interpretation, however, appropriate co-instantiation need not actually occur, at some time or place in the history of the universe, if a certain grade of inductive support is to exist for a generalization. The truth-conditions for monadic support-assessments are given by subjunctive conditional statements, not indicative ones. What is required is that the consequent of the generalization would be co-instantiated if the latter were to occur in any of the appropriate variety of circumstances. Admittedly, if the co-instantiation does not actually occur, it cannot be truthfully reported as occurring. Hence there can certainly then be no test-results from which one can directly infer an appropriate grade of support for the hypothesis. One can at best only conjecture that the support exists, on the basis of test-results for some similar generalizations. Correspondingly the relevance of a particular circumstance does not, on the realist view, entail that at some time it actually causes, or helps to cause, the falsification of one of the generalizations concerned. It entails only that the circumstance would cause, or help to cause, this if the antecedent of the generalization were ever instantiated in such a circumstance.

To put the point from the realist point of view let us suppose, by a familiar metaphor,[5] that one or other of various other worlds are describable, that might conceivably have existed in place of the actual one. Each of these other worlds is to be supposed to have the same causal laws as our actual world, and to differ from the latter only in having different initial conditions at some time for some of these laws. In some of these physically possible worlds, therefore, the antecedent and consequent of a particular generalization might never have been co-instantiated despite being sometimes co-instantiated in the actual world. Yet the same causal laws would have held in all these worlds, and therefore presumably—on the realist interpretation—the same grades of inductive support would

[5] Cf. §66, pp. 240 ff., above. The model given there, however, was a quasi-nominalist, not a realist, one.

have existed for each universally quantified conditional. For when we state the grade of support that exists for a hypothesis, on the realist view, we describe merely the degree to which a certain regularity is immune to causal interference. To say that von Frisch's hypothesis about bees' colour-discrimination is well supported is to say no more than that this capacity is not obstructed, in a population of bees, by any or all of the factors operating according to causal laws in the biotic communities to which bees belong. On the quasi-nominalist interpretation, however, a possible world that differed from the actual one in initial conditions though not in causal laws might also differ from the actual one in regard to the level of support that existed for certain propositions. This is because on a quasi-nominalist interpretation grade of support for a generalization H is determined only by the relevant variety of actually occurring co-instantiations for its antecedent and consequent or for the antecedent and consequent of a generalization that entails H.

But to describe the nominalist-realist difference thus, in terms of alternative possible worlds with identical causal laws and different initial conditions, is essentially to describe the difference from a realist point of view. From a quasi-nominalist point of view the ultimate causal laws are those stated by fully supported generalizations, i.e. by generalizations that are positively instantiated throughout their relevant variety of circumstance. Hence, for a quasi-nominalist, worlds with the same causal laws as one another must share with one another at least that measure of identity in initial conditions which is needed to secure full support for the generalizations that state these causal laws. And, if two alternative possible worlds were as similar to one another as that, it is difficult to see how they could differ from one another in regard to the support that existed for any other generalizations.

Thus the difference between the quasi-nominalist and the realist interpretations of monadic inductive support-assessments issues at one point in a possible difference about the grade of support or reliability that really exists for a generalization H. This point is where H's antecedent and consequent are not co-instantiated because neither is ever instantiated. The quasi-nominalist interpretation treats all such cases (unless at least a certain grade of support for H is inferable from the existence of that grade of support for a more comprehensive generalization) as cases where a certain level of support is not reached. The realist interpretation is prepared to divide these cases into those where the level of support is reached (though we may not know it to have been) and those where it is not. The former cases are where the consequent would be instantiated if the antecedent were: the latter are where the consequent would not be instantiated even if the antecedent were.

It must be emphasized, however, that generalizations for which the two interpretations allow two different monadic support-gradings $\leqslant i$ cannot be consequences of generalizations to which the two interpretations would not also allow correspondingly different support-gradings $\leqslant i$, since inductive support is inherited by consequents in accordance with the consequence principle. So, in order for there actually to be any propositions that have different monadic grades of support according to the two interpretations, we have to suppose either that there are some propositions of great generality that are rather poorly instantiated though—on a realist interpretation—fairly well supported, or that there are similar propositions of lesser generality that are somehow ultimate and not derivable from any well-supported laws of greater generality.

§93. *Can one be a nominalist on some issues but not on others?*

Certainly we could never learn from experience that the realist view was correct and the quasi-nominalist false, or vice versa. Any conceivable test-results fit either interpretation, since generalizations for which the two interpretations allow different monadic support-gradings must always be (and perhaps also derive from) generalizations that never have either their antecedent or their consequent instantiated and are therefore never tested. Nevertheless, though the issue between the two interpretations is not amenable to empirical tests, it is certainly open to philosophical argument, just as are other issues in the long-standing debate between realists and anti-realists.

Consider, by way of comparison, the assessment of legal reasoning from judicial precedent. I have explored the logical structure of such assessments elsewhere, and demonstrated their

conformity to inductive principles:[6] hypotheses about matters
of fact are far from being the only type of hypotheses that are
open to inductive assessment. The point to be made here is
just that the familiar difference between Austin's and Blackstone's philosophy of the common law is strikingly analogous
to the difference just noted between a quasi-nominalist and a
realist conception of inductive support for hypotheses about
matters of fact. According to Austin legal induction is a process

through which a rule made by judicial legislation is gathered from
the decision or decisions whereby it was established.[7]

So for Austin the rule exists if and only if the decisions establish
it (and also, indeed, when and only when they have done so).
But on Blackstone's view judicial precedents are to be regarded
as declaring pre-existing customary law. So for Blackstone a
particular rule of common law exists independently of actual
decisions. It declares or helps to declare what would be the
right decision whenever, or if ever, a case of a certain kind
comes to judgement.

The subsequent judges do not pretend to make a new law, but to
vindicate the old one from misrepresentation. For if it be found
that the former decision is manifestly absurd or unjust, it is declared,
not that such a sentence was *bad law*, but that it was *not law*.[8]

Admittedly, in assessing the grade of support that exists for a
hypothesis about the common law one is not describing the
degree to which a certain regularity is immune from causal
interference, as in the realist evaluation of hypotheses about
matters of fact. But on Blackstone's view one is doing something
rather analogous to this. One is describing the degree to which
a certain duty is intolerant of exemptions.

Now the choice between an Austinian and a Blackstonian
interpretation is not an altogether arbitrary one. Perhaps a
Blackstonian, realist interpretation, for example, tends to
restrain judges from supposing that they have any right to
legislate, while an Austinian, quasi-nominalist interpretation

---

[6] *TIOI*, pp. 155–71.

[7] John Austin, *Lectures on Jurisprudence*, 3rd edn. (1869), p. 66.

[8] A. W. Blackstone, *Commentaries on the Laws of England*, 5th edn. (1773), Bk. I,
p. 70.

tends to encourage this supposition. To at least some extent, therefore, the proper resolution of the issue depends on whether the supposition should be encouraged or discouraged. And that in turn may depend on the branch of law involved, the current trend of judicial opinion, and the current social and political situation.

But is one committed, by adopting a realist, or quasi-nominalist, position in the philosophy of law to adopting a realist, or quasi-nominalist, position, respectively, in one's analysis of dispositional statements and ultimately in one's philosophy of inductive support as a whole? Here two importantly different approaches to the long-standing debate between realists and their opponents need to be noted. According to one approach the issue is a global one, and to fight in either cause on any particular, selected front implies intellectual sympathy for those fighting in the same cause on other fronts. According to this globalist approach realism is a thesis about the nature of reasoning, rather than about the meanings of a certain category of terms. So opposition to realism in the philosophy of mathematics, for example, helps to encourage opposition to it in the philosophy of mind.[9] But according to the other approach there is not so much a single global issue as a set of mutually analogous local issues, some of which may be independent of one another. Each issue concerns the best way to conceive the meanings of a certain category of terms. So for the localist a special connection has to be established between the outcome of realist (or anti-realist) argument on one such issue and the outcome on another, before any interdependence between the two local issues can be admitted. The case against realism in the philosophy of botanical nomenclature, for example, may be quite strong, but its acceptance does not necessarily commit one to oppose realism in the philosophy of law.[10]

Of these two approaches the localist is clearly the more cautious and less question-begging one and I shall assume its correctness. On a localist approach the issues might, or might not, be resolved uniformly in each separate problem-area. But

---

[9] For a hint at such an encouragement cf. B. Rundle, *Perception, Sensation and Verification* (1972), pp. 2 f.

[10] Cf. L. Jonathan Cohen, *The Diversity of Meaning*, 2nd edn. (1966), §§13–15.

on a globalist approach they could not be resolved differently. Indeed the more independent the issues are, in the various problem-areas concerned, the greater the support that would be given to any general realist, or anti-realist, thesis if the issues were in the end resolved uniformly in each separate problem-area. It is as if these main problem-areas were the inductively relevant variables for testing the realist's (or anti-realist's) general hypothesis, since a list of relevant variables must always be independent of one another (§44, p. 139). Accordingly, when I discuss the issue of quasi-nominalism versus realism in the philosophy of inductive reasoning about matters of fact, I shall assume that arguments on the issue need not necessarily have a wider application.

§94. *The nominalist interpretation is epistemologically, not ontologically, superior*

It is often suggested that an anti-realist interpretation is superior in terms of ontological economy. The quasi-nominalist interpretation of inductive reasoning certainly excludes the existence of ultimate causal laws that are uninstantiated. Where the series of relevant variables is finite, therefore, the quasi-nominalist interpretation need not imply the existence of anything besides persons, objects, events, spatio-temporal locations, or other individual subjects of logically first-order predication. And even where the series of relevant variables is infinite the only characteristics to be talked about will be instantiated ones. But to a realist this claim to ontological economy is just a nominalist conceit. In fact, from a realist point of view, the quasi-nominalist interpretation seems enormously extravagant in its ontology. It has apparently to suppose that every bit of inductive support that exists for anything is manifested by appropriate co-instantiations of the antecedent and consequent of a generalization. The realist can suppose much of this support to exist unmanifested, in terms of the truth of counterfactual conditionals about the results of tests that are never performed. But, for every bit of it that exists, the quasi-nominalist has to suppose appropriate actual occurrences in the real world. So the quasi-nominalist interpretation appears, from a realist point of view, to be committed to a very bold principle of plenitude, as Lovejoy called it,[11] just as is Carnap's analysis of dispositional statements. Indeed, it looks as though any truth-functionalist programme—any programme for interpreting the possible, the probable or the necessary in terms of the merely actual—is involved in such a commitment. From his own point of view the truth-functionalist is cutting reality down to size and eliminating everything except the actual. But for a realist he is imprudently ready to expand reality along just that dimension where caution is most advisable—the dimension of the actually occurrent.

The argument from ontological economy is therefore by no means decisive as an arbiter between realist and anti-realist philosophies of dispositional statements. Certainly there is no longer any fairly obvious way of arguing for a principle of plenitude. In a more theistically oriented period it made sense to defend such a principle within a framework of theological argument, though this was by no means always done for nominalistic purposes. For example, Lovejoy shows how Spinoza's philosophy was committed to such a principle. God can conceive of all essences; neither he nor the universe would be rational if existence arbitrarily accrued to some finite essences while others lacked it; 'whatever we conceive to be in the power of God necessarily exists'; and since this power is unlimited (except by the impossibility of conceiving or producing the self-contradictory) it follows that 'from the necessity of the divine nature must follow an infinite number of things in infinite ways—that is, *all* things which can fall within the sphere of an infinite intellect.'[12] Again, Leibniz's principle of sufficient reason does the same work here as Spinoza's determinism. There can be only one ultimate reason, according to Leibniz's philosophy, why anything exists, namely that its essence demands existence and will inevitably attain it unless interfered with by a similar demand on the part of some other essence; and the superiority of the actual world to all the other abstractly conceivable ones consists in the fact that in it this tendency of essences to exist is realized in a greater measure than in any of the others. By creating the actual world 'God

---

[11] Cf. p. 327, n. 3, above. The precise nature of the quasi-nominalist's principle of plenitude is spelt out in §66, p. 241 above.

[12] Cf. A. O. Lovejoy, op. cit., p. 152, and Spinoza, *Ethics*, I. 16 and I. 35.

makes the greatest number of things that he can'.[13] But these arguments carry no weight for agnostics.

So, given that a theological framework is no longer available to buttress a principle of plenitude, it looks as though neither a realist nor an anti-realist has the advantage in appeals to ontological economy. Each indulges, from the other's point of view, in his own characteristic form of ontological extravagance, and each achieves, from his own point of view, his own characteristic form of ontological parsimony.

But epistemological considerations are more helpful here than ontological ones. There is no doubt that a quasi-nominalist interpretation integrates more easily with an epistemology which is preoccupied with inductive modes of justification. When deducibility from self-evident first principles was regarded as a legitimate, and readily available, mode of justification for causal generalizations, it made excellent sense to suppose, as the realist does, that such generalizations might be true of the natural world though uninstantiated within it. These generalizations, and the counterfactuals derivable from them, did not need instantiation in order to be—at least in principle—knowable, since their knowability was ensured in other ways. And it was ultimately again a theistic premiss on which the whole edifice was based. With appropriate Divine provision or necessitation to that effect, self-evidence could reasonably be expected to guarantee truth, as in Descartes's epistemology. Or at any rate there had to be some intimate connection between the Cause of things' being as they are and the Cause of our armchair knowledge of how they are— whether this connection operated like Plato's Idea of the Good, Descartes's benevolent Creator or Spinoza's Infinite Intellect. But if such a theistic premiss is no longer available the alleged non-inductive source of justification has been deprived of any foundation. A realist philosophy that continues to speak of uninstantiated causal generalizations is now caught up in a culture-lag. It has lost touch with any epistemology that can give it credibility. A quasi-nominalist philosophy, on the other hand, is well adapted to the prevailing inductivism and

[13] Cf. A. O. Lovejoy, op. cit., pp. 177–9 and Leibniz, *Philosophischen Schriften*, ed. C. J. Gerhardt (1885), vol. i, pp. 331.

preference for empiricist criteria.[14] The truth conditions for a monadic assessment of inductive support are held to be of essentially similar type to its justification-conditions. For the assessment to be true certain appropriate co-instantiations of a generalization's antecedent and consequent need to occur: for the assessment to be justified these co-instantiations need to be known to occur.

On balance, therefore, the case for a quasi-nominalist interpretation of statements about inductive support is stronger than that for a realist one. So, when we insist that an adequate analysis of dispositional statements must acknowledge their concern with inductive probabilities, we are not implicitly surrendering one of the main points in the nominalist or truth-functionalist programme. We can be construed as merely going a longer way round in order to defend it because a shorter route is not available. It remains defensible that every dispositional truth is rooted in actual, occurrent, non-dispositional ones. But by admitting this we do not thereby claim that every dispositional statement—and along with it every statement about inductive support, inductive probability, and causal necessity—is capable of adequate formulation in a truth-functional, extensional language or in a finite hierarchy of such languages.[15] Certainly no such adequate formulation has yet been produced. On the other hand, to argue its ultimate impossibility, or to determine the ultimate nature of causality, is no part of the present book's purpose. The modal logic of §66 is offered as the most perspicuous representation of inductive syntax—not as its only possible representation.

The point is that the applicability of a modal logic here can be accounted for in at least three different ways. The first is to

[14] But it is inductive logic that justifies a preference for empiricist criteria, not vice versa: cf. L. Jonathan Cohen, 'Why Should the Science of Nature be Empirical?' in *Impressions of Empiricism, Royal Institute of Philosophy Lectures*, vol. 9, ed. G. Vesey, (1976), pp. 168 ff. One should also notice that, while nominalistic philosophies give rise to reductionist research-programmes, which may increase our knowledge even by their failures, realistic philosophies tend to be less fruitful of further research.

[15] However, to accept what I call the quasi-nominalist position is to accept one way out of an important argument of Kneale's for the existence of natural necessity: cf. G. Molnar, 'Kneale's argument Revisited', *Philosophical Review*, lxxviii (1969), pp. 84 f. Bacon himself was a quasi-nominalist: cf. his insistence (*Novum Organum* II. ii) that in Nature nothing really exists besides individual bodies performing individual acts according to law.

adopt a full-blooded realism of the kind that we have just been considering. If principles of natural necessity are a distinct part of the real world, the description of that world involves the modality of necessity. But, if such a realism is rejected because of its epistemological incoherence, at least two other possibilities remain. One is to take causality as a power that is real in the things that have it. For example, an ontology of 'powerful particulars', as Harré and Madden call them,[16] is quite compatible with the quasi-nominalist position. Yet it too generates closer connections between particular individuals than a non-modal logic can represent.[17] The other possibility is to account for the non-extensionality of statements about causal connections and inductive support without supposing causality to be real even in the things that have it. Perhaps any statement of the form 'It is a law of nature that −.−.−' is non-extensional because it is equivalent to a statement about a statement— specifically, to a statement that the truth of '−.−.−' is logically implied by one or more truth-functional statements which satisfy appropriate criteria for maximal simplicity and generality in the description of nature. Such an interpretation also would account for the applicability of modal logic when the two levels of statement are telescoped into one, because it would impose restrictions on substitutivity;[18] and it would, of course, be compatible with the quasi-nominalist position. But, in order to describe the structure and employment of inductive probability-functions—which is the purpose of the present book—one does not need to scrutinize these two versions of

[16] In R. Harré and E. H. Madden, *Causal Powers* (1975). It is interesting to note how analogues for causally powerful particulars may be supposed in other domains of inductive assessment, e.g. bearers of rights and duties, in relation to legal arguments from judicial precedents cf. *TIOI*, pp. 155 ff.

[17] Op. cit., pp. 8 ff. However, these authors do not develop a systematic logic of natural necessity, and it is not clear how they can hold (pp. 132–3) both that natural necessitation may be defined in the same terms as C.I. Lewis defines strict implication and also that it is distinct from logical entailment, as rendered by C. I. Lewis. Nor does their theory offer as complete an exorcism of Hume's problem about induction as they seem to suppose (pp. 75 ff). It is just that in their theory the assumption of an ontology of powerful particulars plays much the same role as does the assumption of natural uniformity in J. S. Mill's inductive logic.

[18] Cf. L. Jonathan Cohen, *The Diversity of Meaning*, 2nd edn. (1966), pp. 211 f. and 319 f. But I should not now wish to defend the theory of natural necessity advocated in the latter passage, since it failed to preserve an adequate distinction between epistemic and alethic modalities.

quasi-nominalism more closely or arbitrate between them. Indeed, on a properly localist approach, it may well be that the appropriateness of one version or the other will vary with the subject matter of inductive assessment. For example, hypotheses about fields of force seem to cry out for an ontology of powerful particulars. But it is not so clear that this kind of ontology is appropriate for hypotheses about molecules, viruses, etc. Admittedly it might be held that, as theories of wider and wider explanatory generality are constructed, inductive support-functions in different areas of scientific enquiry should all ideally be moulded into integration with one another. But the extent to which this is possible raises issues about the unity of science which fall outside the scope of the present book.

24

An Epistemological Corollary

Summary

§95. If a fact that is provable beyond reasonable doubt is inductively certain, the legal assumption that proof beyond reasonable doubt is possible conflicts with the sceptical thesis—held by many modern philosophers of science—that knowledge of general truths about the world is impossible. §96. But if it is possible to know that one hypothesis is inductively more reliable than another, it is certainly possible to know also that a hypothesis is fully reliable. §97. To know that a hypothesis is fully supported does not require knowing that one knows. §98. Prevalence of the sceptical error is due partly to unawareness of the systematic analogy between the structure of inductive support and the structure of logical truth, partly to a confusion between truth-conditions and justification-conditions, partly to an over-reaction to certain shattering events in the history of science, partly to the mistaken view that a correct assessment of how much one proposition supports another must be regarded as an analytic truth, and partly to the mistaken view that any inductive assessment presupposes certain untestable metaphysical assumptions. When all these points are borne in mind it becomes clear that on issues of fact proof beyond reasonable doubt, and scientific knowledge, are at least in principle possible.

§95. *The prevailing scepticism in the philosophy of science*
It was argued in §§67–76 that the concept of probability used in stating the standards of proof in British or American courts is an inductive one. Moreover, since the triers of facts in these courts are often lay juries who are officially urged to assess the evidence in much the same way as they would assess evidence about such issues in their everyday lives, it follows that the concept of inductive probability is assumed by the Anglo-American legal system to be in widespread everyday use. So, unless the treatment of proof in that system is founded on a colossal mistake, we all constantly employ the concept of

inductive probability in reasoning about what has probably, or certainly, happened in a particular situation.

But let us now look more closely at the conditions of inductive certainty, or of reaching conclusions that are beyond inductively reasonable doubt. If a proposition '*a* is *S*' is inductively certain on the evidence of '*a* is *R*', the generalization 'Anything, if it is *R*, is *S*' must have full inductive reliability. So to say that '*a* is *S*' is beyond reasonable doubt on the evidence of '*a* is *R*', is tantamount to saying that there is no known reason to doubt the existence of full support for this generalization. The generalization must be valid for all combinations of circumstances that there is any known reason to think relevant. Hence, if a particular proposition is inductively certain on given evidence, the truth of the corresponding generalization is a possible object of knowledge, since conceivably, if it has full inductive reliability, someone might in fact be aware of test-results that gave it full support. Yet according to most modern philosophers of science the truth of any such generalization is utterly unknowable. Factual generalizations over indefinitely extensive domains are held not to be possible objects of knowledge.

Scepticism, indeed, is in high fashion among modern philosophers of science. One might have supposed that the consistently successful exploitation of a theory was some indication of its truth. But, unimpressed by the aircraft, plastics, computers, or antibiotics of the technology which surrounds them, most modern philosophers of science claim that scientific generalizations do not admit of proof. Uninfluenced by etymology, they claim that science is not knowledge (in any ordinary sense of the word 'knowledge'). Unmoved by the frequency with which distinguished practising scientists claim to 'know' this or to have 'proved' that,[1] they insist that no such claim can be literally true. Instead of justification for belief, they may say (like Popper[2]), a scientist really aims at the

---

[1] Two examples picked at random from a recent book of essays are George Thomson, F.R.S., 'Matter and Radiation' in *Scientific Thought, 1900–1960, A Selective Survey*, ed. R. Harré (1969), p. 52 ('proof' of the nature of radioactivity), and N. W. Pirie, F.R.S., 'The Viruses', ibid., p. 237 ('knowledge' of effects of virus infection). Cf. also A. Einstein and L. Infeld, *The Evolution of Physics* (1938), p. 156 ('proof' of the existence of electromagnetic waves).

[2] e.g. K. R. Popper, *Conjectures and Refutations*, pp. 33 ff.

strongest unrefuted conjecture. Or, perhaps they say (like Lakatos[3]) that he aims at a cumulatively fruitful research-programme. Or they say (like Carnap[4]) that all knowledge is basically guesswork and that instead of seeking proof a scientist cultivates rationality of decision and evaluates the probabilities in a way that is guided by expectations of appropriate utilities. Or perhaps they object to any over-all schema for the analysis of scientific thought, and content themselves with tracing the framework of its history. Such philosophers hold (as does Kuhn[5]) that each major advance in science is a revolution that creates new precedents of legitimacy, or is evolved (as Toulmin has argued[6]) by the forces of natural selection that cause some conceptual innovations to survive and others to die. Or perhaps (like Feyerabend[7]) they view science as a mere tower of babel in which rival theories are linguistically incommensurable and no common standards of arbitration exist. But one thing at least has been common to Popper, Lakatos, Carnap, Kuhn, Toulmin, Feyerabend, and many other modern philosophers of science. They have all in effect denied that the truth of a scientific generalization over an undounded domain is a possible object of proof or knowledge (though most of them, at least, have not denied that the observable characteristics of individual things may be matters of knowledge).

If knowledge that goes beyond the immediate reach of our senses is not to be found in natural or social science—among men professionally dedicated to the comprehension of fact, with vast resources of finance and manpower at their disposal— we can hardly expect to find it elsewhere. If nothing provable ever issues from the refined inquiries of science, then *a fortiori* no general or singular truths of fact are provable in everyday life. We may see what we can see, hear what we can hear, or

[3] I. Lakatos, 'Falsificationism and the Methodology of Scientific Research Programmes', in *Criticism and the Growth of Knowledge*, ed. I. Lakatos and A. E. Musgrave (1970), pp. 91 ff.

[4] R. Carnap, 'Probability and Content Measure', in *Mind, Matter and Method: Essays for Feigl*, ed. P. K. Feyerabend (1966), p. 249; and 'Inductive Logic and Rational Decisions', in *Studies in Inductive Logic and Probability* vol. i, ed. R. Carnap and R. C. Jeffrey (1971), pp. 5 ff.

[5] T. S. Kuhn, *The Structure of Scientific Revolutions* (1962), *passim*.

[6] S. Toulmin, *Human Understanding*, vol. i, (1972), *passim*.

[7] e.g. P. K. Feyerabend, 'Explanation, Reduction and Empiricism', in *Minnesota Studies in the Philosophy of Science*, ed. H. Feigl and G. Maxwell, vol. iii. pp. 28 ff.

remember what we can remember. But if the sceptical philosophers of science are right, there can be no way to set about
proving either the solution of yesterday's crime or the time of
tomorrow's sunset. If no general truths of fact admit of inductive
proof, the premisses of immediate experience can never lead
us, by rational methods, to conclusions that are beyond
reasonable doubt.

There is thus an obvious conflict between the assumptions
on which the Anglo-American law of proof is based and the
claims nowadays advanced, not by most scientists themselves,
but by most philosophers of science. How is this conflict to be
resolved? Well, it would certainly be odd if for nearly two
centuries[8] millions of reasonable men had accepted a standard
of proof in criminal courts that cannot genuinely be reached.
Countless trials would have proceeded on the quite erroneous
assumption that proof beyond reasonable doubt is sometimes
possible. Enormous numbers of citizens would have been
deprived of life, liberty, or property on the basis of a popular
fallacy or intellectual illusion. But fortunately we do not have
to accept so paradoxical a story. The inductivist account not
only makes good sense of the concept of probability in juridical
proof (and better sense than the mathematicist account can
make). It also elucidates why at least some general truths of
fact admit—in principle—of being known. It reconciles
philosophy of science with the ordinary man's conception of
proof and knowledge. And it achieves this without surrendering
the genuine insight that underlies much of the exaggerated
scepticism in modern philosophy of science. It does not
surrender the thesis that in any field, at some level of empirical
enquiry, current reasoning is inconclusive and currently
accepted hypotheses are open to correction.

§96. *If inductive knowledge of comparative reliability is possible,
so is knowledge of complete reliability*

It is sometimes said that we not only cannot, but do not need
to, know the truth of a general hypothesis in the sciences, since
for all worthwhile purposes it suffices to be able to know when
one such hypothesis is more reliable than another. If we can

8 Since at least as early as 1798: cf. E. W. Cleary (ed.), *McCormick's Handbook
of the Law of Evidence*, 2nd edn. (1972), p. 799.

know the latter, it is said, we can know which current proposal offers the most reliable solution for any particular problem that interests us, and by comparing this with the most reliable current solutions for other problems we can come to know the proposal's over-all standing at any one time.

But those who argue thus are deluding themselves, at least so far as inductive support is concerned. Knowledge that one hypothesis is more reliable than another does not differ essentially in ease of attainment from knowledge that a particular hypothesis is fully reliable. If a man really does know that one generalization H is better supported than another H', he must be aware of finite test-results E from which he correctly believes himself entitled to infer that s[H] >s[H']. So he must have in mind a certain finite list of relevant variables which he takes to have been manipulated in these tests, and he must correctly believe that no hidden variables were operative in securing the actual test-results. For, if such a variable had been operating, the belief that H had passed, and H' failed, a test of a certain specific degree of complexity would have been mistaken. A test-result, it will be remembered (cf. §43), gives a certain grade of support to a generalization only so far as no hidden variants of relevant variables are present in the test or the generalization is restricted in its application to domains that are free of such variables. It follows that, if a man really does know H to be more reliable than H', he has in mind a finite list of relevant variables and their variants that is complete at least for certain actually occurring types of situation in which H and H' may be put to the test. But if he really has such a list in mind then he is in a position to know also, from appropriate test-results, either that H or H' itself is fully reliable, or that some version[9] of H or H' which is suitably restricted in application is fully reliable. In either case the point is clear. If we can achieve knowledge that one particular hypothesis is inductively more reliable than another, we can also achieve knowledge that one particular hypothesis is fully reliable. Contrapositively, if knowledge of full support is never possible, knowledge that one hypothesis is better supported than another is equally impossible.

[9] Cf. §54 above.

§97. *Inductive knowledge does not imply knowing that one knows*

In any case the crux of the matter is that a man may conceivably have in mind a complete list of the variables that are inductively relevant in a certain field of inquiry and be aware of test-results that have been structured in accordance with that list. Then he could correctly think that facts of which he was aware were adequate reasons for believing the hypothesis tested to be true, since the test-results might give full support to the hypothesis. Also, if the hypothesis were fully reliable, it would be true, and awareness of the test-results might well be the factor which induced belief that it was true. So sufficient conditions for knowledge would be present, whatever be the rights and wrongs of recent controversy about the precise analysis of the concept of knowledge—for example, about the question whether 'x knows that p' entails 'x believes that p'. The man would know the truth of at least one generalization over an indefinitely extensive domain.

But perhaps neither he nor anyone else would know that he knew this. That is to say, perhaps no one is aware of facts that are adequate reasons for believing the list of relevant variables in question to be complete: no one is aware of test-results establishing a higher-level hypothesis to this effect. The man knows that his first-level hypothesis is true, and correctly believes that he knows this. But, not being aware of any higher level test-results, he does not *know* that he has first-level knowledge. Indeed he could conceivably know that his first-level hypothesis is true without even thinking that he knows this, since he might be aware of test-results that in fact give full support to the hypothesis and also believe the hypothesis to be true because of these test-results, while he himself might not believe that the tests had quite sufficient complexity of structure to give full support: i.e. he might (wrongly) be reluctant to believe that the assumed list of relevant variables was complete. Or again he might think that he knew his first-level hypothesis to be true, but be mistaken, because the list of relevant variables which he believed to be complete was not in fact complete.

Perhaps the third of these three possibilities has been, and perhaps always will be, by far the most frequently realized. Perhaps seekers after scientific knowledge far more often think they have it when they have not, than actually have it when they think they have not, or both have it and think they have it. But what is at issue is the mere possibility of such knowledge, not the actual frequency with which it occurs.

Note too that in order to conceive knowledge in this way we have to be careful to abstract any psychological features from our concept of evidence. We are concerned with certainty as the limiting case of probability, not with certainty as the mental state of conviction.

In the Cartesian tradition, however, what is said to be 'evident' is what strikes one as intellectually obvious. Hence in that tradition, if we are aware of adequate evidence that p, we must also, quite trivially, be aware of adequate evidence that there is adequate evidence that p. If we are certain, we must be certain that we are certain. For, if we find it strikingly obvious that p, we can hardly fail to find it strikingly obvious that we do find it strikingly obvious that p. There is then no serious point to be made by a distinction between knowing and knowing that one knows.[10]

But once we conceive evidence or certainty as something that operates primarily on propositions, not on minds, the distinction between knowing and knowing that one knows acquires much greater importance. For with this conception of evidence, when E and H are both propositions, we can ask quite significantly what evidential support exists for the proposition that E gives top-grade evidential support to H; and the correct answer to our question may not be at all trivial, as the study of inductive reasoning reveals. 'Smith *believes* it true', we can say, 'that H's consequent is provable from H's antecedent with top-grade inductive probability, but does he *know* that it is true?'

§98. *The prevalence of scepticism is due largely to an inadequate understanding of inductive logic*

Why then do so many philosophers of science believe, in effect, that scientific knowledge is impossible? The arguments they actually offer are rather various. But the main underlying reasons are perhaps five.

[10] Cf. H. A. Prichard, *Knowledge and Perception* (1950), pp. 86 ff., and the other references cited in J. Hintikka, *Knowledge and Belief* (1962), pp. 107 ff.

First, if the method of relevant variables and the consequential structure of inductive reasoning are not properly understood, or their importance is not properly recognized, the path to scepticism is a short one. As Hume long ago pointed out, the regular past conjunction of S with R affords no rational justification whatever for believing that S will always accompany R. So enumerative induction is certainly incapable of issuing in knowledge about the truth of a generalization that is true over a domain that is unbounded in size. But the systematic analogy that can be shown to exist between the concept of inductive support and the concept of logical truth is a fact that Hume, and those influenced by him on this point, have failed to notice.[11] And the analogy is also a fact that, as I have argued elsewhere,[12] is fatal to Hume's form of scepticism. Because of the structural analogy between inductive reliability and logical truth, the sense in which it is rational to argue from the antecedent to the consequent of a conditional proposition because that proposition is logically true · is one that may naturally be generalized into a sense in which it is rational to argue from the antecedent to the consequent of a proposition because that proposition enjoys full inductive support, or to be inclined to argue from the antecedent to the consequent of the proposition because the proposition enjoys considerable inductive support.

Secondly, it is easy to suppose that, if we do not know that we know that H is true, it is not true that we know that H is true. For consider[13] the circumstances under which it is prudent to claim that a certain proposition is true. A cautious man might well hold that if you do not know the proposition to be true you should not claim it to be so. On this view it may be rational to believe something yourself on evidence which does not make it completely certain, as was assumed in §§86–9, but it is sensible to require better evidence than this when you are making assertions which, because they tend to generate beliefs in others, may rebound to affect your own credit. A prudent man's assertions, therefore, as distinct from his

11 Cf. *TIOI*, §§21–2.

12 *TIOI*, §§19–20.

13 I disregard here the arguments that rest on some excessively idealized conception of knowers—e.g. on the assumption that the knower is logically omniscient —as in J. Hintikka, *Knowledge and Belief* (1962), *passim*, esp. p. 112.

unexpressed beliefs, should not go beyond what he knows (or believes he knows). So on this view, if your claim is to know that a certain proposition is true, you should know that you know. Your claim to knowledge is justifiable only if you know that you know, since any assertion by x that p is justifiable only if x knows that p (or believes he knows).

But even if this rather cautious ethic were correct—and one can quite easily envisage circumstances to which it does not apply—it would concern the justification-conditions for claims to knowledge, not the truth-conditions for ascriptions of knowledge. It would concern the justification-conditions for assertions by a person, x, that he, x, knows that H is true, not the truth-conditions for propositions of the form 'x knows that H is true'. These are especially easily confused with one another if we concern ourselves with first-person sentences like 'I know that H is true'. But once they are distinguished it becomes quite clear that a man may know that H is true, without knowing that he knows. He knows it because H is true and he is aware of test-results that fully justify the belief in H which they have induced. But he does not know that he knows because he is not omniscient and, specifically, is not aware of facts that justify treating the first-level test-results as full justification for believing in H.

Thirdly, the history of natural science has developed in a way which denies any plausibility to the thesis that theories about the ultimate principles of nature are certifiable once and for all by some particular source of data. For two centuries the unchallenged supremacy of Newtonian mechanics encouraged philosophers to construct epistemologies, like Kant's, that were committed to this thesis, despite Hume's warning of the risks. But in the present century the supremacy of Newtonian principles has been overthrown by the twin onslaught of relativity and quantum theory. So, partly under the pressure of this shattering historical event, philosophical opinion has now swung to the opposite extreme. Every theory, it is said, must be regarded as being corrigible and subject to gradual reform, or revolutionary replacement, in the light of further discoveries. Well, perhaps that is a healthy attitude to adopt and one well worth encouraging in others. But it is quite consistent with the possibility that some one, somewhere, at some time, may actually have some scientific knowledge, even if he does not himself know that he has it. More progress is made by discouraging complacency than by encouraging it. But just occasionally a man's complacency might be well founded even if the adequacy of this foundation could not be proved.

Fourthly, where a system of inductive logic has been supposed applicable to the assessment of scientific hypotheses, this system has very often been conceived to rest on *a priori* foundations of some kind in order to avoid a vicious circle in its justification. Carnap's system of confirmation-theory, for example, issues in assessments that are supposed to be analytic for the language within which they are formulated. But if that is so then conclusively valid assessments ought to be obtainable, and whenever we know a generalization to be true we ought to be able—by a merely logical expertise—to know that we know. Rather than accept the possibility of such conclusive, petrified findings, many philosophers have supposed the whole enterprise of inductive logic to be mistaken. Since its assessments apparently cannot be empirical without being circular, and cannot be *a priori* without being excessively presumptuous, they argue that it has no place at all in the philosophy of science.

The way through this dilemma is to see that inductive assessments can be empirical without being circular, if we are content here to be localists rather than globalists. We must not aim, as the Carnapians do, at a single comprehensive system of assessment. In relation to each first-level field of inquiry a certain mode of grading is—in principle—determined by the appropriate list of relevant variables. But hypotheses about the contents of these lists, and about the terminology of the generalizations to which they are appropriate, are subject to assessment by reference to tests in which appropriate second-level variables are manipulated, and so on. There is thus, in principle, an indefinite regress of justification, but no circle. Inductive logic offers a constantly renewable opportunity for scientists and laymen to get at the right support-criteria for the right terminology, not a once-and-for-all opportunity for philosophers to discover a single comprehensive language-system. Hence even when a first-level hypothesis has in fact been proved, it may be extremely difficult to prove that it has been proved, and even more difficult to prove that such a second-level proof is available. In practice, at any one time, there must always be some level in the hierarchy of proof—normally quite a low level—at which current scientific inquiry is inconclusive and currently accepted hypotheses seem open to correction. But to admit this is quite different from admitting that at no level is scientific knowledge ever possible.

Fifthly, it is sometimes urged that any attempt to justify belief in generalizations over indefinitely extensive domains must rest on certain metaphysical assumptions about the uniformity of causal processes or the existence of a limited variety of independent causal factors. But the answer to this is that if the method of relevant variables is correctly construed it makes assumptions only of a local and empirically testable kind. It has to assume that certain variables are uniformly relevant to hypotheses of a certain kind and that only these variables (in a certain order) are so relevant. And it is prepared to live with the fact that experience often shows some particular assumption of this kind to have been mistaken.

We are now in a position to sum up the situation. If the sceptical philosophers of science are right, matters of fact can never be proved beyond reasonable doubt. But an inductivist analysis of probability and certainty allows such proof to be possible wherever the analysis applies. It therefore sides with the innumerable judges, lawyers, juries, and scientists who have thought it possible, as against the sceptical philosophers who have implied it to be impossible. No doubt mistakes have often been made in British and American courts, about what was or was not beyond reasonable doubt. No doubt scientists have often made false claims to knowledge. But it is neither necessary nor permissible to hold that in seeking proofs which conform to their conventional standard for proof in criminal cases those courts have been pursuing a chimera, or to hold that in seeking knowledge about nature so many distinguished scientists have so grotesquely misconceived the legitimate goal of scientific inquiry.

In fact the sceptical fashion, in modern philosophy of science, has flourished on ignorance about the true structure of inductive reasoning. The generalized method or relevant variables, the empirical character of support-assessments, the systematic analogy of structure between inductive reliability and logical truth, the existence of a concept of inductive probability that grades the weight of evidence—all these features of inductive reasoning have gone largely unnoticed or unacknowledged. Once their importance is recognized it becomes clear how we can, at least in principle, have inferential knowledge about the past, the unobserved present, and the future. It is not the judges and scientists who have been falling into error, through philosophical *naiveté*, but the sceptical philosophers who have fallen into error because of the backwardness of inductive logic.

Index

abnormality, threshold of 185, 212, 293
acceptance, criterion for rational 46, 81, 310 ff.
accessibility, inductive 242
accidental truths 308
Ackerman, R. 124
additivity, conditions for 227 f.
Adler, M. J. 53
adversary procedure 63, 112, 120, 254
agnosticism 341
agreement, method of 146, 246, 302
Anaximenes 187
anomalies in science 135, 162 ff., 179, 189, 242
anti-logicism 126
anti-realism 6, 338 ff.
Aristotle 27
assertion 29 f., 214, 311, 333, 352 f.
assessment, method of 6, 140 ff.
Austin, J. 337
axiomatization of inductive logic, *see* inductive support, axiomatization for
of probability, *see* probability, axiomatization of
of scientific theories 154

Bacon, F. 42, 144 ff., 158, 174, 342
Ball, V. C. 52, 80
Barnard, G. A. 26
belief, rational, *see* acceptance, criterion for rational
Bentham, J. 54 f., 248
Bernoulli, J. 2, 44, 52, 95, 99 f., 199
Best, W. M. 55
betting quotients 7, 26, 55
Blackstone, A. W. 337
Boole, G. 8, 44, 52, 95 ff.
botanical nomenclature, philosophy of 338
Braithwaite, R. B. 9
Brandon, J. 80
Brimnes, The 80

Cajori, F. 163
Carnap, R., *a priori* inductive assessments 24 f., 89, 181, 229, 354
arguments from history of science 124
arguments from intuition 123
betting-quotients 54
confirmation 164 f., 306
dispositional predicates 326 f., 331, 340
instance-confirmation 165, 188 f.
instantial relevance principle 176
polyadic predicables in probability-functors 17
polycriterial account of probability 8
positive-relevance measure 65
quantitative scientific hypotheses 229
range-measures 24 ff., 88 f., 111, 241 f., 276 f.
relevance-measure 104
scientific knowledge 347
symmetry principle 218
total evidence requirement 216, 296
Campbell, N. R. 227
Carter, P. B. 54
causal hypotheses 148 ff., 294, 297, 307 f., 334 f., 341
causation 146, 173 ff., 332, 343
causes, plurality of 150, 302
certainty 83, 212 f., 244, 272 f., 281, 346, 351 f., 355
chance, games of 18 f., 92, 283
Pascal-Fermat calculus of 2, 52, 103, 105, 199, 281
Chisholm, R. M. 124, 322
Chomsky, N. 262
circumstantial evidence, convergence of, *see* evidence, convergence of
Clairaut, A. C. 163
Cleary, E. W. 51, 348
Cohen, L. J. 22, 42, 124, 177, 262, 338, 342 f.
Coleman, R. F. 86
Collingwood, R. G. 285

scepticism in philosophy of science
345 ff.
Scheffler, I. 124
Schreiber, R. 52, 95
science, history of 124, 126, 347,
353
unity of 344
self-evidence 341
semantics, model-theoretic 240 ff.
set-theory, non-Zermelian 39
Settle, T. 8, 30
Sigal, P. 86
signs, hypotheses about 149 ff.
Simon, R. J. 52
Smith, C. A. B. 26
Smokler, H. F, 26
soundness, inferential 14 f., 27 ff., 122
speech-acts 28 f.
Spinoza, B. de 243, 327, 340 f.
Starkie, T. 53, 55
Stephen, J. F. 248
Stoebuck, W. B. 79
Stove, D. C. 151
strict implication 230, 343
structure-dependence, Chomsky's principle of 262
subjunctive conditionals 23, 307 f.,
326 f., 331
Suppes, P. 23, 44, 173, 227
Swinburne, R. G. 163, 177

target predicables 137, 139
tendencies 330 f.
testable generalizations 137, 179, 220,
230, 241

test-results, see inductive support, tests for
Thales 187
Thayer, J. B. 45, 50, 110
theism 340 f.
theories, scientific 152 ff., 288
Thompson, G. 346
Tinbergen N. 149
Toulmin, S. E. 28, 126, 347
Tribe, L. H. 53
truth-functionalism 342 ff.
Tversky, A. 258

uniformity of nature 343
uniformity principle, see inductive
support, uniformity principle for
utilities 310, 322

variables, inductively relevant, see
relevant variables
hidden, see relevant variables, hidden
independent 147
continuous 147
variants, inductively relevant, see
relevant variants
verisimilitude, see Popper, verisimilitude
Vienna Circle 124

Waismann, F. 14
Walls, H. J. 86
weight of evidence 36 f., 80, 213, 215,
225, 254 f., 293, 318, 321, 356
Whewell, W. 125, 512, 157, 281
Wigmore, J. H. 69 f., 248, 268, 281
Wills, W., 55, 77
Wittgenstein, L., 11